TELEVISION TALK

Thomas Schatz, Editor
TEXAS FILM AND MEDIA STUDIES SERIES

TELEVISION

TALK A History of the TV Talk Show

BERNARD M. TIMBERG

with
A Guide to Television Talk
by Robert J. Erler

Introduction by
Horace Newcomb

AUSTIN  UNIVERSITY OF TEXAS PRESS

LIBRARY OF CONGRESS CATALOGING-IN-PUBLICATION DATA
Timberg, Bernard.
Television talk : a history of the TV talk show / Bernard M. Timberg
with Robert J. Erler.
       p.   cm. — (Texas film and media studies series)
Includes bibliographical references and index.
ISBN 0-292-78175-x (hardcover : alk. paper) —
ISBN 0-292-78176-8 (pbk. : alk. paper)
1. Talk shows—United States.   I. Erler, Bob.   II. Title.   III. Series.
PN1992.8.T3   T56   2002
791.45′6—dc21   2002004368

CONTENTS

INTRODUCTION

By Horace Newcomb

Bernard Timberg's book, *Television Talk,* appears at a particularly significant moment in the history of talk shows and, equally importantly, in the history of television. It also appears as part of a significant development in the field of television studies, a development marking and marked by changes in the medium and the social relations it fosters and to which it responds.

As this work makes clear, however, even as those changes occur, the talk show remains a fundamental feature within any economic, social, and cultural formation of television. This long reliance on the form results in part, as Timberg points out, from its status as an efficient and effective commodity. It is relatively cheap to produce. It is often extremely profitable when successful. And those successes need not, in most cases, rely on securing a "mass" audience. Almost always presented to a specific portion of the total viewing public—families shuttling through morning routines, "housewives" during the day, "hip" younger viewers in late-night fringe hours—the talk show, like the game or quiz show, can become a profitable staple of televisual entertainment and interaction within its specific niche.

Moreover, this is true throughout the world. Certainly, if there were time, resources, and research staff sufficient to the task, a version of this book focused on the worldwide implementation of television talk formats would extend to several volumes.

But these economic and simple sociological factors hardly explain the massive amount of attention, both popular and scholarly, paid to talk shows in recent years. And any "formal" notice in print or mediated commentary is merely a portion of a far more widely disseminated general discussion involving parents and teachers, members of Congress and clergy, television executives and television critics. In some ways, talk "about" TV talk has been as prevalent as the talk-oriented programs themselves. Business negotiations surrounding talk shows have been chronicled in the general press, and in the process some of the more significant inner workings of the television industry have been exposed. So, too, have the egos and foibles of familiar television personalities, their guests, their agents, writers, and producers. And in the center of all these accounts have been heated exchanges making clear that the shows are often used as lightening rods for a wider—and far deeper—array of themes.

Surely, argue the most vocal general critics, the topics and issues that began to appear on programs hosted by Geraldo Rivera, and later Oprah Winfrey, and even the more cautious and polite Phil Donahue, were somehow "inappropriate" for "public" exposure. And when "things went too far," on some shows, these prominent personalities themselves, these familiar and successful guides to visible conversation, agreed to adjust their tone and approach. They would become, once again, "more serious," more engaged in "education" and the "informative" aspects of television talk. Or they would quit the business altogether.

But such actions and responses pale before the excesses of a Jerry Springer. While the late-arriving Springer is not a major topic in this book, his program has been consistently cited in current public discussions and will be re-examined in light of the work presented here. This is so because the program has become emblematic of a decline in "proper" discourse, the devolution of all that is proper within publicly performed personal exchange. When some aspects of the Springer-esque displays of verbal and physical violence were exposed as "staged," the arguments were merely confirmed—deception is an even more dangerous step on the slippery slope of social decline. Such charges focus on both the content of "discussions" and the behavior on display within the Springer show and others that approach it in style. Criticism links these factors to old conflicts between "popular" and "high" culture. Viewers as well as the hosts, the producers, the participants, and the medium itself are figured as "low-brow," "anti-intellectual," and "coarse."

Clearly, however, the critique spills outside any academic or general social concern for such categorization. It floods onto those whose lives and issues, troubles and deeds, appearance and attitude are performing "their" talk for the public at large. In other words, these later forms of talk shows and the responses to them expose issues of class, race, sexuality, age, physical appearance—the array of social markers deemed "within" and "outside" the proper boundaries for presence on television or consumption by audiences. These "violations of taste" even call into question the legitimate limits to which corporations may go in search of profit. For some critics such matters reflect a decline in "taste," "propriety," "manners," and, in the most telling commentary, "civility." Society itself is at stake. Sage explanations argue that the creation of such representations, and any delight in them, borders on degeneracy worthy of a failing Roman Empire.

But the defenders of TV talk shows—and there are defenders, even beyond those who profit from them—build their counterclaims around similar topics. They suggest that television has at last assumed a rightful place in the "public sphere." These talk shows, even with—especially with—their rites of excess and displays of grammatical failure, sexual variation, and institutional collapse, have merely brought into the spotlight what those at the "bottom" or on the "fringes" of "civil society" have known all along. Ungrammatical speech can be effective. Sexual behavior can be endlessly reinvented. Institutions, from schools to factories, families to churches, are flawed, often repressive, generally tilted toward privilege.

Thus, the new talk shows are sometimes hailed as democratic and progressive, a welcome change from the prime-time fantasies of perfection and happy endings. They personalize the structural bog-down of society displayed in every evening's news report. From this perspective, those who exhibit dismay at the mid-afternoon spectacle performed all across the land *should* be dismayed. It is their world that is coming apart, not the world of the latest occupant of fringe-town. *That* citizen is finally receiving far more than the pittance of cash paid for mere appearance on television. The real reward is in the TALK—the moment of self-expression, the following moment of being talked about, even the infuriating stage of being talked "down to" by those who never watch the shows in the first place, much less "walk the walk" that precedes the talk.

It is here that the significance of Bernard Timberg's overview of television talk emerges. For this is not a book about sensationalism, except insofar as that category takes its place among many others. It is not a book about the social consequences of talk on TV, except as those consequences are seen as part of a long process. It is not a book about TV talk-show "stars," except as those stars are rightly placed within a galaxy and defined in terms of their function as well as their brightness.

First and foremost, this is a work framing television talk within a detailed historical perspective, an approach placing it within a strong development in the study of television. Perhaps as a result of the enormous technological, industrial, regulatory, and economic changes of recent decades, there is now a sense that it is possible to gain a much-needed clearer perspective on this medium. Indeed, there is a sense that at least one, perhaps more than one, phase of television has passed. Waiting for, living with, the new, we are plunged again into wondering what this thing means. This gives rise to some of the dilemmas and disagreements surrounding current talk shows (and other programming forms, it should be noted). But as usual, historical accounts demonstrate that though they may seem "new," these experiences are certainly not unique. Timberg offers us a guide to what came before the current state of programming related to this genre. His decade-by-decade account of the television talk shows in the three-network era reminds us of the significance of the form in each of those periods. Moreover, the detailed analysis of some thirty-six personalities prominent in these decades is supplemented with Bob Erler's wonderfully comprehensive "Guide to Television Talk." These rich paragraph descriptions cover the work of over 200 talk personalities and shows from 1948 to 1998.

Directly related to this recognition of the ubiquity of television talk is the equal focus on the commodity status of the form. Distinct aspects of earlier talk shows are directly tied to the economic, social, and technological formation of television in different periods, the cycles of talk that Timberg discusses. From three networks we have moved to dozens of options. The consequent demand for more programming requires dipping ever more deeply into the pool of cost-efficient programming such as talk shows, making the search for success more complicated. Thus the talk show emerges as a product that relies on viewer knowledge of the similarities and differences, recombined in yet another attempt to offer the "perfect" specific mix that will draw and hold attention. A new seating arrangement, a different musical style, a wink toward the camera—a thousand other small elements can be altered in the quest for ratings.

One constant, however, clearly delineated by Timberg, is the formation of the talk show around the personality of the host. In this regard a Springer emerges from, combines, recombines, elements of all those other hosts. Oprah, Ricki, Geraldo, Larry King, Roseanne, the tried and the triers, those who survive the competition for one week and those whose weeks extend to what passes for a lifetime are defined by their relation to one another and to all those who came before them. All our speculation about the present can now, with the context provided here, be informed by the details of these past "titans." All our fears of declines in "taste" can be measured by what we meant by that term when Norman Mailer and Gore Vidal spat invective at one another in the presence of Dick Cavett's serenity. All our concerns about the viewer as voyeur can be refined by recognizing the towering presence of Edward R. Murrow leaning in a little too close, almost fawning, in the presence of celebrity.

While the variations sound small, perhaps even simple, Timberg makes it very clear that such changes and experiments result from the collective efforts. His detailed descriptions and analyses of the "behind-the-scenes" aspects of television production point to the elaborate teamwork required to bring these shows to the screen on a regular basis. The commonplace that television is a collaborative medium is given specific meaning in his examples of "entrepreneurial teams" dedicated to shaping the meaning of a program, its place in the expanding "lineup" of other, similar-yet-different offerings. The efforts of these teams are specifically focused on shaping the all-important host persona, adjusting, framing, rewriting until all these efforts disappear in a mask of casual intimacy. That only a few of these programs succeed reminds us that this search for distinction is not an easy task. Indeed, the successes remind us more than anything that the talk show, like all television, must exceed its commodity status even as it confirms it.

These host personalities, these styles, these struggles for "talk" as "conversation" with "us" must finally rely on the meanings associated with the combined elements of the show. In its offer of cultural significance, television draws us to itself with—and draws from us—precisely the engagement that makes some so fearful, others so oblivious, and some so intrigued with its complexities. This means that the "three-network oligopoly" was known in our homes not simply as a technological or economic collusion, but as a link, a connecting device that provided a distinctive type of private-public experience. We watched what all others watched, but we watched within our own small, immediate group. Now, within the multi-channel universe, the same number may have watched a talk show, but not within the familiar, familial circle. Instead, the fans of Springer or Oprah or Dave or Jay may communicate with one another in chat rooms or come together in the office to mention the last outrageous event. To understand these continuities and shifts, it is important to recognize this book as a work of cultural analysis as well as a historical account.

Timberg's explanations, based on specific examples, inform our relation to the shows we watch now by providing descriptive, comparative commentary on what we watched earlier. In "the old days" the role of an early Mike Wallace, Merv Griffin, or Mike Douglas was different from that of Springer—in degree. But it was also similar and in many ways familiar. Were not the personal revelations of movie stars as astonishing in their own way to post–World War II audiences only recently connected to mass culture as the outrageous sexual tales of the working class are today? Were not the wry asides, the nudges and winks of Johnny Carson preparatory to Drew Barrymore's leap onto David Letterman's desk, where she exposed her breasts? And does not the fact that she turned only to Dave, not to the camera, indicate the resilience of some boundaries? Timberg's accounts of those earlier shows refresh the memory of those old enough to have seen them. They also provide valuable fundamental information for those who will never see those shows, even in an archived state.

It is hardly a matter of convenience, then, that Timberg ends the historical survey and the more detailed case studies with an examination of *The Larry Sanders Show*. That program, a comedy "about" television talk shows, is clearly a product of the "post-network era" of television. Aired on HBO, a premium cable channel, it was available only to subscribers. Its ironic perspective assumed a familiarity with the formula made familiar by *The Tonight Show Starring Johnny Carson*. Indeed, some elements of the program—the strong producer reminiscent of Fred de Cordova, the sideman who seemed patterned on Ed McMahon, the lead character's multiple marriages—seemed to indicate that the Carson show and Carson persona were models for this comedic analysis of the genre. But it was the self-reflexive, behind-the-scenes exploration of talk on television that grounded the program in a different television era. Unlike earlier examples of similar techniques in *The George Burns and Gracie Allen Show*, where George regularly observed and commented on the construction of his fictional world, this offering probed the significance of all the details Bernard Timberg identifies in his account: the melding of technology, industrial relations, and "written talk" within the central, explosively fragile personality of "Larry Sanders."

Television Talk, then, a book of details and cases, accounts and descriptions, names and places and times, could have been the bible for *The Larry Sanders Show*. It is the book we need now. No one has looked so closely at the history of talk shows, provided so much information regarding what those shows and the people who made them were like, as has Bernard Timberg. His work will replace neither outraged polemic nor interpretive speculation. But on the foundation established here both may become more precise. This, then, is a book to be talked about.

ONE

HISTORY OF TELEVISION TALK
Defining a Genre

INTRODUCTION

The TV talk show is a creation of twentieth-century broadcasting. It is intensely topical and, like the daily newspaper, has traditionally been considered a disposable form. When one of the founders of the television talk show, Jack Paar, mentioned to his director Hal Gurnee in the early 1960s that he was going to throw away the taped masters from the first years of his show, Gurnee responded, "You're not going to throw away the hubs, are you?" The aluminum hubs of the two-inch video masters were worth $90 at the time.[1] The first ten years of Johnny Carson's *Tonight* show were similarly erased by NBC without any thought of future value.

Until quite recently, the same dismissive attitude toward the television talk show has permeated media scholarship and TV criticism, which traditionally focused on news and drama. However, beginning in the early 1990s new books on the TV talk show began to appear each year.[2] Critical attention and scholarly interest were also reflected in numerous articles, many focusing on the influence of talk shows on American politics. Critics argued that talk-show hosts were usurping traditional functions of journalism.

In the early 1990s, interest in talk shows was also fueled by the talk-show strategies of candidates in national political campaigns. Ross Perot's third-party candidacy in 1992 emerged out of a talk-show appearance on *Larry King Live,* and Bill Clinton was dubbed the first "talk-show President" with appearances on *Donahue, The Arsenio Hall*

Show, and MTV. In every national election since that time, talk shows have increasingly become sites where news, entertainment, and political power converge.

The new awareness of the social impact of TV talk was reflected in a national debate that broke out over "tabloid" talk shows of hosts like Ricki Lake, Jenny Jones, and Jerry Springer. The topic received widespread attention in the media when a mid-1990s coalition led by former Secretary of Education William Bennett announced a national boycott against sponsors of TV "trash talk" and Secretary of Health and Human Services Donna Shalala attended a "talk summit" with hosts, producers, and programming executives to urge them to moderate the excesses of their shows.

Suddenly, it seemed, everyone was talking about talk. How were scholars and critics to make sense of all this talk on the air and the debates swirling around it? Where did these multiplying electronic forms of talk come from, and what were their implications for public discourse? This book is designed to address some of these questions through a decade-by-decade history of the television talk show that traces the talk show's evolution and highlights the work of its most influential hosts.

The history of the TV talk show is marked by a series of distinct cycles, each with a beginning, middle, and end. These cycles are related to broad cultural and economic developments and changes within the broadcasting industry. Each of these cycles fosters certain kinds of talk and certain kinds of hosts. New forms of talk begin to thrive. By the end of each cycle, these kinds of talk have been accepted by viewers, but have often become subsidiary or have begun to fade in their appeal as new kinds of talk emerge within the next cycle.

The range of talk, however, has always been very wide. Talk shows have run the gamut from the polished trans-Atlantic conversations of Edward R. Murrow and Bill Moyers to the verbal mudslinging and parodies that characterized the tabloid talk shows of the 1990s. What has discouraged scholars and critics from treating the TV talk show as a genre has been the difficulty of developing a coherent picture of forms that vary so much from one another and at the same time are so close to normal conversation. However, as I hope to show in this book, the conversations we see on television are anything but normal. However spontaneous they seem, these conversations are always highly planned and structured within the limits of talk-show format and practice. Looking at the TV talk show as a rule-governed form of expression enables us to come up with a definition that embraces all TV talk shows.

UNSPOKEN RULES

The TV talk show is governed by a set of rules or guiding principles that make it distinct from any other form of TV—soap opera, news, or game shows, for instance—and also from daily conversation. Before examining the rules of the TV talk show, however, it is useful to distinguish *television talk*, a set of principles that governs all talk on television, from *talk shows*.[3]

Television talk emerges out of fifty years of television practice and the preceding three decades of radio. It is unscripted yet highly planned and invariably anchored by an announcer, host, or team of hosts. It is based on what sociologist Erving Goffman calls "fresh talk": talk that appears to be spontaneous, no matter how planned or formatted it actually may be.

The range of TV talk is much broader than that of "talk shows." TV talk covers every kind of talk on television: cooking shows, book-review shows, station announcements, home shopping channels, Miss America pageants, live political investigations like the Watergate and Iran-Contra hearings. It covers such a wide territory that I have not attempted to cover it in the narrative section of this book. However, the full range of TV talk is covered in the final Guide to Television Talk by Robert Erler. The television *talk show*, as opposed to *television talk*, is the television show that is entirely structured around the act of conversation itself.

The first principle of the television talk show is that it is anchored by a host (or team of hosts) who is responsible for the tone and direction, and for guiding and setting limits on the talk that is elicited from guests on the air. In most successful national television talk shows, the host has rarely been simply the "star" of the program. Major talk-show hosts have traditionally attained a high degree of control over their shows and the production teams that run them. From a production standpoint, the host frequently acts as managing editor. From a marketing standpoint, the host is the label, the trademark, that sells the product. From the organizational standpoint, the host's personal power as entrepreneur is pivotal. The host deals with advertisers, network executives, and syndicators. The host is the one irreplaceable part. With a new "brand-name" host, the show may continue, as *The Tonight Show* continued with Johnny Carson replacing Jack Paar in 1962, and with Jay Leno replacing Johnny Carson in 1992, but the show will inevitably change with each new host. Network executives have been acutely aware of this since the days of Arthur Godfrey, Dave Garroway, and Edward R. Murrow.

The second principle of the television talk show is that it is experienced in the present tense as "conversation." Live, taped, or shown in reruns, talk shows always maintain the illusion of the present tense. For talk-show reruns, this requires a "willing suspension of disbelief." For example, in 1998, more than twenty-six years after it first aired, a Dick Cavett show in which Norman Mailer confronted Gore Vidal live on the air was played to an audience at Ithaca College in Ithaca, New York. As members of the audience watched the show, they picked up levels of subtext in Mailer's homophobic taunts of Vidal and were alternately amazed and appalled, vocally supporting Vidal's responses to Mailer's behavior. It was as if the audience were sharing the room once again with the verbal contestants. Viewers relive the present-tense moment even when topical events—news, catastrophes, sports events, talk, or elections—clearly are dated.

A corollary to the talk show's daily present-tense immediacy is its present-tense intimacy. The host speaks to millions as if to each alone. Host and audience share a moment in time, but they share more than that. The intimacy of the moment is tied to the history and continuity of the host's relationship with the audience. On his last *Tonight* show in 1992, after thirty years on the air, Johnny Carson referred frequently to his long history with his audience. Several times his voice choked with emotion as he spoke. This indeed was a powerful form of present-tense immediacy for many in the television audience.

A third principle is that television talk is a product—a commodity competing with other broadcast commodities. Johnny Carson joked in the monologue of his final show: "When we started this show, the total population of the earth was 3 billion, 100 million. This summer it is 5 billion, 500 million people, which is a net increase of 2 billion, 400 million people. . . . A more amazing statistic is that half of those 2 billion, 400 million people will soon have their own late-night talk show." This reference to the proliferation of talk shows suggests that, even at the very end of his career, Johnny Carson's eye was on the competition.

Television talk has proven over time to be a valuable commodity, and talk-show hosts themselves are valuable commodities. Their worth to networks and advertisers is reflected in their salaries. To take a single year in the early 1990s, for example, in 1991 NBC paid Carson approximately $30 million, and according to *Forbes* magazine's annual survey, Oprah Winfrey was, like Johnny Carson, one of America's wealthiest four hundred people. By 2000, Oprah Winfrey's net worth was estimated at $900 million.[4]

Successful talk-show hosts are also profit centers for their own producing or distributing companies. In 1993, most of the income of Multimedia's Entertainment Division ($63.3 million) came from two talk shows run by well-known hosts: Phil Donahue and Sally Jessy Raphaël. In 1994 Oprah Winfrey made about half the profits of her syndicator, King World, with $180 million in revenue at that time. When Oprah Winfrey's contract was up for negotiation with King World, it was estimated that the loss of her program might drop King World's stock 30 percent in one day.[5]

A commodity as valuable as a talk show hosted by a major star must be carefully managed. It must fit the commercial imperatives and time limits of syndicators, packagers, and network programmers. Though it can be entertaining, even outrageous, it must never seriously alienate advertisers or viewers.[6] For this reason television talk is always regulated by invisible rules of acceptability. Guests are carefully chosen and questions prescreened. When comedian Richard Pryor appeared on the Letterman show in 1986, as much as 80 percent of the interview was set up in advance,[7] which was standard procedure.

A fourth principle is that the give-and-take on a talk show, while it must appear to be spontaneous, must also be highly structured. Scores of invisible hands shape each show. One good example is Carson's final show, which listed a production staff of fifty-five, including writers, producers, set designers, graphics coordinators, makeup artists, hairdressers, wardrobe specialists, propmasters, and other technicians. This represented only the employees of Carson Productions, not the NBC camera crews and technicians in Burbank. Nor did the credits include scores of network officials who oversaw, budgeted, did legal work, and publicized the show. More than a hundred talk-show professionals put a show like *Tonight* on the air every day.

Although hosts and shows change over time, the core principles remain the same. For fifty years, the television talk show has been host-centered and defined, forged in the present tense, spontaneous but highly structured, churned out within the strict formulas and measured segments of costly network time, and designed to air topics appealing to the widest possible audience. Whoever the host and whatever the format, these are the defining characteristics of the TV talk show.

HISTORY

Perhaps we tend not to see the talk show as a genre because, so far, no comprehensive history has defined its evolution and illustrated the variations within its common structures. Many of the best examples of early talk-show hosts and formats are gone, or available only in archives or from the hands of private collectors.

This situation is changing. Yesterday's trash becomes today's history. Old talk shows are now running on cable channels. Through Peabody and Emmy awards, books, articles, and more recent scholarly attention, the television talk show has begun to receive recognition for its role in helping to define American life over five decades. Influential talk-show hosts are beginning to receive serious attention. Hosts are now being defined as entrepreneurs as well as entertainers, owners and managing editors as well as catalysts within the TV industry. Ultimately, certain talk-show figures have become acknowledged titans of talk and shapers of American culture.

This history of the television talk show will define the genre as it emerged from radio and other precedents in American popular culture. It will show how influential hosts shaped talk-show forms and were themselves influenced by previous talk traditions, by sponsors and network officials, and by the writers, producers, and directors with whom they worked. It will describe the larger forces that shape the TV talk show, including the economics that dictate the terms of the hosts' relationships with their audiences.

A history of the television talk show, then, has multiple purposes. It provides an overview of talk shows' unspoken rules, forms, formats, and landmark figures, tracing the intricate web of forces, people, and technology that put a talk show on the air. It leads to historically informed definitions of the major subgenres of the TV talk show seen on television today.

THREE MAJOR SUBGENRES

Three major subgenres of television talk developed specific identities over time: the late-night entertainment talk show (modeled on *The Tonight Show* of Steve Allen and Jack Paar, 1954–1961), the daytime audience-participation talk show (modeled on *The Phil Donahue Show*, 1967–1995), and the morning magazine-format show (modeled on the first *Today* show of Dave Garroway, 1952–1959). Because of their prominence, these subgenres have influenced many other forms of talk on television and are the focus of this book.

The Late-Night Entertainment Talk Show

This is the subgenre that many people picture when they think of talk shows—a celebrity host chatting with one guest, possibly with other guests seated nearby. The celebrity chat show takes on different characteristics depending upon the time of day it is broadcast. The late-night version is based on congenial, playful encounters between guests and the host, who is more often than not a singer or comedian. The late-night entertainment talk/variety show became dominant on network television in the 1950s with *Broadway Open House* and *The Tonight Show*, and in the 1960s *Tonight* became the flagship late-night talk program of NBC. The audience for late night increased during the late 1960s and early 1970s with the publicity of the first late-night talk-show wars between *Tonight* host Johnny Carson and his competitors. David Letterman brought a new sensibility to the subgenre with his program following Carson's on NBC in the late-night program schedule of the 1980s. Drawing on the earlier comedy talk traditions of Ernie Kovacs and Steve Allen, Letterman's version of late-night entertainment talk, which played with the talk show as a form, became increasingly mainstream through the 1980s. Later, Jay Leno and others integrated Letterman's innovations into the more traditional elements of Carson's format. With many contenders entering and leaving late-night talk, but only a few holding steady, the late-night entertainment talk show grew steadily in popularity among viewers throughout its first five decades on the air.

The Daytime Audience-Participation Show

This format, founded by Phil Donahue in 1967 in Dayton, Ohio, and based on Donahue's earlier hot-topic radio call-in show (*Conversation Piece*, 1963–1967), made the studio audience a full participant by putting the audience in direct dialogue with guest experts or celebrities. Donahue's young production team was willing to try new approaches to reach a largely female audience at home during the day. Donahue pioneered the role of the host as a peripatetic mediator who stirs a live studio audience to question and speak up to celebrities and experts. Donahue's commercial success in national syndication in the 1970s and 1980s spawned many imitators. His competition with Oprah Winfrey in the mid- and late 1980s brought new viewers, publicity, and attention to the form. By the late 1980s and early 1990s, however, the intermittent public-service orientation of daytime talk shows like Donahue's was supplanted by the purely entertainment-oriented commercial values of tabloid shows like *Ricki Lake, Jerry Springer,* and other forms of "reality-based" talk programming.

The Early-Morning News Talk Magazine Show

Whether presenting news or entertainment, every television talk show that rose to prominence in the first decades of television was influenced by the time of day it was offered and the audience it appealed to at that time of day (what programmers call "the day part"). The morning show provides a good example of the trial-and-error method by which talk subgenres emerged in their respective time periods.

By the late 1940s, radio had a wide variety of talk formats in the morning, but television was just beginning to experiment with early morning viewers. Television still reached a limited number of households, and there was not much programming of any kind on television in the morning in 1947–1948. In 1948, however, NBC scheduled a popular morning radio talk couple, Tex and Jinx, at 1 P.M., then the earliest hour on the TV schedule. By fall 1948 the fourth TV network, DuMont, began to experiment with a series of variety and informational shows that aired before noon. CBS began its first morning TV programming with *Two Sleepy People,* starring Mike Wallace and Buff Cobb.[8] These experiments in early-morning programming took lasting form in January 1952 with the creation of *The Today Show* with host Dave Garroway, under programming chief Pat Weaver's direction, on NBC. Arthur Godfrey's daytime program, *Arthur Godfrey Time,* began on CBS the same week, with both hosts going on to become founders of television talk and creating major profit centers for their networks.

By the end of the 1950s, most of network television's major subgenres were in place, though occasionally new formats emerged out of syndication (*The Phil Donahue Show,* 1967), cable (Bill Maher's *Politically Incorrect,* 1993), or independent network competition (Fox Broadcasting's *Fox in the Morning,* 1996–1997, which attempted to update the early-morning talk magazine for an MTV audience). New forms of TV talk are rare. Instead, talk subgenres are periodically modified or brought up to date within each cycle of television industry practice.

CYCLES

Before the invention of television, broadcasting began to influence popular speech. Although David Sarnoff, later head of RCA and NBC, was not one of the operators relaying signals from the sinking *Titanic*, as later legend proclaimed, he saw the effect of the instantaneous transmission of news on the listening and reading public. When radio turned broadcasting into a mass medium in the 1920s and 1930s, advertising agencies, producers, and performers brought diverse forms of radio programming to the air, paving the way for the television talk of the late 1940s and early 1950s. The founders of network talk had extensive experience in radio, and some, like Edward R. Murrow and Arthur Godfrey, maintained careers in both media.

Television added sight to sound. One could now see as well as hear the host and his guests. From 1948 to the present, thousands of talk shows have been produced by hundreds of hosts. The history of the major subgenres of the TV talk show can be broken down into five major periods, or cycles, of development, which correspond roughly to the last five decades of the twentieth century. Within each cycle, a handful of hosts played leading roles both on and off camera. During each cycle, technological, economic, and cultural changes within the television industry affected how emerging subgenres of talk shows were produced.

The first cycle of television talk, from 1948 to 1962, was the era of the founders. Arthur Godfrey, Edward R. Murrow, Dave Garroway, Arlene Francis, Mike Wallace, and Jack Paar all played significant roles in founding major subgenres of TV talk. The decade began with experiments in television programming, sometimes decentralized, and moved rapidly into reliance on a few powerful, independent hosts. This period, from 1948 to 1953, was a time when television-set ownership exploded from 1 percent of the population to 53 percent. By the end of the 1950s, with the saturation of American households by television reaching 90 percent, talk programming was rigorously controlled by bottom-line corporate managers. By 1962, the founders of TV talk in the 1950s were all gone, often after being tragically stripped of their former independence and initiative. The excitement of television talk in the early

1950s is illustrated by Edward R. Murrow's narration of the split-screen joining of the New York harbor and San Francisco's Golden Gate Bridge on the first *See It Now*, using the first coast-to-coast coaxial cable for television in 1951. An image that ends the period is Murrow, head in hands, worn out by struggles with the network and unable to execute his weekly radio broadcast. Two other images that capture the end of the era are Jack Paar's famous walk off *The Tonight Show* after being censored by network officials for a water-closet joke in 1960, and his retirement two years later as he dramatically walked off the stage, followed by his dog and with his talk-show stool in hand.

The second and third cycles of television talk ran from 1962 to 1974 and from 1974 to 1980. These cycles represent the rise of network power and the beginning of its fall. From 1962 to 1974 the three big networks consolidated their power. Network coffers were overflowing. Network decision-makers were firmly in control of programming, intent on making sure that nothing would upset sponsors or advertisers. Network officials had the additional control of videotape, which is how they flagged the Jack Paar water-closet joke, and much "live" dramatic and talk programming was no longer truly live. A small but vigorous syndicated talk industry grew up beside the networks in the period, but only three hosts emerged as stars with staying power in the network structures of the day: Johnny Carson, Barbara Walters, and Mike Wallace. These stars established themselves with programs that were steady profit-makers for their networks and used their network bases to become stars of TV talk for more than three decades.

Johnny Carson's career spanned the rise and fall of network power. In 1963 he was the network's hand-picked successor to Paar. When Carson retired in 1992, the network's falling clout was signified by its dilemma in finding his successor. Jay Leno was contractually bound to NBC, but David Letterman, becoming a free agent from his NBC contract in 1993, was courted by other networks and national syndication companies like King World. He eventually chose CBS, for its tradition and stability, but his choice was by no means a foregone conclusion. The balance of power had shifted away from the networks and toward individual stars and new broadcasting entities in national television.

Some of the shift was already under way in the third cycle of television talk. Though the networks still dominated the industry, they began to receive challenges from new competitors: syndicators, independent station groups, cable, and PBS. Another series of images brings back the competitive ferment of the period: Phil Donahue sneaking back to his former radio station in 1967 to steal back his Rolodex for his new daytime television show; Joey Bishop, Merv Griffin, David Frost, and Dick Cavett battling Johnny Carson to dominate late-night TV from 1967 to 1974; Cavett bucking Emmy Award ritual in 1972, when he refused to accept the Emmy to protest the networks' lack of news, documentary, and public-affairs talk programming. Another image from the period is that of Bill Moyers' amazement as he received a flood of letters after his 1973 "Watergate Essay" on *Bill Moyers' Journal*. He had no idea that a PBS television show could have that much impact.

Of the new competitive forces, syndication turned out to be the most significant. Since the 1950s, syndicators had produced television shows inexpensively in their own studios and sold them to independent stations around the country or to network affiliates for off-peak hours. Until 1969, however, the number of new talk shows rarely exceeded five. Twenty new talk shows came on the market in 1969, most of them syndicated.[9] New technologies of production (cheaper television studios and lower production costs), new methods of distribution (satellite transmission), new distribution systems (HBO and cable), and key regulatory decisions by the Federal Communications Commission (FCC) made nationally syndicated talk shows increasingly profitable and attractive to investors.

The fourth and fifth cycles of television talk, from 1980 to 1990 and 1990 to 2000, took place in the post-network era of TV. Traditional distinctions between news and entertainment began to break down. Hosts, programs, and formats continued to exploit the steady expansion of cable and syndicated talk outlets through the 1990s. Films like *Wayne's World* appropriated and satirized talk shows, while arguments about the impact of talk shows as forums of social expression raged among politicians, journalists, academics, and talk professionals.

The end of each decade brought ferment in the talk-show industry, but the early 1980s reflected particularly deep changes in the way audiences watched TV. In the 1979 introduction to the television reference book *The Complete Directory to Prime Time Network TV Shows*, authors Tim Brook and Earle Marsh confidently remarked that "little had changed" in network television programming since the demise of the fourth network (DuMont) in 1956.[10] Five years later, in the preface to the second edition of *Total Television*, Alex McNeil noted the remarkable growth of cable television from 1980 to 1984 as a major development in broadcasting.[11] With cable came a steady stream of reality-based programming and infotainment.

The term *infotainment* was a marketing ploy at the 1980 National Association of Television Programming Executives (NATPE) conference, applying particularly to real-life cop shows. The term encompassed much more, however, in the next two decades as blended forms of information, news, and entertainment became more prominent. With increasing regularity, starting in the early 1980s, five to ten channels suddenly expanded to fifty to a hundred or more for many viewers, and, with the advent of the remote control, audiences no longer had to get up to switch channels. Zipping through programs with the remote control became the normal way of viewing television, and the lines between information and entertainment began to blur in viewing experiences at the same time they were blurring in programming. Infotainment in talk programming encompassed news as entertainment (*The McLaughlin Group*); carnivalesque relationship shows (*Ricki Lake* and *Jerry Springer*); blends of comedy, opinion, and public-affairs discussion (Bill Maher's *Politically Incorrect*); news parodies (the *Dennis Miller Show* and Jon Stewart's *The Daily Show*); blends of dramatically scripted and improvised talk (*The Larry Sanders Show*); and specialized topics that blended information and entertainment (the *Dr. Ruth Show* or MTV's *Loveline*). These hybrid programs often made money, and while some were transitory, others marked a more permanent change on the landscape of television.

By the time Johnny Carson retired in the early 1990s, most talk programming was coming from cable television or syndication. Although the exact contours of TV talk could not be predicted by the end of the 1990s, the talk show was clearly a vigorous and expanding form. New strategies were being developed for recycling talk shows, and certain major hosts established their own national magazines (*Oprah* and *Rosie*). TV talk could now be integrated with websites and other forms of interactive computer communications.

STAR HOSTS

In an industry in which talk shows are plentiful but the variety of talk-show forms relatively limited, individual hosts have played an enormous role in inventing and refining the talk show's most influential subgenres. Who those star hosts have been, what they have said, and the kinds of ideas they have represented are particularly relevant to a history of TV talk. The person and on-air persona of the talk-show host are closely intertwined. This is why the following chapters trace so closely the careers of individual hosts.

The period from 1980 to 1990 marked breakthroughs in ethnic and racial representation among star hosts of TV talk. Oprah Winfrey, Geraldo Rivera, Sally Jessy Raphaël, Arsenio Hall, Montel Williams, and others put new class, ethnic, racial, and cultural diversity on a television screen that was still limited, but certainly now included much more of a range than in the 1950s when canceled African American entertainer Nat King Cole made his famous remark: "Madison Avenue is afraid of the dark." Oprah Winfrey led the field of new hosts in the 1980s, grossing over $100 million her first year in national syndication. The networks were looking for new formulas and new audiences and to redefine traditional day parts in the face of the competition. Ted Koppel and David Letterman emerged as major talk-show stars during this period as well.

The show-business biographies, key programs, and business history of each host reveal some of the cultural, technological, and commercial forces that constituted each cycle. These forces first supported the host and program, then shaped them, and eventually were influential in taking them off the air. The profiles also illustrate the cultural role of the national TV talk-show host. Late-night entertainment hosts, most of whom had their training in stand-up comedy, performed balancing acts as comedy monologists, social commentators, and masters of ceremony introducing celebrity and non-celebrity guests. As interviewers they asked questions designed to represent the probing curiosities of the viewer at home. The star hosts of daytime audience-participation talk shows performed a different kind of balancing. The big four of daytime talk in the 1980s—Donahue, Winfrey, Rivera, and Raphaël—all had their early training in radio public-affairs broadcasting and journalism. While often playing the role of reporter, they also served as catalyst, mediator, teacher, preacher, counselor, confessor, or ombudsperson in the midst of contesting views and personalities on their shows. Trained in theater techniques, Sally Jessy Raphaël was quoted as saying that her skills, and the skills of other daytime hosts, were the skills of a theater director as well.

In general, late-night and daytime hosts draw on interview techniques that test their abilities to listen and their skills at repartee. They bring the force of their own personalities to the sociability rituals of television talk. As culture critic Michael Arlen has pointed out, the talk-show hosts reinforce, almost obsessively, rules of social decorum that are disappearing from other places in American life.[12]

Star hosts also set social, political, and cultural agendas. In the 1970s, 1980s, and 1990s, the comedy monologues of Johnny Carson, David Letterman, and Jay Leno were repeatedly cited by news critics and political commentators as barometers of public opinion, helping to define what constituted common sense for many Americans. Serious issues were always just beneath the surface of entertainment, and entertainment values permeated the news. News and entertainment hosts faced the same pressures for audiences and ratings, and complemented one another in their treatment of the day's news topics. The explosion of interest in the O. J. Simpson case as a national media event, from June 1994 through the verdict of the criminal trial in October 1995, was as much a creation of talk shows as news headlines. Twenty years previously, Phil Donahue's airing of issues raised by the women's movement had helped turn what were formerly considered private issues into public ones. In the 1980s, Oprah Winfrey's programs on incest and child abuse, drawing on her own authority as an incest victim, had extended the limits of public discussion around those issues. The agenda-setting potential of television talk shows increased in each decade as the number of TV sets multiplied and television became a more pervasive influence in American life. Frank Mankiewicz, former president of National Public Radio, argues that by the 1980s entertainment and news talk hosts on television had overtaken the voices of the printed press and radio as the most important shapers of public opinion. Mankiewicz cites Johnny Carson and David Letterman as two of the ten most powerful molders of public opinion in the 1980s. "Like Johnny Carson's jokes," Mankiewicz said, "David Letterman's famous lists are almost always a form of commentary on the news. . . . He is making sense of the news just as surely as some thrice-weekly foreign policy expert delivering the latest assessment of glasnost or medium-range missiles."[13] By the 1990s, Jay Leno had joined the ranks of national comedy news commentators as well.

With this larger view of the role of star hosts in the televised talk worlds of contemporary America, we can begin to think about the talk show in relation to the recorded conversation of earlier eras.

TALK WORLDS

A *talk world* is a point of intersection or site in which a small group talks to itself while simultaneously addressing an invisible but clearly defined collective audience. Talk worlds may be captured by writing, audio recording, film, or television and relayed to their audiences at the distance of centuries, or in an electronic instant. In its most immediate form the talk of television takes place within a small group and within the relatively confined space of a TV studio, but it is simultaneously directed to a mass audience at various locations around the world. Because talk shows address an immediate and public audience at the same time, they are characterized by a dual consciousness. They are a form of rhetoric that is both private and public, personal and mass. To borrow a metaphor from quantum physics, talk shows are wave and particle at the same time.

In one sense, dual consciousness characterizes all talk worlds of private conversations made public. In every age bards, scribes, writers, and amanuenses have reflected this dual consciousness by recording the words of influential speakers and relaying them to widening circles. The difference between earlier recorded talk worlds and the talk shows of today is one of speed, totality, and impact. Modern participants are aware of the intersection of their small circle of talk with the larger cultural one and, with major network television shows, they are aware that millions are listening to the same conversation.

A talk world is completed by its last participant, its last decoder. In the case of written accounts of talk worlds, that decoder may read a written description of spoken words at a distance of centuries and through various filters of translation and narrative framing. The last decoder—the reader or listener—imaginatively re-frames or "hears" the words that are spoken *as if they are being spoken in the present tense.* The reader may contextualize the words being read as part of a historical document, a religious teaching, or a piece of literature, but the power of the spoken word reverts to its origins as a spoken act. One of the major principles of TV talk—present-tense immediacy—maps in this sense onto the way ancient, medieval, and modern talk worlds have been relived for centuries.

Of course, earlier talk worlds occupy gray areas between fictional and real. Biblical dialogues, such as the encounter between Moses and God on Sinai, can be understood as purely literary documents, as real on the level of myth (collectively condensed sagas of real people in real historical circumstances), or, as biblical literalists maintain, as the actual words spoken in biblical times.

The highly selected and canonized talk worlds of ancient cultures often made powerful statements. These talk worlds were passed down by bards and scribes. The authorship or recording of these dialogues was often placed under the name of a single interlocutor. For example, the Five Books of Moses are ascribed to Moses, the dialogues of Socrates to Plato, the dialogue between Krishna and Arjuna in the *Bhagavad-Gita* of Hinduism to the poet sage Vyasa. Taken collectively, these ancient talk worlds show how important certain basic dialogues—private conversations made public—have been to the history of publicized talk.

The eighteenth century marked a turning point in the history of public conversation. Members of the emerging middle class debated the scientific, political, social, and artistic issues of the day in taverns, in coffee houses, at private dinner parties, in salons, and within discussion societies of all kinds. Journalists and essayists converted this talk into print, and that, too, was disseminated.

The commodification of talk by a vigorous publishing industry and the rise of a celebrity system accompanying the public talk of the eighteenth century played a decisive part in the rise of modern democracies. Posthumous battles over the words of Samuel Johnson, for example, resulted in dozens of biographies, sketches, and portraits of Johnson's conversations.[14] The commodification of talk in the eighteenth century prefigured the TV talk worlds of today.

While the role of public talk in the eighteenth century has now been recognized by many scholars and writers, the impact of public talk on television today has been harder to see. By the 1990s, however, social critics were beginning to recognize the power of the TV talk show as cultural institution and social text as well as performance event and profitable form of entertainment. Media critics, editorial writers, and scholars began asking questions about how TV talk shows affected public judgments about what was and was not newsworthy. A new round of articles and books appeared concerning the eighteenth-century ideal of common public space and rational debate and what had happened to it. Television's role in defining topics of national interest and identification for Americans, and for an increasing number of viewers worldwide, made television talk, by the end of the 1990s, one of the nation's leading forums for working out national values and ideas.

Modern media critics recognize that the public space of television is subject to enormous corporate influence and that powerful filters are operating all the time.[15] Alternative ideas—direct critiques of the fundamental premises of a capitalist system and consumer society, for example—are marginalized or not discussed at all. Intensifying the trend toward univocal public discussion was the increasing consolidation and concentration of mass media ownership. Talk shows were being produced within larger and larger corporate systems of production and distribution.

By the late 1980s, General Electric had taken over NBC, Cap Cities had become the new corporate owner of ABC, and CBS was bought by Laurence Tisch from previous stockholders and Paley family interests.[16] By the mid-1990s Walt Disney acquired ABC–Cap Cities with the worldwide ESPN network for $18.84 billion, and Time Warner purchased Turner Broadcasting with the worldwide Cable News Network for $6.88 billion. Westinghouse merged with CBS in another $5.04 billion mega-deal.[17] At the end of the decade the CBS merger with Viacom dwarfed these earlier deals, at $37 billion,[18] and soon afterward America Online bought Time Warner for the new record merger price of $166 billion.[19] These acquisitions represented new pressures for immediate returns on capital invested, stepped up the drive for ratings and mass audiences, and favored forms of talk that were profitable and easy to produce.

Still, some social critics have seen rays of promise in all this talk.[20] Although there are limits to what can be said and done in all commercial television formats, new constituencies were able to appear on shows like *Donahue* and *Oprah* and speak directly for themselves and their groups without experts or professional broadcasters re-framing their words. Sometimes these citizens challenged the experts. Political candidates spoke more directly to hosts and audiences on talk shows as opposed to the more rigidly controlled formats of traditional press conferences or press panels. Though new levels of spin have developed on the talk-show circuit as handlers guide their candidates through the maze of talk forums, critics and audiences have become more knowledgeable about these rhetorical strategies. Talk shows can sometimes put the spotlight on social issues, catching candidates off guard or taking them away from their positions and highly rehearsed campaign images.

Historically, TV talk has occasionally weighed in on important national issues. The shows of hosts like Edward R. Murrow, Phil Donahue, and Oprah Winfrey have on occasion raised important social and political issues for debate. For example, Murrow's 1954 confrontation with Senator Joseph R. McCarthy represented a turning point in national politics. Similarly, public debate on television, along with direct views of warfare and casualties on TV news, contributed to the serious questions that were being raised about the war in Vietnam.[21]

How television talk functions as an "ideology machine" can only be understood by a close examination of its texts. By the time of the O. J. Simpson verdict in October 1995, for example, it was clear that network decision-makers, producers, and talk-show hosts were conceiving of the television talk show as one of the last truly national centers of public opinion in a market-segmented public sphere. Major news commentators got it wrong at the time of the verdict, though it seemed to faze them only momentarily. For it was clear at the time of the verdict that the white population and the African American population did not see the trial the same way. The man-and-woman-in-the-street interview, the discussions with legal and forensic experts, constitutional scholars, and political analysts, and the joke factory of TV talk comedians attempted to simulate the old town meeting on a national scale, but television talk often provided more spectacle than analysis. Its main goal, it appeared, was to create a consensus narrative that would allow all viewers to feel comfortable with the verdict when it was rendered. That proved impossible.

Viewers saw powerful consensus narratives during other national and international media events: the outbreak of the Gulf War in 1991, for example, or the flood of news and talk commentary that accompanied the announcement of the "War on Terrorism" after the World Trade Center attack on September 11, 2001. The appearance of veteran news anchor Dan Rather on *The David Letterman Show* the week after the attack, when Letterman dropped his characteristic irony and reserve and Rather cried on the air, represented a moment when TV news talk and TV entertainment talk fused.

With all its limitations, dangers, potentials, and pitfalls, the TV talk show is now part of the fabric of modern society. Talk shows represent skewed but instantly recognizable constructions of American experience. Their political and cultural importance can no longer be discounted. An understanding of the TV talk show is now crucial to an understanding of American public life itself.

TWO

THE FIRST CYCLE (1948–1962)

Experimentation, Consolidation, and Network Control — CBS

INTRODUCTION TO THE FIRST CYCLE

Before there were "talk shows" or talk-show hosts, before the term was even invented or had entered standard dictionaries,[1] there were talk personalities. Without exception, the major talk personalities who appeared on television in the late 1940s and early 1950s had already distinguished themselves on radio. The founders of television talk — Edward R. Murrow and Arthur Godfrey on CBS; Dave Garroway, Arlene Francis, Steve Allen, and Jack Paar on NBC; and Mike Wallace on Du-Mont — were already pre-sold commodities in that sense. Their reputations as radio hosts helped them raise funds, enlist advertisers, and create new programs. They understood broadcast time and could serve as managing editors as well as stars of their shows. Television simply gave them a new venue.

The radio traditions out of which the founders of television talk emerged were diverse. They came out of news (Murrow); variety talk/humor (Godfrey); disc jockeying, experimental radio, and avant garde comedy (Garroway); live theater and panel/quiz show traditions (Francis); intriguing mixtures of news, interview, and stand-up and sketch comedy (Paar). All of these radio talk traditions played a part in the emerging forms of television talk.[2]

The late 1940s and early 1950s were a time of unusual openness to experiment and the creation of new forms for television. In its early years television time was still relatively cheap.[3] Ad agencies and sponsors found themselves racing to catch up with the new medium's potentialities, and the 1948 television season saw such special-interest talk programs as *Photographic Horizons,* which explored the world of photography; cultural talk of shows like *Omnibus;* and public-interest discussion shows like *America's Town Meeting* and *We, the People.* Reading was promoted on such shows as *Teenage Book Club* and *Author Meets the Critics.* Serious public-affairs discussions could be seen on *Meet the Press* in prime time, and aesthetic experiments as well as hard-hitting original-for-television social dramas appeared on *Studio One.* Some experiments in interactive television appeared in the early 1950s as well. Kids could draw pictures directly from images on the screen, and *The Continental* (1952) had a Don Juan–style talk-show host who would speak ingratiatingly to housewives at home. It was indeed a lively time in television, and a time in which many of the ongoing forms of television talk, including some of its principal genres in entertainment and news, were established.

The early 1950s were also a time that favored the rise of the first major talk personalities on television. If an individual star or creator was able to obtain solid backing from a substantial sponsor—as Edward R. Murrow had done with his *See It Now* series from Alcoa— the program could be sustained over a long period of time, and the major networks were still willing to support "sustaining" public-service shows even if they did not generate immediate profits. Commercial forces were nakedly evident in the early days of commercial sponsorship, but strong-minded hosts who were also master sales people rose to immense popularity. They could even bait their own sponsors, as did Arthur Godfrey with his frequent acerbic jests at his sponsors' expense. In the 1950s, writer-producers like Rod Serling and well-known filmmakers like Alfred Hitchcock managed to engage in and win censorship battles with network programmers as well. As a result, a certain amount of offbeat, innovative programming made it to the nation's television screens.

Television had been experimental at first, a weak adjunct to radio, but by 1951 ten sponsors were each billing over $4 million in television advertising and a total of $77.1 million was spent.[4] Coaxial cable united West and East Coasts by the fall of 1951 when Edward R. Murrow's first *See It Now* went on the air, and the number of television stations leaped meteorically when the FCC lifted its freeze in 1952. From 38 stations on the air in May 1949 the number rose to 422 in 1955.[5] Most of these stations belonged to the four national television networks: NBC, CBS, ABC, and DuMont.[6] The number of households with television sets grew from 3.8 million in 1950 to 38.9 million by 1955, reaching 78.6 percent of the U.S. population. The United States was becoming "one nation under television."[7]

The history of talk programming in its first cycle follows closely the history of the television industry itself. It comprises three stages: the experimental phase from the late 1940s into the early 1950s; a period of consolidation in the mid- and late 1950s, when the networks began vying with powerful advertising agencies and sponsors for control; and the period following the quiz-show scandals at the end of the decade, when the networks assumed full control. Two television networks dominated this period: CBS and NBC. Between them they produced many of the television talk show's most enduring forms.

In this first cycle, 1948–1962, seven founders—Murrow, Godfrey, Garroway, Francis, Allen, Paar, and Wallace—laid the groundwork for future subgenres of talk. Chapters 2 and 3, covering the first cycle, profile these seven talk-show hosts, highlighting their achievements in the first decade of television. With the occasional assistance of an imaginative television executive, these seven hosts extended the financial possibilities, scope, and tone of television talk and influenced its development for years to come. They truly deserve the appellation of "founders."

FOUNDERS AT CBS: Murrow and Godfrey

Edward R. Murrow, 1948–1961

Edward R. Murrow pioneered three forms of news talk: live investigative reporting, celebrity journalism, and live trans-oceanic dialogue. As executive producer, newscaster, and host, Murrow charted new territory in television. He joined CBS radio in 1935 as Director of Talks, after an earlier career working with student groups and international education. Over the next twenty-five years he assumed near-statesmanlike status in broadcast journalism at CBS. When he moved to CBS television in 1951, Murrow used his status as CBS's premier radio news broadcaster and his close relationship with CBS founder William Paley to establish several innovative news talk formats.

As a host, Edward R. Murrow illustrated the power of the spoken word as no one had done before or has done since, demonstrating in terse but eloquent first-person narrations that the boundary between the written and spoken word is at best a fragile one. As the host of *See It*

Now (1951–1958), *Person to Person* (1953–1959), and *Small World* (1958–1960), he showed that a single host could pass back and forth among three kinds of talk show and do justice to each. Finally, he exemplified the multiple roles of the talk-show host as character, creator, star-commodity, and entrepreneur.

Murrow's biographers describe the roots of his verbal power in the story-telling traditions he absorbed growing up in Guildford County, North Carolina.[8] The oral tradition was strong on both sides of the Murrow family. By many accounts, the person who had the most to do with molding Murrow's character and his ability as a speaker was his mother, Ethel Lamb Murrow, a strong-minded woman who instilled in her three sons a compulsion for hard work and a respect for the sounds and rhythms of the English language. "At home, the boys had to read aloud from the Bible, a chapter every night. . . . a first encounter with formal speech in the strong, rhythmic measures of the King James Version of the Bible."[9] Murrow's speech, like his mother's, never lost its Southern intonation and Spenserian quality. It was the kind of English that was spoken in Elizabethan times and that still survives in isolated cultural pockets of the South. The exact choice of words and their precise use, inverted phrases like "this I believe," and verb forms like "I'd not" and "it pleasures me," which Ed Murrow used on and off the air, came directly from his earliest years.[10]

In his London "blitzkrieg" reports during World War II, Murrow established himself as the foremost radio foreign correspondent of his day. In crisp, condensed cadences he employed vivid metaphors to paint verbal pictures of what he was seeing. Describing a plane taking off at sunset, Murrow spoke of "rivers and lakes of fire atop the clouds." Small bombs fell "like a fistful of white rice thrown on a piece of black velvet," and bigger ones went off "like great sunflowers gone mad." Looking down on a burning Berlin, he described fires that merged and spread "like butter on a hot plate."[11]

Murrow's broadcasts from London brought radio listeners an intensity they had rarely experienced before. BBC correspondent Frank Gillard remembers Murrow's agonies as he hunched "over his typewriter, enveloped and isolated in cigarette smoke, oblivious to all around him." Murrow's intensity on the air was lifelong, and it is what many viewers recall from his famous *See It Now* broadcasts on Senator Joseph McCarthy.[12]

The sense that Murrow forged his words as he spoke them came from his method of composition. Unlike Eric Sevareid and other reporters of the day, who wrote drafts and then polished them, Murrow dictated his broadcasts to long-time secretary Kay Campbell shortly before delivering them. This was to remain his practice for twenty-five years on the air. The words were copied down exactly as he spoke them. Though the syntax might seem awkward on the page, when Murrow spoke, the words emerged in smooth and perfect cadences.

In looking back at Murrow's remarkable career on television in the 1950s, we can now see his contribution: he demonstrated the power of the written-as-spoken word on television, a tradition that extended itself on television in the work of veteran broadcasters like Eric Sevareid, Charles Kuralt, David Brinkley, Bill Moyers, and Charles Osgood. By the early 1990s this tradition had all but died out on network television, but Murrow's legacy remained. His contribution was not just to television news but to talk on television, with three major talk traditions emerging from his three most influential shows: *See It Now*, *Person to Person*, and *Small World*.

***See It Now* (1951–1958)** *See It Now*, coproduced by Murrow with Fred Friendly, went on the air at 3:30 P.M., Sunday, November 18, 1951, sponsored by Alcoa Aluminum, then attempting to bolster its corporate image with a "class act" on national television.[13] Murrow's personal relationship with Alcoa executives was a good one,[14] and survived, for a time, the battering he took from rabid anti-Communists after his McCarthy broadcasts. He also had a long-standing and intimate relationship with CBS founder and president William Paley, who appointed Murrow a CBS vice president when he returned from London in 1947. Murrow's position within the executive hierarchy of CBS gave him an unusual degree of control and authority over his first television show.

Looking up from an odd, cramped corner of the *See It Now* control room, cigarette smoke curling up from the bottom of the screen, Murrow introduced the first edition of *See It Now* in 1951 as follows:

> "This is an old team, trying to learn a new trade," Murrow told his viewers. "We are fully conscious that there is no such thing as a wholly objective reporter. We are all the prisoners of our own experience, of our leanings, of our indoctrination and our travels."[15]

The cramped control room setting was a last-minute decision. It was characteristic of the chaotic, spur-of-the-moment conditions under which *See It Now* was produced. Those conditions helped give the program a sweaty, present-tense, improvisational feeling. The first program included a shot of both coasts, the Golden Gate Bridge in San Francisco and the Brooklyn Bridge in New York, captured in split screen at the same moment. It was a scene made possible by the coaxial cable that had just been completed. "Three thousand miles compressed to a vanishing point," said one critic.[16] Along with interviews of major newsmakers, Murrow and Friendly had sent *See It Now* crews to Korea to interview soldiers on the front. It was, wrote one critic, "the first Korea picture report that actually brought the war home to us,"[17] and it displayed the kind of intimacy and authority that were to become Murrow's trademark on *See It Now*.

CLOSE-UP: "THE CASE OF MILO RADULOVICH," *SEE IT NOW,* OCTOBER 20, 1953

Of all Murrow's work on the air, it was the five programs Murrow did on Senator Joseph McCarthy that insured his place in television history. The first program in this series focused on the dismissal of Air Force lieutenant Milo Radulovich for the alleged "Communist associations" of family members, and aired October 20, 1953.[18] It was one of Murrow's finest programs, and it is worth reconsidering for two reasons. It shows the importance of the historical and social context of television talk, and demonstrates the power of the written word when, in the Murrow tradition, it takes on the force of the spoken word.

The charges of "Communist" sympathies leveled against Milo Radulovich, a young Air Force ROTC officer, were similar to charges that affected tens of thousands during the McCarthy period, causing many to lose their jobs without proof, evidence, or the ability to confront their accusers. The television networks themselves had been the targets of "anti-Red" campaigns. Names were listed in *Red Channels: The Report of Communists in Radio and Television,* a pamphlet distributed by three former FBI agents,[19] putting hundreds in jeopardy of losing their jobs and causing hundreds of others to be fired. Before the Radulovich program went on the air, Murrow had been under some pressure to act as Eric Sevareid and a few other responsible journalists had done, to oppose the smear and innuendo tactics of McCarthy and his committee. Murrow and Friendly decided the time was right in October 1953, and the veteran newscaster gathered his staff before the show to ask if any had a reason to think he or she might be the target of an investigation. Production manager Palmer Williams said that he had been formerly married to someone engaged in Communist Party activities in the 1920s and 1930s. Murrow didn't think it would be a problem. Every person in the room, however, knew that *See It Now* was taking on a powerful and vengeful foe. CBS management had distanced itself from the program, and Murrow and Friendly had gone into their own pockets to promote the show in an ad in the *New York Times*. Murrow said that the terror was right there in the room.

Much of the show was based on the live, in-the-field testimony of people who lived in the small town where Radulovich resided. Field producer Joseph Wershba had found a chorus of support for the young career officer among the citizens of Dexter, Michigan. His camera recorded their comments. A carefully coiffured young woman spoke directly to the camera: "I felt like so many others in Dexter that Milo was getting a pretty bad deal." [20] An older man in rimless glasses, standing very upright, spoke forcefully: "My viewpoint: I can't see how you can hold a man responsible for the views and actions of his relatives." A middle-aged man with a crew cut and wearing a worker's shirt told the camera: "I know I wouldn't want to be held responsible for what my father did." Then the camera came to a guy who, in Wershba's words, "evidently had just come out of a bar with a face to match, and he was the head of the American Legion. I figured this guy is really going to tear him apart." [21] This t-shirted man made one of the program's strongest statements: "If the Air Corps or the United States Army or who they are that are purging this man—I believe they're purging him, gets away with it, they're entitled to do it to anybody— you, me or anyone else." Murrow ended the program with a biblical injunction: "We believe that the son shall not bear the iniquity of the father, even though the iniquity be proved, and, in this case, it is not."

The "Case of Milo Radulovich" was one of Murrow's most important shows and, in a tradition that *60 Minutes* would continue, it effected changes at the highest level. The culmination came when Murrow received a call at home at 8:00 A.M. in late November.[22] It was from Secretary of the Air Force Harold Talbott. He asked that Murrow's camera operator, Charlie Mack, be sent to the Pentagon by 9:00 A.M. to take a statement.[23] Hours later in the *See It Now* screening room the staff let out a cheer and Murrow broke out the scotch. The Air Force exonerated Radulovich.[24]

The citizen-crusader/star-reporter formula of *See It Now* was to inspire *60 Minutes* sixteen years later when it aired under the direction of Murrow's old studio director, Don Hewitt, with many of the old *See It Now* team still on board. Over time the formula would become, some would argue, stale, even a parody of itself. However, during the period from 1951 to 1954, Murrow and his team established a "fresh talk" news show that brought investigative reporting to a new level with the power and immediacy of live TV. The live, on-camera introductions and the filmed as-if-live television talk of *See It Now* set a standard for broadcast journalists.

Person to Person (1953–1961) *See It Now* and those that followed in its tradition were not talk shows per se; they were magazine news shows featuring a distinctive kind of television talk. In contrast, Murrow's next major venture on the air, *Person to Person,* was a show based entirely on conversation between individuals. It certainly wasn't news, but it wasn't just entertainment either. It had informational value as well. The show is perhaps best described as celebrity talk.

Person to Person was an idea brought to Murrow by his longtime associates and friends, Johnny Aaron and Jesse Zousmer, who had been with Murrow in radio and produced remote interview work for *See It Now,* including interviews with Senator Estes Kefauver in Tennessee and Senator Robert A. Taft in Ohio. Aaron and Zousmer believed that people were fascinated with the private lives of famous people, and eventually persuaded Murrow that a show based on weekly visits to the homes of celebrities would be successful.

Person to Person ran from October 1953 to September 1961 on CBS.[25] Murrow's stature and the innovative technology of the show attracted some of the world's great newsmakers and stars. It was also commercially one of CBS's most successful shows. Conducting two fifteen-minute interviews a week with Aaron and Zousmer as associate producers, Murrow introduced his first *Person to Person* as follows:

> Now this is really an ordinary studio in midtown Manhattan. We have no applause meter. We have no jackpot. We have no audience. We have no scripts.[26]

The program did not have a "gimmick," he said, but it would have a "device."

> The device is that window [pointing to the interview screen] and we hope to make it something of a long range window in order that you may . . . look into the homes of some interesting people doing usual things.[27]

Murrow, Aaron, and Zousmer would characteristically pair guests from very different worlds. In the first program, for instance, Murrow interviewed catcher Roy Campanella of the Brooklyn Dodgers in his

179th Street home in St. Albans, Long Island, and then went to the fashionable Upper East Side apartment home of conductor Leopold Stokowski and his socialite wife, Gloria Vanderbilt.[28]

From 1953 to 1961, 312 guests appeared on *Person to Person*.[29] Some of Murrow's most notable guests were Marilyn Monroe, Senator John F. Kennedy and his wife, Jacqueline, ex-President Harry Truman, film stars Humphrey Bogart and Lauren Bacall, Supreme Court Judge William O. Douglas, and the president of NBC, David Sarnoff. Notably lacking from this list were the ordinary citizens who had been part of Murrow's "small picture" news accounts on radio and *See It Now*. Murrow himself had wanted to interview non-celebrities, but ratings were poor for these shows and the host eventually succumbed to his producers' arguments that non-celebrities did not work in this format.

The technical conditions for producing *Person to Person* were formidable. It took twelve technicians several days to set up the broadcast with five cameras, ten stage lights, miles of wire, and several tons of portable control-room equipment packed into twenty suitcases. On the day of the broadcast the interview subject's home was invaded by six members of a camera crew, six more technicians for microwave relay, electricians, producers, directors, makeup artists, and telephone company engineers. As many as twenty-six technicians were on standby at the studio to receive incoming pictures.[30]

Murrow's comments often dipped into the banal on *Person to Person*, and critics became more and more severe. Gilbert Seldes of *The New Yorker*, for example, who admired *See It Now*, attacked *Person to Person*, saying, "the Edward R. Murrow [of *Person to Person*] is not to be confused with the man of the same name who is the star and co-producer of *See It Now*. One of them is an imposter."[31]

Stung by these criticisms, but unwilling to give up a show that had given him financial returns and a good deal of clout with the network, Murrow continued his grueling schedule of working on both *See It Now* and *Person to Person*. Then, to complete his legacy at CBS, in the spring of 1958 Murrow added a third show: a Sunday afternoon interview program called *Small World*.

Small World (1958–1959) *Small World* appeared on CBS from October 1958 to April 1959.[32] Using phone lines and location cameras on separate continents, Murrow captured live exchanges with such noted contemporaries as philosopher Bertrand Russell and nuclear scientist Edward Teller on the prospects for nuclear disarmament. Playwright

Noel Coward, writer James Thurber, and actress Siobhan McKenna discussed the essence of theatrical performance. Irish dramatist Brendan Behan, American comedian Jackie Gleason, and English literary critic John Mason Brown debated the nature of humor. It was a high-order engagement in the world of ideas that equaled anything Bill Moyers was to do three decades later on PBS.

Small World was broadcast with a high order of civility, wit, and charm. The guests and ideas expressed were not always predictable. Irish playwright and humorist Brendan Behan became so inebriated in the course of a discussion that he simply dropped out before it ended. "The art of conversation is gone," Behan wailed in one of his last lucid comments, "murdered by lunatics—most of them in the United States."

As important as *Small World* was in enlarging the scope and tone of talk on television, it is scarcely mentioned in standard Murrow biographies.[33] A footnote in television history, *Small World* established a precedent. It showed that a host could balance serious news talk with light-touch celebrity journalism, while encountering some of the world's greatest thinkers on the air and recording them for posterity.

The "Higher Murrow" vs. "Lower Murrow" Debate   As Edward R. Murrow's career on television in the 1950s developed, the "higher Murrow" vs. "lower Murrow" debate among TV critics dragged on. This debate refused to acknowledge how intimately Edward R. Murrow had always been involved with the commercial side of broadcasting. From his earliest days as CBS administrator, managing news editor, host, and newscaster, Murrow had close working relationships with sponsors. In London he had defended America's free enterprise system against Harold Laski and others who proposed the BBC model for broadcasting, with programming supported by the sale of receivers and government funding. For all its failings, Murrow argued, commercial broadcasting had the ability to produce the best kind of programming as well as the worst, and it was inherently more democratic.

In an overview essay on *Person to Person* in *Journalism Monographs* (1988), Jeffrey Merron argued that Murrow's apparently contradictory roles on *See It Now* and *Person to Person* were actually a successful attempt to bridge two different audiences. Using Dwight Macdonald's terms, Merron suggested that *See It Now* was Edward R. Murrow's "midcult" attempt to attract to television an informed, aware, and news-conscious viewership, whereas *Person to Person* was a "masscult" program, regularly attracting eight to nine million viewers a week, a mass audience for the time.[34]

A gender element played a role in the "higher" Murrow vs. "lower" Murrow debate as well. The news world that Murrow lived and worked in was dominated by men. Hard news and the serious issues of the day were associated almost exclusively with male newscaster figures. The parlor-room interviews of *Person to Person* entered a feminine space. No matter how much a husband or male partner may have dominated many of these conversations, the home was the woman's domain. A newsman entering that world, especially a newsman with a cultivated image as a tough, independent war correspondent who knew how to handle his cigarettes and his scotch, produced an interesting series of gender tensions in 1950s television. It was one thing for Arlene Francis or later Barbara Walters to do these kinds of interviews. It was quite another thing for the country's foremost war correspondent, a man considered to be one of the most serious news broadcasters of his time, to engage in this parlor talk.

While the critical debates continued, with his trilogy of shows in the 1950s—*See It Now, Person to Person,* and *Small World*—Murrow established three major trajectories in the history of television talk.

Arthur Godfrey (1948–1959)

What Murrow was to news broadcasting at CBS in its first decade, Arthur Godfrey was to entertainment programming. "Broadcasting's Forgotten Giant," as he was called in Arthur Singer's 1996 documentary on his life and broadcasting career,[35] Godfrey institutionalized a form of intimacy and wry, rebellious charm that has set a standard for entertainment talk on television.

In *Arthur Godfrey and His Friends* (1949–1957), *Arthur Godfrey and His Ukulele* (1950), *Arthur Godfrey Time* (1952–1959), and *The Arthur Godfrey Show* (1958–1959), and in time slots that occurred in almost every part of the day on radio and on television, Arthur Godfrey was one of the most popular entertainers of the 1950s. At the height of his career Godfrey had two prime-time shows on television with an estimated weekly audience of 82 million viewers. He brought in 12 percent of CBS's total revenues.[36] *Variety* estimated that Godfrey was responsible for $159 million in billings by 1959, with more than eighty on-air sponsors.[37] He was also broadcasting's "big, bad boy," famed for his sudden bursts of anger and jealousy, for feuds with members of his broadcast "family" and with other major stars (including Ed Sullivan), and for headline-provoking off-camera episodes (he once buzzed an airport control tower in his private plane). A photo recognition poll taken before the 1960 elections registered 71 percent for Presidential candidate John F. Kennedy, 86 percent for Vice President Richard M. Nixon— and 91 percent for Godfrey.[38]

Godfrey's major contribution to the history of television talk was the persuasive, intimate, sometimes sarcastic person-to-person tone he brought to broadcasting. It is a tone that viewers of David Letterman and his followers in the 1980s and 1990s will immediately recognize. Indeed, it was specifically Godfrey's morning show that NBC executive Fred Silverman had in mind when he negotiated the original Letterman morning show on NBC in the early 1980s. But Godfrey brought to television more than a style. He was a master salesperson as well, selling, and selling very well, the same products that he would sometimes mock over the air.

Arthur Godfrey was born in 1903. His father was a freelance writer and lecturer, an expert on horses, his mother an aspiring piano player who had played at silent movie theaters. His father's work dried up, and the family was very poor through his early life, his mother selling jams door to door. Godfrey himself resorted to stealing milk bottles. Eventually, the children were split up and sent to foster parents. At ten, Godfrey went to work after school, and he quit school entirely at fifteen, moving across the country in a succession of jobs. He worked as a coal miner in Pennsylvania, a typist in an army camp, a tire finisher in Akron. In 1920, at the age of seventeen, he enlisted in the Navy. The Navy sent him to radio school, where he went up in an airplane for the first time (flying later became a lifelong passion), and learned to play the ukulele. When he got out of the Navy in 1924, he drifted again, for a time selling cemetery plots door to door. Signing up for the Coast Guard in 1927 as a radioman, he was sent to Baltimore to design radio equipment, and it was there that his career as a radio performer took off.[39]

He had always had a gift for talk, serving as captain of his school's debating team before he left school to work. Godfrey's broadcasting career began in radio in Baltimore in 1929 at the rate of $5 a day. He answered a call for amateur talent as "Red Godfrey: The Warbling Banjo and His Ukulele Club." The station manager who heard him do his own commercials on the air told him, "You talk twenty times better than you sing," and hired him for a regular spot.[40] In 1931, after the Coast Guard let him go and his first marriage broke up, Godfrey moved from Baltimore to the local NBC affiliate in Washington, D.C. Here a life-changing event occurred. A severe car accident shattered his knees and broke both hips and six ribs. The accident left him with ongoing pain, a permanent limp, and a prolonged hospital stay. It was there, Godfrey said, listening to radio announcers from his hospital bed, that he realized the old oratorical styles of broadcasting no longer had relevance for the small audiences gathered around their Philcos and Emersons. What the old-time announcers with their "Good eeeevening, ladies and gentlemen" did not know, Godfrey decided, "was that the audience is one person sitting in a room and if there's two they're probably fighting. I saw that you have to talk to that one person."[41]

Eventually Godfrey was picked up by the CBS network and began to build a national reputation. Another turning point in his career arrived when he was assigned to cover Franklin Delano Roosevelt's funeral procession in April 1945. His relaxed, reassuring broadcast and his heart-felt delivery (at several points his voice cracked as he described the funeral) made him a national figure. In 1947 a humorous song Godfrey recorded, "The Too Fat Polka," went to the top of the hit parade, beating out Bing Crosby and Frank Sinatra, the most popular singers of the day. In a characteristic downplaying mode Godfrey said, "Never in my life did I waste so much time over junk. Gosh it was awful."[42] But the record sold 3.5 million copies. When in 1948 radio/television simulcasts became economically feasible,[43] Godfrey took his radio show in front of the television cameras of CBS, and he was an immediate success.

Godfrey's broadcasting style is documented in a rare 1948 film recording of an early rehearsal simulcast for television of his radio show.[44] The film shows Godfrey sitting at his desk with his radio headphones on, a somewhat dyspeptic smile on his face as his announcer, Tony Marvin, intones the opening: "Yes, it's Arthur Godfrey and all the little Godfreys . . . and now here's that man himself, Arthur 'you'll-be-tickled-pink,' Godfrey."[45] Godfrey's first lines reflect the combination of rambunctiousness and sarcasm that made him famous:

Thank you, Tony, thank you very much. This is the Godfrey bringing you a whole hour of entertainment through the miracle of radio. Isn't it wonderful? If this stuff entertains you, it's a miracle.

He commented on the conversion of the studio for television that day.

> This morning we've got lights all around this joint—they're
> driving us crazy with 'em. They said we'll come in, Arthur,
> and you won't even know we're there. We'll just take the pic-
> tures. [Godfrey grimaces and, with a carefully timed gesture,
> thumbs his nose at the studio camera, and the studio audience
> breaks into laughter.] A penny postcard, I'll explain that laugh
> to you folks.

Throughout the program Godfrey pitches products: Chesterfield
cigarettes, Glass Wax cleaners, Nabisco foods. He reads letters on the
air from fans and letter writers who ask questions but also try to emu-
late Godfrey's humor. One of the show's sponsors, Nabisco, sends him
a turkey and parsley for the Thanksgiving season. Godfrey is apparently
not amused: "I know just what to do with that parsley. If you folks can
guess where I just shoved the parsley." An explosion of laughter from
the studio audience greets this remark. "Really," says Godfrey, eyeing
the fowl caustically, "it's a very nice bird. I thank you very much for
giving me the bird, Mr. Nabisco."

Just as Edward R. Murrow articulated a characteristic tone and
broadcast tradition for news and celebrity journalism, Arthur Godfrey's
rebellious word play also influenced generations of talk-show hosts. His
spontaneity—"you never knew what Godfrey was going to say, because
Godfrey never knew what he was going to say"[46]—is evident in every
appearance. Godfrey himself seemed to be aware of his equivocal position as a talk-show personality, an immediate presence to millions of
viewers with no discernible special ability in any one particular form
of entertainment, yet someone who was able to seize and hold the attention of his viewers. As Godfrey put it in a later interview:

> I knew that I didn't have any talent. I knew that if I were to have
> any longevity at all I would have to be someone upon whom you
> would depend, somebody—whether you liked me or not—you
> had to believe what I told you because it was true.[47]

Godfrey's Irish wit and rebellious honesty enabled him to sell
products as no one had done before him. His agent said he never sold
a product he didn't totally believe in. But it also got him in trouble, increasingly so as his career soared. His flippant, caustic personality had

a darker side. Millions of his fans saw this side when he fired his young lead singer, Julius LaRosa.[48]

On October 19, 1953, Arthur Godfrey fired Julius LaRosa, live, on the air, and it was front-page news. LaRosa had been a popular member of Godfrey's broadcast family—too popular, for Godfrey's taste, as he saw him parlay his appearances on the Godfrey show into nightclub engagements and a record contract, get more fan mail than Godfrey himself, and hire a lawyer to represent his interests.[49] When LaRosa missed one of the ballet lessons that Godfrey had mandated for all cast members to develop their physical agility and grace, Godfrey decided to take action.[50]

The show of October 19, 1953, was in its sixth segment, which was broadcast nationally on radio only. Godfrey's voice asked LaRosa to sing a song. "I would like Julie, if he would, to sing that song called 'Manhattan,'" he said. "Have you got that?" An attentive listener could pick up a note of coldness in Godfrey's voice; most considered it a simple introduction. When LaRosa finished his song, Godfrey announced: "That was Julie's swan song. He goes out now as his own star, soon to be seen in his own programs, and I know that you wish him Godspeed same as I do." Andy Rooney, a writer on the show at the time, recalls LaRosa coming backstage and asking, "Was I just fired?" Newspaper headlines fanned the flames. LaRosa called a press conference, and Godfrey called his own press conference to answer him. Julius had lost his humility, Godfrey said. Never noted for humility himself, he triggered a backlash from critics and fans. The largely favorable press he had received began to turn against him. Biographer Arthur Singer feels this was a turning point for Godfrey. The "bad boy" image that was so attractive at first had been allied to a certain innocence. The innocence was gone.

Grandiloquent gestures such as the firing of Julius LaRosa on the air and its attendant publicity could only happen in live television, and only an established titan of live television could obtain front-page headline publicity from such a moment. At CBS in the 1950s, William Paley was building the network's fortunes, in part, on talk stars like Godfrey and Edward R. Murrow. Over at NBC another television executive was building recognition and profits with stars of TV talk. The executive was Sylvester "Pat" Weaver, and the programs Weaver founded—*Today* (1952–), *Home* (1954–1957), and *Tonight* (1954–)—proved to be three of the most influential and durable on television.

THREE

THE FIRST CYCLE, PART II

Experimentation, Consolidation, and
Network Control—NBC and DuMont

SYLVESTER "PAT" WEAVER: NBC's Executive Visionary of Television Talk (1949–1955)

It is fitting that Sylvester "Pat" Weaver, the television executive who had the most to do with the founding forms of television talk, was himself a noted talker. A *New Yorker* "Profile" on Weaver that appeared in the fall of 1954 describes him as a man constantly in motion, issuing a stream of memos and directives from an L-shaped desk in a big, bleached-mahogany-paneled office on the sixth floor of the RCA Building. Sessions with Weaver were stimulating if sometimes confusing. "It's rough," said one of his assistants. "Right in the middle of a meeting, the guy will start acting out some bit from an old Greek play to illustrate a point he wants to make about a show we're working on."[1]

Weaver's success rate was remarkable. *Your Show of Shows, Today, Home, Tonight, Wide Wide World,* and *Operation Wisdom* went on the air within a few years of each other. Beginning in 1954 NBC began to gain on arch-rival CBS and by 1956 NBC had overtaken CBS in the ratings. NBC's new management team, which included Pat Weaver, had, according to the *New York Times,* "raised NBC to the undisputed leadership of television broadcasting."[2]

A key to Weaver's success was his implementation of multiple sponsorship—individual participations of thirty- and sixty-second "spots" by sponsors rather than a sponsor or group of sponsors buying time for a single show. This new method of financing shows was an important development in the first cycle of television talk. It gave the network more power to control technology, experimentation, and content. More sponsors participated at lower individual rates in this system, but with a higher overall return to the network. The network was thus able to support its own programming, which included "extravagant" new forms of television technology like the electronic moving set built for the Arlene Francis *Home* show on NBC, and Weaver promoted each of the network's new programs and technological wonders in the waves of publicity that accompanied new shows.

Weaver's twenty-year background in broadcasting was an important ingredient of his success. He had worked on every level of the broadcasting business. He had been a radio announcer, scriptwriter, radio and television production executive, advertising account director (at the age of thirty, he handled all accounts for the American Tobacco Company), and before coming to NBC he was the executive in charge of production at one of the largest advertising agencies in the country. He had also acquired a reputation as someone who could negotiate effectively between the "creative" people who wrote and produced the shows and the sponsors and advertising executives who put them on the air.[3]

Before Weaver came to NBC there had been three vice presidents in charge of television production in as many years, none with extensive production experience. Weaver's experience in the industry and his self-confidence made him willing to experiment, to take short-term losses for long-term gains.

By 1954 NBC had 390 affiliates and, under Pat Weaver's direction, led the way in national talk programming. Some of Weaver's shows, like *Home* (1954–1957) and *Wide Wide World* (1955–1958), lasted only a few years. Others, like *Today* and *Tonight,* have become network staples and institutions of television talk. Weaver's shows laid the foundation for news, public affairs, and entertainment traditions on television that would eventually fill the early-morning talk hours with shows like *Today,* late morning and afternoon with public service talk on the *Home* show model, and late night with comedy/variety talk based on *The Tonight Show* model. The *Today* show was founded in 1951 and hosted by Dave Garroway. It became the model for the morning shows that followed.

DAVE GARROWAY (1952–1961)

Dave Garroway extended the tone and scope of the morning news/information show and created a model for all future TV morning talk.

That model was the *Today* show, which was network television's first and, as of this writing, longest-running morning program. The first *Today* show under Garroway (1952–1961) was very much a function of the unique broadcasting personality of its founding host.

Dave Garroway's broadcasting career began inauspiciously. He graduated twenty-third in a class of twenty-four from the NBC announcers school in New York City in 1939.[4] He worked briefly for KDKA in Pittsburgh, did stints in radio news departments in New York and Chicago, and joined the Army at the beginning of World War II. The eccentric Garroway style—"rambling commentaries in curious start-stop cadence"[5]—was developed on his midnight jazz show in the Army. After returning to WMAQ in Chicago with Army buddy and fellow jazz enthusiast Charlie Andrews, Garroway worked with Andrews to create *Garroway at Large,* a half-hour experimental television talk/variety show out of Chicago on the new NBC television network.[6] *Garroway at Large* went on the air in June 1949 and ran until June 1951. Critics took immediate notice. Garroway and Andrews executed conceptual comedy bits and black-out sketches similar to the ones Ernie Kovacs and Steve Allen developed on *The Tonight Show* several years later. On one show, for instance, just as the announcer began, "This show came to you from Chicago . . ." Garroway whacked a television cable with a hatchet and the screen went black. On another night, the announcer introduced the show as coming from "Chicago . . . the friendly city." The camera moved around to reveal the handle of a knife sticking conspicuously out of Garroway's back.[7]

Despite a loyal following from its unpredictable, high-spirited comedy ideas and forms of jazz not normally heard on network TV, *Garroway at Large* lost its sponsor in June 1951, and Garroway was looking for work. Hearing about a new national morning show being planned in New York, he went there and convinced Mort Werner, NBC's chief talent executive, that he was the person for the job.

Contemporary viewers rarely have a chance to see what made Dave Garroway such a compelling television personality. Few recordings of the *Today* show survive, but the ones that do give us glimpses of a slightly odd figure. In many ways an ordinary, shy Midwesterner, Garroway later described what happened to him when the camera light went on.

> When we got on the air I felt very warm and comfortable—
> strangely so—instead of being frightened. The lens seemed to be

so direct and friendly, really, almost as if I could see somebody there. It was a black channel to the people, a neutron star. I still think that way. It stuck with me all my life. I am much more comfortable with whoever is at the end of that black hole than I am with someone in person.[8]

Garroway's opening remarks on the first *Today* show, January 14, 1952, capture his earnestness and jazz cantata style of delivery.

We'll be with you every day for two hours in the morning, just about the time you get up—7 to 9 A.M. We're going to try, very much, to put you more closely in touch with the world we live in by the magnificent, unparalleled means of communication which NBC has assembled in a single room in New York. . . . We'll put you in touch with the whole world, and not only with news, which we will cover as no program ever has been able to cover before, because they didn't have the many tools, but we'll give you music—music of today—what good records are coming out tomorrow. Tomorrow in art, tomorrow in science, tomorrow and today in sports, all fields of human endeavor we think we'll be able to inform you better about, and the people who are close to you, than you had a chance to be informed before. So as you leave the house into the day, you're close to it at the beginning of the day, knowing where you're going and what the world is like that you're going into.[9]

The syntax may have been tangled, but Garroway and the *Today* show were popular with critics and viewers from the beginning. That did not translate into advertising dollars at first. The network was willing to support a "sustaining" show for a short time (the network footing the costs), but no show would remain on the air indefinitely unless it found sponsors.

Selling the show became a team effort, with executive producer Richard Pinkham, NBC executive John Kingsley Herbert, and an aggressive sales representative named Matthew Culligan playing key roles. It was Garroway himself, however, who was the one of the show's chief persuaders. The team relied on him again and again in their pitches to sponsors, advertisers, and network officials. The viewer mail —65,000 unsolicited letters came in the show's first two weeks[10]—belied the ratings, and the staff used the mail to back their case.

Garroway traveled to the West Coast with Pinkham for exhausting show-and-tell sessions with potential clients. Garroway would employ his "pleasantly eccentric manner," telling stories or relaying amusing anecdotes, and Pinkham would make the pitch. Finally, after a year on the air and a boost from a chimpanzee named J. Fred Muggs (who lightened up the show and brought in younger listeners, though he occasionally bit people), the *Today* show was established on solid advertising footing. It became one of NBC's chief moneymakers.

Entertainment hosts like Godfrey and Garroway sold products on the air in the 1950s, and Garroway, like Godfrey, was a master salesman. While Godfrey employed his sly Irish charm and reputation for outspoken opinions to sell products, Garroway's sales technique was understated.

> Garroway spoke quietly, in a mellifluous baritone. . . . He pitched products well but refused to pander to a sponsor. Nor would he eat a product on camera, having once tasted frosting on a sponsor's cake and discovered it was shaving cream. A reservoir of information, he was dignified in presenting his knowledge and was somehow handsome, peering owlishly through his gigantic horn-rimmed glasses.[11]

One of the *Today* show's products, Saran Wrap, became a household name when Garroway took to holding the clear plastic wrap over the camera lens and saying, "See how clear it is."[12] But Garroway, like Murrow and a number of other hosts who had authority over their programs, placed limits on what products and campaigns he would represent. For example, Garroway refused to read an advertising line that read, "Tuffy Pads remove icky dirt" declaring he would not say "icky" on the air even if Tuffy canceled. Finally, it was agreed that Dave would say, "Tuffy Pads remove *sticky* dirt," though the line on the TV screen read "icky."[13]

Garroway presided over the *Today* show for nine years, from January 1952 to July 1961. After the suicide of his second wife, his behavior became increasingly erratic. The last days of Dave Garroway's career on the air provide a tragic example of a host who could not survive the pressures of a daily broadcasting schedule. According to an account in Robert Metz' anecdotal history of the *Today* show, Garroway lay down on the floor one day and refused to get up if he did not get the conditions he demanded.[14] Shortly thereafter, in May 1961, Garroway's retirement was announced by NBC, ostensibly so that he could spend more time with his family. Like Godfrey, who was never an easy personality for the network to handle and who left for health reasons in 1959, after he was taken off the air Garroway was never given a steady berth on the network again and never regained his popularity. He did, however, appear intermittently on a number of talk vehicles until the end of his life in 1982.

The *Today* show was Pat Weaver's first "communicator" experiment on NBC. By September 1954 he was preparing another one. This one would appeal to women audiences at home during the day and be hosted by Arlene Francis, a well-known actress and long-time radio and television personality.

ARLENE FRANCIS AND *HOME* (1954–1957)

Arlene Francis was one of the most prominent women talk-show hosts of the 1950s. She set a standard for "intelligent" programming, focusing on public issues as well as issues of domestic life in America. Her career illustrates the importance of power and control in the role of a 1950s talk-show host, and the uphill battle faced by a woman host during this time.

For three and a half years Francis was the nationally acclaimed host of the *Home* show, one of the most successful public-service information shows of the 1950s. She was thus a founder of one of television talk's major subgenres.

Many women played significant behind-the-scenes roles in fifties television—women like Mili Lerner Bonsignori, Edward R. Murrow and Fred Friendly's film editor, who shaped many of Murrow's most important *See It Now* shows and television documentaries from her editing bench.[15] But one way women could shine in front of the camera was as talk-show hosts. Faye Emerson, Wendy Barrie, and Ilka Chase, for example, hosted widely viewed shows out of New York.[16] Faye Emerson was a particularly important early host. An actress who became active in politics after marrying Elliott Roosevelt, the son of President Franklin Delano Roosevelt, she was one of the five Emmy nominees for outstanding television personality of 1950.[17] Other prominent hosts were Dinah Shore, who hosted an evening variety hour sponsored by Chevrolet, and Eleanor Roosevelt, whose first guest was Albert Einstein and who fought, unsuccessfully, within the climate of virulent anti-

Communism in the early 1950s, to have Paul Robeson appear as a guest on her television show in New York.

Network officials and advertisers were well aware that women constituted a large part of the audience, especially during the day. Arlene Francis' *Home* show, however, was the first major effort by a national network to capture the daytime audience of women with a woman host and a serious informational format. Pat Weaver's "communicator" would now be a woman who relayed to other women the world's latest information using the world's most advanced television technology.

Arlene Francis' career as an actress began in the thirties on stage and in film,[18] and among early television talk-show hosts, only Edward R. Murrow is now represented by more programs in the Museum of Television and Radio in New York. At the Museum one can listen to Francis reading a poem by Keats on the Columbia Radio Workshop in 1937,[19] or tune into *Blind Date,* a panel show she hosted during World War II featuring service personnel. *Blind Date* was a forerunner of *The Dating Game.*[20] Arlene Francis was also one of the first panelists of *What's My Line?,* joining the Goodson-Todman production on its third show and remaining with it throughout its twenty-five-year run on television. Each week Francis would trade witty repartee in her distinctive, theatrical Broadway voice with such figures as columnist Dorothy Kilgallen, publisher Bennett Cerf, and poet Louis Untermeyer.[21] In September 1950, shortly after she joined the panel of *What's My Line?,* Arlene Francis also became the first "mistress" of ceremonies for *Saturday Night Revue: Your Show of Shows.* She appeared throughout the 1950s as guest or guest host on numerous shows, including Mike Wallace's *Night Beat,* Edward R. Murrow's *Person to Person* (with husband Martin Gabel, a producer, and son Peter), and in a *Hallmark Hall of Fame* production of *Harvey* with Jimmy Stewart. Later in life Francis was a frequent commentator, narrator, and guest on broadcasting tributes and retrospectives.[22]

Arlene Francis' role as host and managing editor of the *Home* show, the second of Pat Weaver's trilogy, made her, according to a mid-1950s poll, the third most recognized woman of her time. The first *Home* show on March 1, 1954, reveals the structure of the show and its ambitions. Announcer Hugh Downs opens the show:

> Good morning everyone, and it is a good morning. You're looking at NBC's newest television studio in New York—a studio

especially designed for *Home*. And from this television laboratory—which is what it really is—each week day at this hour [11:00 A.M.], a staff of electronic editors is going to bring you news and information that applies to your home and your family. Now I'd like to let you meet the editor-in-chief of our electronic magazine, Arlene Francis.[23]

As Downs speaks, a circular platform revolves revealing staff members—over 120 people worked on the show—one or two at a time in tableau-like settings shaped like wedges in a pie. Each section of the revolving platform represented a segment of the show—health, cooking, fashion, education, and current events. The revolving set cost NBC approximately $200,000—an astounding figure for a television stage at that time.

As managing editor, Arlene Francis always had a firm hand on this "electronic magazine of the air." *Home* covered a wide range of topics, including such controversial fifties social issues as divorce, the "menace of tranquilizers," the "blackboard jungle," and "crisis in the schools." It featured newsmakers like Senator John Kennedy, Supreme Court Justice William O. Douglas, Attorney General Herbert Brownell, Vice President Richard Nixon, and Maine Senator Margaret Chase Smith. When Senator Smith appeared, she spoke about what the term *home* meant to her ("the place where we store far more important things than furniture . . . where we store our hopes and our fondest memories"),[24] but she also talked about hard policy decisions she had to make in office.

Like *Today* and *Tonight, Home* traveled. Francis took it to Japan (where she appeared in a kimono on New Year's Day), to Monaco and Holland (where she visited a houseboat), to Paris (where she visited the Eiffel Tower with actress Jean Seberg), to Nassau in the Bahamas (where she went diving with her son Peter and water skiing on one of the world's fastest speedboats).

The decision to take *Home* off the air in 1957 was a shock to the staff and many of its viewers, and the decision is still somewhat shrouded. Though Francis was told the program was a victim of ratings decline, it may just as well have been a victim of NBC founder David Sarnoff's desire to "clean house" and purge the slate of programs promoted by Pat Weaver, whom Sarnoff had replaced with his son Robert Sarnoff a year before *Home* was taken from the air.

The last *Home* show, broadcast August 9, 1957, was like Johnny

Carson's last *Tonight* show in 1992, an emotional experience. It reveals quite a bit about the show and its appeal to viewers.

CLOSE-UP: ARLENE FRANCIS' LAST *HOME* SHOW, AUGUST 9, 1957

After opening with a clip from the first *Home* show, Arlene Francis appears before the camera.

> Three and a half years later, we are starting the final edition. [She gestures to Downs.] My left hand, right hand, my all around man about *Home,* Mr. Hugh Downs. . . . After all this time he still continues to amaze me about how much information he carries in that little head. [She looks toward Downs.] And you certainly do. And maybe that is why some of your hair is falling out. [Downs replies good naturedly off-mike, "Could be."] But it is a good, solid level head, and if I've embarrassed you— I'm glad!

It is rather startling even today to see a woman talk-show host ribbing a male second banana. Now Downs steps in. "It is the names of television programs that are mortal," he says. "The programs and the ideas are immortal— like people are." The final *Home* show featured highlight clips from many of its past shows, and at the end invited a long-time viewer and contributor to the show to appear: the editor of the *Cleveland Free Press.* He is known to his followers and fans as "Mr. Cleveland," Francis says, a "citizen philosopher" who had done many guest editorials for *Home* over the years. The editor from Cleveland comes on stage and says that in times of stress and the breakdowns that accompany change—changes between management and labor, parent and child, husband and wife, government and people—the most important thing is that relationships remain solid. He speaks of his relationship to the *Home* show. It has been "truly magnificent," he says, and he regrets, "as do millions of others" that it is going off the air. Arlene Francis fights back the tears:

> Yes, . . . *Home* is going off the air. After 893 hours, editions, adventures, hellos, and good-byes and see-you-tomorrows, *Home* is going off the air in 113 cities and four time zones, plus Alaska and Hawaii. When I said, what are we going to do the last day, they just said, Arlene, the most important thing is don't weep. Well, I don't want to weep, certainly. I know that I'm just supposed to feel wonderful and gay, and everything will go on—but this is a big family of 120 people and we have all gotten very attached. . . .

She closes the program with inspirational music and the prayer of St. Francis of Assisi: "Where there is hatred, make me sow love / Where there is injury, pardon / Where there is doubt, faith / Where there is despair, hope . . ."

NBC eased the transition by giving her a thirty-minute daytime show for a while, a blend of "chitchat" and features called The Arlene Francis Show.[25] It lasted only six months. Afterward Francis went back to her usual busy schedule of theatrical work, guest appearances, and her regular panel duties on What's My Line?

What happened to Arlene Francis' *Home*? Was there any way the show could have remained on the air, as *Today* and *Tonight* did? Francis' autobiography intimates that unresolved power issues were involved, and gives us an idea of just how hard it was to be a woman talk-show host in the 1950s with no real power, authority, or leverage within the network system. Her description of the end of the *Home* show also indicates how important the business side was—how the talk-show hosts who remained on the air had to speak the language of television business, as Weaver did, to maintain their positions on the air.

An interview Arlene Francis did with Mike Wallace on *The Mike Wallace Interview* in 1957 is particularly revealing. Wallace begins the interview by saying that a lot had been written recently about what happened to career women in America, "not you particularly, but others." He asked her if she could explain what "happens to so many career women that makes them so brittle? That makes them almost a kind of third sex?" Do you "never find yourself losing your identity then as a woman in the—let's face it—male-dominated world of television?" he asks.[26]

Francis thinks before replying and then answers: "What happens to some of [the women] who have these qualities you've just spoken of, is that I suppose they feel a very competitive thing with men and they take on a masculine viewpoint." They "forget primarily that they are women. . . . Instead they become aggressive and opinionated." She goes on to deliver her own theory on the different genders. "While men do it, it is part of the makeup of a man, and a man has always done it all his life. Therefore he has other qualities that soften the edges. Whereas women are maybe doing it for the first time and they go farther ahead, and they are so determined and they are so sure that they know everything, so that they can win the race . . ." Her own position, she says, is that it is not "a woman's position to dominate. I have no desire to do some great world's work, except through my own family and my own peace, and to connect that back with the world."

Francis' position seems quite clear here, but her memoir reveals that the pull between private and public life for Francis was filled with tension and ambiguity. In the early 1960s, David Tebet and a group of executives from NBC came to Francis and made her an offer to succeed Garroway as cohost of the *Today* show, working with her old "right-hand man," Hugh Downs. "I heard them out," Francis says, "and said flatly no, n-o, no. (And of course, thank you.)"

> It was bad enough getting up at four in the morning when we
> did remotes on *Home*. . . . I felt (rightly or wrongly) that it would
> have caused too great an upheaval in my relationships with
> family and friends. . . . I thought about Martin being on his own
> most evenings—what sort of life would that be for him? (Maybe
> marvelous, which would make it even worse!) Thus, although
> I had always been accustomed to talking such career decisions
> over with Martin, this was the time I decided to make my deci-
> sion independent of his advice. I was afraid that in his desire not
> to stand in the way, he might try to be "gallant" and persuade me
> to do something he didn't want me to do.[27]

Furthermore, Francis adds, "It was a time during which I was riding the crest of a wave—guest appearances, Woman of the Year, award shows, and *What's My Line?* . . . I saw no reason why I should be a 'co-host'!"[28] That decision became, however, one of what Francis calls the great "If Idas" of her life ("if Ida done this or Ida done that"[29]). Barbara Walters got the job, and though most of the time Francis felt happy for her, she had severe twinges afterward when, for example, Walters accompanied President Richard and Pat Nixon on their ground-breaking trip to China.

Lacking a firm grip on the business side of her show (she relied on her husband for that), Arlene Francis was not able to manage her career as Barbara Walters managed hers in the 1960s and 1970s. In the Mike Wallace interview Francis recounts a dream she had repeatedly, and she ends her memoirs with the same dream. "I pick up a phone to make a call, and discover it has no mouthpiece. I seek another phone, and it is the same—there is no mouthpiece. In panic, I go from phone booth to phone booth, in and out of rooms, unable to find a telephone with a mouthpiece, frantic in my drive to communicate with someone—anyone." She felt earlier in her life, she says, that the dream represented her anxiety about her career as an actress, but by the time she wrote her memoirs, she felt it meant more than that. "I realized how deeply my inability to express myself without becoming apprehensive about what 'they' might think had affected me. In short, my 'don't make waves' philosophy had inhibited my life to an incalculable extent. . . . I had forgotten that a few waves are necessary to keep the water from becoming stagnant. . . ."

STEVE ALLEN, JACK PAAR, AND *TONIGHT!*
Founding Traditions of Late-Night Entertainment Talk (1954–1962)

Many of the traditions of late-night entertainment talk, so familiar to television viewers of the 1970s, 1980s, and 1990s, were established by two important talk-show hosts, Steve Allen and Jack Paar, during the eight years from 1954 to 1962, on *Tonight!*, the third of Pat Weaver's daily "communicator" shows.

Steve Allen's *Tonight!*, 1954–1957

Pat Weaver's *Tonight!* was originally to be a late-night version of the mix of information, public service, and entertainment represented by the *Today* show, founded two and a half years earlier, with some elements of the previous variety format in the late-night time slot, *Broadway Open House.* But the *Tonight!* show's first host, Steve Allen, fought to carry the show in the direction of his own strength—improvisational comedy. Although some NBC executives resisted this concept, Allen received the backing of Weaver, who correctly saw the show as being built around a strong host with proven comedy ideas.

The show Steve Allen and his team put on national television in the *Broadway Open House* time slot on September 27, 1954, was structured in a way that was comfortable to Allen himself. It included a piece of business at the piano and an opening monologue by the host, a talented pianist and composer, followed by segments that involved the studio audience through banter, impromptu interviews, and games such as Stump the Band. Using a simple desk and chair for the host, and chairs or a couch for the guests, the *Tonight!* show featured occasional on-the-road broadcasts and impromptu madcap bits by the host—such as the time he ran outside the studio, followed by the camera, to direct traffic. The Steve Allen *Tonight!* show had a serious side as well. The host would occasionally entertain a single guest for the entire evening, as he did when poet Carl Sandburg appeared on the show, or when he had such rare-for-television guests as "beat generation" novelist and poet Jack Kerouac. The practice of paying guests "scale," the minimum fee required by union network contracts, originated with the first *Tonight!* show. Indeed, Allen's format set many of the standards for future late-night entertainment talk/variety shows.

The First *Tonight!* Show

The very first *Tonight!* show gives the viewer its flavor.[30] Allen energized the old performance traditions of vaudeville and his more intimate "found comedy" on radio by using the unique resources of television as a medium. Indeed, the filmed opening of the first *Tonight!* show bears a strong resemblance to David Letterman's NBC show in the early 1980s.[31] The camera wanders down Broadway to the flashing lights of the Hudson Theater marquee as announcer Gene Rayburn booms: "Just off the crossroads of the world, Times Square, is NBC's Hudson Theater. That's where we're taking you now, tonight and every night. Now to meet the star of our show, Steve Allen." As the applause dies down, the camera trains in on a pair of heavy, dark-frame glasses (Allen's trademark), a hand picks them up and the camera racks focus to Allen, who says, "Boy, we've been making last-minute changes." He reports to the audience that the audience remote unit has had a flat tire and there have been numerous other mishaps ("four engineers committed suicide this week preparing for this show"). The show was not a spectacular, Allen said, but "a mild little show in a theater that sleeps 800 people." Like Murrow on his first *See It Now*, Allen professes humility in the face of NBC's "technological wonders," and moves over to his piano for a boogie-woogie piece. The piano was to become part of a standard opening.[32]

From September 1954 to January 1957, Allen would create an atmosphere of performance excitement and comic improvisation with such guests as new comedians Mort Sahl, Lenny Bruce, and Shelley Berman; unusual personalities, like Joe Interleggi, "the human termite"; and "civilians" from the audience, like Mrs. Sterling and Miss Dorothy Miller, who became regulars.[33] Allen made full use of his wide-ranging musical talents as well. Sometimes he would compose a melody on the piano using notes suggested by the audience.

Allen's entry into the world of late-night entertainment on television was almost accidental. He intended to study journalism at Drake University, but after a course in radio production he moved over to broadcasting.

Allen's transition to television was not effortless. His work in radio, starting at KNX in Los Angeles in 1948, came out of written comedy routines that he worked hard to perfect. Hired only to play records, he began to write short comedy scripts that he then read as if they were improvised.

Turning written comedy ideas into spoken comedy was to remain the tradition of late-night entertainment talk well into David Letterman's time, with Allen's two writers on the *Tonight!* show expanding to twelve on Letterman by the end of the 1980s. Allen's late-night show on Los Angeles radio in the early 1950s was at first, like Letterman's late-night show following Johnny Carson, something of a cult item. But the show began to attract an impromptu audience at the station, beginning with ten or twelve people who came to participate in the fun, and building eventually into a late-night audience in a studio that seated up to a thousand people. The Steve Allen radio show became a performance "event" in Los Angeles, and a lot of the comedy ideas used on the *Tonight!* show (interviewing "just plain folks" from the audience, for instance)[34] were developed there.

By the time Allen came to the *Tonight!* show in 1954 he had, along with his radio experience, a fourteen-month trial run on local New York television[35] and was working with a production team he knew well: director Dwight Hemion, described appreciatively by Allen as one of the "best camera directors in television"; producer Bill Harbach; financial manager Jules Green, Allen's agent since his Hollywood radio days; and writers Stan Burns and Herb Sargent, both of whom went on to long careers as comedy writers.

Though Steve Allen established the format and many of the comedy elements of the late-night variety talk show, Allen's successor on *Tonight!*, Jack Paar, made "talk" itself the ongoing center and focus of the show. In his autobiography, Allen describes himself as running an "experimental TV laboratory," but credits Paar with setting late-night talk in its present mold.

Jack Paar and *Tonight* (1957–1962)

By the time he was eighteen, Jack Paar was already a radio announcer and newsreader in Jackson, Michigan, and by the time he was twenty, working out of WGAR in Cleveland, he was the youngest announcer on the CBS network.[36] It was as a monologist and stand-up comedian that he first began to make a national name for himself. He became more widely known when his stand-up comedy act for troops in the special-services entertainment division during World War II received a glowing review in *Esquire*. He had a series of acting roles in Hollywood after that and a television guest appearance in the early 1950s that got good reviews. CBS signed him as host of its morning show to compete with Dave Garroway's *Today*. Paar started the morning show with a salary of $200,000 a year, an enormous sum at that time and an indication of his perceived worth to the network.

Indeed, Jack Paar was an original, a conversationalist whose private and public personae merged on the air. He talked to entertain but also to reveal himself. He was a man who was willing to follow the flow of his thoughts and vulnerabilities wherever they might lead him, to share half-private, half-public thoughts and ideas with his audience and treat the millions who tuned in as if they were company in his home. Nothing better illustrates the bond Paar forged with his audience and members of the press than the national furor that greeted his famous walk off the set of the *Tonight* show in 1960 at the height of his popularity as a TV host. The incident illustrates not only Paar's power and appeal as a host, but the tensions that had developed by this time between strong-minded stars of the fifties and network hierarchies that were increasingly sensitive to pressure from advertisers or governmental overseers, and who wanted nothing to disturb or interfere with smooth delivery of their entertainment product to a mass audience.

CLOSE-UP: JACK PAAR'S WALK OFF THE SET OF *THE TONIGHT SHOW*, FEBRUARY 1960

Here is Paar's own account of his "walk" off the set of *The Tonight Show* after the censorship of one of his jokes:

> One night, in February 1960, I read something that I thought was funny in an earthy, outhouse genre, yet rather sophisticated in its double entendre. I told a harmless story, the kind of story that could practically be read at a Wednesday-night church social. [The joke played on the use of "W.C." in England to stand for "wayside chapel" as well as "water closet," or toilet.] An NBC censor ordered the three-minute segment cut and re-

placed it with news bulletins. I never knew the story was cut until I got home and watched the show.[37]

At that point Paar was outraged when he saw the censorship that had taken place, without his consent, on his show. He was even more angered when he read press accounts that the joke that had been taken out was "obscene." He was under a lot of pressure at the time, and he blew up at the network hierarchy itself.

> I called NBC's president and asked him to review the tape. He did, said it was harmless, and that I was to forget it. I insisted that since he felt it was harmless or mildly questionable, I should be allowed to rerun the edited portion the following night. . . . I was told by Bob Kintner, the president of NBC, not to be so thin-skinned and sensitive. He said it was a mistake to cut it in view of the trouble it caused, but their decision would have to stand. . . . I knew the only thing to do would be to explain my position to the audience that night and then walk off the show.

And that's what Paar did—to front-page headlines. Hugh Downs, Paar's announcer and sidekick, was as stunned as everyone else when Paar left the show after only three minutes. Downs later said that he thought Paar would reappear, and was surprised that he had to continue the show alone. This show too, like the one in which the "water closet" joke had been edited, had been taped "as-if live" before an audience, and immediately the question arose as to whether or not the network would allow the show to air. There was a tense standoff afterward, as Downs recalls the meeting:

> It was seriously discussed to run a movie and not to run that tape and I said that if you don't run that tape, I quit. It would be like going out to cover a blizzard and freezing two fingers off and not having them run the recording.[38]

Whether it was Downs' self-proclaimed forcefulness or other factors that tipped the balance, the network decided to run the tape.

The rest of the story is not so well known, though Paar recounted the aftermath in his memoirs.

> For days my home was surrounded by press cars, television crews, and police to protect the property. . . . Bob Hope and Jack Benny called and

said it was the damnedest publicity stunt ever in show business. This really hurt, as there was no thought of publicity. . . . The truth was that I became quite ill. My wife knew we had to get away somehow, but for two days we could not open our front door.[39]

The Paar family managed to suppress news of the host's breakdown and whisked him off by private plane to a secluded hotel in Palm Beach. "I wanted to watch the *Tonight* program but was kept so sedated that I could never stay awake," Paar says. In all, it was "the most melancholy experience" he had ever had in television.[40]

After days of frantic searching, network officials were tipped off to his whereabouts. Paar tells the story of his discovery:

> I was sitting out by the empty pool, wondering what I was going to do with my life, when I saw a large limousine pull into the driveway. I thought it was the press and began running down the road. Two men got out of the car and yelled, "Jack, we want to talk to you."
>
> I recognized the two men as Bob Kintner and Bob Sarnoff, the top two men of the National Broadcasting Company. I felt very foolish, since I liked both of them, and walked back. Either Bob (Kintner or Sarnoff) explained that the National Broadcasting Company was not going to release me from the contract. I had become an important personality to the network . . . They then said something that I did not know: Miriam [Paar's wife], whom everyone loves, had phoned them and told them where we were hiding and that she was worried about my emotional state. They wanted me to go away for a while and forget the program. They did not want me back in New York for a few weeks. But then I had to return and fulfill my commitment.[41]

Paar and his wife went to Hong Kong for a two-week vacation. He returned to the United States and his show approximately a month after he had gone off the air. He returned with the line, "As I was saying," and that night *The Tonight Show* garnered the highest ratings it had ever had.

Jack Paar remained host of *Tonight* until March 1962, when he decided he was finally worn out by the network's constant interference. By this time not only had the thin-skinned, ever-surprising Jack Paar established late-night talk as a site of intimate late-night conversation with a range of celebrities and performers, he had also—inadvertently perhaps—demonstrated "star power" in television talk. It was a lesson others, Johnny Carson principal among them, would heed.

MIKE WALLACE: The Grand Inquisitor of Television Talk (1956–1958)

If Arlene Francis was in some ways the fifties "ideal woman," Mike Wallace represented the decade's ideal "masculine" image. That image proved durable for Wallace for over five decades of network television. The November 1993 cover of *TV Guide* carried a beaming picture of the well-known host, his face in front of the *60 Minutes* stopwatch, with a headline celebrating "25 Years of Tough Guys and Gritty Scoops."[42] Though confrontational hosts had come and gone in the years between Wallace's first *Night Beat* and the 1993 *TV Guide* cover—Joe Pyne, Alan Burke, and Morton Downey Jr., to name three of the more notorious— only Mike Wallace had been able to transform hard-edged confrontation into a durable talk commodity. Wallace's career spanned the period of the founders of talk in the 1950s, the corporate era of the 1960s, the emergence of new talk formulas in the 1980s, and the new cycle of talk spurred by the technological and economic developments of the 1990s. He survived in part because of a series of decisions in which he reinvented himself at key moments in his career. These moments illustrate once again that control over business decisions is as important to the career of the talk-show host as performance on the air.

Mike Wallace grew up in Brookline, Massachusetts, the same suburb of Boston that produced several other prominent figures of television talk, including Arlene Francis, Barbara Walters, and David Susskind. Indeed, Brookline in the early middle decades of the twentieth century was described as "a hotbed for over-achievers."[43] Myron Leon Wallace, the son of Russian-Jewish immigrants, went to the University of Michigan, where he majored in English, intending to pursue a career in teaching or law. At the University of Michigan he discovered the university's broadcast center and decided broadcasting would be his career.[44]

Wallace's first professional job was in 1939, at the age of twenty-one, at radio station WOOD in Grand Rapids, Michigan.[45] There he had a chance to do everything: announce, read on-air news, host community affairs and quiz shows, work on the station's commercials. This jack-of-all-trades quality would characterize Wallace's broadcast work for the next twenty years.

From WOOD Wallace moved to WXYZ in Detroit, a major broadcasting outlet in the early 1940s,[46] and again Wallace not only read the news, but also did commercials, announced for the station, and acted in dramatic programs. Moving to Chicago in 1941, Wallace became a local radio celebrity. It was in Chicago that he met Buff Cobb, an actress and the granddaughter of well-known humorist Irvin S. Cobb.[47] Wallace and Cobb developed an on-air as well as off-air relationship, cohosting *The Chez Show* (named after the popular Chicago nightclub from which they broadcast). In 1951, they launched the *Mike and Buff* show on the new CBS television network out of New York.[48]

Husband-and-wife teams were in vogue in the 1940s and 1950s. Tex McCrary and Jinx Falkenburg, Faye Emerson and Skitch Henderson, Dorothy Kilgallen and Dick Kohlmar, Peter Lind Hayes and Mary Healy—all were couples with successful shows at the time. The *Mike and Buff* show alternated light themes and entertainment banter with more serious, controversial issues, and played on the couple's amusing on-air bickering.[49] Wallace was already displaying a confrontational edge to the breezy raconteur image he cultivated on the air. Off-screen, however, things were not going well. The marriage to Buff Cobb fell apart. Wallace began to take stock of his situation and decided that he had spread himself too thin. Reviewing all the jobs he had done since his apprenticeship in Grand Rapids, Wallace decided that what had given him the most satisfaction was his work as a newsman. He had particularly enjoyed working on *The Air Edition* of the *Chicago Sun.* There was not as much money in it, but he found news challenging, and it would give him the kind of stability entertainment lacked.

Wallace decided to take his career firmly in this new direction of public affairs and news. In 1956, working with an innovative television executive named Ted Cott and a twenty-six-year-old news director named Ted Yates, Wallace premiered *Night Beat* on WABD, an independent station in New York that was part of the DuMont chain. Says Wallace:

> From the moment we put *Night Beat* on the air—live—at 11:00 P.M. on October 9, 1956, we had a hunch that we were caught up in something special. . . . Our guests would be thoroughly, painstakingly researched and then, once we got them on the air, I'd go at them as hard as I could. If they appeared to be hiding behind evasive answers, I'd press them—or cajole them—to knock it off, to come clean. If, in response to pressure, they became

embarrassed or irritated or sullen, I'd try to exploit that mood instead of retreating into amiable reassurance. Oversimplified, that was the formula we had in mind: candor, ours and theirs, with enough time to draw them out.[50]

Night Beat was unusual for TV in visual terms. The *Night Beat* staff did not want the traditional cheerful living room set, with the soft lights, comfortable sofa, and fake flowers. Instead, the *Night Beat* studio was stark, pitch black except for one large white klieg light that glared over Wallace's shoulder "into the guest's eyes—and psyche."[51] *Night Beat* used searching, tight close-ups to record "the tentative glances, the nervous tics, the beads of perspiration." In the context of American television in the mid-fifties, says Wallace with his characteristic lack of modesty, this kind of third-degree television "was revolutionary."[52]

The formula worked, and by 1957 the show had an estimated nightly audience of about a million and a half viewers.[53] It worked for critics, too. They loved its no-holds-barred approach as an antidote to the tepid "happy talk" of television.

Despite his bluntness, Wallace had a charm and sense of limits that softened the blows of his questions. One critic noted:

> Wallace's guests rarely get upset. He does thorough research on their backgrounds and personalities before he talks to them, and seems to sense just about how far he can go with each one.[54]

By the end of 1956, both NBC and ABC began bargaining with Wallace for long-term contracts.[55] He ended up signing with ABC, though he was soon to regret it. Instead of a one-hour fringe-time program four days a week with eight interview subjects, which allowed Wallace to explore any avenue he wanted that came within his research and prosecutorial zeal, the ABC show limited him to one guest a week, in prime time, with network pressures unlike anything he had encountered before. When he went to ABC he had been assured by ABC President Leonard Goldenson that if he didn't "make the building shake every couple of weeks" he wasn't doing his job.[56] He soon found out even small tremors elicited panic reaction. A case in point was his interview with "gangster" Mickey Cohen. On the program Cohen made unsupported allegations that Los Angeles Police Chief William Parker was on the take. Parker filed suit. ABC was terrified. The suit never came to trial (six months after the interview, Parker settled out of court for $45,000), but ABC and its insurers instituted a new policy. This is the way Wallace described it. "Each night we went on the air, a lawyer would sit in the studio where, facing me, he would hold up cue cards at sensitive moments warning me to BE CAREFUL or STOP or RETREAT."[57]

Wallace's ABC version of *Night Beat* was an intensive course in the broadcaster's education about what sociologist Muriel Cantor calls network television's "prime-time content and control."[58] *The Mike Wallace Interview* continued until September 1958, after which he continued in syndication for another two years,[59] but a regular news or public-affairs programming job was not open to him. He engaged in a number of other broadcasting jobs until 1968, when Don Hewitt invited him to join the new staff of *60 Minutes*, where once again Wallace would re-create the persona of *Night Beat*.

CONCLUSION

"By 1960," as broadcast historian J. Fred MacDonald put it, "television had become a mature and streamlined business, a great 'cash cow.'"[60] The focus had shifted from "invention to convention," and the networks' concerns had gone from carving out an acceptable social role for themselves "to counting the rewards of investment, planning, and monopoly."[61]

In this first cycle of television talk shows, none of the founders had originally aspired to be television personalities—television had not even existed when they were growing up. Television was in every case simply a natural extension of radio careers. Some of the founders, like Murrow and Godfrey, continued to work in both television and radio as their national reputations grew. What the hosts of the 1950s had in common was that they were entrepreneurs who controlled their own shows and ran them in ways that were consistent with their broadcasting personalities. Edward R. Murrow, Arthur Godfrey, Dave Garroway, Arlene Francis, and Mike Wallace all formed tight-knit teams that put new combinations of talk on the air. Murrow established first-person news, investigative reporting, celebrity interviews, and trans-oceanic dialogue. Garroway's light touch guided the creation of the morning news/information show. Godfrey established the tone of the boyish and rebellious entertainment host amidst the toys and splendors of a television studio. Arlene Francis established the daytime talk show as an educational public-service forum for discussing home, family, and public issues—focusing on the concerns of women. Mike Wallace honed television as a tool of confrontation, using background research, verbal agility, and charm to reveal aspects of his guests not revealed in formats that favored prepared statements.

By the beginning of the 1960s the era of the founders was over. The strong-minded talk-show hosts of the fifties discovered that, without the leverage of ownership of their own programs and without the backing of powerful individual sponsors or advertising agencies, network packagers called the shots. When the system began to change, they did not change with it. By the time of the Jack Paar retrospective show in 1962, all of the major talk hosts of the 1950s were gone. Arlene Francis left in 1957 when *Home* was canceled. Arthur Godfrey, who had been an unassailable profit center for CBS through most of the decade, left for health reasons in 1959 and never returned. Dave Garroway's slow breakdown and "retirement" from *Today* was finalized in May 1961. Edward R. Murrow had been gone from any regular hosting duty on CBS for two years. Mike Wallace, the lone survivor of the founding generation who would reappear to work in the 1970s, 1980s, and 1990s, was also out of network television. He reemerged as a national figure a decade later only after repackaging himself on an established network.

The networks had taken over the shows that had been created or personally managed by the strong-willed hosts of television talk's first generation. Conforming to corporate imperatives and devotion to the bottom line, new managements at CBS, NBC, and ABC supported established talk formulas that did not cause controversy among advertisers or viewers. From this point of view, Jack Paar's "water closet" joke and Edward R. Murrow's hard-hitting investigative reports were the same— they caused "problems." They were the kind of things that gave network executives like William Paley "stomach aches." The first cycle of television talk was over. The second, which was to last through the era of corporate consolidation in network television, was just beginning.

FOUR
THE SECOND CYCLE (1962–1974)
Network Consolidation and New Challenges

INTRODUCTION

What Sylvester "Pat" Weaver set in motion in the mid-1950s had become the dominant pattern in the television industry by the early 1960s. The networks had assumed control over almost every aspect of programming. Although a national economic recession had slowed television's growth, by the late 1950s almost every American had access to a television—six million sets being sold in 1957 alone.[1] Television now played a dominant role in many areas of American life. For instance, though television news and advertising had influenced the 1952 and 1956 Presidential campaigns,[2] the "Great Debates" between Richard M. Nixon and John F. Kennedy in 1960 were major television talk events and proved that television had acquired a new level of power in American politics. Kennedy's vitality and charm in these debates fairly "crackled" over the tube, in the words of broadcast historian Erik Barnouw,[3] but Nixon had also learned to use television to his advantage. Despite his poor appearance in the 1960 debates, Nixon's famous "Checkers" speech in 1952 had first brought him to the attention of many Republican party leaders, and his "kitchen debate" with Soviet Premier Nikita Khrushchev—videotaped on a special Ampex system at the "American Life" exhibit in Moscow—had gained national headlines.[4]

Videotape was in regular use by the networks by 1960, making live shows "as-if live" and giving the network executives another measure of power over live programming. Videotape brought the networks a new tool of censorship and control at precisely the time network managements were increasingly worried about Congressional oversight and interference in the wake of the quiz-show scandals.

Revenues from advertising on daytime television in 1962 had risen to $225 million.[5] The advertising was aimed at a consuming audience that was spending $160 billion a year, and all programming decisions were scrutinized by network executives with the mass consumer in mind. They were not, as talk-show host Merv Griffin put it, going to put "all those millions up for grabs."[6] David Halberstam describes the corporate climate:

> Companies like CBS became increasingly dominated by a new generation of bright young men who knew systems, how to take an existing structure and make it far more profitable, cutting quality here, adding a minute or two of advertising there, little changes which, when carried through for an entire year, might mean millions and millions of dollars. Their loyalty was to the bottom line.[7]

In the 1960s, the hosts who were engaged in new forms of talk—David Susskind, Phil Donahue, and Bill Moyers, for example—were beginning to look outside the networks for outlets, principally in syndication and PBS. The network talk-show stars who did survive in the 1960s were individuals like Johnny Carson, Barbara Walters, and Mike Wallace who had the patience, durability, business acumen, and skills to maintain themselves within the new corporate environment. These talk-show hosts usually came to network television with substantial show-business experience and became stars on established shows. They were not, like the founders of television talk, innovators. Rarely did they create a show. Rather they were forceful personalities who managed to make themselves indispensable to the networks within their own particular network vehicles. The stories of Johnny Carson, Barbara Walters, and Mike Wallace reveal how the network system functioned during the 1960s, and what it took to emerge as and remain a national talk-show star during that time.

In his thirty years as host of *Tonight*, Johnny Carson institutionalized the late-night entertainment talk show founded by Steve Allen and Jack Paar. As entertainer Dan Aykroyd put it, "In the year 3000, Johnny Carson will be the lodestone researchers will covet when studying our popular culture."[8] Carson, his authority periodically challenged in contract negotiations with the network and in talk-show "wars" with other hosts, raised the profile of the late-night television talk show. With his down-to-earth Midwestern persona, boyish charm, and tinge of urban sophistication, and with a reputation for independence enhanced by iron-willed battles with the network, Johnny Carson was for nearly thirty years the "king" of late-night television.[9]

The son of a lineman for an electric company, Carson moved frequently in his boyhood through small towns in the rural Midwest, ending up at the age of eight in Norfolk, Nebraska.[10] After stints as a magician, comedian, and radio announcer in Norfolk, he became a radio and television host and announcer in Omaha. There he hosted a forty-five-minute morning radio show, *The John Carson Show*, that mixed music with offbeat comedy, and a daily fifteen-minute comedy "chatter" show called *The Squirrel's Nest* on Omaha's new TV station, WOW-TV. At the time of its earliest broadcasts, WOW-TV reached about thirty-five homes, a couple of taverns, and TV displays in local department stores.[11]

Moving to Los Angeles in 1951, Carson joined the staff of KNXT-TV, where he hosted a Sunday afternoon comedy/variety talk show called *Carson's Cellar*, which lasted until mid-1953.[12] The show became something of a cult favorite, with celebrities like Red Skelton and Jack Benny frequently dropping in. Typically the show would present Carson doing comedy commentary on current news or entertainment topics, or zany stunts followed by parodies of other television shows.[13] A later half-hour variety hour on CBS, *The John Carson Show*, lasted only thirty-nine weeks.[14]

In 1956 Carson moved to New York with money borrowed from his father and landed a job on the ABC game show *Who Do You Trust?* Carson's run on this show, from 1957 to 1962, brought him national attention. Two NBC executives, looking for a host to replace Jack Paar on the *Tonight* show after Paar stepped down in 1962, were intrigued with the possibility of signing Carson. Former NBC executive David Tebet tells the story of watching Carson on *Who Do You Trust?* and then bringing the young comedian, with then head of NBC programming Mort Werner, to a brand-name convention at the Green Brier. "He tore up the place," says Tebet. "He decimated it. They were screaming, carrying on like a bunch of animals."[15]

Werner and Tebet went to NBC President Robert Kintner and Chairman Robert Sarnoff for the go-ahead. Carson, who was represented at the time by David "Sonny" Werblin of MCA, still had twenty-six weeks left on his ABC *Who Do You Trust?* contract. ABC President Leonard Goldenson did not want to let him go. In addition, Carson himself originally balked at the idea. "What do I need that for?" he said.[16] He was earning $2,500 a week on *Who Do You Trust?* and had a steady renewable contract.[17] But NBC offered to redesign the show for him and pay him over $100,000 a year. After two weeks of mulling it over, and a good deal of back and forth between Carson, Werblin, and NBC, Carson signed. He had more security at ABC, he said, but wanted "to try something a little more creative."[18] This was to be Carson's negotiating pattern for the next thirty years: tough bargaining and eventual compromise, usually to Carson's advantage.[19]

During the twenty-six-week interim period before Carson's contract with ABC expired, David Tebet worked frantically to keep the *Tonight* show on the air with guest hosts. Meanwhile, NBC "test marketed" Carson again at a meeting of its affiliates in Chicago. The results were positive. Afterward, Carson met with Tebet at the Drake Hotel in Chicago and told him about the team from *Who Do You Trust?* he wanted to bring with him, including producer Art Stark, sidekick Ed McMahon, and writer Herb Sargent. Before the new *Tonight* show went on the air, Carson took his team down to Fort Lauderdale to design strategies for the new show.[20] What they came up with, adapting Steve Allen's *Tonight* to their own specifications, was the format Carson would use for the next thirty years. *Tonight* show historian Paul Corkery describes the format as follows:

> A fifteen minute monologue followed by guests from the entertainment world (a regular *Tonight* show feature); sketches and skits (something borrowed from the Allen format); stunts in which Johnny would participate (an idea borrowed from *Who Do You Trust?*); adventures among the audience (also from the old *Tonight* show); guests with books or ideas to discuss (from the *Today* show version of *The Tonight Show*); and musical acts (a

segment borrowed from all versions of *The Tonight Show* and designed to give the host at least a short breathing spell during the 105-minute show).[21]

With a steady promotional drumbeat from NBC, the thirty-seven-year-old comedian's first *Tonight* aired on October 1, 1962. In its first week *The Tonight Show* with Johnny Carson registered 40.9 percent of the viewing audience.[22] Jack Paar had topped that only once—the night he returned from his walkout. Carson continued his strong showing through his first year, playing to over 7.5 million viewers a week, doubling Paar's audience.

In his first years Carson did stunts and took risks. His off-screen image was that of a bon vivant, playboy, and drinker. With second banana Ed McMahon, who joined him for escapades around New York, he created a madcap atmosphere on the show.

How the Camera Shaped *Tonight*

The way the camera operated illustrates the "classic" model of the late-night talk show institutionalized by Carson in the 1960s, and how camera and staging went together to create a "talk world." On Carson's *Tonight* show, as distinct from the new format instituted by David Letterman on *Late Night with David Letterman* in the early 1980s, the camera recorded the action but did not participate in it. The Carson opening, like the start of most late-night entertainment talk shows, always included a fanfare, the introduction of the band and guests, and Johnny's entry, kicked off by sidekick announcer Ed McMahon's stentorian roar: "Heeeere's Johnny!" *The Tonight Show*'s rainbow curtain would part to cries of "Hey-yo!" from McMahon and pandemonium from the studio audience. Carson would enter, his demeanor mock heroic, pleased but seemingly embarrassed by the hoopla. He would then attempt to quiet the demonstration with a gesture of his hand. Though clearly a celebrity receiving celebrity treatment, he did not really seem to believe it. He put himself neither above the audience nor beneath it, but presented himself rather as an Everyman figure directly in contact with the sensibilities of his audience.

Eventually managing to silence the crowd, and, after a few asides to flanking minions Ed McMahon and Doc Severinsen, Carson would begin his famous monologue. The monologue could run as long as ten to fifteen minutes and would always have between sixteen and twenty-two sure-fire jokes[23] culled by his writers from a perusal of over sixty newspapers and periodicals.[24] The camera remained absolutely fixed and frontal on Carson during his monologue, with no movement in the frame except that of the host. Carson's gestures were familiar to his audience as he nervously touched his tie, pulled at his sleeves, clasped his hands together or thrust them behind his back. Though static, the camera work suited Carson. His physical presence was, like the camera, formal, reserved, buttoned-down, vertical. It was as if the rectangular frame in which he operated was designed to contain the bursts of energy and gesture that darted from the perimeter of his body.

The camera isolated Carson spatially on the television screen. It underscored his reputation for being a loner and emphasized his firm control of the proceedings. A man who had long resisted invasions of his emotional privacy, Carson seldom fraternized with colleagues or guests before the show.[25] His barbs to McMahon and Severinsen, his seismographically sensitive responses to the studio audience, and his mock disparagement of his writers' material were delivered in the same steady, unrelenting camera isolation. Sidekicks McMahon and Severinsen were seen briefly in separate shots (cutaways) but never in over-the-shoulder or crossover shots that would include them with Carson in the frame. During the entire opening the home audience would hear but never see the studio audience at all.

Carson normally avoided direct eye contact with the camera during his monologue. His head would continually swivel back and forth, occasionally acknowledging his announcer and bandleader or making comments to his writers behind the scenes, but most of his remarks were addressed directly to the studio audience in front of him. This was a less personal engagement with the camera than Jack Paar's, for example, or David Letterman's.

Carson's enduring legacy to late-night talk moving into the late 1960s and early 1970s was his comedic mastery of political and social topics that were considered "safe" for network television and his institutionalization of the late-night comedy monologue.

Safe Topics

In the course of his long career Carson learned what *not* to talk about: how far to go with jokes, how to balance his barbs, how to turn controversial social and political issues into items of personal parody. By the time Alex Haley interviewed him for *Playboy* in 1967 he said he had learned to keep "personal liberal political opinions to himself."[26] Ten years later, with the turbulence of the 1960s and the Vietnam War safely in the past, Carson welcomed anti–Vietnam War activist Jane Fonda on the show, congratulating her for "having lived to see her views on Vietnam fully justified by history."[27] "Ms. Fonda," says Carson biographer Kenneth Tynan, "refrained from reminding him that when she most needed a television outlet for her ideas the doors of *The Tonight Show* studio were closed."[28]

Carson's hold on late-night television talk-show ratings remained secure through most of the mid-1960s, but toward the end of the decade he faced a series of new challengers. Some of these challengers were willing to take on the controversial issues Carson avoided. The other two network hosts who rose to the top in 1960s television, Mike Wallace and Barbara Walters, were able to bring controversy to news talk, but at the same time make those forms of controversy palatable to a national audience. Mike Wallace employed a hard, head-on, "masculine" style of confrontational interview; and Walters developed a softer, but still assertive "feminine" approach to her political and lifestyle interviews.

MIKE WALLACE: "The Grand Inquisitor" Returns (1962–1967)

The year 1962 represented a turning point for Mike Wallace, precipitated by a family tragedy that forced him to reevaluate his life. His nineteen-year-old son, Peter, a Yale student who had begun working in news, died in a mountain-climbing accident in Europe. Wallace vowed to concentrate his energies on journalism, though it meant a major cut in income from his previous dramatic, commercials, and game-show career, and no income at all for a while. Wallace decided to reinvent himself on television as a working journalist with no ties outside journalism.[29]

It took several months to get his foot in the door of the highly bureaucratized network news business—turning down $150,000 to host a game show along the way. Wallace wrote letters to the network news heads at CBS, ABC, and NBC, receiving nothing but polite messages, ritual meetings, and handshakes. He grew more anxious and depressed about his prospects. In early February 1963, however, he got a call from KTLA in Los Angeles, which needed a host for a late-night newscast. He was about to accept when a call arrived from Dick Salant at CBS, who, against the advice of other CBS executives, made Wallace a modest offer. He could take a "starter" job at the local New York affiliate WCBS doing an interview series on the local radio network at a salary of $40,000 a year. It was a fraction of what he could earn doing commercials and entertainment shows, but Wallace accepted.

Wallace's long trek back to being a full-fledged "newsman" on the networks took five years. He worked on *The CBS Morning News* and a series of other CBS news vehicles until finally, in 1968, Don Hewitt invited him to *60 Minutes,* where he joined some of Edward R. Murrow's original *See It Now* staff. There Wallace's most successful talk persona—the persona of his earlier live show, *Night Beat*—was repackaged to fit the conventions of a filmed newsmagazine interview show. By the 1970s, the show would come to have higher ratings than any other news show on the air.

Though not a talk show per se, the drama of *60 Minutes* pivoted on as-if-live television talk—filmed and edited for later airing. Carefully staged verbal confrontations between *60 Minutes* correspondents and their prey—a mixed cast of public officials, quacks, and perpetrators of fraud—were presented each Sunday evening. As time went on, the live, present-tense quality of these confrontational interviews became increasingly formulaic. The *60 Minutes* crusader/reporter always won. In his persona as the grand inquisitor of *Night Beat* fame, Wallace maintained a hard-edged advantage over his interviewee victims week after week, and viewers returned week after week to see whom Wallace would chew up next.

On another network, at approximately the same time, another reporter was establishing herself on a network news vehicle, but with a considerably different approach. Barbara Walters was beginning to make a name for herself through her own distinctive television interviewing style.

BARBARA WALTERS: "The Tender Trap" (1962–1967)

On NBC's *Today* show Barbara Walters rose to widespread public attention by asking hard questions in a soft, "feminine" way. Walters became the nation's premiere woman news talk host in the 1960s and continued to refine her reputation and persona until 1976, when she was successfully courted by ABC with a highly publicized million-dollar-a-year contract.

All of the 1960s talk figures discussed above had pre-established reputations from radio or television, or performing in other kinds of show business. Walters was an exception. Born to precarious wealth and privilege as the daughter of a prosperous nightclub owner who gained and lost a fortune managing nightclubs in Florida, Boston, and New York, Walters went to some of the best private schools in the United States. With the help of a television executive who had been a family friend,[30] she managed to get a series of secretarial, writing, and public relations positions in television, including a steady five-year stint on the staff of *The CBS Morning News* before being let go for economy reasons in 1957. She also worked as a publicist for radio talk personality Tex McCrary.[31]

In 1961, Walters became a freelance writer on the *Today* show.[32] Through persistent effort she advanced from freelance writer to regular staff writer, to reporter, and in 1964, the third time she had asked producer Al Morgan for the job, she became the sixteenth *"Today* girl," a job which consisted of sitting decoratively at the desk and assisting the main anchor with lively talk and light features. Walters took over the position from actress Maureen O'Sullivan and built it into a permanent spot for herself as reporter and cohost of the show. By the mid-1960s Walters had succeeded her friend Arlene Francis as the best-known female news talk host in an industry dominated by men.

Barbara Walters' rise was associated to some extent with the feminist movement in the United States in the 1960s. She was a transitional figure in this regard, as her own comments and comments of friends and colleagues indicate. "I suppose we need some extremists," she told a 1972 interviewer, "so the middle will change."[33] She favored legalized abortion but would not sign a petition for free choice. "Because of my image as a reporter, I can't take a stand," she said. Echoing some of Arlene Francis' comments a decade earlier, she said in the same interview in 1972 that "militant feminists have done a lot, but they've also given American women a kind of national inferiority complex. . . . There's something unattractive about the way they spar on television."[34] Answers to questions about how she saw herself as an interviewer and working journalist often centered on how she posed questions to appear soft and unthreatening while maintaining a line of persistent questioning. She explained, "I have developed a particular type of interview. I'm good at drawing people out—there's a thin line between asking critical questions well and making someone mad."[35]

Like Mike Wallace, Barbara Walters worked out her interviewing style through an on-air, trial-and-error process. "I didn't intend to be in front of the camera," she said in a later interview. "I like to write. When I was young I guess I would have been considered—we all use the word shy—maybe overly sensitive. When I first went on television I had a very different look. I was very serious—I still am too serious sometimes, I keep thinking I should smile—and I worked very hard."[36]

Barbara Walters had no illusions about what she was up against, and with persistence and hard work, she made a place for herself within the NBC news division. When she took over interviewing assignments on *Today* from cohost Hugh Downs after 1964, it was, according to producer Al Morgan, largely because Walters had the energy and drive to do the interviews Downs simply wasn't interested in doing.[37]

By going after hard news interviews—and getting them—Walters became more than a decorative item on the *Today* show set. At the same time she was unhappy about the interviews she was doing, and having to boil them down to four minutes. "What you'd get is the 'news' but you wouldn't get any of the stuff that made the person a person, or that qualified the statement, or that explained it."[38] Thus Walters had already begun to develop her own signature "personalized" interviews in the 1960s. These longer interviews were both persistent and deferential, curious and acutely tuned to the sensitivities of the person interviewed. Her Boston accent and "r's" that sounded like "w's," along with her extreme deference to notable news figures, were easy to parody, and by the mid-1970s Barbara Walters' interview style was so well known that Gilda Radner's "Baba Wawa" parodies had become a staple of *Saturday Night Live.*

In effect, Barbara Walters was performing the same "feminine" function as Edward R. Murrow on his popular *Person to Person* shows. When she asked questions like "What is the biggest misconception about you?" she was providing her interview subjects with a chance to set the record straight and tell the story as *they* saw it. Long before Deborah Tannen's best-selling book on the different ways men and women speak to and understand each other,[39] a series of women talk-show hosts brought "feminine" ways of speaking to news and entertainment. As we have seen, Arlene Francis' blend of public and private information, news and home affairs, had a significant impact on audiences in the 1950s. Faye Emerson, Virginia Graham, and others spoke to women audiences as well. Barbara Walters' approach to the television interview of political and cultural celebrities provided an intersection of women's and men's talk that captured the public imagination. The blend she created was powerful enough not only to make her the first woman news talk star but, for a time, the only woman news talk star on national television.

By the late 1960s Johnny Carson, Mike Wallace, and Barbara Walters were consolidating network talk traditions. All three hosts had risen to prominence on network vehicles that became profit centers for their respective networks. The fact that so few major new stars emerged in the 1960s in network television talk was no accident. Hosts who chafed at network restrictions were soon replaced. Successful hosts learned to battle for their rights within the network, but choose their fights carefully. If they were not persistent or assertive enough, or had not developed a power base within the network, their time on the air was limited. The survivors of television talk in the 1960s learned to work within the limits and commercial mandates of network television while steadily maintaining visibility and audience. They shared a certain toughness, these hosts of the mid-sixties, a resilience but also an ability to charm and "play the game."[40] By the end of the 1960s the rules of the game were changing. Despite their surface stability and considerable profit margins, the networks were facing a series of cultural, economic, and political challenges as talk shows responded to the cultural ferment of the late sixties and new competition in the talk-show industry.

CHALLENGES TO NETWORK DOMINATION (1969–1974)

In 1969 twenty new talk shows went on the air—sixteen of them in syndication. In the fifteen years prior to that time the number of new talk shows, including network offerings, had rarely been more than six per year.[41] This talk-show explosion was the result of many things: new television technology for production and distribution; impending regulatory changes that threatened network hegemony and made syndication more profitable for talk programming; an explosive cultural climate that gave hosts and shows a lot more to talk about. These forces moved the second cycle of the television talk show into a transitional stage that included new kinds of talk shows and talk-show wars.

Though the networks went to great lengths at the end of the 1960s to avoid controversy, it could not be avoided—not at a time when the rising tide of the civil rights movement, the emergent women's movement, and protests against the war in Vietnam provoked national division and debate. By 1970 the networks were responding to a consuming public that was less docile, younger, more urban, and more outspoken than previous generations. A few executives realized that these audiences responded to social issues. CBS President Robert Wood, for example, saw the need for such shows, and as a consequence backed Norman Lear's *All in the Family* against considerable opposition within CBS itself.[42]

Though produced as a situation comedy, *All in the Family* was something of a "talk show" as well. The lead character, Archie Bunker, represented a pre-1960s set of values and attitudes, and his son-in-law, Michael Stivic, was a product of the sixties. The real drama of each show was often the debate between the two of them about the most hotly contested social issues of the day.

Prime-time and late-night television also attempted to capitalize on social controversy, with the networks testing the waters (as they did with the Smothers Brothers variety hour), then fitfully withdrawing.[43] Indeed, network television was undergoing what television critic Sally Bedell called a "sea change," and the year 1970 was referred to by another television critic as the most "chaotic" in television history.[44]

This ferment was fueled in part by significant new technological developments. Cable television was a small but growing force. Experimental satellite technology was already in use. As early as 1965, a Sunday afternoon news program on CBS produced by Don Hewitt and sponsored by IBM featured speakers from across the Atlantic Ocean talking to each other over satellite in live electronic debate.[45] Political developments also fostered a wider range of talk. The Carnegie Commission and citizens' committees for public television, along with a wide range of critics, had assailed the networks for years for their stale, trite programming and lack of vision. The Public Broadcasting Service, founded in 1967, had received its first major funding from the Ford Foundation, with Congress promising supplemental funds to promote new forms of programming.

On the regulatory front, significant cracks appeared in the networks' monopoly over the syndication market. Two FCC decisions, the Prime Time Access Rule (PTAR) and the Financial Interest and Syndication ("fin-syn") Rules helped loosen the networks' grip. The Prime Time Access Rule meant that the networks lost three and a half hours a week from their profitable prime-time schedules. Local stations were now free to buy whatever talk programming they wanted to fill those hours.

The success of talk radio in the 1960s was another factor that encouraged the new explosion of talk on television. The voices and viewpoints of talk radio, in which listeners would call in and speak directly to the host, were, as they were again in the late 1980s and 1990s, often those of outrageous hosts or hurt and angry citizens who felt marginalized or trivialized by the mainstream media. Local radio stations sensed profits in the controversy generated by live talk radio and had much less to lose from this controversy than consensus-seeking national programmers and advertisers. Local radio was therefore more permeable to voices of national debate and cultural topics (the sexual revolution, for instance) than the more conservative national television networks.

PHIL DONAHUE (1967–1974)

One of the most important new talk-show figures to come out of local talk broadcasting at this time was Phil Donahue. To understand Donahue's emergence, broadcasting first from Dayton, Ohio, and after 1974 from WGN-TV in Chicago, we need to understand his roots in 1960s talk radio and the ways in which "hot topic" radio talk paved the way to new forms of talk on television.[46]

KABC in Los Angeles was one of the first stations to go to an all-talk format, making this move as early as 1961, but it was soon followed by KMOX in St. Louis and KVOR in Colorado Springs. By mid-decade the "audience-connected radio" format was extremely popular. Talk radio sought the moving target of a young audience with disposable income and went after it with such "hot" topics as prostitutes, drug addicts, and drug dealing. The search for new demographics also played a role in the emergence of "topless radio." "Female-only, two-way talk," as it was called in 1970 by KGBS, a station in Los Angeles, was designed for a female audience in the eighteen to thirty-four age group who wanted explicit sexual conversation. Within three years, fifty to sixty stations were running "topless" shows of this kind, though they were regularly denounced by critics inside and outside the industry. Psychological self-help call-in shows, like that of Dr. Toni Grant on the ABC talk stations, were also popular, as were a wide range of political commentary, news, and sports talk shows. By 1974 over 100 radio stations had talk formats on the air.

Television was also seeing new daytime activity, and into the daytime television syndication market stepped the host who had made a name for himself on a small "hot topic" call-in radio talk show in Dayton, Ohio.[47] Phil Donahue brought to television the kind of audience participation and involvement that had been popular on radio for over a decade.

Donahue's entry into the world of daytime television was startling for those who had been used to nothing but formula game shows and soap operas. His new format and syndication business acumen—with videotapes of the show "bicycled" around the United States and later to other countries in the days before satellite distribution—enabled the *Donahue* show to become the nation's number one syndicated talk show by 1979. Donahue converted "talk radio" into "talk television" and was one of the prime forces in the regeneration of the TV talk show that took place during its third cycle and third decade on the air.

Born in 1935 in Cleveland to a strongly church-affiliated, lower-middle-class Catholic family, Phil Donahue was the son of a furniture sales clerk and a department store shoe clerk. Attending Catholic schools in Cleveland and graduating from St. Edward High, a newly established Catholic prep school, Donahue went on to Notre Dame from 1953 to 1957, majoring in business but preferring his courses in philosophy and theology. Those courses at Notre Dame represented a heady atmosphere of liberal intellectualism, philosophy, and religion, and Donahue responded to it.

Donahue's own break with the Church in the 1960s and early 1970s was an agonizing one. As he reported the "gender wars" of his era on his talk show, his own marriage of fifteen years, which had produced five children, was falling apart. Donahue visibly carried his own personal pain to the shows he moderated. As he later explained,

> I graduated from college in 1957 after having been prepared for a world that never materialized. Nobody told us that Mom would go out, leave the house. Nobody told me I'd get divorced. Nobody told me that the Catholic Church would face this tremendous crisis of the evaporation of what we used to call vocations. . . . It's a little bit like believing in Santa Claus, and then suddenly looking up and having the feeling, sort of, that you've been had.[48]

Donahue ends his 1979 autobiography in the Grotto of St. Mary at Notre Dame, his alma mater. "I had moved in my forty-three years," he says, "from certainty to doubt, from devotion to rebellion."[49]

The television show Donahue and his team developed represented and recorded these changes in American life. Though the civil rights and women's movements had affected many levels of American society by the 1970s, direct expressions of those movements were rarely seen

on television. Viewers were unaccustomed to witnessing ordinary people arguing, debating, and questioning authorities on the air on issues
that centered on power relations between husband and wife, the "right
to life" versus "the right to choose" in abortion debates, or arguments
for and against lifestyles outside traditional heterosexual monogamous
ones.

This revolution in television talk, which has variously been called
participatory television, talk-back television, or tele-democracy, was
launched by Donahue and his team in Dayton, Ohio, in 1967. The team
included producer-director Richard Mincer, who went on to become
the show's executive producer and then parent company executive;
Patricia McMillen, who started as a secretary and went on to become
the show's producer and then executive producer; and a staff of women
producers that grew over the years. Producers often had a great deal of
autonomy to decide who and what topics and guests were to air.[50] Donahue was always the hands-on managing editor of the show, however.
He decided early on to concentrate on women's issues and themes, and
from the beginning worked out a balance between more serious and
more sensational entertainment topics.

Television gave Donahue a much wider audience than his radio
show, and television revealed faces, expressions, and gestures that, together with Donahue's frenetic, probing style, brought tension and
drama to his own patented form of talk drama in the studio. Indeed, on
Donahue the studio audience itself was the protagonist each day. A live
studio audience could not be manipulated as easily as one held at bay
through a telephone switchboard. The show reversed Mike Wallace's
formula. Rather than the star host grilling the guest or expert witness,
the audience itself became the show's prime "inquisitorial" force.

Richard Mincer, Donahue's first director, remembers the moment
the show "discovered" the audience. It was during a commercial break
during one of the first weeks of the show when a member of the audience asked the fashion model who was appearing why she didn't braid
her hair. The model replied that she had never learned to do so and accepted the woman's offer to show her how. As the show came back from
the commercial break, the audience member came up to the stage and
began braiding the model's hair on camera. "There was a new electricity
in the room," says Mincer. "Phil and I talked about it later in the day
and decided to make the audience a part of the process every day."[51]

The design of the set in the Dayton television studio facilitated
this kind of interaction. It was an open stage area with the audience

seated at one end—a kind of theater in the round, hexagonal in shape. From two cameras *Donahue* went to three when the show moved to the larger studio at WGN in Chicago in 1974. A new director, Ron Weiner, added a fourth camera, which created an even greater sense of theater-in-the-round. Traditional "screen right" and "screen left" were abandoned. The "180 degree rule" that normally locates speakers in film and television space was also abandoned as Donahue bounded around the studio fielding questions, provoking responses from the audience, and catalyzing new issues of debate. Weiner, who was responsible for the "look" of the *Donahue* show, won a number of Emmys for his directing.

From the beginning, Donahue dealt with topics that few daytime television shows would touch. As he later put it:

> It all began in the sixties when I realized out there were all these women with questions. Bloating. Spotting. Yeast. Discharge. Everything! All the things they were afraid to ask their own doctor. Remember how patronizing we were, then? You know, doctors would pat 'em on the head and send 'em along to get some . . . something at the drugstore. And women were enraged.[52]

Not since Arlene Francis' *Home* show had a talk show presented such a stimulating mix to a predominantly women's audience. Working with a team of women producers, Donahue showed once again that intelligent programming for women could pay off in commercial television. His show registered a hefty fifty "share" its first month in Dayton (meaning that it was viewed by over half the audience that had television sets on at the time)[53] and remained popular in Dayton and its Midwest sister stations while Donahue and his team searched for new markets.

The *Donahue* show was one sign of changing times in the national talk-show market of the late 1960s. There were other, equally compelling signs. Indeed, the period of the late-night talk-show wars from 1967 to 1974 was one of the most interesting transitional periods in the history of the television talk show.

FIVE

COMPETITIVE FERMENT IN THE LATE SECOND CYCLE

The First Late-Night Talk-Show Wars (1967–1974)

INTRODUCTION

By the end of the 1960s, television viewing was an established fact of life in the United States. By 1967 color television was a strong force in the market, with the number of color sets sold that year equaling the number of monochrome receivers and many families using more than one television set. Late-night television and early fringe-time television were increasingly profitable as more and more viewers integrated television into their daily lives. The talk show took on new visibility particularly during late-night fringe time periods (after 11 P.M.), and nationally syndicated talk began to provide more competition to the networks as well. It was under these circumstances that the first late-night talk-show wars broke out.

The talk-show wars centered on the comparative Nielsen ratings of competitive shows, but they were essentially publicity wars. The fighting took place in the pages of the national press. Articles on the late-night talk-show wars in the late 1960s and early 1970s appeared in *Time, Newsweek, Ladies' Home Journal, Life,* and other national news and entertainment publications, with numerous commentaries in editorials and opinion pieces by writers such as *New York Daily News* television critic Jack Gould. All of this publicity focused new attention on the talk show and helped to refine the public's understanding of the late-night talk show as a genre.

It was no mere coincidence, perhaps, that the first late-night talk-show wars heated up just as the Presidential election campaigns of 1968 were gaining momentum. The same thing occurred again a quarter of a century later in 1992, when a second round of late-night entertainment talk-show wars took place at exactly the same time as the national political campaigns that eventually put Bill Clinton in the White House. The talk-show wars of 1967–1972 and 1992–1993 took place during times of national political conflict and change. The controversies of 1967–1972 focused on the new "youth culture," the civil rights movement, the rise of feminism, and the early anti–Vietnam War movement. During the bitterly contested election of 1968, Republican candidate Richard Nixon faced a series of Democratic challengers, including antiwar candidates Eugene McCarthy and Robert F. Kennedy. During that year, which featured nationally televised police riots at the Democratic Convention in Chicago, the entertainment talk-show wars provided late-night viewers with a series of simpler choices as to who would "speak" for them.

THE CHALLENGERS: Bishop, Frost, Griffin, and Cavett

At first glance the contenders to Johnny Carson's throne in late-night television did not have much in common: Joey Bishop, a fifty-two-year-old stand-up comedian; Dick Cavett, a Yale graduate and thirty-four-year-old comedy writer from Nebraska; David Frost, a thirty-one-year-old English television personality; and Merv Griffin, a singer who had developed two game shows and had, for four years, run a successful nationally syndicated talk show for the Westinghouse network. From 1967 to 1972 each of these figures found himself, at one time or another, competing with Johnny Carson for the late-night talk-show audience.

ABC entered the competition first. Leonard Goldenson and other top executives at ABC, still smarting from the loss of Carson to NBC in 1962, were determined to find a host who could attract audiences away from Carson. Their first venture into late-night talk had been *The Les Crane Show*, and though the show got good reviews, it lasted only four months, from November 1964 to March 1965. Crane, an innovator, invited such rarely seen television guests as singer/poet Bob Dylan to his show, and three years before Donahue went on the air he had already begun engaging members of the studio audience as participants, using a shotgun microphone. Thereafter, ABC tried out a series of late-night hosts, finally settling on comedian Joey Bishop, who in April 1967 took over the time slot opposite Johnny Carson.

Bishop was already a veteran of the Eastern burlesque and nightclub circuit when he came to television.[1] He had starred in two TV situation comedies, done guest stints on Jack Paar's *Tonight*, and guest hosted for Carson. He had evolved on television, as one critic described him, from "a tough Jewish comic from South Philadelphia" to "the friendly Jewish merchant you used to see in John Wayne movies, delivering quips that never wounded."[2] ABC's choice of Bishop threw a new challenger into a talk-show field dominated by Midwesterners with standard American accents.[3]

Bishop's show was in the *Broadway Open House* tradition, featuring guests, music, and comedy performances, and was livened up by second banana Regis Philbin, who was later to host *The Regis Philbin Show, Live! with Regis and Kathie Lee, Who Wants to Be a Millionaire?,* and *Live! with Regis and Kelly. The Joey Bishop Show* had a two-and-a-half-year run on ABC, but lagged in the ratings, and ABC replaced him in December 1969 with its second entry to the talk-show wars, stand-up comedian Dick Cavett. Cavett had done a little bit of every kind of comedy by the late 1960s, working as a standup and writing for such diverse talents as Jack Paar, Groucho Marx, Jack E. Leonard, and Jerry Lewis. By 1966 Cavett was commanding a salary of $1,000 a week for stand-up appearances and performing his own material.[4] Having launched Cavett in the spring of 1968 with a ninety-minute morning show, ABC elevated him to a thrice-weekly prime-time show in the summer of 1969 and put him in Joey Bishop's place opposite Carson. Cavett brought wit, erudition, and a sense of verbal play to a medium that viewers and critics found lacking in all of these areas. He talked "up" to his viewers, appealing to a younger, more sophisticated audience, and his show produced some of the most memorable moments in talk-show history. (One of these moments, a confrontation in December 1970 between writers Norman Mailer, Gore Vidal, and Janet Flanner, is included in a Close-up at the end of this section.)

Carson had two other challengers during this period: David Frost, an already successful English talk-show host, and ex-singer and syndicated talk-show host Merv Griffin. Frost had been introduced to American audiences in two episodes of the satirical program *That Was the Week That Was* and through interviews he had conducted with American Presidential candidates in 1968. The Westinghouse syndication network signed Frost to replace Griffin in 1969, when Griffin went to the CBS late-night show to challenge Carson.

Coming to the United States in the wake of the Beatles and the "British invasion" in music, movies, and fashion, Frost was the kind of second-generation talk-show host whose material was designed to appeal to the new urban audiences Cavett was drawing.[5] Frost, dubbed "TV's Intercontinental Man" by a *Look* magazine article in 1970, had a wider range of guests than most hosts of the day and one of his specialties was in-depth interviews that lasted forty minutes to an hour. Like Donahue, Frost would walk out into the audience to take questions or lead discussions with audience members from the stage.

It was Merv Griffin on CBS, however, who mounted Carson's stiffest competition. In 1969, Griffin, at forty-five, was a show-business veteran with two decades of television experience as singer, game-show host, and syndicated talk-show host. Born the same year as Carson,[6] Griffin had guest hosted for Paar in the early 1960s and run his own morning talk show on NBC in 1962. Griffin's daytime NBC show started October 1, 1962, the same day as Carson's *Tonight* show. Despite interesting and controversial guests and much critical acclaim, Griffin's first network outing lasted only six months. He re-entered the talk-show world on the Westinghouse circuit in 1965 with *The Merv Griffin Show*, broadcasting from New York's Little Theatre off Times Square. It was the success of this show over a four-year period that made Griffin a candidate for CBS's foray into the late-night talk-show wars.[7]

Up to this time CBS had been content to run old movies after 11 P.M. By 1969, however, supplies of feature-length films were waning, their costs were rising, and affiliates were taking a disproportionate share of the late-night revenues. A successful talk show owned by the network would be considerably more profitable and draw viewers to other shows. "Tapping Griffin," *Newsweek* said, "was in keeping with the traditionally safe, conservative CBS approach."[8] The network "combed the business and rejected every potentially new and different face." They settled "on the one pretested, prepackaged show in the country." CBS offered Griffin a $25,000 a week contract, a salary reportedly equal to Carson's.

With Griffin, the final gauntlet had been thrown down. "For the first time," *Newsweek* proclaimed, "the three networks are matching essentially the same show in the same time slot—putting credit or blame for the results squarely on the drawing power of the hosts."[9] NBC responded with full-page ads for Carson in papers across the country, and the talk-show wars were now a three-way battle between Griffin, Cavett, and Carson.

The talk-show wars of 1967–1972 highlighted the problem of free speech in network television. Talk on television had never been unfettered, and part of Carson's success as reigning monarch was his canny ability to shy away from hard-edged political and social controversy while remaining hip and "contemporary." There were, however, hosts in the 1960s who did engage in the controversies that were part of the era: Jack Paar at the beginning of the decade, then Les Crane on ABC, David Susskind on *Open End,* Dick Cavett on ABC, and—with varying degrees of success—regional "shock" talk hosts like Joe Pyne and Alan Burke, who were able to go past network-imposed limits in syndicated settings. Surprisingly, for those who knew him only in his later mild-mannered days, Merv Griffin gave CBS network executives headaches in the late 1960s by pushing controversial guests and topics on his show.

Griffin saw himself as following in Jack Paar's footsteps in this respect. Well aware that the same controversy that had made Paar a network pariah had also made him a rich and successful broadcaster—one of the first major stars of television talk—Griffin decided to mix a potent brew of controversial topics with standard show-business patter on his new CBS show. He invited guests who opposed the war in Vietnam, supported liberal sexual morals, and argued for the legalization of marijuana. If Carson's approach to television came out of playing it safe in the Los Angeles entertainment community, Griffin, who came to New York as a singer in the early 1950s, was subject to other influences. He had watched shows like Mike Wallace's *Night Beat* and David Susskind's *Open End* and enjoyed socializing with some of the feistier spirits in the New York theater community.[10]

On his syndicated show from the mid- to late 1960s, and also on his network show, Griffin capitalized on the ferment of the era. As early as 1965 he had aired a syndicated theme show from London featuring English philosopher Bertrand Russell issuing a strong indictment of growing U.S. involvement in Vietnam. Russell told Griffin that the "strategic hamlet" policy forced Vietnamese farmers into "virtual concentration camps" and recited atrocities that were taking place in the name of "pacification." Griffin himself was shocked by these statements, and the studio audience in the United States booed the segment as "anti-American" when it was played back. But Griffin reminded his audience that it was part of free speech and necessary for robust debate on these issues.

This kind of programming did not sit well with CBS executives. In 1969, concerned with the number of statements being made on the Griffin show against the war in Vietnam, network lawyers shot Griffin a memo: "In the past six weeks 34 antiwar statements have been made and only one pro-war statement, by John Wayne." Griffin replied: "Find me someone as famous as Mr. Wayne to speak in favor of the war and we'll book him."[11] "The irony of the situation," Griffin recalls in his memoirs, "wasn't wasted on me; in 1965 I'm called a traitor by the press for presenting Bertrand Russell, and four years later we are hard-pressed to find *anybody* to speak in favor of the Vietnam war."[12]

Network battles continued. In March 1970, antiwar activist Abbie Hoffman visited the show wearing a red, white, and blue shirt that resembled an American flag. Network censors aired the tape but blurred Hoffman's image electronically so that his voice emanated from a "jumble of lines."[13] Network executives interfered in other ways as well. They told Griffin to get rid of sidekick Arthur Treacher because he was too old. When Griffin asked Desi Arnaz Jr., then eighteen, to guest host the show, the network argued that he was too young. This time Griffin held his ground, and Arnaz was allowed to appear.

By the beginning of 1972, his ratings sagging and his spirits flagging from constant network interference, Griffin signed a secret syndication deal with Metromedia and waited for the network to cancel him. Ever attentive to business details, Griffin stood to collect a quarter of a million dollars from the penalty clause that he had inserted in his 1971 contract, but only if the network canceled him, not if he quit. The expected boom was lowered in February 1972, and Griffin went on to host his commercially successful Metromedia show for another fourteen years, until 1986, when he retired to devote himself full time to profitable real estate holdings and game shows. On Merv Griffin's farewell show, retrospective clips failed to include any of the dissident writers, artists, or the men and women of ideas who had appeared. Only at the end did viewers glimpse guests who had been what Griffin called the "heavy furniture" of the show: brief shots of an unidentified Gore Vidal and actress/anti-war activist Jane Fonda.[14]

On ABC, it was Dick Cavett who insisted on bringing to audiences the "heavy furniture" of relevant social and cultural issues through visits with some of the more important writers, thinkers, and intellectuals of the time. Cavett, too, faced constant network interference and restrictions. This interference began the first day he went on the air with a morning show featuring writer Gore Vidal, boxer Muhammad Ali, and actress Angela Lansbury. An ABC network executive approached Cavett after the show and excoriated him for not delivering to the network what it had "bought, bargained for," or wanted. "Nobody in the world wants to hear what Gore Vidal or Muhammad Ali thinks about the Vietnam war,"[15] the executive said. But Cavett persisted, and in a show seen originally five nights a week on ABC in 1969, Cavett brought to the screen some of television talk's most lively and interesting moments. One of those moments was a confrontation between writers Norman Mailer, Gore Vidal, and Janet Flanner that occurred in late 1971.

CLOSE-UP: NORMAN MAILER VS. GORE VIDAL ON *THE DICK CAVETT SHOW,* ABC, DECEMBER 1, 1971[16]

From the moment that noted writer Norman Mailer appeared on the set of *The Dick Cavett Show* of December 1, 1971, with his literary nemesis Gore Vidal it was clear that sparks were going to fly. Mailer was seething over Vidal's review of his recent book, *The Prisoner of Sex.* Mailer made it clear in his first seconds on the screen that he felt wounded and was out for revenge. The third member of the panel was Janet Flanner, seventy-nine years old at the time and a brilliant conversationalist herself. As "Genêt," she had been writing the "Letter from Paris" feature for *The New Yorker* since 1925. She provided an ironic chorus to Mailer's bombast and display of testosterone that evening. Mailer self-consciously promoted himself, in the course of the evening, as the proverbial bull in the china shop of talk-show conventions. He was as truculent and offensive as he could possibly be. Before the evening was over, he had managed to offend almost everyone in the studio audience and break almost every one of the talk show's unspoken rules.

The encounter between Mailer and Vidal was like a prize fight. Cavett acted as a referee, with Mailer consciously playing on his image as an amateur boxer.

Round One

After a witty and urbane conversation with Janet Flanner, Cavett announces Mailer's appearance with some trepidation. He is "an unpredictable and brilliant man," Cavett tells the audience, but someone "who hardly ever has a predictable or cliché opinion about anything" and whose unpredictability once extended to punching one of Cavett's guests. Mailer saunters on stage in Italian leather boots, clearly in a foul mood, angry because Cavett's staff has misinformed him about the show's start time. Coming early, he was forced to cool his heels in one of his favorite "watering spots," he says. How much he has had to drink is unclear, but now, hands jammed deep in his pockets, he refuses to observe the customary talk-show ritual of shaking hands with Vidal. Mailer also refuses to acknowledge the presence of the cameras. As the studio audience audibly gasps, he slips sullenly into his chair, turning his back to Vidal and the audience, and addresses Cavett alone. He talks about Vidal in the third person as if he weren't there:

> We were friends two to three years ago, but since then we have done nothing but write atrocious things about each other. I am so mad at Gore by now that I came on the show prepared to break the exceptionally wondrous and lovely mood that Genêt [Flanner] has given us.

It is only two minutes into the show and Mailer has made it clear that he is not playing by the rules. He knows those rules. Indeed, he describes himself as a "student of television," a "particularly obdurate art" in his opinion, and praises Flanner's performance before the camera. She is "splendid at it," he says. He is "overcome" with just how good she was, he says. Vidal, on the other hand, has continually proved himself "shameless in intellectual argument . . . absolutely without character or moral foundation or even intellectual substance." As Mailer continues his tirade against Vidal, never looking in the direction of his rival, his literary opponent listens silently, chin in hand, waiting patiently for an opening. Mailer gives him few opportunities. Finally, no longer able to contain himself, Mailer turns directly to his foe.

> You can do anything you want to any piece I ever write. You can rip it apart and by God I may be bloody on the floor, but if you taught me anything about writing, I'll look up and I'll love you for having taught me something about *writing*. But when you teach me something about the—tricks of adulteration—when you pollute the intellectual rivers, good God . . .

Vidal finally intercedes. "Well, you know, I must say. I think it worries you that I made some comments about your recent writing"—he pauses to look down at the by-now-crumpled review Mailer has passed Flanner—"not being very good." Each word is cool, reserved. At the moment, Vidal sounds quite a bit like conservative talk-show host William Buckley. "I wasn't setting myself up as the Famous Writers School to give you any hints. It's just that I thought your subject—"

Mailer breaks in: "Why don't you talk, for once, Gore, without yuks? Why don't you just talk to me—instead of talking to the audience?"

"Well," Vidal replies, "by a curious circumstance we have not found each other in a friendly neighborhood bar, but we are both sitting here with an audience, so therefore it would be dishonest of us to pretend otherwise."

"All right," says Mailer, "we are here with an audience by choice, but let us at least"—he suddenly looks over to Janet Flanner, who has said something quietly to Vidal. "Hey, Miss Flanner, are you workin' as the referee or as Mr. Vidal's manager?" Flanner breaks into a hearty laugh. "His manager!" she says.

"My mind is fragile," Mailer tells her in a wounded voice. "I find it hard to think," he tells her, if she is "muttering in the background." It was only "the slightest mutter," she replies, "a tiny mutter." "Yes, *dear*," says Mailer, his voice dripping sarcasm. Flanner pretends not to notice and promises not to "mutter" again.

Mailer continues to rip into Vidal while describing their literary feud. "Gore's entries have been long and mine have been short," he says. Gore intercedes, "but they *seemed* long." After several more minutes of this Flanner can contain herself no longer. "You men insult each other not only in public but act as if you were in private. That's the odd thing. You act as if you're the only people here." "Aren't we?" says Mailer. "*They* are here," says Flanner, gesturing to the studio audience. "*He* is here [looking over to Cavett], and *I* am here, and I am becoming very, very bored." Flanner's comment gets the biggest response of the evening as members of the studio audience roar their approval. She blows them a kiss.

This seems to push Mailer further into his intransigence. He turns and addresses the audience directly. "This audience has been curiously hostile to me from the word go. Are you all truly idiots or is it me?"

"You!" the audience thunders.

"Oh," says Cavett. "That was the easy answer," and then, looking at the clock, "There is an exigency of time." He turns to Mailer. "I remind you of your earlier vow not to punch anyone. We'll be back after this message from our sponsor."

Round 2

Cavett tells viewers that during the commercial break the four of them had sat on stage in "stony silence." "No," Vidal corrects him, "someone in the audience shouted 'Your argument is immature' to all four of us." Mailer pays no heed and is anxious to pursue his interrogation of the audience.

"What do you have against me?" he asks. The audience response is immediate: he's been "rude," a "snot," a "male chauvinist pig."

Mailer seizes upon the last phrase. "Oh!" he says. "The joint is loaded with 'libbies!'" he cries. "Gore, my God, it wasn't enough to trundle Janet Flanner along, the most formidable presence in the history of television, but you had to load the balcony with 'libbies.'" He turns again to the audience.

What all this is about is that I wrote a book called *The Prisoner of Sex,* which started off to be a book about women's liberation and what I thought about it for *Harper's* magazine. And in the course of it I found that I couldn't begin to talk about what I thought about women's liberation until I began to start to say what I thought about sex. This was complex. My thoughts went back and forth. I had a large number of feelings about women's liberation. I admired aspects of it and detested other aspects of it, and wrestled with it, and my mind changed a bit as I thought about it. This book was an attempt to write about these things and think about these things and talk about them. And after the book was written it was as if I had not written the book. The word came out that I was "a male chauvinist pig." Well that's dull. It's just dull. It's beneath us as Americans to think in thick, frozen terms of intellectual pollution . . . Gore comes along—on his toes, he's a marvelous little boxer, as you saw— and starts polluting the waters further. But he knows what he's doing. That's the trouble. He's a bad man.

Cavett tries to interrupt, but Mailer ignores him.

In prize fighting terms, Gore is like a fellow who has been ranked anywhere from #9 to #3, #2 once in a while. And he's been around, so it's not as if he doesn't know the ropes. And then suddenly after all these years—he's suddenly developed a particularly dirty literary game. Well it enflames me. I've been so bold as to pretend to be the presumptive literary champ, whether I deserve to be or not. . . . Hemingway said, people who write books take as much punishment as prize fighters and one of them has got to be champion. . . . [Vidal and others] can't knock me off because they're too damn simply yellow—

Cavett finally cuts in. "We will finish this sentence, whether we like it or not, after a message from the sponsor."

It is worth noting here that, with all the dramatics and violations of talk-show decorum, one rule has remained unquestioned: commercial breaks have occurred at each point in their accustomed place and the requisite number of commercial spots that pay for the program have had their play on the air. There will be one more round, however, before the final commercial break.

Round 3

Cavett announces there are only "three and a half minutes left" in the show. "I insist," he says, turning to Vidal, "that you get them." Vidal has by this time been assaulted by Mailer continuously for almost half an hour with little or no chance to reply. He measures his words carefully now, aiming them directly to Mailer, who is now facing him.

> What I detest in you—and I like many things in you, as you know, I'm a constant friend, despite this—but your violence, your love of murder, your celebration of rage, hate . . . this violence, this knocking people down, this carrying-on, is a terrible thing. It may make you an interesting artist, I'm not saying that [it doesn't], but to the extent one is interested in the way the society is going, there is quite enough of this without your celebration of it. . . . I said [in the review] Henry Miller in his way, Norman in his, and Manson in his far-out mad way, are each reflecting a hatred of women—and a hatred of flesh.

The studio audience is quiet, though someone claps after Vidal's statement. Mailer wishes to rebut, but Cavett says the show is definitively out of time. Vidal manages one parting shot: "Give you a few minutes more on the program and you will [again] prove my point."

The Norman Mailer/Gore Vidal/Janet Flanner show of December 1, 1970, was many things. It was a stunning example of Cavett's skill as a host in stepping back and letting his guests take over the show. It was a brilliant example of how a show's "mix"—in this case the combination of Mailer, Vidal, and Flanner—can make for great television. It showed that substance—passionate intensity around an issue or theme—can at times cut through the clutter and mindless "chatter" of much television talk. A well-known author was not simply on a show to sell books—though that was certainly a subtext of Mailer's appearance. An intellectual engagement occurred in which the character of the author and the character of each of the speakers was heightened, revealed. And the discussion did not revolve around fluff, but an issue of central importance to American culture.

The show revealed something else: the forms of television talk itself. Here, as in other self-reflexive moments, rules are revealed when they are parodied, challenged, or broken. David Letterman by no means invented "reflexivity" in TV talk, though he took it in interesting new directions in the 1980s. Ernie Kovacs constantly put the spotlight on his own cameras and crew. Carson, too, was self-reflexive from his earliest days on television. But on this Dick Cavett show in the early 1970s it is the guest who calls attention to talk-show forms and subverts them. One after the other, Mailer breaks the unspoken rules of television talk. He displaces the host, taking over the direction and pacing of the show. Aware that Cavett is an old friend of Vidal and a supporter of his "civility," Mailer pushes Cavett aside and strips him of his guise of genial objectivity. Finally, Cavett can no longer assume the guise of obectivity and is forced to declare himself in the camp of Mailer's "opposition." Mailer also challenges the studio audience. He refuses to let it play its role as an invisible surrogate for the audience at home, an unquestioned presence and responsive but essentially silent chorus to the talk on the stage. Mailer forces the audience to articulate its own position. Finally, Mailer puts the spotlight on something else that is normally left unspoken in TV talk—the degree to which private conversations on stage are also always public. Are we talking to each other, he asks Vidal, or playing to the audience? How much of this "talk" is "show"? The questions Mailer raises about the talk show as a form are as interesting as the literary and social issues revealed in his verbal duel with Vidal. Mailer later summarized many of his thoughts and arguments about television as a medium and the talk show as a form in an article in *Pieces and Pontifications,* his collected essays from the 1970s.

The Mailer/Vidal/Flanner confrontation reminds us that television talk occurs in cycles, and it does not progress in an orderly, linear fashion. Breakout moments in television talk-show history, when certain shows challenge the form and substance of TV talk, tend to come out of periods of social and cultural conflict. There were a lot of issues to talk about during the period from 1967 to 1972, as the issues of the 1960s spilled into television and challengers to Johnny Carson—such as Joey Bishop, Merv Griffin, David Frost, and Dick Cavett—found new ways of talking about them. The talk-show wars gave the networks both an opportunity to build new audiences for late-night television, making the advertisers happy, and a dilemma, since they kicked up social and political controversy that network programmers and advertisers would just as soon avoid. Reconsidered thirty years after it first aired, the Mailer/Vidal confrontation is a fascinating social document as well as an extraordinary moment in the history of TV talk.

The Gay Subtext

The exchange of December 1, 1971, between Norman Mailer and Gore Vidal had a subtext that often left the audience, and Cavett himself, perplexed. The dominant frame of the confrontation was the literary rivalry between Mailer and Vidal. But there was something else going on. Mailer had another agenda—one that revealed itself in the coded language of the closet. Vidal and Flanner were both prominent "out" members of the literary intellectual gay community, and Mailer, playing his *enfant terrible* role to the hilt, was constantly making veiled, taunting references to their homosexuality.

Mailer began his sexual innuendo soon after he appeared with a reference to rival talk show host David Frost. He found he got bigger in Frost's presence, he said, and in Cavett's he shrank and felt very small and weak. "My, I wonder why that is," Cavett retorted. "Perhaps you're eating the wrong thing." Mailer came back, "Keep the conversation clean now." This became the first of many references to oral sex. Minutes later, speaking about his literary opponent in the third person, Mailer said: "Gore can bring up everything [about his recent published attacks on me] because the contents of his stomach are no more interesting than an intellectual cow's"—a reference to fellatio. Later "eating" comes up again. This time Mailer addresses Janet Flanner. "I know when I came to your house for dinner I wasn't going to get anything to eat." Flanner, a central figure in the Parisian Left Bank literary and artistic scene of the 1920s, '30s, and '40s, catches the meaning immediately and roars with laughter.

"Eating," then, was Mailer's coded reference to both Vidal and Flanner's homosexuality. He alternates these mocking references to remarks on male tumescence. Mailer claims, for example, that perhaps he intimidates the other three people on the show because he is "bigger" than they are. Cavett goes for the bait. "Bigger in what way, Norman?" Mailer replies, "Bigger in intellect, of course." At this point, Cavett turns his chair to align himself with Vidal and Flanner. He quips: "Well, maybe we should bring two more chairs, Norman, so that you have something to contain your giant intellect." Mailer rejoins, "I'll accept the two chairs, if the rest of you will accept the finger bowls" (an allusion to both masturbation and hand-sex in same sex acts). Cavett picks up the cue this time and pushes Mailer to explain himself. "I know it means something," Cavett says, adding, "Finger bowls are things you dip your fingers in when you've gotten filthy from eating." "Am I getting warm?" Cavett asks Mailer. Then, becoming agitated, Mailer suggests Cavett return to his prepared question and answer sheet and ask him a real question. Cavett's reply, one of the remembered lines of the evening, is: "Why don't you fold it five ways and put it where the sun don't shine?"

This level of sexual subtext and innuendo was just one strand in the confrontation between Norman Mailer and the other guests, but it struck an odd, mystifying note for those not picking up the allusions.[17]

For Mailer, commercial television itself was a great cancer, a Limbo, as he called it, a dragon to be slain. Homosexuals were also an obsession for Mailer. Vidal always thought Mailer was angry with him because Mailer felt he had "buggered" Jack Kerouac and ruined him as a writer. On the evening of December 1, 1971, Mailer's dragon-slaying performance was reckless.

What is even more remarkable than the evening itself is that what was meant to be ephemeral, a consumable daily talk show, became an object of permanent rediscovery, a "classic," a moment frozen in time. Visitors to the Museum of Television and Radio have made the show one of the most frequently watched in the Museum's "Greatest Hits" series. Audiences of all ages can watch the verbal duel again and again, on all its levels of text and subtext, re-entering this talk world of 1971 with a simple push of a button.

While Dick Cavett was performing his balancing act as a public intellectual on network television, the television industry itself was facing a series of major political, social, and economic challenges. Within the world of late-night television talk, despite all the challenges, Johnny Carson helped to restore a sense of continuity and order within the industry. He did so by persistence, by constantly re-negotiating a place for himself within the NBC network, and by moving his operation to the West Coast as the industry consolidated itself there.

JOHNNY CARSON (1967–1974)

The turning point for Johnny Carson as talk-show host and entrepreneur took place in 1967, right at the beginning of the challenges that were mounted against him as "king of late night." As opposition to the Vietnam War began to mount, and as the culture wars flared, Carson was engaged in his own battles with NBC executives. Up to this time Carson's network salary had been quite substantial, almost three-quarters of a million dollars a year. Out of that amount, however, he had to pay salaries not only to his personal staff but also to a number of other *Tonight* show staffers.[18] His offices and dressing room were small and shabby, "just a little bigger than closets,"[19] one secretary recalled, and more importantly, Carson did not make the larger financial decisions that affected his show. NBC owned the show and called the shots.

In the meantime, Carson continued his work as a top-billed nightclub act in the 1960s. It was the way he hedged his bets against the kind of sudden cancellation he had experienced on his 1955 CBS show, and it kept him in touch with his audience by bringing him not only to Las Vegas but to arenas, auditoriums, and fairgrounds around the country. His experience on the road, and the figures he was commanding to perform, convinced him that he had become by this point a star, not just a hired voice. He had been an interested observer of Jack Paar's walk off the air in 1960, and he knew that NBC would be convinced, in the final analysis, only by confrontation.

The turning point came in March 1967 when the American Federation of Television and Radio Artists (AFTRA), representing all on-air performers, including Carson, called a strike. Carson flew down to Fort Lauderdale with several colleagues and friends to wait out the strike. There he was surprised to see that NBC was rebroadcasting a tape of his show from the 1966 Christmas season. Carson thought the replay of a Christmas show in the spring was "ludicrous" and fired off a memo to NBC telling them so.[20] The network's refusal to stop the rebroadcasts, or compensate Carson for the reruns, was the last straw. Carson went public. "What is the price that should be paid for a rerun when it's used while your union is on strike?"[21] he asked the press, and the press gleefully jumped on the story of a major star's battle with the network.

Over the next month, the negotiations between Carson and the network continued. Once Joey Bishop's ABC challenge had been launched, the network realized it had no one with anything close to Carson's following or reputation to replace him on short notice. Executives at NBC capitulated. Under Carson's new contract, negotiated by his lawyer, Arnold Grant, he was given complete control of the show, including the power to hire and fire personnel (the network's prerogative up till then) and a reported increase of salary to $1 million a year, with additional funds to pay staff. It was a three-year contract that put Carson, for the first time, fully in the driver's seat. When Carson returned to the air in May 1967, *Time* magazine made him the cover story, dubbing him television's first "midnight idol."[22] As he would characteristically do throughout his career, Carson marked the change by firing one of his staff who had been closest to him. When he returned to NBC after the strike, he fired long-time producer Art Stark, who had become identified, in Carson's mind, with the NBC executives he had been battling.[23]

Two hard-fought contracts with NBC and a move to his new Burbank studios on the West Coast in 1972 put Carson even more in control of his show. His West Coast location differentiated him from the hosts whose shows were being produced on the East Coast like Griffin, Cavett, and Frost and opened up to his talent coordinators a set of new faces and guests from the Hollywood entertainment community. In personal terms, the move marked a clear division from his past life with his first wife in New York. The divorce was finalized in the summer of 1972 with a sizable settlement. This part of his life now became comedy material for his show, as Carson's "divorce" jokes became a standard part of his monologue.

Carson's move to Los Angeles paralleled an economic and population shift to the West and the Sun Belt states. It was in tune with other developments in the television industry. Despite all the ferment that occurred in 1960s television talk, the networks continually clawed back to standardized entertainment products that would offend no one. In September 1970, Vice President Marvin Antonowsky of ABC spoke in high rhetorical terms of networks meeting their "obligations to the American public" by giving them "entertainment of substance and broad appeal that is relevant, timely, entertaining, and exciting,"[24] but the rhetoric was quickly superseded by ratings realities. By the next season the networks had retrenched on much of their innovative programming. A few new programs survived the axe, notably Norman Lear's *All in the Family*, with the backing of CBS executive Robert Wood, but shows like the liberal *Storefront Lawyers*, with White lawyers working in a Black ghetto, were taken off the air.[25] According to broadcast historian J. Fred MacDonald, "Within three months overt social relevancy was rejected by the audience, and the networks scrambled for replacement programs." By 1972, it was business as usual.[26] *The Tonight Show*'s move to the heart of the entertainment production community in Los Angeles marked the show's acceptance as part of the Hollywood establishment. Carson reassumed the dominant position in late-night television. His institutionalization as *the* successful host of late-night talk was a sign of the successful consolidation of the television industry.

CONCLUSION

The network talk-show wars of 1967–1974 encouraged critics and audiences to reconsider the talk show as a genre—its history, its economics, its importance to the television industry. With growing late-night audiences, leading contenders in the late-night talk-show sweepstakes were now seen as steady moneymakers for the networks. In 1969 Carson's *Tonight* show received $17,550 a minute for commercial spots, Griffin's CBS show $10,500, Joey Bishop's ABC show $7,500, with the combined profits from all three shows totaling over $50 million a year, a major portion of network profits.[27] Some industry sources were worried about "overexposure of the genre," and some critics, like Woody Allen, who had logged over fifty appearances on talk shows by this time and had written comedy material for television, felt the genre might eventually wear itself out. "One show works and everyone tries to shove it down the viewers' throats," he said. "The format is a durable one, but eventually they may kill it."[28]

In the years from 1974 to 1980, major network talk-show hosts like Johnny Carson, Mike Wallace, and Barbara Walters would tenaciously build their positions within their respective networks. Meanwhile, hosts like Bill Moyers, Phil Donahue, Dinah Shore, and Mike Douglas were rising up through PBS and national syndication to pose new challenges to the networks.

SIX

THE THIRD CYCLE (1974–1980)

Transitions

1974: A Year of Change

At the end of 1974 the television industry in general was still in turbulence, but several broad patterns had emerged. For one thing, national syndication was making itself increasingly felt as a competitor to the networks for national talk audiences. In addition, by 1974 public television had proved surprisingly durable and supported a range of new voices and formats in talk television. And 1974 was unusual in that a single national talk event dominated the landscape: the Senate Watergate hearings that led to President Richard Nixon's resignation. For a time, this single news event, covered selectively by all of the major networks but given complete coverage by PBS, dominated television news and talk space. In a period of economic and political uncertainty, the power of TV and the press, which had uncovered the constitutional abuses of the Nixon administration, was most dramatically revealed in this year.

As social, political, and economic issues caused uncertainty in the broadcasting industry, enterprising talk-show hosts found a range of new vehicles to make themselves known to a national audience. Barbara Walters, for example, built a national reputation through "talk" exposures that were actually not directly connected with her normal daily duties on her NBC morning newsmagazine show. She increased her visibility by arranging special *Today* show interviews with England's Prince Philip, Presidential aide H. R. Haldeman, and, in front of 6 million viewers, President Richard Nixon himself. She also supplemented her *Today* schedule by hosting a nationally syndicated show out of New York, *Not For Women Only*, and she authored a best-selling book, *How to Talk with Practically Anybody about Practically Anything*. Using these print and syndicated television exposures for leverage, Walters was finally able to get NBC to recognize her as not just as the *"Today* girl" but the official cohost of *Today* when Frank McGee was replaced by Jim Hartz in 1974.[1] What she increasingly wanted, however, was sole-host status, which she did not receive, and this was one of the factors in her move to ABC in 1976.

Another host who used multimedia strategies to expand his base as a host of news and public affairs was Bill Moyers. Moyers had taken breaks in his career at several crucial junctures, and May 1974 was one of them, as he left public television to review his options. One of those options was hosting *Today*, but that was not what he really wanted to do. Moyers ended up writing for *Newsweek* and working part time for public television and part time for CBS as a senior reporter on a series of news and talk specials for PBS. For Barbara Walters and Bill Moyers, as for a number of other talk-show hosts in the turbulent mid-1970s, building a career in TV talk involved a series of choices among shifting network affiliations and new syndication possibilities.

By the mid-1970s, hosts like Phil Donahue, Mike Douglas, and Dinah Shore were reaching national audiences through national syndication. The new competition made the networks increasingly nervous. In negotiations they tried to put binders on the talk stars they had and were reluctant to try new formats of talk. Within this atmosphere, stars like Barbara Walters or Johnny Carson could remain stars only by periodically threatening to leave.

The television industry as a whole was clearly in malaise in 1974. While profits held steady, an air of uneasiness hung over the industry. *Variety* reported in its first issue of 1974 that though "the broadcast industry was rolling in green in 1973" with "revenues and profits skyrocketing," the networks were actually cutting back expense accounts and tightening their fiscal belts. The energy crisis, the uncertain state of the American presidency, and the apparently bleak future of the economy—inflation was rampant and the stock market stagnant—all "dampened optimism." Stock market values of all three major network shares were down, and investors were pessimismistic about the profit potential of broadcasting in a fragmenting market.[2]

In addition to these problems, fears of government interference and regulation were giving industry leaders "ulcers."[3] The White House was putting pressure on the networks through Clay T. Whitehead's Office of Telecommunications Policy while at the same time network power was being challenged by a wide range of citizen interest groups. Legal actions were part of this pressure. An anti–Vietnam War group had attempted to buy time on WTOP in Washington, D.C. When they were refused, they allied themselves with the Democratic National Committee and, relying on the First Amendment, tried to force broadcasters to sell time to all "responsible entities."[4] In 1974 the case was still pending.

Women's issues were particularly hot. *Newsweek* magazine dubbed 1974 as "the year of the woman" in national and local politics, pointing out that a record number of women, 800, were running for office.[5] The women's movement raised questions about the representation of women in positions of power and authority, and the television industry responded by putting more women broadcasters in front of the camera. In the mid-1960s only three African American women newscasters were in major markets across the country. By the early 1970s, that number had grown to thirty-four.[6] By the 1970s, ten of twenty-one syndicated shows, or 47 percent, had women hosts. Virginia Graham's *Girl Talk* (1962–1970) became *The Virginia Graham Show* in 1970. *For Women Only* became *Not For Women Only* when it was taken over by Barbara Walters in 1971, and other shows in a wide range of formats were hosted by women for primarily women audiences.[7]

Within the gender wars and new identifications that were taking place in the mid-1970s, national television audiences were being offered paired role models. If Barbara Walters served as a model for a woman entering the professional news world of men, Dinah Shore represented a woman's traditional role as hostess and homemaker. Indeed, Shore's talk-show studio on NBC was designed to replicate her home kitchen and living room in California and highlighted her domestic skills. If Phil Donahue represented "the new male," profoundly affected by the women's movement, Mike Douglas, still the "king" of nationally syndicated daytime talk in the mid-1970s, represented the traditional *pater familias.*

The networks had to respond to the post-sixties political and cultural controversies in some way and did so by looking for escape valves for national talk. One was fringe time, in which the networks could experiment with controversial talk for smaller, more tolerant audiences.[8] In the fall of 1973 NBC put Tom Snyder and the *Tomorrow* show in the time slot after Johnny Carson,[9] bringing Snyder back to New York from Los Angeles by the end of 1974 to coanchor the New York station's news desk as well as broadcast this more controversial material from a city that traditionally supported controversy. Still, the networks were wary about going too far. With annual billings of over $4 billion by the end of 1972,[10] they were not anxious to offend mainstream audiences or jeopardize advertising dollars.

In addition to syndication and PBS, the networks now had to worry about cable TV. Although in 1970 there were only 2,490 cable systems with about 4.5 million subscribers, mostly in rural environments, by the end of the decade the cable audience had quadrupled. It was becoming clear that the networks were beginning to lose their dominance, and this at a period when the presidency itself faced a crisis.

WATERGATE AS NATIONAL TALK EVENT

"Be not deceived," Senator Sam Ervin had thundered. "As they have sown, so shall they reap." The Watergate hearings of 1974 were covered gavel to gavel by PBS and were the premier news talk event of television in 1974. Never before had the spoken word been analyzed with such overwhelming thoroughness. Never had so much airtime been devoted to a single story. CBS ran a special program during this time entitled "The Seventh Crisis: Nixon on Nixon," referring pointedly to Nixon's book *The Six Crises.* It used Nixon's own filmed and taped words to analyze the trajectory of his embattled presidency.[11] This preoccupation with the spoken words of the Nixon administration intensified with the release in May 1974 of the transcripts of Nixon's surreptitiously taped phone calls. These transcripts were almost half as long as *War and Peace* —350,000 words by *Time* magazine's estimate—and their transmission to news media clogged the high-speed wires of the day, which operated at 1,050 words a minute.[12] While the print media raced to excerpt and comment upon the transcripts, CBS used clips from the Watergate hearings to stage readings of key conversations acted out by CBS newsmen playing the parts of key Presidential officials and aides.[13] Though the newsmen stood behind nineteenth-century lecterns and read tonelessly "to avoid possible inaccurate inflections," news was transformed into talk docudrama. The rendering of private conversations as part of the public record—the essence of TV talk—had now been dramatically forefronted in national consciousness.

The Watergate affair had another powerful effect on television. The embattled White House under Office of Telecommunications Policy head Clay T. Whitehead was arguing for lifting all governmental restrictions on cable TV to allow it to grow in competition with the networks. Major producers and network officials were alternately cowering and fighting back. This is what the battle over the FCC's prime-time access rule was about.[14]

It was in this climate that Merv Griffin gave up his attempt to experiment with forms of controversial talk on network television and went back to his lucrative national syndication deal with Metromedia. It was in this climate that Phil Donahue and his team stepped up their struggle to enter the national syndication market and to provide an alternative to the current pabulum of daytime programming. And it was in this climate that PBS became for the first time a major player in national talk programming.

By the end of March 1974, *Newsweek* was billing PBS as "the Fourth Network." It then reached an estimated 33 million Americans weekly, up 37 percent from the year before. The PBS *Newsroom* extended the range of news talk by allowing reporters to engage in roundtable discussions of how and what they wrote and put their news reports in perspective. William F. Buckley's *Firing Line*, which had begun in syndication in 1966 and moved to PBS in 1971,[15] was building a loyal following and providing a contrast to the more liberal Moyers. Buckley's show remained on public television for over three decades, one of PBS's longest-running talk shows. *Black Journal*, hosted by Tony Brown,[16] was opening up new ground for African Americans in television talk. PBS was addressing a range of lifestyles, topics, and themes that the networks would formerly not touch.

Some hosts hung onto network spots during this period—Dick Cavett, for instance, although he increasingly chafed at network restrictions. In a *Newsweek* piece written in the fall of 1974, Cavett complained, "I have found TV censorship to be so petty, niggling, small-minded, and silly that it is well-nigh impossible to wax eloquent on the subject." The network was not a "giant predatory bird blacking out the sun," said Cavett, but "swarms of tiny insects, nipping you to death."[17]

NEW VOICES IN SYNDICATION: Phil Donahue and Mike Douglas

As syndicated talk upped the ante in verbal confrontation in the 1960s and 1970s with such confrontational and acerbic individuals as Al Capp, Alan Burke, David Susskind, Joe Pyne, Oscar Levant, and Joan Rivers now on the air,[18] one syndicated talk show host stood out from the rest and indeed went on to become one of the most successful hosts in television history and to create a new subgenre of daytime talk.

Beginning in Dayton, Ohio, in 1967, Phil Donahue was by the mid-1970s competing for women listeners with a large number of other syndicated talk-show hosts, including Virginia Graham, Joan Rivers, Gypsy Rose Lee, Bess Myerson, Dinah Shore, and Barbara Walters. Phil Donahue, however, was the first *male* host to speak effectively to this growing female audience, a male host who took the issues raised by the women's movement seriously. By the mid-1970s the *Donahue* show, from WGN in Chicago, still needed markets in Los Angeles or New York to be truly national, and in October 1977 it got a break. WNBC-TV, a network owned and operated affiliate, was looking for a show to go up against WABC's popular *A.M. New York*, hosted by Stanley Siegel. The *Donahue* show came to New York and was immediately successful. Donahue signed a new six-year contract with Multimedia and soon was seen on 178 markets nationwide, more than any other talk show. *Donahue* had by now become the number one talk show in syndication. The three major daytime talk-show hosts who followed Donahue in the 1980s—Sally Jessy Raphaël, Geraldo Rivera, and Oprah Winfrey—all built on the format he established. *Donahue* was a compelling example of how a single show could redefine the talk-show industry.

If Phil Donahue represented the insurgent in daytime syndicated talk by 1974, Mike Douglas, along with Merv Griffin, represented the reigning establishment. Born Michael Delaney Dowd Jr., the son of a railroad freight agent in Chicago,[19] Douglas began his career as a singer and band leader, singing for five dollars a night in the American Legion Hall in Forest Park, Illinois, and working Great Lakes cruise ships and Midwest night clubs, as well as traveling around the country as a band soloist.[20] Douglas had experience with early TV shows out of Chicago, including *The Music Show* (1953–1954) and *Club 60* (1957–1958). By the early 1960s Douglas was on the verge of deciding to leave show business to begin a career as a real estate broker. Then, in 1961, an offer came through for a position hosting a new 90-minute television show out of KYW-TV in Cleveland. *The Mike Douglas Show* featured a mixture of singing, celebrity guests, and conversation. Eventually the show moved from Cleveland to Philadelphia in a national syndication deal with Group W/Westinghouse. His show lasted until 1982, over twenty years on the air.[21]

Donahue and Douglas confronted the cultural issues of their time in very different ways. Whereas Phil Donahue's marriage had resulted in single fatherhood for the talk-show host, and a reappraisal of his role as a father and husband, Mike Douglas' reaction to the women's movement, the youth culture, and issues of minority representation was more subdued. His show was geared toward entertainment, not social issues—Following the standard format of the Carson/Griffin model of entertainment chitchat and cameo performances by guests. "Despite the rapidly changing role of women," he told a *Good Housekeeping* reporter, "in many cases the man is still considered the senior partner in a union." The talk show's recipe for an ideal marriage was that "both partners must work together as equals toward a common goal, building a happy life, each involved, each growing all the time."[22]

Even a "soft" talk-show host like Mike Douglas had to confront the issues of the time, however. A major counterculture event occurred the week of February 14–18,1972, when *The Mike Douglas Show* was cohosted by John Lennon and Yoko Ono. These five segments featured such figures as consumer advocate Ralph Nader, Surgeon General Dr. Jesse Steinfeld, "Yippie" Jerry Rubin, and musical performers the Ace Trucking Company, the Chambers Brothers, Chuck Berry, and Lennon and Yoko Ono's own Plastic Ono Band. Douglas played the mediator role in these sessions, which he described later as "the most challenging thing I had ever done."[23] For a moment, viewers might have been thinking they were watching a rip-roaring session of *The Dick Cavett Show*, not Mike Douglas. But, in general, Douglas was known for his conservative and patriotic defense of traditional American values, for the things that had made America "great."

While Phil Donahue was interrogating and questioning and Mike Douglas was reaffirming traditional American values and gender roles in the face of counter-cultural and feminist revolt, another talk host was asking fundamental questions about the American system, using PBS as his platform for inquiry.

AN INDEPENDENT VOICE: Bill Moyers

In the 1970s Bill Moyers' program did as much as any other single talk show to change the direction, nature, and intellectual depth of television talk. Moyers did this by raising his own funding, which left him free to stretch the boundaries of talk on television. In 1970, when he first appeared on WNET-TV, New York's PBS station, Moyers was more familiar to the worlds of politics and publishing than television. He worked alternately out of the Public Broadcasting Service and CBS in a variety of settings and formats. In filmed and taped interviews, he extended the "think-piece" tradition of Edward R. Murrow. His dedication to the written word, his ability to provide historical context for central themes in American life, and his moral passion recalled Murrow at his best. In interviews with artists, scientists, politicians, and provocative thinkers of all kinds, Moyers brought to television what he called the "conversation of democracy."[24]

Just as Edward R. Murrow had found it increasingly difficult to explore controversial themes on commercial television so, too, did Moyers. Murrow moved into government service. Moyers had another avenue in the early 1970s, and a standing in public life that allowed him to take a more entrepreneurial approach. The foundation support and funding he elicited in the 1970s and early 1980s gave him a degree of freedom few broadcasters possessed, and he was constantly working to consolidate his position of independence from both network and governmental control. Never a "talk-show host" in conventional terms, he produced some of the most interesting talk of the 1970s and 1980s on television. Over time, it became increasingly apparent that the shows Moyers produced were a significant body of work. It added up: six hundred hours of programming (filmed and videotaped conversations and documentary interviews) between 1971 and 1989 alone, coming to about thirty-three hours of programming a year, or the equivalent of more than half an hour of programming a week for eighteen years.[25]

Bill Moyers always had a clear idea of what he wanted to do on the air, and he was able to maintain a consistency of purpose and programming working with a wide range of producers, some twenty-seven of them on the first two *World of Ideas* series.[26] Many of Moyers' programs had significant afterlives as well. Filmed conversations with mythology scholar Joseph Campbell and poet Robert Bly sold tens of thousands of copies in videocassette after they were aired. Moyers produced books to accompany many of his most successful television series, for example, *The Secret Government*, 1988; *A World of Ideas*, 1989; *A World of Ideas II*, 1990; and *Healing the Mind*, 1992. These books consistently placed Moyers on the *New York Times* bestseller list. By the late 1980s and early 1990s, Moyers had established himself as one of TV talk's most significant figures.

Born in Hugo, Oklahoma, in 1934, Bill Moyers grew up in Marshall, a small, very conservative town in the Piney Woods of East Texas. Books were Moyers' entry into the larger world outside his home. Moyers proved to be a precocious student, reading journalism, politics, and whatever else he could get his hands on. He attributes his love of the spoken and written word to growing up among storytellers in East Texas, including his father, who had only a fourth-grade education but was a well-known spinner of yarns. Reflecting on this later in his journalism career, Moyers said, "It's all story, isn't it? The oral tradition is the oldest, and the video medium is the newest, but it's always a matter of story."[27]

Moyers' own first stories were as a print journalist, beginning with a part-time job at the age of fifteen on the local *Marshall Messenger*. He later attended Southwestern Baptist Theological Seminary in Fort Worth, Texas, and became a fully ordained Baptist minister. Journalistic and ministerial careers were followed by a third one in politics. In 1959, he joined the staff of Texas Senator Lyndon B. Johnson, serving Johnson in one capacity or another until 1966. As Johnson's Press Secretary during the early part of the war in Vietnam, Moyers later joked that the administration faced a credibility gap "so bad we didn't believe our own press releases." It was an ironic position for him to be in—considering his later image as journalistic truth-seeker—and it occasioned some bitter controversies with Moyers' critics in later years.

After leaving the Johnson administration Moyers re-entered the newspaper business for three years as publisher of the Long Island *Newsday*. When the paper was bought by the *Los Angeles Times*, Moyers was replaced. The year was 1970. By this time Moyers had served on the boards of private foundations and had contacts at the highest levels of government. Now he was unemployed and looking around for what to do next. Willie Morris, editor of *Harper's*, offered to publish an account of Moyers' travels if he would go about the country in a bus.

Moyers' travels resulted in *Listening to America*, a title that was suggested by his wife, Judith Moyers, who was his partner and the co-producer of many of his ventures. The book became a bestseller by January 1971. The book also led to his first job in public television, a program called *This Week*, funded by the Ford Foundation.

The Ford Foundation had been looking for a host with an established name to anchor public-affairs broadcasts on issues of national importance, and Moyers fit the bill. But broadcasting did not come easily for Moyers at first. He was a print journalist, and his apprenticeship to the medium of television was a difficult one. A turning point occurred halfway through the first season when he began doing interviews with well-known people, usually intellectuals, the first one being historian Barbara Tuchman.

This was the beginning of Moyers' "conversations with" series. The session with Tuchman turned out well, but had to be edited. In the editing sessions, Moyers found the silences particularly interesting. "You could see her thinking, you could experience her thinking. A mind at work, my God, what a marvelous instrument it is [and] the human face is the most marvelous production value I've ever experienced. The way the eyes speak. The way silence communicates."[28]

Moyers joined other hosts of TV talk who learned that, whatever the content of their shows, it was their names and personalities as hosts that sold the show. Altogether, Moyers spent six years producing programs for public television—the last two, from 1974 to 1976, he also served as a regular contributor to *Newsweek.* In 1976 Moyers moved to CBS as reporter and chief correspondent, and alternated over the next ten years between commercial and public television. He describes the difference: "Public television has the freedom but not the money; commercial television has the money but not the freedom."[29] Moyers, working closely with his wife, Judith Moyers, used his political and foundation experience to escape the hackneyed formulas that he despised by functioning on several levels at once: as fundraiser, grant writer, and liaison to private and public sponsors, as well as reporter, writer, producer, managing editor, and executive producer. He was especially successful with governmental agencies like the National Endowment for the Humanities as his reputation grew and as his "prestige" programs gained new audiences.

Despite his soft demeanor, Moyers was known as a perfectionist and tough in-fighter in the Johnson administration and later at CBS in the mid-1980s.[30] In a profile by Jonathan Alter, Moyers described the last-minute pitch he made to CBS Broadcast Group president Gene Jankowski before resigning to return to public broadcasting in 1986:

> Jankowski asked me what would keep me at CBS. I said, "You own the title to the best known name in broadcasting history: *See It Now.* Resurrect it. Give me a 52-week commitment, your worst time slot—a slot you haven't won for years. Give me call on some of CBS News's best producers and reporters, and a little patience. In return, this is what you'll get: ratings as good as or better than you've had in that slot, and—because of the lower costs—profits better than you can get in the same slot, the prestige of a first-class broadcast and the next generation of

60 Minutes correspondents. . . . At the end of one year, you decide the success or failure. If it fails, send me $1 in the mail. If it succeeds, give me any payment you want—no agents.[31]

Jankowski turned down the offer.

A chance encounter between Moyers and the older Edward R. Murrow—where Murrow warned Moyers that "Sooner or later they'll get you"[32]—signaled the end of one era in broadcast history and the beginning of another. The technologies Murrow used for his commentaries were the typewriter, 16mm film, and the cumbersome equipment used for his electronic "picture window" remote interviews. Murrow entered broadcasting when a small number of companies would take responsibility for and pride in "prestige" programs. Bill Moyers came of broadcasting age when new technologies and new forms of distribution were developing, but he had to go outside the mainstream to produce prestige programs. He was an entrepreneur of the spoken word, and became a major figure of television talk by creating an audience for the kind of talk he wanted to pursue. He did so with a conscientiousness that bordered on obsession. He questioned his own abilities and worried about every detail, but when the time came to go on the air, Moyers was always ready, marked-up script in hand. "How much he knew," said producer Jon Katz, who worked with him at CBS, "how great he sounded, how well he wrote, how much more he added than any of the usual think-tank policy freaks and pallid academics."[33] The same intensity extended to his contacts with the public. Katz recalls his own amazement at one scene:

> Everywhere we went, people came up to him—waitresses, cabbies, casino dealers, blue-rinse ladies—to touch him, praise his work, cluck about one commentary or another. He shook every hand and listened to every comment, scribbled their names down and promised to send scripts, articles, letters. He did, too. He urged them to write.[34]

Eschewing limos, Moyers would ride to work each day in the subway or drive his car. He was interested in what he could learn from people directly, not through polls, public relations handlers, or experts. He was very sensitive to the charge that public television was an exclusive citadel of an intellectual elite, and he vigorously denied it. His introduction to *A World of Ideas* quotes a letter from an inmate of a federal prison who expresses his "heartfelt gratitude" for the PBS series *Six Great Ideas* and explains how important the series had been for him as an "institutionalized intellectual."[35] When Moyers wrote the introduction for his book *A World of Ideas II,* he quoted a letter from a plumber to philosopher Mortimer Adler:

> I am writing on behalf of a group of construction workers . . . who have finally found a teacher worth listening to. While we cannot all agree whether or not we would hire you as an apprentice, we can all agree that we would love to listen to you during our lunch breaks. . . . *We never knew a world of ideas existed.*[36]

As an entrepreneur of ideas Moyers moved skillfully between the worlds of commercial and public broadcasting to put together series and specials that extended the journalistic traditions of Murrow's *See It Now, Small World,* and *Harvest of Shame.* By going this route he was able to tackle controversies too "hot" for the major networks to handle. In the space between commercial and public television Moyers was able to build, in his own words, new "constituencies" for television talk. The irony here was indeed considerable. The man who scored the news and public opinion industries of the 1980s for defining the truth as what "sells,"[37] had himself learned the marketing lessons of the 1980s.

From 1989 to 1992 Bill Moyers sold 125 programs, all created by his own production company, to public or commercial television.[38] Thirty million people tuned in to watch the *Power of Myth* series with Joseph Campbell.[39] Hundreds of thousands bought books or videotapes.[40] What Bill Moyers did for television talk, beginning in the 1970s but leading into the 1980s and 1990s, was prove that it could be both subtle and profound—and much more versatile than most people thought. He showed that despite limitations imposed on televised talk by the "commodification" of most talk-show formats, the range of what could be said on television need not be limited to the superficialities and "cookie-cutter" formulas he abhorred. Once again, a single individual with a well-organized business and production team had been able to take TV talk in new directions.

THE VOICES OF WOMEN: Barbara Walters and Dinah Shore

Barbara Walters did not have her own show to host until the late 1970s, though by that time she was clearly established as one of the preeminent figures of TV news talk. She had been working hard ever since she came to the *Today* show in 1961, working even harder after her father declared bankruptcy in 1966 and Walters found herself in the position of supporting her parents and sister.[41] But there was more than money involved in Barbara Walters' drive to become one of television's top newswomen. Some of her first anchors and cohosts on the *Today* show caused problems as they resisted her ambitions. She had a good relationship with Hugh Downs, who had also worked well with Arlene Francis as her announcer on the NBC *Home* show. But Downs left *Today* in October 1971. His successor was Frank McGee, a tough, well-respected reporter who had worked in Oklahoma City, Montgomery, Washington, and New York. He appeared to get along with Walters on camera, but relations between the two were strained.[42] McGee insisted on opening and closing the show himself, and initiating all studio interviews that had been assigned to Walters. "If we did political interviews from Washington," Walters said, "Frank insisted on asking the first three questions. Then I was allowed to step in." She had more leeway in interviews from the field. "If I were able to get them on my own and I could then do them on film, outside the studio, I could do more hard-news interviews, which I enjoyed."[43]

Turning necessity to advantage, Walters began her series of interviews with famous personalities, including Presidents Nixon and Ford. Though NBC wouldn't give her sole-host status on the *Today* show, she obtained that goal when she took over hosting duties for the syndicated show *Not For Women Only* in 1971. Initiated as a response to the growing demand of advertisers to reach the new daytime women's audience, *Not For Women Only* was a talk/discussion show that focused on a single topic for the entire week's five half-hour programs. It turned out to be one of the most durable woman-oriented programs of the 1970s, running for eight years in syndication. It also proved that Barbara Walters was up to the task of running a show herself.

Though not entirely happy with the limits placed on her at NBC, Walters stayed with the network through the first part of the decade. When Frank McGee left *Today* in 1974, suffering from terminal cancer, it looked as if things might improve for Walters with the appointment of new anchor Jim Hartz. Hartz had Walter's approval, and she was finally elevated to an official cohost status. By 1974 Walters had been named "Woman of the Year" by the *Ladies' Home Journal* and made the cover of *Newsweek*. The *Today* show was very profitable for the network. In the preceding four years it had netted $10 million a year, making it

NBC's most lucrative daytime venture and leaving the other network morning shows far behind. Still Walters did not have the one thing she wanted: control of her own show and of her broadcasting image.

Several blocks away in midtown Manhattan major changes were occurring at ABC. Fred Pierce was named president of ABC Television in 1974, determined to turn the fortunes of the network around. Under programming "genius" Fred Silverman, Pierce launched such hit entertainment shows as *Happy Days, Starsky and Hutch,* and *Laverne and Shirley,* and ABC finally achieved parity with the two stronger commercial networks, becoming for a time the top-rated network in prime time. In November 1975, ABC launched *Good Morning, America* with David Hartman to challenge *Today.* In 1976, Pierce signed Barbara Walters for ABC in a "raid" that stunned the industry. ABC lured Walters from NBC with a $1 million yearly salary contract ($500,000 from ABC News and $500,000 from the Entertainment Division) and the promise to allow her to develop her own shows. She was at first to cohost the evening news with Harry Reasoner and produce a series of Barbara Walters interview specials.[44]

The news of Walters' hire and million-dollar salary was greeted with the "avalanche of publicity" the ABC brass had hoped for, but the adjustment was not as smooth as they had hoped. The odd-couple pairing of Harry Reasoner and Barbara Walters did not work out; nor did the new format, which was to emphasize Walters' personality profiles. Pierce and News Division head Bill Sheehan had expected to expand national news from half an hour to forty-five minutes or an hour; in fact, the expansion was announced to the press, but affiliates resisted because they did not want to lose advertising time, and ABC retreated. Walters' interview pieces would radically reduce the time ABC had for hard news. Reasoner objected. The veteran newsman, acerbic about the arrangement from the beginning, engaged in behind-the-scene battles for camera and air time. When Roone Arledge entered the picture, he attempted to salvage the situation by putting veteran CBS news producer Av Westin in charge of the show. "When I got there," said Westin, "I was told that Reasoner was owed a five-minute, thirty-second piece because she had done a five-minute, thirty-second piece several weeks before. It was terrible."[45] Westin ordered director Charlie Heinz to stop shooting both anchors at the same time and to check their facial expressions, since both anchors frequently registered disgust with one another. Walters and Reasoner marked out their space on different ends of the set.

Press coverage did not help. The *Washington Post* billed Walters as "A Million-Dollar Baby Handling 5-and-10 Cent News,"[46] and broadcasting traditionalists were appalled at the entertainment orientation of ABC News. CBS's Walter Cronkite, who had been a supporter of Walters on the *Today* show, confessed to a "sickening sensation that we were all going under, that all of our efforts to hold television news aloof from show business had failed."[47] ABC upped its spending on the evening news, *Time* noted, to about $44 million a year versus about $47 million each for CBS and NBC.[48] The addition of a single ratings point for ABC could be worth as much as $2.7 million a year in extra advertising revenue, the article pointed out, and that would mean a "170% profit on the Walters investment."[49]

By fall 1976, before Walters went on the air, ABC had commissioned a Frank Magid survey to determine audience reaction to a woman news host. Forty-six percent said they would like to see a woman deliver the news, 41 percent did not care, and only thirteen percent said they would prefer a man.[50] Now ABC commissioned another Magid survey. This one reported that reaction to Barbara Walters was negative. Complaints were that she was ineffective as an anchor, she was overpaid, and she had a bad voice.[51] Walters was devastated. News division chief Roone Arledge, feeling Walters had "star quality" and sensing an ally in his efforts to bring entertainment values to the news, discounted the Magid report and made it clear he was willing to stick with her. Though Arledge was to hire and develop a number of new major stars of news talk at ABC, including Geraldo Rivera, Ted Koppel, and Diane Sawyer, Walters was the first major star he had to work with in developing the new, entertainment-oriented news division of the network, and for a while she was an expensive liability.

Arledge and his assistants worked to try to place Walters in vehicles that suited her talents, including an ill-fated entertainment/variety special with Howard Cosell. Other programming exposures, following her natural bent in interviewing, were more successful. Though often ridiculed at first, her celebrity interview specials garnered good ratings. Her first special, with President Jimmy Carter, became a parody item when she ended the program by saying, "Be good to us, Mr. President, be kind,"[52] but millions watched. Walters was able to tap personal revelations from off-guard moments in these interviews, and she was able to interview some of Hollywood's biggest stars—Jimmy Stewart, John Wayne, Bing Crosby, Paul Newman, Clint Eastwood, and Bette Davis, among others.

In the end, the move from NBC to ABC paid off for Walters and ABC. By 1980, through the force of her personality, her celebrity interview profiles, and her cohosting duties on the ABC newsmagazine, *20/20,* with her old *Today*-show companion Hugh Downs, Walters had reconstructed herself on television. After four years of trial and error, supported by the ABC executives who had invested in her, she reasserted her position as a titan of talk.

Dinah Shore's emergence as a daytime talk-show host for NBC in August 1970 represented her fourth career in show business. She had already had three: as a singer of blues, jazz, and pop hits; as a Hollywood actress who appeared in eight pictures while married to actor/producer George Montgomery; and finally, starting in 1951, as the host of *The Chevy Show Starring Dinah Shore,* a fifteen-minute variety show that aired twice weekly until July 1957, and resumed as a weekly variety hour in color on NBC until 1961.[53] That show had made her one of the best-known celebrities in the United States.

Shore was known for her bubbly brand of Southern hospitality and intimacy with her audience (she developed a trademark of a waved kiss to the audience at the end of each show). In the 1950s, she won several Emmys and was named television personality of the year. She left series television in the early 1960s to devote herself to her family and charity interests. Shore's comeback talk show, *Dinah's Place,* aired on August 3, 1970, and ran on NBC until July 26, 1974.

Despite their differences, Barbara Walters and Dinah Shore had a number of things in common. Both were Jewish. Both were extremely hard workers, something noted by all who knew them. Both had good educations, and both had felt like outsiders growing up, with early setbacks in their lives, and then a redoubled determination and will to succeed.

Born Frances Rose Shore in 1917 and known as "Fanny," "Dinah" adopted her stage name shortly before launching her professional singing career. Her father was an immigrant furniture merchant, and her mother had been an aspiring opera singer. Until the family moved to Nashville, in 1923 when Shore was six, they lived in Winchester, Tennessee, where they were the town's only Jewish family. As a child, Shore suffered from polio, which affected her right foot and leg. Six years of arduous therapy were needed to overcome an awkward walk and limp, which remained well into her elementary school days in Nashville. This was one of the principal reasons she adopted an early regimen of tennis, swimming, and ballet. Her mother encouraged her performing talents, and this, too, helped her overcome her feelings of being an outsider and "an ugly duckling."

By the time she began her new career as a daytime talk-show host, at the age of fifty-three, Dinah Shore was well known as a singer, celebrity, host, homemaker, and cook. All of Shore's previous identities came into play in her *Dinah's Place* and her later syndicated version of the show, *Dinah!*, which ran from 1974 to 1980.

A blend of talk, music, home improvement, and cooking tips,[54] her talk show also highlighted her domestic role. *Dinah's Place*, produced with long-term business agent Henry Jaffe, aired at 10:00 A.M. It was addressed primarily to a female audience and gave tips on how to stay attractive, young, and beautiful, and how to cook special recipes, diet, sew clothes, apply makeup, and take care of husbands and children in a modern world. The set was modeled on Dinah Shore's own Beverly Hills living room and kitchen.[55] Though some critics were not terribly excited about the show, it developed a loyal following. The show was as much a "do show" as a "talk show," Shore said, naming the activities of some of the celebrities who had appeared. "Ethel Kennedy played the piano. Joanne Woodward did some beautiful needlepoint. Cliff Robertson made a linguine . . . Leslie Uggams made sweet potato pie . . . Senator Muskie hypnotized a lobster."[56] She felt that the social movements of the 1960s had encouraged "the thinking that the young people have put on us today—that there's a terrible impermanence in the world," but she generally avoided political and religious controversy. Occasionally she would have on her show "heavier" guests, like scientist/peace activist Linus Pauling or *Ms. Magazine* editor Gloria Steinem, and she generally handled these more serious guests with aplomb. But when Steinem was on the show, Shore was taken aback by the anger of some of the women in the audience toward men. "I don't understand this violence," she said. "We're in the world together, you know. . . . If women have been exploited it's been a collaborative effort and not a giant conspiracy on the part of men. Being a homemaker is a lovely, marvelous role and only denigrating if you yourself make it that way."[57]

Shore, like Arlene Francis in the 1950s and Barbara Walters in the 1970s, represented a series of contradictions. A woman who was ambitious and headstrong, and who had by all accounts achieved four highly successful show-business careers, earning a star's salary approaching a million dollars and with nineteen golden records, credited it all to others. Acknowledging her first pianist and arranger, Ticker Freeman, her producer, Henry Jaffe, her husband, and other men who had given her her first breaks in show business, she said, "All of my life, on radio, in recording studios, in films and on television, men have made the decisions for me, and they've usually been the right ones."[58] At the same time Shore herself was a hard-driving perfectionist who knew what she wanted in each case and clearly directed her own career. However much she relied on close advisors, America's girl-next-door had engineered her own success. Hosting her own national talk shows over a ten-year period, from ages fifty-three to sixty-three, Shore proved that it was not just younger women who could command a national audience in daytime talk, and that the palette of women hosts on the air could include one who operated as a traditional hostess from her own living room.

BATTLING FROM WITHIN: Johnny Carson and NBC (1974–1980)

Johnny Carson's *Tonight* show audience continued to grow throughout the 1960s and 1970s. He had begun his long reign on *The Tonight Show* with an average nightly audience of 7.5 million viewers. By 1972, when he moved to the West Coast, his audience had grown to 11 million. By the end of 1977, *The Tonight Show* audience averaged 17.3 million viewers a night. At the same time, Carson was becoming increasingly discontented with his relationship to NBC. He was continually re-establishing the terms of his contract and the limits of what he could and could not do on the air, in essence redefining his star power within the network every two or three years. Some battles he lost, however. An example is recounted in the following close-up, demonstrating limits in network television to which even a major star had to accede.

CLOSE-UP: JOHNNY CARSON'S *TONIGHT:* "THE EXECUTION GAME," A CENSORED MONOLOGUE ROUTINE, JANUARY 18, 1977, NBC

In his definitive 1978 "Profile" of Carson in *The New Yorker,* drama critic Kenneth Tynan describes the careful course Carson and his advisors charted regarding guests and topics. Carson's producer Fred de Cordova told Tynan that Carson had "an in-built sense of what his audience will take," and that Carson was "the best self-editor" in the business.[59] This, Tynan points out, was only partially true. He relates an incident he observed in 1977 when, upon arriving for an interview with Carson, he found the host "making copious notes" for a new routine.[60]

I ask what he is writing. He says he has had an idea for tonight's monologue. In Utah, yesterday, the convicted murderer Gary Gilmore . . . got
his wish by facing a firing squad. Carson's comment on this macabre
situation takes the form of black comedy . . . [he] proposes a new TV
show, to be called *The Execution Game.* It would work something like
this: Curtains part to reveal the death chamber, in the middle of which is
an enormous wheel, equipped with glittering lights and a large golden
arrow, to be spun by the condemned man to decide the nature of his
fate. For mouth-watering prizes—ranging from a holiday for two in the
lovely Munich suburb of Dachau to a pair of front-row seats at the victim's terminal throes—members of the audience vie with one another
to guess whether the arrow will come to rest on the electric chair, the
gas chamber, the firing squad, the garrote, or the noose.[61]

Tynan looked for the routine that evening, the night of January 18, 1977, but it
did not appear. The only reference to it was a terse sentence, "Capital punishment is a great deterrent to monologues," inserted without buildup or comic
payoff. A couple of nights later when one of his guests, Shelley Winters, broke
into an attack on the death penalty, specifically referring to the Gilmore case,
Carson showed a "distinctly nervous reluctance to commit himself" and shied
away from the subject. He cut off discussion with an abrupt, "There are no abso-
lutes." "I called up Fred de Cordova," Tynan says, "who admitted, after some
hesitation, that he had disliked the 'Execution Game' idea and that the network
had backed him up. There had been a convulsive row with Carson, but in the
end 'Johnny saw reason' and the item was dropped."[62]

What is revealing about this anecdote is the degree to which Johnny
Carson, however much of a "self-editor" he might have been, was still under
the network's authority concerning what he could or could not say on the air.
In 1977, at the height of his power, when he was garnering 32 percent of the
late-night audience against 24 percent and 23 percent for the other two networks, Carson could not put on the air material his producer and network censors found offensive. The "king of late night" answered to powers higher than
himself.

Despite his apparent stability and success on network television, the
years from 1978 to 1980 were far from placid ones for Carson. At the
1979 Academy Awards, the first time he was asked to host the show,
ABC set up a campaign to woo him.[63] Of all the "raids" it had attempted
on CBS and NBC, the idea of attracting Johnny Carson to return to
the network he had left in the early 1960s was one of the most attrac-

tive. NBC officials, on the other hand, chief among them Fred Silverman, had been pressuring Carson to return to a four-day-a-week schedule from the three-day schedule he had recently negotiated. "It doesn't take a mastermind to figure out that when Carson is on the program it does better than when he isn't on," Silverman told *Newsweek* in March 1979.[64] Carson was furious at these efforts, and, as Letterman was to do a decade later, responded with anti-NBC and anti-Silverman jokes on the air. Silverman and other NBC executives pushed Carson to book more stars and help shore up NBC's promotional image. Carson resented this, too. Since NBC executive David Tebet had retired from the network (Carson later hired him to work for Johnny Carson Productions), the network had not treated their premier evening talk star with the kind of respect he felt he deserved. In an April 1979 interview prepared for CBS's *60 Minutes*, Carson dropped a bombshell: he was quitting *Tonight*. The stock prices of RCA, NBC's corporate owner, fell three-eighths of a point as the *New York Times* headlined, "Carson Leaving 'Tonight Show': Setback to NBC."[65]

Leaving *The Tonight Show* would mean cutting his new three-year contract by two years, however, and a new round of negotiations took place. The negotiations were handled by Henry Bushkin, the Beverly Hills lawyer who by now handled all of Carson's finances. The lawyer invoked an obscure provision of California law that forbade contracts longer than seven years between a performer and a company. Its application to Carson's contract with NBC was unclear, since he had repeatedly renewed short-term contracts with the network. But Bushkin, who had a firm mandate from Carson to find a way out so that the talk-show star could pursue other business interests, wrested a compromise from NBC. The compromise gave Carson, and to some degree the network, what each wanted. On May 7, 1980, almost a year after Carson had threatened to quit, Carson signed a new three-year contract.[66] He would return to *The Tonight Show* and do the show four times a week, as Silverman had wanted, but at a salary of $6 million a year. NBC would provide him an additional $12 million to fund Carson Productions, his own production company that would not only produce *The Tonight Show* but also a number of movies and other television specials. One of the movies the new company would soon produce was *The Big Chill*, and one of its first television shows, designed to replace Tom Snyder's *Tomorrow* in the 12:30 A.M. time slot after Carson, was *Late Night with David Letterman*.

CONCLUSION: The End of the Network Era

By the late 1970s the "years of plenty"[67] for network television were coming to an end. The 1970s were a transitional decade. New talk-show stars were emerging: Phil Donahue, Dinah Shore, and, from PBS, Bill Moyers. Other hosts consolidated their positions as network or syndicated talk-show hosts: Mike Douglas, Merv Griffin, Johnny Carson, and Barbara Walters, for example. Hosts like Donahue, Shore, and Douglas showed how a well-known host and a smart production team could compete with the networks in national syndication. Hosts like Bill Moyers showed that a fourth network, PBS, though relatively weak in the ratings, could serve as a springboard for new forms of talk.

The cultural ferment of the late 1960s and early 1970s meant that there was more to talk about: the effects of the civil rights movement, affirmative action, the increasingly visible role of women in politics and public life, the crisis in governmental authority occasioned by Watergate and the growing war in Vietnam. It was perhaps inevitable that the host who was seen as most representing middle-American values, Mike Douglas, would stage a series of shows with the two figures who perhaps best represented the counter-cultural insurgency of the 1960s—John Lennon and Yoko Ono. In the wake of the late-night talk-show wars between Johnny Carson and his challengers, and the controversial but fascinating talkfests sponsored by hosts like Dick Cavett, Douglas felt compelled to wander into the maelstrom of controversy so as not to be deemed irrelevant. As always, talk shows influenced each other and competed to supply what talk audiences seemed to demand.

Not only did the talk itself change during this period, in some cases raising the decibel level and the level of confrontation on the air, but the talk-show industry was beginning to change. In the coming decade technological and structural developments would threaten to do what "no regulation or critic had ever accomplished: loosen the grip of monopoly television on the nation."[68] As the third, transitional cycle of TV talk drew to a close at the end of the 1970s, the fourth cycle was already under way. Looking into the face of increasing competition from syndication, cable, and independent station groups, the networks would attempt innovations of their own, fighting back with new formats and new talk stars such as Ted Koppel on ABC's *Nightline* and *Late Night with David Letterman* on NBC. In the world of daytime talk, Geraldo

Rivera, Sally Jessy Raphaël, and Oprah Winfrey would extend the audiences for daytime talk with new topics and audiences. Arsenio Hall would bring Black guests and music groups to late-night television. The post-network era was under way, with the hosts of the 1980s taking established talk subgenres in new directions.

SEVEN

THE FOURTH CYCLE (1980–1990)
The Post-Network Era

INTRODUCTION

In the early 1980s once again technology and economics drove changes in talk programming. With new video production and distribution systems requiring smaller outlays for producers and marketers, syndicated talk shows became cheaper and easier to produce. In 1981 *The Merv Griffin Show* became the first daily talk series to be distributed by satellite, beaming its programs to syndicated stations the same day they were taped—"day and date" as the process was called.[1] No longer did film prints or videotapes need to be "bicycled" from one location to another. The technological changes in the 1950s unified TV talk in a single broadcasting system. The production and distribution technologies of the 1980s fragmented the market for talk, increasing the ways audience members could see talk shows in their homes, in their workplaces, or in places of recreation like bars or airport terminals.

Cracks in the monolith of network domination widened further as multi-channel cable operations and a burgeoning videotape industry gave viewers new options. The new stars of TV talk in the mid- to late 1980s (Sally Jessy Raphaël, Geraldo Rivera, Oprah Winfrey, Arsenio Hall) rose to prominence not through network vehicles but through national syndication. Previously underrepresented racial, social class, and ethnic communities began to receive recognition. Two Hispanic Americans (Raphaël and Rivera) and two African Americans (Winfrey and Hall) were now prominent in the talk market, and talk shows were no longer representing only White, middle-class faces and voices.

The technological revolution and expanding demographic base of TV talk brought other changes. From 1980 to 1990, as the broadcast networks' prime-time share of audience fell from 90 percent to 65 percent of those watching television[2] and cable penetration went from 22 percent to over 60 percent, the networks worked frantically to create new talk vehicles that would be successful with a national audience. David Letterman's *Late Night* on NBC and Ted Koppel's *Nightline* were two early 1980s successful attempts against a string of failures. Meanwhile, talk syndicators, working with non-union crews and lower production costs, and not encumbered by network censorship rules, expanded their offerings.

By the early 1980s, entertainment marketers were increasingly interested in "infotainment" and "reality programming."[3] The search for new audiences and better demographics for advertisers dominated the syndicated television trade meetings.[4] The trend continued through the 1980s, as women, ethnic and racial minorities (Hispanic and African American), and lower-middle-class and working-class viewers became increasingly desirable demographic targets for marketers with Nielsen ratings showing that these groups were heavy television watchers and consumers of certain nationally advertised products. Sensationalized "trash talk" gave visual representation to formerly invisible economic, ethnic, and "lifestyle" groups on television. The representation these groups received, however, was often highly stereotyped, and the political and economic structures of commercial television itself were hardly even challenged.

Five of the talk-show hosts profiled in this book—Ted Koppel, David Letterman, Joan Rivers, Oprah Winfrey, and Geraldo Rivera—rose to prominence in the new competitive environment of the 1980s. It was a broadcasting environment that, in its headlong quest for ratings, started to engage new blends of talk, building and sometimes twisting old subgenres into new shapes. Profiles of the leading hosts in the fourth cycle of television talk reflect not so much changes in program formats—though Letterman and Koppel did represent significant format changes—but changes in the make-up of national talk-show audiences. Some of these changes horrified critics, but successful ratings and profits continued to stoke the hot engine of talk-show industry growth. One of the most significant hosts to emerge in the early 1980s—particularly appealing to a younger generation of viewers—was David Letterman.

DAVID LETTERMAN AND THE REINVENTION OF THE LATE-NIGHT TALK SHOW

As a comedian, writer, artist, organizer, and shaper of ensemble comedy, David Letterman was a key figure in the shifting sensibility of late-night talk during the 1980s. Reformulating the entertainment talk-show model developed by Johnny Carson on *The Tonight Show*, Letterman defined a new "ironic" mode of late-night comedy talk. *Late Night with David Letterman* gradually became the paradigm that influenced all other late-night talk-show hosts—including, eventually, the "King," Johnny Carson himself, in his last years on the air.

Searching out the biographical roots of Letterman's complex comedy talk persona is a daunting task. Letterman himself was never very forthcoming about his origins, though he has responded to questions in published interviews. Two biographies and a feature interview in *Playboy* provide much of what was known about the host by the end of the century.

Born April 12, 1947, a second child between an older and a younger sister, Letterman grew up in the Broad Ripple section of Indianapolis, Indiana. His father was a florist and his mother a homemaker who worked as a secretary for the Second Presbyterian Church in Broad Ripple.[5] When Letterman lived there, Indianapolis was growing, eventually reaching a population of over one million, but it was still surrounded by rural areas. Letterman's parents were themselves the children of farmers, both grandfathers having been coal miners before turning to farming.[6]

Letterman's family life was not particularly eventful, and his performance in school, in most cases, not much more than average. He did, however, manifest a bizarre sense of humor from an early age. When asked to write a theme in English on a significant event in someone's life, Letterman wrote about a man who committed suicide by swallowing paper towels. The other thing that Letterman enjoyed was TV—despite the fact that his parents placed a severe time limit on television watching.[7]

When Letterman was not yet ten, he got a Tinkertoy set and built a microphone like the one he had seen on Arthur Godfrey and Garry Moore. He was also an avid viewer of Johnny Carson's *Who Do You Trust?* and Steve Allen's syndicated show.[8] He could picture himself as a wisecracking host, and it helped him overcome feelings of being a loner and an outsider. "I never had a whole lot of friends, I was in the group of people that was always making fun of everybody else," he later said. "You know, we weren't in the honor society, so we made fun of the honor society."[9]

Letterman's interest in broadcasting as an outlet for his creativity began to take more serious shape in college at Ball State in nearby Muncie, Indiana. His first broadcasting experience was on the student radio station, WBST, where he was eventually fired by the program manager for making fun of the classical music he was playing. He later transferred his comedy talents to a pirate radio station, and then got a job as a substitute announcer on a legitimate commercial radio station (WERK in Muncie), moving on to a summer job as booth announcer at the ABC television affiliate in Indianapolis, WLWI-TV (Channel 13). Letterman organized, with fellow radio and television majors Ron Pearson and Joyce DeWitt, a comedy group known as the "Dirty Laundry Company."[10] Letterman wrote much of the group's material, a mixture of skits and monologues modeled on the comedy improvisations of Chicago's Second City.[11]

After graduation in 1969, Letterman returned to Indianapolis with his wife, a choral music major named Michelle Cook, whom he married his senior year. They found an apartment in Indianapolis, and Letterman parlayed his summer job as booth announcer into a six-month temporary position and later a permanent position at Channel 13. His assignments included hosting the late-night movie, interviewing kids on a Saturday afternoon show for the 4-H Club (*Clover Power*), and acting as a substitute weatherman.[12]

One of Letterman's early assignments allowed him to be more creative: a fringe-time late-movie slot Letterman renamed *Freeze-Dried Movies*. The show developed a cult following in Indianapolis, but Letterman left Channel 13 in 1974 to go to an all-talk radio station in Indianapolis where for $16,000 a year he anchored his own afternoon drive-time program and call-in show.[13] He practiced his interview technique on the show and began to make a name for himself locally. But he soon learned he disliked traditional news and public affairs programming and felt "miscast" in the role.[14]

Meanwhile, his comedy ambitions continued to grow.[15] His friends told him he should try his luck on one of the coasts. Responding to an ad in a Hollywood trade paper, Letterman wrote to an agent, who promised to talk to him if he came to Los Angeles.[16] On Memorial Day weekend 1975, Letterman, still waffling about whether this was the right decision, packed up his Indianapolis home, and headed with his wife for Los Angeles.

Soon after his arrival in Los Angeles, Letterman started to sell material to other comedians. Jimmie Walker, popular from his role as "J.J." on television's *Good Times*, paid the young comedy writer $150 a week for fifteen jokes. Letterman also began to present material at the Comedy Store, where Jay Leno, one of the featured comedians, admired his work. Leno and Letterman became friends. Buddy Morra of Morra, Joffe, and Rollins—one of the top personal management companies in Los Angeles—saw Letterman's work at the Comedy Store and signed him to a contract in 1977. *Tonight* show talent scouts saw him at this time as well, but felt he was not ready. "I was just thrilled they'd been watching me," Letterman later said. "The last thing you want to do is go on and not be ready. So I kept working and building my act, and the next year, they called for me."[17]

By the time of Letterman's first appearance on *The Tonight Show* in 1978, he had honed a half-hour of "A-quality" material and he impressed Carson and others who saw him that night. Comedian Tom Driesen called it "the strongest first shot" he had ever seen.[18] After two more successful appearances on the Carson show, Letterman was asked to guest host for Johnny—something he would do twenty-nine times over the next few years, becoming one of Carson's most frequent replacements.

At the Comedy Store, Letterman met a young comedy writer named Merrill Markoe. Markoe had come to Los Angeles from the San Francisco Bay Area after being a student at Berkeley. She had been teaching art at USC and, like Letterman, was performing her own comedy material at the Comedy Store. Letterman and Markoe teamed up for what turned out to be a ten-year personal/professional relationship. It lasted through Letterman's first morning show on NBC and the formative years of *Late Night with David Letterman*, and Markoe was a cofounder of both shows.[19]

Letterman's first morning show on NBC came through programming executive Fred Silverman. He had been impressed by a stand-up performance he had seen Letterman deliver at a B'nai Brith dinner in early 1980.[20] Silverman had in mind an Arthur Godfrey type of show, a mid-morning service/information/humor show that would appeal to housewives and have a "family feeling" to it.[21] But within days, not liking the direction it was taking, Letterman, who owned the show, replaced the original game-show producer and director. Head writer Merrill Markoe became interim producer. Letterman and Markoe reshaped the show, moving it progressively in the direction of "found" comedy and the kind of work they had done at the Comedy Store.

The morning show was Letterman's first full-fledged effort in experimental TV comedy. Much of it hearkened back to Ernie Kovacs and Steve Allen's work on the early *Tonight* show. One of the first episodes features Letterman beginning a spot at his desk and then becoming disconcerted when he finds on the monitor that his TV image is beginning to "roll" (the TV's horizontal setting is off).[22] Viewers at first might think that their own sets are rolling, but when the camera pulls back we see Letterman's rolling image on the television monitor placed beside him while he remains perfectly steady. Letterman fusses and fumes, and a technician comes out and whams the set with the top of his fist. The image stabilizes and Letterman continues, only to have to repeat this procedure several more times during the show as his image begins to slip again. It was the kind of play with the television image itself that would become a trademark of *Late Night with David Letterman* and differentiate it from other talk shows on the air.

NBC canceled the Letterman morning show months before its six-month preliminary contract was up, but comedically, the show was just beginning to take off. By the time it was taken off the air the show had developed an extensive word-of-mouth reputation. Letters poured in, and college students hitched across the country with petitions to save it. A group of housewives from Long Island tried to block traffic in Manhattan to protest the cancellation.[23] Letterman and Markoe won two Emmys for the show—one for best daytime talk show; the other, to Markoe, for outstanding achievement in writing. The critical success of the morning show led to its rebirth, sixteen months later, as *Late Night with David Letterman.*

Though the Letterman morning show was off the air by fall 1980, NBC saw the young comedian's promise and signed him to a one-year holding contract for $625,000.[24] The network considered Letterman a viable successor to Johnny Carson and agreed to pay him a penalty fee of a million dollars if they did not come up with a new show for him by the time his holding contract ran out. Less than a year later, which turned out to be one of the most anxious periods in Letterman's career, the network found a spot for him in the fringe-time hour that followed *Tonight.* Members of the morning show returned from "exile" to put

Late Night with David Letterman on the air on February 1, 1982. Letterman had finally found a time slot, a format, and a repertory team that worked. At first audiences were small, but after two and a half years on the air, no one knew why, ratings started to rise. It had taken fifteen years and repeated failures and false starts, but a new star in late-night TV talk had finally arrived.

In light of Letterman's enormous influence over late-night talk and my unusual personal access to the show through *Late Night* director Hal Gurnee, a study of how the show was put together in its NBC Rockefeller Center studios in the early and mid-1980s is included in the following Close-up.

CLOSE-UP: LATE NIGHT WITH DAVID LETTERMAN

From fall 1983 to winter 1986 I had the unusual opportunity to visit the Letterman show numerous times, observe tapings, and interview members of the production team just as the show was beginning to receive national recognition. By that time it was already clear that Letterman was an important innovator in late-night talk.

Under the aegis of director Hal Gurnee, I was allowed to observe backstage. I found members of the crew articulate and eager to explain to me what made the show work, what its rules were, and how each of their roles shaped the final product. I interviewed scores of people, almost everyone involved with the production, and what emerged was a production ethnography—a composite picture of what went on behind the scenes of late-night talk. This was my education in the kind of work that goes into structuring the spontaneity of TV talk, before, during, and after the show goes on the air. I include only a few brief scenes here.

Structuring the Flow: The Role of the Producer and Segment Producer

The producer provides the day-to-day direction for the ongoing operation of a show like *Late Night with David Letterman*. In the early and mid-1980s, the producer of the Letterman show was Barry Sand. The timing for each program began with a run-down sheet passed out by Sand at the daily 11:00 A.M. meeting. The sheet contained tentative timings for the nine segments of the show (opening, closing, and seven "acts" in between), and Sand and head writer Steve O'Donnell would run over the guests, comedy ideas, and potential problems for set designers, stagehands, and other members of the team. For show #814 on January 15, 1987, for example, Act 1 was allotted eleven minutes. That segment was to include a "Top 10" list and "Viewer Mail" segment with two pre-taped inserts. Twelve minutes was assigned for Acts 2–4 with the celebrity guest, comedian Richard Pryor. The Act 5 comedy piece ("The Superbowl Quiz") was assigned six minutes.

From the first production meeting, it was clear that the Letterman show adhered to a fairly standard formula. *Late Night* would try to match a celebrity who appeared early in the show (the major guest of the evening) with a lesser-known guest, a "civilian" (an unusual personality or guest who was not a professional performer) or a lesser-known singer, character actor, or comedian who appeared in the later acts. The important thing was that everyone on the production team know in advance what was supposed to happen during the show's forty-three minutes and thirty seconds of actual running time and be prepared for surprises.[25] That was Letterman's job—to manage the surprises. From the original timing blueprint of the show, specified in the run-down sheet, came all the last-minute scene adjustments.

The topics of Letterman's interview segments had been rehearsed and prioritized as well. Segment producer Robert "Morty" Morton had talked to each guest and prepared a list of questions for Letterman to work from.

On the night of January 15, 1987, Morton's questions for guest comedian Richard Pryor were typed out neatly in capitals and appended to the run-down sheet. They would later be transferred to blue index note cards for Letterman's use on the air. Morty's notes were as follows:

1. IN N.Y. . . . GOOD MEMORIES HERE? FIRST ED SULLIVAN SHOW . . . WHAT LIKE?
2. EARLY DAYS . . . STRANGE CLUBS YOU WORKED?
3. TV SHOW ON THIS NETWORK . . . WHAT WAS THIS PHOTO? (show) OTHERS CENSORED?
4. STAND UP . . . MISS IT MUCH? MISS THE HECKLING?
5. CONCERT FILMS . . . THAT RED SUIT . . . STILL FIT?
6. NEW MOVIE . . . EVER WANT TO BE A DOCTOR? JOBS OUT OF COMEDY?
- -CLIP- -
7. MARRIED AGAIN? WHAT #? HOW OLD? REALLY ONCE SHOOT UP CAR?
8. WIFE, BABY, HOME . . . ANY PETS? REALLY ONCE HAVE A PET MONKEY?[26]

Pryor's appearance that night was a coup for the talent department. He had been hard to get, and this was the first time they had been able to persuade him to appear. Morton's questions were designed to lead Pryor gently through his history in comedy—and then push him a little at the end, without seriously offending him.

When Letterman went on the air that evening, he followed Morton's suggestions to the letter, and the strategy worked well. Although most viewers were vaguely aware that Letterman relied on note cards, few were aware of how specifically he targeted his questions to the celebrity as a result of his segment producer's pre-interview.

The line between scripted and unscripted is a thin one in television talk. Obviously scripted material on Letterman was often subverted and turned into a kind of ironic "fresh talk." The "scripted" lines of a hammy skit sounded exactly like what they were—lines being read—and that was the point. Also problematic was the distinction between spontaneous and "completely" spontaneous. Though Letterman's questions and probes for Richard Pryor had been scripted, how questions were delivered, the degree of intimacy and challenge implied in the questions—these brought out Letterman's distinctive style and talents as a performer. Crucial to the success of the show was the chemistry between the host and the interviewee. The viewer's enjoyment centered on watching how Letterman did it, how he applied his own particular brand of comedy talk on the air, how he juggled and played with words and with the forms and conventions of late-night TV talk. For Letterman, all of these talk-show conventions were malleable, to be assembled, mocked, and reassembled at will.

Most of all the timing had to be right. Commercial breaks allowed time for producer and host to check signals on actual running times versus the rundown sheet's projected times for each segment. They could then make adjustments as needed.

The moment the show went on the air was the moment that everything changed. The show was now "live." In the adrenaline rush of a single concentrated hour, the production team and millions of television viewers experienced the same event: a talk world come to life in an electronic present tense.

Structuring the "Real": The Writer-Director Team

An example of how present-tense talk-show worlds are shaped invisibly by writer-director teams behind the scenes can be found on a David Letterman show broadcast October 15, 1986. It was the night of the New York Mets and Houston Astros baseball playoff game for the National League baseball title, and the baseball game being broadcast on another network became the focus of one of the major comedy routines of the evening.

Letterman, quite aware that the playoff game was competing with his own show for television viewers, concluded his opening remarks by asking Hal Gurnee, the director of the show, "The last we heard, the ball game between the Astros and the Mets is tied three-three in the bottom of the tenth. Is that right?" Looking up to an undefined space overhead, Letterman continued, "Hal, oh Hal—this will be our director Hal Gertner [Letterman's comedy name for

Gurnee]—can you keep us posted if there are any developments in that ball game?" The New York Mets had not been in a World Series since 1973 and had not won a pennant since the "Miracle Mets" of 1969, and there had been great excitement on the set before the show, with many of the staff and crew deeply involved baseball fans.

The off-screen Gurnee replies, "Yeah, Dave, and by the way, it's three-three in the tenth."

Letterman, a little annoyed, shoots back: "I just announced that, Hal." The director calmly replies that he just wanted to be sure everyone knew. A suspicion forming on his brow, Letterman asks, "Are you watching the game in there?"

The director's response is instantaneous, "Sure we are!" The studio audience breaks into laughter, and Letterman himself begins to laugh at the thought of his director, feet on the console, paying more attention to the Mets game than his own star.

"But that shouldn't affect the quality of tonight's show, should it?" Letterman asks.

"Not at all, Dave. Craig Reynolds is up, by the way."

"OK, OK." Letterman attempts to break off and go back to the show, but he can't get his vagrant director off his mind. "Do you guys have snacks in there?"

"They're on their way," Gurnee replies. Another explosion of laughter from the studio audience. Letterman himself cackles at this latest effrontery. "Well, just let us know what happens," he trails off.

When Letterman announces his first guest, NBC news anchor Tom Brokaw, Gurnee interrupts again. His voice is quiet, polite, assured. "Excuse me, Dave. He fouled one off." (A new roar of laughter from the studio audience.)

Letterman waits for the laughter to die down. Then, sarcastically, "All right, fine, Hal. Let us know if there are any broken bats, too, all right?"

These interruptions by Letterman's wayward director with updates on the baseball game continue throughout the show when they are least expected or welcome. They become a running gag eventually taking up about a minute and forty-five seconds of airtime.

But were these interruptions as spontaneous as they seemed? In fact, all of the interruptions that evening were planned. They were directed by writer Jeff Martin and director Hal Gurnee from the control room.

The Mets-Astros game routine was not in the production notes for the evening. Martin had suggested the idea to Gurnee minutes before the show was to air. The bit was spontaneous in a sense—the present-tense involvement was real enough. Yet the gag was also highly constructed. Martin guided Gurnee through the entire routine. Gurnee had some leeway, as he teased out his lines off screen. When he sensed later in the show that Letterman's annoyance was real, he backed off. The dramas that occur in front of the camera and behind the scenes are related, but the "spontaneity" of the evening had been carefully structured by professionals behind the scenes.

Structuring the Permissible: Executives, Censors, and Informal Controls

In addition to producers and segment producers who plan TV talk, and writers and directors who shape it, a range of middle managers "manage" the talk seen by viewers over the air each evening. They make sure the talk that appears on the air fits the time and institutional requirements of network television and in no way interferes with the commercial imperative of sponsors who foot the bill.

The job of network middle managers is to see that nothing goes out that will offend viewers or sponsors or violate established network practice. Comedy writers for the Letterman show found ingenious ways to test the limits of network "censors." A "top secret" comedy segment of the show on October 8, 1985 (Show #609), was designed to do just that: it was called at various times "Project X," "Test the Censors," and "The Show That Went Too Far." The story of how this segment was produced, and what happened when the Letterman team tried to get it on the air, highlights the fundamental tension that exists between a network management that wants attractive but stable programming and a team of comedy writers testing the limits in the quest for new ideas.

Guarding against infractions of the rules at NBC in the mid-1980s were three departments: Legal Affairs, Compliance and Practices, and Standards. The departments sometimes overlapped, but each had a separate oversight function. Legal Affairs screened scripts and rehearsals for potential libel and product liability suits.[27] Compliance and Practices made sure the program was in compliance with FCC regulations and company policies regarding such things as payola, free endorsements of products, and political partisanship. The Standards department, the old-fashioned censor, was charged with screening rude language, sacrilegious jokes, jokes promoting drug use, or anything else deemed in "bad taste."

The network kept an eye on a show like Letterman's in a well-regulated process that usually included advance review by network officials of all scripted comedy ideas or sketches. On the night of October 8, 1985, however, the Letterman show decided to run its "Test the Censors" segment without submitting it for pre-show review.

Letterman explained to his studio audience that the show would look one way to them—they would see everything—and another way to viewers at home, who would not see or hear material removed by the censors. Then he proceeded to violate each of the network's standard rules, beginning with commercial solicitation.

He began by asking for money from his viewers for a worthy cause—himself. Four million viewers at $10 a head, he reasoned, would be enough to buy himself a new house and an Olympic-sized swimming pool. Bill Wendell boomed the announcement: "Send cash or money order to 'Money for Dave.'" For viewers at home that evening a sudden gap appeared on the screen, ten seconds of a giant yellow X blocking the solicitation address and silence on the audio track where Wendell's voice read the address. Only viewers in the studio audience, rocking in laughter, heard and saw the full written address for this fundraising "gimmick."

The rest of the segment continued in this vein. Other areas tested were "explicit" language, four-letter words, plugs and slanders of specific commercial products, and "graphic sexual material." With the aid of an old high school biology film, Letterman introduced several levels of sexual activity, from simple to complex. He began by showing "one cell sex between a paramecium and itself" (the cell division is shown graphically on the screen), moved on to "plant sex" (the science film narrator intones, "these are the pollen grains, this is the anther, the stamen . . ."), then stepped up to "bunny and bedroom slipper" sex (a bunny humping a furry bedroom slipper in what appeared to be a home video)—then, suddenly, all that appears on the screen is a PLEASE STAND BY sign and five seconds of studio audience pandemonium.

At a meeting of the National Academy of Television Arts (NATAS) in New York, head writer Steve O'Donnell and producer Barry Sand later described the phone calls and agitation that occurred in frantic post-production meetings with network officials before the censored segment was aired. O'Donnell and Sand emphasized the "scientific" nature of the experiment. Said Sand: "We progressed in increments: cell reproduction, plant reproduction, bunny, sniffing around the slipper, not humping the slipper, humping the slipper. . . . We really didn't know where they would draw the line." Looking back, O'Donnell said, he still could not comprehend the reaction. "To see grown men fighting over whether the rabbit can be shown humping the slipper—these were grown men, lawyers . . ."

Though the network officials considered pulling the show and using a replacement, the compromise was the censored piece that went on the air. The behind-the-scenes maneuvering could have been a Letterman show skit in itself, but it was deadly serious to the network officials involved. Some clearly felt it could have cost them their jobs.[28]

RUNNING TIME	SEGMENT TIME	ITEM	PROPS AND GRAPHICS
Opening 12:30:30	(2:45)	Show Opening — Main Titles Dave — Opening Remarks	VTR/Audio From Band and Announce Dave comes down to Monologue Mark
ACT 1	(11:00)	TOP TEN SIGNS THAT SOVIET SOCIETY IS LOOSENING UP VIEWER MAIL	CHYRON ⊢SNAPPY ⊢PRE-TAPE PEOPLE IN AUDIENCE ⊢SNAPPY ⊢PRE-TAPE PAUL & DAVE IN GARAGE ⊢PRE-TAPE PAUL & DAVE IN SAILOR
12:44:15		Bumper	SUITS / CHRIS WALK ON
12:46:20	2:05 Black Slug	Commercial Position #1 (Network 1:30 + Local :30)	
ACT 2	(6:00)	RICHARD PRYOR	Homebase/Talk CLIP: "CRITICAL CONDITION" Chyron: RICHARD PRYOR
12:52:20		Bumper	
12:54:25	2:05 Black Slug	Commercial Position #2 (Network 1:00 + Local 1:00)	

Excerpt from *Late Night with David Letterman* rundown sheet. For show #814, Thursday, January 15, 1987.

is this show."

TRUE FACTS ABOUT DAVE

DAVID LETTERMAN USED TO CHAIN-SMOKE. NOW HE refuses almost everything: alcohol, drugs, caffeine. He does, however, smoke cigars. "I'll probably have to stop that, too," he says. "It could get out of control."

His first TV show – he's had three – was a pilot called *Leave It to Dave*. The set was constructed to resemble the inside of a pyramid. Letterman's chair was a throne. He hated it.

Letterman was once a substitute weatherman in Indiana, where he was born (Indianapolis) and attended college (Ball State). He once predicted hail the size of canned hams. He left Indiana in 1975 and moved to Los Angeles to write comedy.

Jay Leno, the stand-up comedian, is one of his best friends and favorite guests on the show. Letterman has never invited him to his house for dinner.

David Letterman believes he could break out of prison. He isn't optimistic about much else.

LYNN HIRSCHBERG *is a contributing editor of* ROLLING STONE. *Her last story, a profile of Daryl Hall and John Oates, appeared in RS 439.*

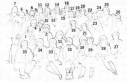

(1) David Letterman, host; (2) Merrill Markoe, writer and onscreen-segment producer; (3) Paul Shaffer, bandleader; (4) Jeff Martin, writer; (5) Neena Beber, talent assistant; (6) Larry Jacobson, writer; (7) Bill Wendell, announcer; (8) Chris Elliott, writer; (9) Paula Niedert, casting coordinator; (10) Darcy Hettrick, talent researcher; (11) Hal Gurnee, director; (12) Steve O'Donnell, head writer; (13) Fred Graver, writer; (14) Gerard Mulligan, writer; (15) Kevin Curran, writer; (16) Matt Wickline, writer; (17) Laurie Lennard, talent researcher; (18) Randy Cohen, writer; (19) Sandy Frank, writer; (20) Joe Toplyn, writer; (21) Rick Scheckman, film coordinator; (22) Marie O'Donnell, assistant to David Letterman; (23) Barry Sand, producer; (24) Betsy Steyer, assistant to associate producers; (25) Robert Morton, segment producer; (26) Peter Fatovich, associate director; (27) Gae Morris, talent coordinator; (28) Sandra Furton, talent coordinator; (29) Lisbeth Anderson, associate producer; (30) Sue Hall, production assistant; (31) Edd Hall, visuals coordinator; (32) Brian McAloon, second associate director; (33) Maria Pope, writers' assistant; (34) Barbara Gaines, production assistant; (35) Jude Brennan, production coordinator. Missing from the photograph are Laurie Guthrie, assistant to the producer, and Laurie Diamond, receptionist.

'WE'RE JUST TRYING TO SELL PINTOS'

DRESSED IN BLUE SHORTS PULLED OVER BLUE SWEAT pants, a baseball jersey and Adidas sneakers, David Letterman is throwing a toy football across his office. He tosses it to one of *Late Night's* segment producers, Robert Morton, whom everyone calls Morty. They are in the middle of a meeting. Morty talks to guests to prepare questions for Letterman and now is briefing him on actor Tony Danza and sportscaster Bob Costas. Letterman seems very serious, which is how he seems most of the time. Around the office, he wears glasses, is obviously shy and looks on the verge of anxiety. But since he's also constantly tossing a ball and almost always wearing sweat clothes, the final Letterman effect is appealingly contradictory. He's an oversize Little Leaguer with an editorial point of view, and he never stops watching – you or himself. There just aren't many false moves with this guy.

Which also means he's not exactly the David Letterman you see on TV. There are similarities – they're both very fast and rather elusive – but the Letterman on television wears suits and ties and is a high-octane version of the real-life Letterman. And though the sep-

Late Night with David Letterman production team. The Letterman show took self-reference to new heights at NBC in the mid-1980s. Here is a group portrait of thirty-five members of *Late Night's* production team. The photograph does not show the scores of others at NBC — make-up artists, props and stage crew, camera crew and technicians, pages, unit managers, accountants, publicists, programmers, legal staff, and standards and practices officers — who worked on the show as well. (*Rolling Stone,* June 20, 1985, p. 27; photo by Deborah Feingold)

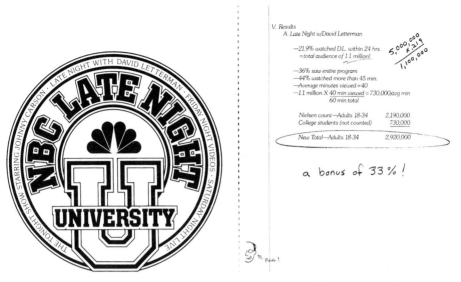

V. Results
  A. Late Night w/David Letterman

    —21.9% watched D.L. within 24 hrs.
      =total audience of 1.1 million!

        5,000,000
        X .219
        1,100,000

    —36% saw entire program
    —44% watched more than 45 min.
    —Average minutes viewed =40
    —1.1 million X 40 min viewed = 730,000/avg min
        60 min total

Nielsen count—Adults 18-34	2,190,000
College students (not counted)	730,000
New Total—Adults 18-34	2,920,000

a bonus of 33% !

Psst !

NBC Research Department catches the "creative" spirit of the Letterman show. This sales document uses Letterman themes and emulates a college notebook to document findings from a survey conducted March 31–April 9, 1987, by Survey Design and Analysis of Ann Arbor, Michigan.

Overleaf: *Late Night with David Letterman* organizational chart, November 24, 1986. (Produced from credits and discussion with production staff)

"LATE NIGHT WITH DAVID LETTERMAN" • PRODUCED BY NBC ENTERTAINMENT IN ASSOCIATION WITH CARSON PRODUCTIONS • ORGANIZATIONAL CHART *

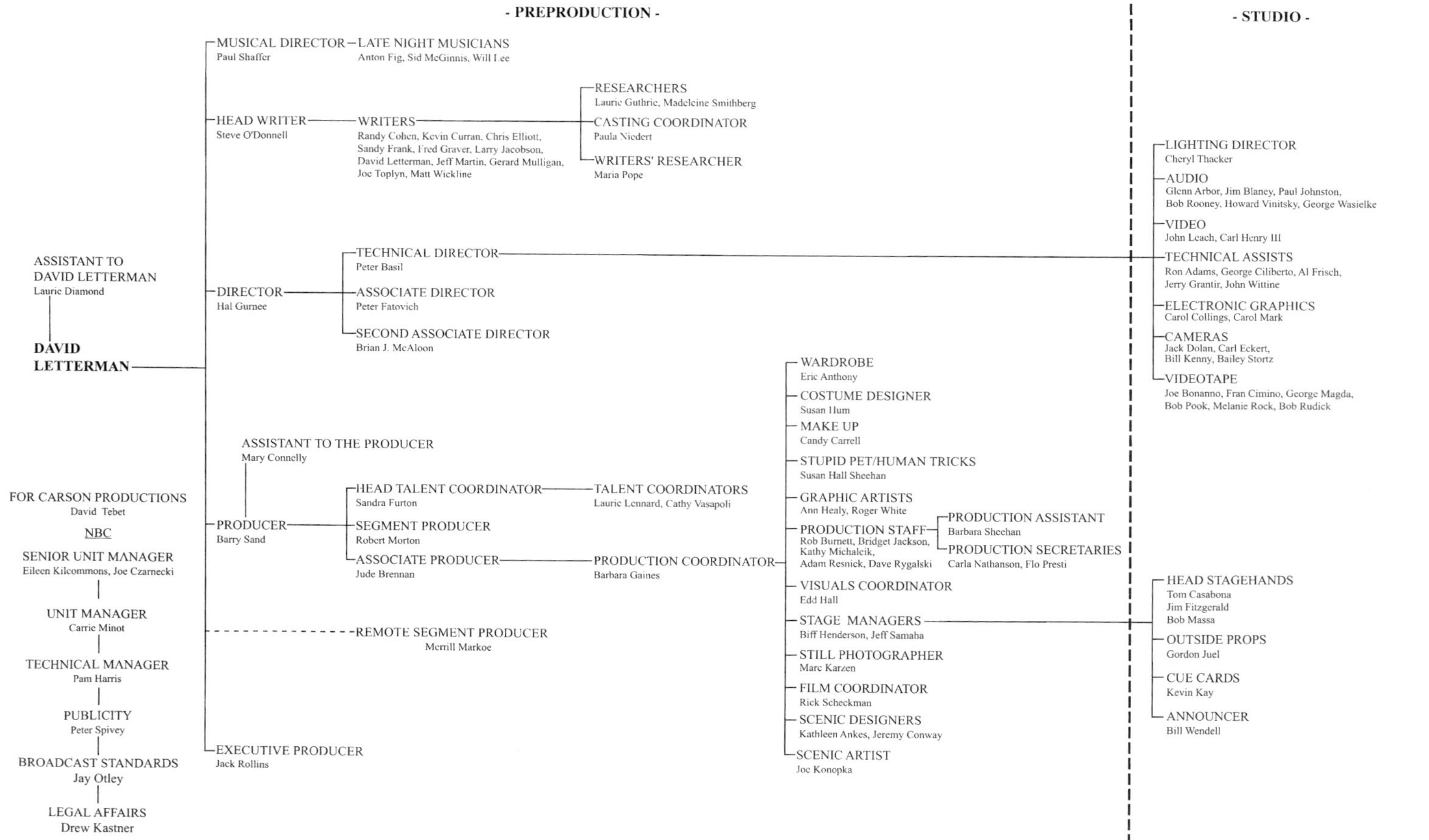

- PREPRODUCTION -

MUSICAL DIRECTOR – LATE NIGHT MUSICIANS
Paul Shaffer

LATE NIGHT MUSICIANS
Anton Fig, Sid McGinnis, Will Lee

HEAD WRITER
Steve O'Donnell

WRITERS
Randy Cohen, Kevin Curran, Chris Elliott, Sandy Frank, Fred Graver, Larry Jacobson, David Letterman, Jeff Martin, Gerard Mulligan, Joe Toplyn, Matt Wickline

RESEARCHERS
Laurie Guthrie, Madeleine Smithberg

CASTING COORDINATOR
Paula Niedert

WRITERS' RESEARCHER
Maria Pope

TECHNICAL DIRECTOR
Peter Basil

ASSOCIATE DIRECTOR
Peter Fatovich

SECOND ASSOCIATE DIRECTOR
Brian J. McAloon

DIRECTOR
Hal Gurnee

ASSISTANT TO DAVID LETTERMAN
Laurie Diamond

DAVID LETTERMAN

ASSISTANT TO THE PRODUCER
Mary Connelly

HEAD TALENT COORDINATOR
Sandra Furton

TALENT COORDINATORS
Laurie Lennard, Cathy Vasapoli

SEGMENT PRODUCER
Robert Morton

PRODUCTION COORDINATOR
Barbara Gaines

ASSOCIATE PRODUCER
Jude Brennan

PRODUCER
Barry Sand

REMOTE SEGMENT PRODUCER
Merrill Markoe

EXECUTIVE PRODUCER
Jack Rollins

FOR CARSON PRODUCTIONS
David Tebet

NBC

SENIOR UNIT MANAGER
Eileen Kilcommons, Joe Czarnecki

UNIT MANAGER
Carrie Minot

TECHNICAL MANAGER
Pam Harris

PUBLICITY
Peter Spivey

BROADCAST STANDARDS
Jay Otley

LEGAL AFFAIRS
Drew Kastner

- STUDIO -

LIGHTING DIRECTOR
Cheryl Thacker

AUDIO
Glenn Arbor, Jim Blaney, Paul Johnston, Bob Rooney, Howard Vinitsky, George Wasielke

VIDEO
John Leach, Carl Henry III

TECHNICAL ASSISTS
Ron Adams, George Ciliberto, Al Frisch, Jerry Grantir, John Wittine

ELECTRONIC GRAPHICS
Carol Collings, Carol Mark

CAMERAS
Jack Dolan, Carl Eckert, Bill Kenny, Bailey Stortz

VIDEOTAPE
Joe Bonanno, Fran Cimino, George Magda, Bob Pook, Melanie Rock, Bob Radick

WARDROBE
Eric Anthony

COSTUME DESIGNER
Susan Hum

MAKE UP
Candy Carrell

STUPID PET/HUMAN TRICKS
Susan Hall Sheehan

GRAPHIC ARTISTS
Ann Healy, Roger White

PRODUCTION STAFF
Rob Burnett, Bridget Jackson, Kathy Michalcik, Adam Resnick, Dave Rygalski

PRODUCTION ASSISTANT
Barbara Sheehan

PRODUCTION SECRETARIES
Carla Nathanson, Flo Presti

VISUALS COORDINATOR
Edd Hall

STAGE MANAGERS
Biff Henderson, Jeff Samaha

HEAD STAGEHANDS
Tom Casabona, Jim Fitzgerald, Bob Massa

STILL PHOTOGRAPHER
Marc Karzen

OUTSIDE PROPS
Gordon Juel

FILM COORDINATOR
Rick Scheckman

CUE CARDS
Kevin Kay

SCENIC DESIGNERS
Kathleen Ankes, Jeremy Conway

ANNOUNCER
Bill Wendell

SCENIC ARTIST
Joe Konopka

* as of November 24, 1986

During this period the Letterman show actively fostered unexpected events such as this "Test the Censor" show, even courting screwups on camera. It was one of the things that made the show interesting. Ultimately, however, *Late Night with David Letterman*, like any other show on television, had to stay within the prescribed limits of network practice. With all its antic moments and anarchic disruptions, the TV talk of one of the most inventive shows the 1980s was never completely unfettered.

As Letterman was redefining late-night comedy, another TV talk team was redefining news. Ted Koppel, a veteran news reporter in the ABC News Division, became the host of a late-night news show that arose from a single news event to reshape late-night television news talk.

"AMERICA HELD HOSTAGE": The Genesis of ABC's *Nightline* with Ted Koppel

Into the new competitive environment of the early 1980s came a television executive, a host, and a format that would change the face of late-night TV news talk. ABC took a traditionally conservative form of TV news—the late-night newscast—and wed it to a glitzy new entertainment package developed by the sports/talk division.

Nightline first aired at 11:30 P.M. on March 24, 1980,[29] an extension of the nightly "America Held Hostage" broadcasts that had followed the takeover by Islamic militants of the American Embassy in Tehran in the fall of 1979. Roone Arledge was the executive innovator behind the program. As head of the network's sports division, he had instituted the "color" commentaries of Howard Cosell and Don Meredith on *Monday Night Football* and developed a wide range of techniques to dramatize sports figures and contests. Upon his appointment as Vice President for News in 1977,[30] Arledge set his sights on dramatically enlivening the news division. He brought with him associates from sports and a series of sports production techniques: split screens, live satellite relays, remote trucks, and exciting computer graphics. He worked assiduously to develop Barbara Walters and Geraldo Rivera as new talk stars for ABC. Ted Koppel, however, an earnest, disciplined senior diplomatic correspondent, seemed at first an unlikely candidate for stardom.

Koppel was regarded by colleagues as a highly competent journalist, but also as one of the "old guard" at ABC. He resisted Arledge's changes at first. In the summer of 1977, unable to reach Arledge about a demotion from anchor to his former senior diplomatic correspondent role, Koppel quit.

The story of Ted Koppel's rise from the nadir of his career to its height hosting *Nightline* shows how quickly programming decisions, technology, and economics can come together in TV talk. In this case, the reporter's resourcefulness, persistence, and strong-minded personality simply rode out the tides of network change and ultimately won Roone Arledge's respect.

Ted Koppel was born in England in 1940. He was the only child of wealthy German-Jewish parents who fled Hitler in 1938. As a boy, Koppel listened to re-broadcasts of Edward R. Murrow's wartime reports from London and decided that he too wanted to become a broadcaster. He never wavered from that decision.

After moving with his family to New York in 1953 at the age of thirteen, he attended the private McBurney School and Syracuse University. He did graduate work at Stanford, earning a master's in Mass Communications Research and Political Science in 1963. That year he went to New York looking for a job in broadcasting.[31]

What he found was a $90-a-week copyboy position. He auditioned for ABC Radio, but the producer told him that he was good but too young. He offered Koppel a $175-a-week job as a writer instead. Koppel turned it down. "I didn't apply for that job. I want the on-air job," Koppel told him, "and I think you are being shortsighted because no one is going to know on the air how old I am."[32] A few days later the producer phoned back offering him the reporter's job. He learned a valuable lesson, Koppel later said. "No one is that confident in reality, but ours is a business of appearances, and it's terribly important to appear self-confident."[33]

The twenty-three-year-old Koppel became ABC's youngest reporter. Over the next fifteen years Koppel focused on a series of increasingly responsible jobs at ABC, serving as general assignment reporter, reporter in Vietnam, diplomatic correspondent to Hong Kong, and, in 1968, ABC's Miami bureau chief. He returned in 1971 to Washington to become the network's senior diplomatic correspondent.[34]

When Roone Arledge became head of the news division in 1977, Koppel's future at ABC seemed dim at best. Nothing about Koppel suggested he was the kind of TV personality Arledge was looking for. And when Arledge demoted him, Koppel resigned.

Bill Sheehan, the Vice President of ABC News who had signed

Koppel to his new contract, urged him to reconsider. Koppel was firm. When Arledge received Koppel's resignation, he ignored it at first.

But Sheehan did not give up. Arledge's secretary, Carol Grisanti, also spoke on Koppel's behalf. Eventually, Arledge agreed to have lunch with the senior diplomatic correspondent. Over a three-hour lunch Koppel became one of the first people at ABC News to experience what he later described as "the treatment." Arledge said he would like Koppel to stay, and Koppel readily agreed. Then Arledge got Koppel to talk about his career. ABC historian Marc Gunther says, "Arledge turned on the charm, and in a one-on-one setting few could be more charming." Koppel was impressed. Arledge still thought that Koppel should continue covering the State Department. However, the stage was now set for Arledge and Koppel to get together two years down the road at the time of the Iran hostage crisis.

In the meantime, though many journalists and news critics were horrified by Roone Arledge's "showboating" at ABC News, the ratings went up.[35] And the Iran hostage crisis in November 1979 was exactly the kind of story Arledge was looking for. ABC had the edge on this story from the beginning, since reporter Bob Dyk and photographer David Greene had managed to slip into Tehran before the Iranian regime cut contact with the West.[36] Four days into the crisis, ABC News began a series of late-night specials anchored by Frank Reynolds in New York. "Look at this," Reynolds began his first report. "One American, blindfolded, handcuffed, today in the courtyard of the American Embassy in Tehran."[37] The picture of Barry Rosen became the unofficial symbol of the Iran hostage crisis, and the special news reports turned into a nightly news program: *The Iran Crisis: America Held Hostage.*[38] Koppel, a regular reporter on the hostage crisis from the beginning, moved into the permanent anchor spot at the end of November when it became clear that Frank Reynolds, who was then hosting the regular *ABC Evening News,* could not do both. Koppel was not Roone Arledge's first choice for *Nightline.* But Koppel had the support of others in the news division and there was really no one else to do the job.

Pre-publicity for the premiere of *Nightline* was deliberately low key, but Roone Arledge had provided plenty of trumpet and drum fanfare in the graphics, musical theme, and dramatic presentation strategies.

The show was a team effort, and Arledge spared no expense or technological gimmick in seizing the time slot (originally twenty minutes, later expanded to a half-hour)[39] and putting the show together. Veteran producer Bill Lord persistently urged on exhausted troops through the long days that characterized *Nightline*'s first year on the air, and Koppel proved a smart managing editor as well as anchor.[40] *Nightline* was a ratings success, consistently beating the competition on CBS and frequently coming in a close second to Johnny Carson's *Tonight* show.

By November 1980, a year after the program had gone on the air, television critic William Henry III was proclaiming *Nightline* "TV's most innovative news show" and Koppel its "genuine boss."[41] Henry attributed *Nightline*'s success to a number of factors. For one, Koppel had a format that allowed him, unlike practically everyone else in television news, "to express his opinions, to be both reporter and commentator."[42] For another, *Nightline* was the first commercial TV news show to be aimed at an "upscale" late-night audience. Though Koppel always insisted his show tried to reach "cab drivers, truckers, waitresses, everybody,"[43] Henry pointed to different demographics.

> News and public affairs, Nielsen surveys tell us, always appeal more to the middle-aged than the young, more to the rich than the poor, more to professionals and managers than to blue-collar workers, more to college graduates than to the common man. *Nightline* maximizes that appeal by airing at an hour when almost all upscale people are home. Dinner or the theater or a long commute, even a late stay at the office, keep many "opinion leaders" from seeing nightly news at 7 P.M. (6 P.M. in the Midwest). By 11:30 they are ready for the day's final briefing, in *Nightline*.[44]

Over the next ten years Ted Koppel and *Nightline* continued to receive favorable press. The anchor was dubbed "the smartest man in television"[45] and the show won a number of awards, including in its first year an Emmy, a Dupont-Columbia award, and a Christopher award.[46] *Nightline* also became a forum for many of the world's most prominent figures, and it introduced a new programming idea—an international electronic "town meeting" that combined panelists, call-ins, and simulcasting to create a unique participatory event. "Town Meeting" topics included AIDS, Wall Street and the economy, the question of legalizing drugs, the Palestinian-Israeli conflict, and the South African freedom movement. By the mid-1980s Ted Koppel was a recognized star of late-night talk.

In late-night TV talk programming, news and entertainment—especially late-night comedy monologues—often work together in a complementary fashion. The following Close-up compares Ted Koppel's news talk on *Nightline* with the kinds of comedy talk being broadcast at the same time.

CLOSE-UP: NEWS TALK, ENTERTAINMENT TALK, AND THE CHERNOBYL NUCLEAR REACTOR DISASTER OF 1986

Three Takes on Chernobyl

On April 26, 1986, a tremendous explosion occurred in the Chernobyl nuclear reactor in the Ukraine. The disaster dominated world headlines for months. Details of what had occurred—including the number of victims and the ecological damage caused by the accident—were hotly contested.[47] The accident precipitated a new level of public awareness about the dangers of nuclear radioactivity. Initial news coverage of Chernobyl was highly melodramatic, spreading fears of worldwide ecological disaster. The Soviet government worked hard to counteract these fears.

After two weeks of sifting through contradictory reports, Ted Koppel on *Nightline* addressed the issue of how much the world knew about the disaster and from what sources. The same evening Johnny Carson devoted the first part of his comedy monologue to Chernobyl, and several weeks later David Letterman, who characteristically responded to headlines obliquely and after the fact, provided his own satiric commentary on the disaster. The three hosts treated Chernobyl from within their own talk traditions, their own talk subgenres, and each host's comments became part of the mosaic of public opinion taking shape at the time.

Nightline began its broadcast on the evening of May 14, 1986, with a picture of Soviet Premier Mikhail Gorbachev on Soviet television being translated as saying:

> For the first time we've come up against such a dangerous force as that of nuclear energy getting out of control. Radiation in the station's area, and the immediately adjacent territory is still dangerous for human health. [A *New York Post* headline—"15,000 Buried"—is flashed on the screen as Gorbachev continues]. . . . We encountered a tremendous accumulation of lies—the most shameless kinds of lies.[48]

The image of Ted Koppel now appears with the *Nightline* theme music mixed under:

The Soviet leader breaks his silence on the disaster at Chernobyl. Good evening, I'm Ted Koppel, and this is *Nightline*.

Koppel continues:

Is Mikhail Gorbachev really aiming at a new level of openness, or is it just another tactic of the Soviet propaganda machine? Our guests tonight, live from Moscow, Genadi Gerasimov, commentator for Soviet News Agency Novosti, and in New York, former Secretary of State Henry Kissinger.

This is a typical *Nightline* opening. Beginning with the "tease" from Gorbachev's speech, Koppel's commentary has all the standard features of television news talk. It begins with the reporter's personal introduction ("Good evening, I'm Ted Koppel"), announces his topic for the night, and continually emphasizes the topicality and "liveness" of the event discussed. Koppel's serious, stentorian announcing style and clipped dramatic cadences also mark this as a hard newscast. It is presented in formal, third-person address, with no side comments, digressions, or diversions from the factual material he is reporting. Koppel speaks directly into the camera at a medium close-up distance. In standard news form he posits "two sides" to the story and two authorities who will speak to them. However, it is Koppel himself who "anchors" the event. The host gives us the context for the story and tells us what Gorbachev is doing. Through a series of pointed questions he sets the frame for interpreting Gorbachev's words.

Koppel and his producers frame the news event visually with flashy computer graphics. In the initial stages of Gorbachev's speech, the Soviet premier is seen on a computer-drawn television monitor that takes up about two-thirds of the screen. The monitor is set against another computer-generated image: a glowing red background. Though Koppel speaks disdainfully of early press reports that conjured up "apocalyptic visions" of thousands dead in an "atomic wasteland," *Nightline*'s visuals deliver the same apocalyptic message. The television monitor has been placed on a spread-out global grid, bright red, in front of a horizon line that looks like a fire that is raging around the edge of the world.

As Gorbachev continues to speak, the outline of the monitor is flattened into a blue-rimmed rectangle, and computer-generated stars shoot past him into a black void that now surrounds his image on the screen. The image of Gorbachev now resembles a space ship shooting deep into space. The image echoes George Lucas' *Star Wars*.[49] Never—anywhere—do Koppel or the writers and producers of *Nightline* use the words "Evil Empire," the phrase popularly attributed to President Ronald Reagan to characterize his view of the Communist world during this time. The graphics do that much more subtly and effectively.

The same evening Johnny Carson approached the topic of Chernobyl from a comedy perspective. After making his ritual entry through the rainbow-colored curtains of *The Tonight Show,* Carson quelled the studio audience demonstration and began his monologue with the first of a series of Chernobyl references:

> Are you applauding or just trying to scatter the nuclear fallout we have out here?

> Speaking of the nuclear fallout, did you read that it has reached Los Angeles? The good news is: it is killing the cancer-causing agents in the hamburgers. [Carson waits for laughing to die down.]

> Los Angeles was ready for that—we're laid back out here. We have a defense line-up of leaf blowers on the beach [audience begins to laugh] blowing the stuff back to the Soviet Union! [more laughter][50]

Carson and his writers go on to make a few more humorous comments on the futility of the West's response—the lack of a safety plan or even the most rudimentary ideas about how to survive radioactive fallout. The three jokes quoted here run for about forty seconds on the screen. In all, Carson's comments on Chernobyl account for six of the fifteen jokes of that evening and fit comfortably into the grooves of a monologue he had honed for twenty-four years.[51]

Carson's relationship to his audience through the camera is quite different from Koppel's. In contrast to the visual energy of *Nightline*'s zooms and computer graphics, the audiovisual space that Carson inhabits is static. His jokes are entirely verbal, and he presents them from a traditional stage setting.

Letterman's comment on Chernobyl comes weeks later and is briefer and more visual. The Letterman show had a regular feature in which the host would sit in front of a television screen and search the channels to see what was playing on other stations. What appeared was often old film stock footage (from the 1940s, 1950s, and 1960s), to which Letterman attached outlandish captions.[52]

Seated at his desk over a month after the first news headlines on Chernobyl, Letterman announces that it is about time to search "other channels." Among the wacky images this produces is a straitlaced First Lady Nancy Reagan doing the "frug" at a Motown benefit (Letterman's comment: "Guess who the white person is") and a bizarre image shot from several vantage points that remains on the screen about fifteen seconds. The image is of a small-town parade, shot in black and white, with three lead marchers in flouncing hoop skirts and papier-mâché cow heads.

In mocking tones but adopting the voice of a news announcer, Letterman narrates the footage as follows: "Here we have the Cable News Network satellite pictures from the Soviet Union of the finalists in the Miss Kiev Beauty Pageant." Scattered laughter drifts up from the audience as several people "get" the allusion to radioactive genetic mutation.

It is characteristic of Letterman and his staff that he waited over a month to mention Chernobyl. It is also characteristic of Letterman that his comment was primarily visual—you had to see the footage of the small-town parade and cow heads to get the point. Where this strange footage came from is hard to say, though it appeared from the cars and the clothes that it had been shot in the 1950s.

As seen in these examples, Ted Koppel, Johnny Carson, and David Letterman comment on Chernobyl from different frameworks and different subgenre traditions of TV talk. Ted Koppel's discussion of Chernobyl comes from news; Letterman's verbal/visual irony represents one part of the spectrum of late-night entertainment talk; Johnny Carson's word-oriented, stand-up monologue presents another. Each host participates in a talk tradition that he himself has helped to define and redefine in network practice. Each show represents a particular subgenre of news and entertainment talk. In the much wider world of popular culture and public opinion, they work together.

NEW HOSTS, NEW AUDIENCES

The late 1980s saw an explosive expansion of national talk stars, including the first woman to challenge Carson in late-night comedy talk (Joan Rivers); the first African American to host a successful daytime talk show (Oprah Winfrey); the first self-identified Hispanic American to host a national talk show (Geraldo Rivera); and the first African American to host a late-night comedy talk show (Arsenio Hall). Viewers were being treated to hosts who were decidedly not the "button-down" Midwestern broadcasting types so popular on American television screens in the 1950s, 1960s, and 1970s. The hosts of the 1980s challenged the notion of a single conventional broadcast personality and extended the range of racial, ethnic, and gender representation in national TV talk.

The complexion of studio audiences changed as well. African Americans, Hispanic Americans, "inner city" types, and "trailer park" people were now appearing regularly on television screens as guests or as part of talk-show audiences. Though hosts like Johnny Carson and Phil Donahue still reigned in many markets, gender challenges occurred as well. Joan Rivers took on Johnny Carson with her late-night Fox Television show and became the emblem of the "unruly woman" up against one of show business' most powerful male patriarchs. Launching her nationally syndicated show out of Chicago in 1986, Oprah Winfrey challenged Phil Donahue, and beat him in the ratings in many markets, including Chicago, his own home base. The battle between Donahue and Winfrey signaled an enormous change in the culture and in TV talk—the public moment in which a Black woman from humble origins in the South was able to wrest the throne of daytime TV talk from a middle-class White male star who had been number one in daytime talk for almost a decade.

Late night saw the rise of African American talk-show star Arsenio Hall. When Joan Rivers' late-night talk show faltered in the ratings, Hall took over to a burst of critical and viewer acclaim. For six years, Arsenio Hall was one of the most talked about hosts on television.

As daytime and late-night talk gained more viewers, an estimated 75 million by the end of the decade, the role of national talk-show hosts took on new significance. As during the time of the Chernobyl incident, these hosts were more than show-business figures. They were also mediators and focal points of public opinion.

JOAN RIVERS AND THE LATE-NIGHT TALK-SHOW WARS OF 1986–1987

Joan Rivers was part of a rising movement of women stand-up comics in the 1980s.[53] They included comedians like Rita Rudner, Abby Stein, Beverly Mickins, and Kate Clinton, some of whom survived into the 1990s. But Joan Rivers was the only one of this group to become a national talk-show host and even to challenge Johnny Carson himself. Although she failed in her late-night bid, Rivers opened up territory on television for other women comedians—like Roseanne Connor and Rosie O'Donnell—and for new forms of ethnic comedy as well. It was no mere fluke that Arsenio Hall followed Rivers in her time slot on the Fox Television Network, and with her blessing. African Americans and women were knocking on the doors of late-night talk.

Joan Rivers' career began to change in 1983 when she was named Carson's first "permanent guest host." Her contract specified that she appear once every seven weeks, eight weeks a year. "Joan Rivers Gets

Even with Laughs," proclaimed *Newsweek* that fall, describing her as "television's most outrageous funny woman."[54] Rivers' schedule at the time was rigorous. She was on the road with her comedy act forty weeks a year, including ten weeks in Las Vegas, where she commanded up to $200,000 per week. Her comedy album *What Becomes a Semi-Legend Most?* had sold more than 500,000 copies and her one-woman show at Carnegie Hall was sold out within a week. She had also been named cohost of the Emmy Awards with *Saturday Night Live* star Eddie Murphy.[55] Joan Rivers was, said the *Ladies' Home Journal,* the reigning "Queen of Comedy."[56]

Before her rebirth on the *Tonight* show, Rivers was seen by some as a "has-been." Television critic James Wolcott described her as a "rude, fussing anachronism, a tatty-feathered parrot who needed a dark cloth dropped over her cage."[57] When she appeared on *The Tonight Show* in the early 1980s, however, her act suddenly caught on. Part of it was the stark contrast to Carson. Whereas Carson tended to get his laughs with the constrained, buttoned-down humor of the Midwest, Rivers' style was pure karate. "She *whacks* her lines with a war cry," Wolcott said, "then finishes off the viewer with a mean knee to the naughty bits."[58] Critic Michael Pollan concurred. "Where [Carson] is scrupulously polite, [Rivers] is bitchy; where he is low-key, she is overheated; where he is Midwest, Waspy and proper, she is urban, ethnic and gossipy. Carson conducts interviews as if he were at the country club; Rivers does hers at the kitchen table."[59] Rivers versus Carson, then, was not just a battle of two veteran comedians; it was a gender battle, a battle of comedy icons of masculinity and femininity, and it was a battle that took on a personal edge when Carson found out his protégée was going to compete against him in his own time slot.

The explosion came in May 1986, the day Rivers announced her new three-year contract with Fox. Rivers tried to reach Carson as soon as the contract was signed, but an aide told him first. Rivers had been leery of talking to Carson before the contract was signed. She saw what had happened to David Brenner when he told the Carson organization about his upcoming syndicated talk show. He had been angrily and summarily fired. Carson was "kept in cotton, everybody afraid to say anything that might disturb him," Rivers later said. Others echo this account of Carson's isolation and dependence on advisors in the mid-1980s. In describing negotiations for their divorce, ex-wife Joanna Carson said she was never quite sure whom she was talking to. She often felt she was dealing with two personalities—Carson's and that of

Henry Bushkin, his lawyer, also going through a divorce at the time. Journalist Bill Carter, in his book on the power negotiations that swirled around Carson in the 1980s, describes meetings Carson knew about and meetings he did not. Carson would joke about his competition and the "succession" question on the air, but his concern with competition was serious. The timing of Rivers' announcement was particularly volatile for the "King of Comedy."

The offer Joan Rivers accepted from Rupert Murdoch's new Fox network for her new late-night talk show was for $10 million and three years. The Fox network had a nucleus of six "owned and operated" stations in New York, Los Angeles, Washington, Chicago, Dallas, and Houston, covering 22 percent of the national audience.[60] Fox hoped to build its base to include over a hundred stations and more than 80 percent of the national viewing audience. Owner Murdoch committed $100 million to the project.

The Carson/Rivers "talk-show war" hit the press resoundingly soon after the announcement of the new show in the spring of 1986. *Time* and *Newsweek* came out the same week with lead stories. "Can We Talk? (Crash, Click, Buzz)" headlined *Newsweek*.[61] "Carson Gets a New Rival," said *Time*. Rivers had bragged that her ratings were higher than Carson's and that she could now book offbeat guests *The Tonight Show* never allowed.[62] In October, *USA Today* delivered its own front-page report on the "Late-night Lulu" between the hosts, and the *New York Post* ran a "Johnny vs. Joanie" scoreboard that included a checklist for viewers to fill out on their predictions for the upcoming "jaw wars" (see photo section). "Will Johnny jab at Joanie?" "Will Joanie return the punch?" "Will Joanie jab at Jody, Joanne, and Joanna [Carson's ex-wives]?" "Will Joanie say 'Can We Talk'?" "Will Johnny say 'Oh, grow up'?" "Will Anybody Care?"

Had Joan Rivers succeeded, she would have been the first woman comedy host to secure a successful long-term slot in late-night comedy. But her show did not succeed. Afterward producers, advertisers, critics, and pundits tried to sort out why. The NBC publicity department loyal to Carson had sought to characterize Rivers as an ungrateful employee who had hidden her true intentions from her boss, but it is not clear what effect this negative publicity had on the new show. The threat to "blacklist" guests who appeared on Rivers' show was certainly damaging.[63] In addition, the Fox executives who signed Rivers had little experience with national talk shows. When the show showed a large loss its first half year, Fox executives panicked and decided to pull the plug. They were willing to pay a large severance fee to get out of the $10 million contract. Fox also lost $1.6 million in compensation fees the network had been forced to pay advertisers for not meeting the 6 percent audience share it had promised. The show, said one executive, was "a bomb of Hiroshima-like dimensions."[64]

In the end, Rivers' flamboyant brand of talk may simply have been too strong a taste for everyday TV consumption. As her reappearance in TV talk in the 1990s indicated, however, there was still room in the spectrum for Rivers. In fact, she hosted talk shows several times in her long career; however, she never achieved the status of a titan. Other hosts, however, were opening up new spaces for talk in the 1980s, and one of them would become one of the most popular talk-show hosts of the decade.

OPRAH WINFREY

While many new daytime talk shows were successful, Oprah Winfrey's rise was perhaps the most dramatic. She had come seemingly out of nowhere to challenge Phil Donahue in the talk format he had personally created and in the city (Chicago) that had been his home base for the previous twelve years. And Winfrey was the first successful African American daytime talk-show host, the most commercially successful daytime talk-show host of the 1980s. Thus Oprah Winfrey, like Jackie Robinson forty years before, broke the color line in a major U.S. institution—this time daytime TV talk.

As soon as Oprah Winfrey came on national television screens in 1986 it was obvious that a significant change had occurred. As one critic put it:

> The reigning champion was a white male, born in 1935, from a solid middle-class background, had been raised a Catholic, had married, divorced, and married again. The challenger was a black female, born out of wedlock in 1954, into an impoverished farm family, was sexually abused as a child, was raised a Protestant, and was unmarried.[65]

Born out of what Winfrey later described as a "one-night stand" between a serviceman and a seventeen-year-old girl from Kosciusko, Mississippi, Oprah's name came from the biblical "Orpah" with two letters accidentally transposed when her birth certificate was written. Her mother went north to look for work, and she was raised in her earliest years by her devout Baptist grandmother. Oprah had little contact with her father until the early 1960s when, at the age of seven, she was sent to live with him for a year in Nashville. It was a relatively happy and stable year, but her mother wanted her to rejoin the family in Milwaukee, where she now lived and worked, and at the age of eight Oprah Winfrey traveled to her third home. There she shined academically and was awarded a scholarship to a high school on Milwaukee's affluent North Shore.[66] She also started getting into trouble. She later ascribed her "wildness" as a teenager to a rape at the age of nine and sexual abuse within her family that left her confused, humiliated, and angry.[67] As a talk-show host, talking to another victim of childhood sexual abuse, she referred to this incident of incest and sexual abuse on the air.[68] This was a first: a major personal disclosure by a nationally known television personality live, on the air. In 1992 she narrated a powerful documentary on the subject that was aired on the three major commercial networks and PBS.[69]

At the age of fourteen, Winfrey was sent once again to live with her stepmother and her father, now a well-respected barber and city council member in Nashville. Her father and stepmother put her on an academic regimen that included reading and reporting on two books a week outside of school. Under their strict guidance and supervision, Winfrey became a high academic achiever and high school leader and went on to Tennessee State University on full scholarship.

In high school Oprah Winfrey showed promise as a performer as well. Her first major public recognition came at seventeen when she was named "Miss Fire Prevention" in Nashville. She was prepared to say in her interview concerning career goals that she wanted to be a fourth-grade teacher.[70] The morning of the competition, however, she had tuned in to the *Today* show with Barbara Walters and had a change of heart. She told the judges she wanted to be a journalist.

Winfrey worked at a local Black radio station in high school and while going to college was invited to apply and accepted a news position at the local CBS affiliate. Here again Barbara Walters was a model.

> I would sit like Barbara, or like I imagined Barbara to sit, and I'd look at the script and up to the camera because I thought that's what you do, how you act. You try to have as much eye contact as you can—at least it seemed that way from what I had seen Barbara do.[71]

From a $15,000-a-year job in Nashville, Winfrey went in 1976, at the age of twenty-two, to an anchor job in a larger market, WJZ-TV in Baltimore,[72] which turned out to be a much tougher market for the young reporter. She was paired with a veteran Baltimore newscaster, and right away the chemistry didn't work.[73] The biggest problem revolved around Oprah Winfrey's on-air personality. As biographer Norman King put it, "She *really* wanted to be an actress—a person whose job it was to *show* emotion and to *live* a story. She never really wanted to be *outside* things that were happening, an observer equipped with cold-blooded objectivity."[74]

The Baltimore station had invested a six-figure contract in its new minority newscaster, and in 1977 they sent her to New York for a "make-over." "Your hair's too thick," the assistant news director told her. "Your eyes are too far apart. Your nose is too wide. Your chin is too long. You have to do something about it."[75] At the station's expense, a New York salon decided to try something stronger to thin her hair.

> I felt the lotion burning my skull. I kept telling them, "Excuse me, this is beginning to burn a little." Hell, it wasn't burning—it was *flaming*.[76]

When she went back to Baltimore, her hair started falling out. In a week she was bald. It was a turning point, said Winfrey.

> They wanted to make me a Puerto Rican. Or something. What I should have said then, and what I would say now, is that nobody can tell me how to wear my hair. I've since vowed to live my own life, to always be myself.[77]

Winfrey worked with a voice coach, building up her determination to face her employers with her own style. She applied for the job of cohosting the local morning talk show, *People Are Talking*. This time the format and chemistry with cohost Richard Sher worked much better. From the first show Winfrey knew this was more the kind of talk format she felt comfortable with.

> I was interviewing some of the cast from *All My Children* and maybe the Carvel ice-cream man—really big-time stuff, you know!—but I'm telling you, I finished that show, and the

minute it was over, I thought, "Thank God! This is *it*. This is like *breathing!*"[78]

Winfrey spent seven years in Baltimore, steadily building her ratings. By 1984 she was ready once again for a larger market. WLS-TV in Chicago had hired her former producer, Debra DiMaio. DiMaio showed the WLS station manager, Dennis Swanson, Winfrey's audition tape, and he was impressed. He went to the ratings books and found out Winfrey had been regularly outscoring Donahue in the Baltimore market.[79] In January 1984, he hired her.

From that point Winfrey's rise was rapid. By the middle of March she had bypassed Donahue in Chicago in Donahue's time slot, garnering 265,000 viewers to Donahue's 147,230.[80] Four months later the station doubled the length of her show from thirty minutes to an hour. In December Winfrey received her first major national recognition: she was dubbed "Chicago's Grand New Oprah," in a feature article in *Newsweek*.[81] By September 1985 the show had changed its name from *A.M. Chicago* to *The Oprah Winfrey Show*, and in the fall of 1986 Jeffrey Jacobs, Winfrey's attorney-manager, concluded a national deal with King World, one of the country's leading syndicators. Her show was designed to go national, with a major publicity/marketing campaign scheduled for summer and early fall 1986.

Executives at King World, working with publicist Anne McGee, felt the media were looking for "a war with Donahue," and they were ready to oblige.[82] Once again, a "talk-show war" fueled by publicists spurred change in the talk-show world. King World's first step was to send tapes of the pilot of Oprah's show to "focus groups" across the country.[83] Collating the results, King World sent tapes to small station groups—network alliances of a half-dozen or more stations under a single owner. As reactions came in, King World again adapted its strategy. Rather than making blanket offers to station groups, the syndicator opened separate negotiations in each market. This paid off, since the new Oprah show was now considered a hot enough commodity to win better deals station by station. Ads in major media outlets trumpeted Oprah's ratings victories over Donahue in Baltimore and Chicago, although the "Donahue-buster" strategy was played lightly by Winfrey herself, who tried hard not to appear too boastful or overconfident. When asked about the head-on competition with Donahue, she would reply, "In the majority of markets I do not compete directly with him. . . . Donahue will certainly remain the king, and I just would like a part of the monarchy."[84]

By the time *The Oprah Winfrey Show* was aired nationally in September 1986, it had signed over 180 stations—somewhat less than Donahue's 200-plus but approaching that number.[85] Still, questions remained. How many signed-up stations would stick with her? How many stations would renew for the full year? These questions were soon answered. *The Oprah Winfrey Show* was an undisputed ratings success in its first three months.[86] By November *Oprah* was averaging a 5.1 national Nielsen rating and its clearance rate (the percentage of stations choosing to run it nationally) was "the best among the new shows, 94% of the U.S."[87] The show, which cost less than $100,000 a week to produce, was highly profitable. The success of *The Oprah Winfrey Show* encouraged a wave of new talk shows, and helped build audiences for Sally Jessy Raphaël and Geraldo Rivera as well.

By 1986, the year she broke into national syndication, Oprah Winfrey had assumed full control of her business affairs. She had her own company, Harpo Productions, and attorney-representative Jeffrey Jacobs was a full-time manager. Harpo Productions was designed to produce films and television shows devoted to African American themes.[88] Winfrey had also established herself as a character actress by this time, playing the role of Sophia in the Quincy Jones/Steven Spielberg production of Alice Walker's *The Color Purple*. She received an Academy Award nomination for that role.[89]

Winfrey's African American identity was central to her coverage in the national press. Bill Zehme's profile in *Spy* magazine in December 1986 described her as "capaciously built, black, and extremely noisy." She would make, said Zehme, gratuitous "down-home" references to men who had left her "'cow-faced' from sobbing," while "tugging at her trademark big-mama earrings."[90] These and other race-conscious comments were common in the press coverage of Winfrey. She was confronted with the issue of race constantly in interviews and was very aware of her image as an African American role model.

In August 1986, for example, a *USA Today* reporter asked Winfrey, "As someone who is not pencil-thin, white, nor blond, you are transcending barriers that have hindered many in television. How were you able to do it?" Winfrey replied,

> I've been able to do it because my race and gender have never been an issue for me. I've been blessed in knowing who I am,

and I am a part of a great legacy. I've crossed over on the backs of Sojourner Truth, and Harriet Tubman, and Fannie Lou Hamer, and Madam C. J. Walker. Because of them I can now soar. Because of them I can now live the dream. I am the seed of the free, and I know it. I intend to bear great fruit.[91]

Much of Oprah Winfrey's facility in speaking and performing, she later explained, had come from her African American roots, beginning with her experience in her grandmother's church in Mississippi. Between Sunday school, Baptist Training Union (BTU), and two church services, she spent almost all day every Sunday in church. She was very often on the program for a recitation.

Winfrey was so precociously verbal at church that she was known as "The Preacher."[92] She was raised in the "call and response" tradition of the South, where the speaker's statements or "calls" were punctuated by expressions or "responses" from the listener. Like Donahue, Winfrey would later refer to her show as her "ministry," but rather than a confessional orchestrated by an analytical White male, Winfrey's show drew forth antiphonal confessions of empathy from a largely female audience of "sisters." She was a woman speaking to other women who had themselves experienced victimization and powerlessness.

As she became more and more successful in mainstream broadcasting, Winfrey came increasingly to represent a "double-voiced" identity as an African American woman. As Henry Louis Gates put it, echoing W. E. B. Du Bois, the successful African American has to demonstrate "his or her own membership in the human community and then to demonstrate her resistance to that community."[93] Feminist critic Gloria-Jean Mascariotte commented on this "double-voiced" identity.

> Media gossip delighted in Winfrey's battles with food, her troublesome relationship with a good-looking guy, that foregrounds and (according to the common wisdom of white patriarchal aesthetics) contradicts her own more "mammy-like" appearance and function, and her fluctuating hairstyles and fashion choices . . .[94]

Winfrey's "battles with food" centered on weight loss campaigns, which figured prominently in press accounts. The African American "big momma" was a powerful, earthy figure represented by the Sophia character in *The Color Purple,* and this contrasted significantly with the asexual Aunt Jemima of "white patriarchal aesthetics," where slenderness and beauty were equated.[95] In the battle over body image, Winfrey came firmly down on the side of slimness, but she was continually playing off of and against the perceptions of her by both White and Black America—mediating both systems of values and aesthetics.

After Oprah Winfrey broke the color line in TV talk, other racial and ethnic barriers began to fall, and another major host of daytime talk rose to national prominence: Geraldo Rivera.

GERALDO RIVERA

As a Puerto Rican American, Geraldo Rivera renegotiated his identification with the Hispanic community not once but several times in the development of his prolific on-air broadcasting career. Known originally for his role as an aggressive investigative television reporter for ABC News, Rivera came to his national TV talk show as a flamboyant television personality with an off-screen reputation as a ladies' man. Rivera's overwrought style and curious mixture of empathy, bravado, exploitation, and crusading journalism were easy to parody, but his viewers rewarded this mixture with ratings that were consistently good.

Rivera's talk-show persona had its roots in a childhood in West Babylon, Long Island, where he was constantly vying for attention from family and friends. The family moved to Long Island from Brooklyn, and he never truly felt at home in his new suburban environment. He began his autobiography bluntly: "Aesthetically speaking, growing up in Long Island sucked."[96] The rest of the autobiography shows Rivera constantly uncomfortable with his identity and upbringing, constantly trying to prove himself to family, girlfriends, peers, and especially his father. Rivera's father was one of nineteen children of a Puerto Rican sugar plantation worker who had never been able to achieve success in the United States. Rivera's own childhood was also complicated by his ambivalence over his mixed ethnic identity—his father was Puerto Rican and his mother was Jewish. Rivera describes the scene in which his Puerto Rican family attended his Bar Mitzvah in a Long Island temple. When he began to read from the Hebrew, the assembled Rivera clan, unfamiliar with Jewish ritual, wanted to treat the moment with respect. "They removed their yarmulkes and placed the skullcaps over their hearts."[97] Growing up in a strange mix of "whitefish and *pasteles,*"

Rivera found that he "started to approach my Judaism the way I approached acne, as something to cover up."

Rivera was also ambivalent about his Puerto Rican heritage. His mother had filled in his last name on his birth certificate with an extra "i," so that it read Riviera. "I came to realize she was deeply embarrassed" with the Puerto Rican name, he later said. He decided that she had added the "i" to make the name sound less Puerto Rican and more Spanish. Rivera decided to capitalize on the confusion.

> Until I was twenty-four, I was Gerry Riviera, Americanized Latin lover in search of greater expectations and better scenery. . . . The beauty of the name was its ambiguity, which also allowed me to allay any anti-Semitic attacks . . . Access to the alternative spelling allowed me all the social mobility I could afford. . . . I would pose as someone more elegantly continental, still vaguely Hispanic, perhaps the son of a businessman from Spain or Argentina.[98]

During summers in Puerto Rico, however, Rivera came directly into contact with his Puerto Rican family and culture, and spurred by an intense desire to succeed, he decided to take advantage of his new-found Puerto Rican identity to apply for a minority scholarship to Brooklyn Law School. Rivera relates this story about his law school interview, in which a Penn Law School professor and aide came to Brooklyn to search for minority attorneys to work in low-income communities:

> "Are you sure you're brown?" the aide asked timidly at the conclusion of our interview. "What the hell kind of question is that?" I shot back. "It's just, you know, your name," the putz fumbled, "Riviera." "I'm Puerto Rican," I said proudly, defiantly. "My real name is Rivera. Riviera was my slave name."[99]

Rivera completed his degree at Brooklyn Law School, finishing nineteenth in a class of 330. As a young activist lawyer in New York in the 1960s, he represented the "Young Lords." He became New York's Channel 7 *Eyewitness News* affirmative action reporter covering the Puerto Rican community. This TV job allowed him to take advantage of another opportunity—a minority training program in the Graduate

School of Journalism at Columbia University under the direction of Edward R. Murrow's old friend and coproducer, Fred Friendly.

In a school formerly devoted to the "high road" journalism represented by Murrow and Friendly, Geraldo Rivera received basic training in the dramatization-of-news-stories journalism that was later to make his name. Rivera's favorite instructor was John Parsons, a former news director who had changed his name from John Perdito. Parsons had an instinct for the kind of TV news that would garner ratings in the New York area. Here is Parsons' account of Rivera's apprenticeship:

> Geraldo came to me with certain handicaps. He had a very high, squeaky voice. And he was thin. And I said to him, "Geraldo, you're gonna have to be forceful and powerful," and I gave him tips on how to do that. Close-ups. To unbutton his shirt. Not to wear a tie. To have the camera shoot him low-angle so that he dominated the screen. I thought his appeal would be to women, and he should imagine that he was talking to a woman when he did a report. Let the wind blow in the hair. Be casual . . . Remember, these were the first minorities going out there, so it was important to come on strong. It's like Jackie Robinson. He had to be outstanding, and so I stressed that. And looking for causes.[100]

Rivera shaped himself according to Parsons' advice. First with Channel 7, the ABC flagship station in New York, and later on national ABC News, Rivera became a regular contributor to ABC's *Good Morning, America* (1974–1978) and a senior correspondent to *20/20* through the late 1970s and early 1980s. He did a series of late-night news commentary specials for the network (*Geraldo Rivera: Good Night, America*) and a documentary on the substandard conditions of a state institution for retarded children ("Willowbrook: The Last Disgrace"). The documentary won awards and favorable criticism.

After fifteen years of flamboyant exposure on ABC, in December 1985, with Rivera holding a contract close to a million dollars a year, he was fired. Rivera's brashness took him too far when he challenged ABC News Vice President Roone Arledge's decision not to run colleague Sylvia Chase's story about Marilyn Monroe's affairs with John and Robert Kennedy. Rivera charged that Arledge censored the story because of close ties to the Kennedy family.

After being dismissed by ABC, Rivera went through a period of uncertainty and doubt. He began a series of freelance ventures, including a syndicated special, "The Mystery of Al Capone's Vault," in which he found—on the air, in front of millions of viewers—virtually nothing in the legendary gangster's sealed private vault. It was a tacky publicity stunt from top to bottom, and Rivera himself was embarrassed by it. But it gained huge ratings and played a role in his broadcasting comeback. By the time he launched his own nationally syndicated talk show in 1987, he was once again a "household name." He had proved himself the master of the pseudo-event, as well as a hardworking journalist, someone who could simultaneously take the high road and low road in journalism. It was a role he would play, with some tacking and weaving, through the next decade on television.

Under Winfrey, Rivera, and others such as Sally Jessy Raphaël, the daytime talk show began to change. The public-service traditions of Arlene Francis and Phil Donahue began to move toward carnivalesque exploitation. The trash talk and "freak shows" of Ricki Lake, Jerry Springer, and others in the 1990s had their roots in the 1980s. By the end of the decade, daytime TV talk was clearly taking a baroque turn. Jerry Springer had taken the desire for spectacle exploited by Ricki Lake and others and the proletarian anger of Morton Downey Jr. and transformed them into a single highly profitable form of television, a carnival of conflict with no pretense of public information or therapeutic "solutions." But in the wake of the new competition for Johnny Carson's position in late-night television, late-night talk TV was changing as well, and no one had more of an impact on late-night TV at this time than a young African American comedian named Arsenio Hall.

ARSENIO HALL

Arsenio Hall was the "hottest" new talk-show host in entertainment television in 1989. He was also the first African American to become a star of late-night talk, and at the age of thirty, one of the youngest to crack the circle of nationally syndicated late-night entertainers. For thirteen weeks on Fox Television, as a replacement for Joan Rivers, and then for five and a half years on his own nationally syndicated show for Paramount,[101] Arsenio Hall gave audiences a "high voltage" act that was also a full-fledged representation of African American speech, musical acts, topics, and themes. Although faulted by some for his exaggerated interview style (he was called "Obsequio" for his fawning over guests), Arsenio Hall proved that showcasing Black culture and Black entertainment figures could appeal to mainstream White American audiences. *The Arsenio Hall Show* consistently beat Ted Koppel's *Nightline* and frequently came in number two in the ratings to Johnny Carson's *Tonight* show, often ranking number one with young audiences in the eighteen-to-thirty-four age group.

The Arsenio Hall show featured an over-the-top entrance on the huge sound stage of Paramount Studios in Los Angeles. To the sound of theme music he himself had composed, Hall entered the arena, weaving and dancing through rows of cheering fans, hugging, kissing, joking with members of the audience, and waving his index finger in circles. He had no sidekick, no band, nor a desk to sit behind, which he felt would separate him from his guests and the audience, and was a sign of authority not appropriate for his young audience. Arsenio Hall continued as one of late night's successful talk-show hosts until 1993, when the show ran into head-on competition with David Letterman. That was the year CBS used all its clout with its affiliates to "clear" stations for the new talk-show star in the 11:30 P.M. time slot in order to fulfill the conditions of its $14 million contract with Letterman.

Before the appearance of Arsenio Hall, late-night television had been the preserve of White talk-show hosts, an almost exclusively male preserve, with a tradition of hosts who came from the heart of the Midwest (Carson, Paar, Cavett, Letterman). When Nat King Cole's 1950s talk show went off the air after only a few weeks, he was quoted as saying that Madison Avenue was "afraid of the Dark."[102] Arsenio Hall, at least for a time, proved him wrong.

When Hall first appeared on Fox Television in 1987, replacing Joan Rivers' unsuccessful attempt to compete with Carson, he was an immediate hit with young audiences and hailed by critics as the nation's first new Black presence in TV talk since Oprah Winfrey. He expanded the limits of ethnic and racial representation on television and in the press with cover stories appearing in *Time, TV Guide, Ebony,* and the *Village Voice.*[103] Hall made a point, from his very first shows, to book not only African American celebrities like actor-comedian Eddie Murphy and film director Spike Lee, but also less well known African Americans like motivational speaker Les Brown and Johnetta Cole, the president of Spelman College.[104] He was willing to take risks and did theme shows on subjects like the environmental movement during Earth Day and the Los Angeles riots in 1992. As one of the first broadcasters to take his talk show out of the studio to talk to people in the streets of the Black community, he won national recognition and critical acclaim. Hall also broke Black musical acts like Snoop Doggy Dogg and Tupac, who were generally not given exposure on television, and he discussed issues affecting African American community life that had been up until then effectively excluded from late night.

Arsenio Hall got his biggest break with his own nationally syndicated show in part because of his close association with film star Eddie Murphy, a major power in Hollywood at the time. Hall was offered the syndication deal by the Paramount TV Studios, with executive producer status and creative control, after a starring role with Murphy in Paramount's *Coming to America*. Hall was a member of an influential group of young African Americans in Hollywood, the so-called "Black Pack," which included Robert Townsend (director of *Hollywood Shuffle*), Keenen Ivory Wayans (writer-producer of *In Living Color*), and Paul Mooney (for fifteen years head writer for comedian Richard Pryor). And Hall was, like Oprah Winfrey, quite conscious of being an African American role model. He felt he could identify with the "hip-hop" generation and use his personal influence to open doors for other African American entertainers and artists. In 1988, when he announced his new contract with Paramount for a reported $12 million, he told reporters, "As a Black man I see myself making an attempt to not only make people laugh, but to make history . . . That's what my deal [with Paramount] is all about. It gives me an opportunity to bring a lot of minority performers into a situation they might not normally get . . . without me pushing it."[105] On another occasion he described his show as "a party at a black man's house."[106]

Indeed, when Arsenio Hall left the air in May 1994, his departure left a void in late-night TV. In between his first exciting years on the air (he was named *TV Guide*'s "TV Person of the Year" in 1990) and his departure from television in 1994, bitter and defiant, Arsenio Hall participated in expanding the notion of who and what could appear on late-night TV.

NEW CONSCIOUSNESS OF THE POWER OF TV TALK

By the end of the 1980s and beginning of the 1990s, and then into the 1990s, a number of new books began to appear about the TV talk show. Students of journalism and public sphere theorists debated the power of TV talk to expand or contain public discourse. Patricia Priest's *Public Intimacies* highlighted the experiences of guests on daytime talk shows, finding that they often had their own very clear strategies in their appearances on nationwide television. Jeanne Heaton and Nona Wilson debated the impact of talk shows on mental health. Jane Shattuc's *The Talking Cure* analyzed the history, production, and social issues dealt with by TV talk shows, and included several close studies of TV talk texts. Wayne Munson attempted to give a panoramic view of the TV talk show and its cultural history in *All Talk: The Talkshow in Media Culture.* This list is by no means inclusive. This new awareness of the talk show as a cultural and social force encouraged a reevaluation of the history of the talk show as a genre. The next chapters look at the kinds of talk that were occurring in the 1990s as audiences and critics became increasingly aware of the form and as trends in the economics and distribution networks affected all talk formats.

Major talk-show hosts remain visual as well as verbal icons long after their shows go off the air. New generations of viewers become aware of these hosts through kinescopes or videotapes of their shows, through clips of "classic" talk shows they have seen in retrospectives and reruns, and through the lingering image of the publicity photograph. These illustrations document the careers of major talk-show hosts over five decades of television. The publicity image, a carefully staged moment frozen in time, does much to reveal the talk-show host's persona as the viewer knows it. Such images, used in press packets for journalists, featured in articles by newspapers and magazines, and adorning the covers of mass circulation magazines, also reveal the role of the press in not simply informing but promoting the talk-show host's image, amplifying and reinforcing that image to a public that loves to read about, talk about, follow (and sometimes stalk) the personal lives of its stars.

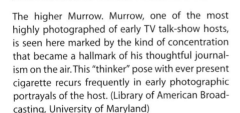

SEE IT NOW:
A RETROSPECTIVE

Photograph of Edward R. Murrow courtesy of CBS Inc.

The higher Murrow. Murrow, one of the most highly photographed of early TV talk-show hosts, is seen here marked by the kind of concentration that became a hallmark of his thoughtful journalism on the air. This "thinker" pose with ever present cigarette recurs frequently in early photographic portrayals of the host. (Library of American Broadcasting, University of Maryland)

The lower Murrow. The "lower" Murrow was garrulous, witty, and quite charming as he inserted himself into the homes of his guests from the comfort of his "picture window" in the New York studio of *Person to Person*. (Library of American Broadcasting, University of Maryland)

The collaborative Murrow. An informal moment of Murrow at work with *Person to Person* coproducers John Aaron and Jesse Zousmer. Most viewers never saw Aaron and Zousmer. This photograph shows the kind of coordination and teamwork that went into each production of *Person to Person*. (Library of American Broadcasting, University of Maryland)

Arthur Godfrey. Godfrey is represented here in a characteristically impish pose, head resting on hand while holding the radio headset that became the trademark of his first radio/television simulcasts on CBS. (Postcard used to publicize the Arts and Entertainment Biography, *Arthur Godfrey: Broadcasting's Forgotten Giant*)

Dave Garroway. Garroway would say "peace" and flash this sign at the end of each show. Garroway inhabited a world of his own invention on *Today*. (Library of American Broadcasting, University of Maryland)

Monkey business on *Today*. Though Garroway's animal companion was important in building children and family viewership for *Today* on NBC, the chimpanzee "J. Fred Muggs" was also problematic. J. Fred could get into ugly moods and occasionally bit people, leaving wounds and lawsuit worries for the legal department. (Library of American Broadcasting, University of Maryland)

Arlene Francis. Francis presented intelligent public and cultural affairs discussions for daytime audiences. Her *Home* show served as a precursor to Phil Donahue's audience-participation talk show two decades later. (Library of American Broadcasting, University of Maryland)

Steve Allen: in performance under the marquee of the Ed Sullivan theater and preparing copy to go on the air. Allen was a comedy writer as well as announcer. What sounded like spontaneous witticisms were often written comedy sketches. (Library of American Broadcasting, University of Maryland)

Jack Paar on set, talking with celebrity gossip columnist Elsa Maxwell during a commercial break. (Library of American Broadcasting, University of Maryland)

Paar's portrait on the cover of his informally written autobiography captures the host's geniality and charm, and reminds viewers of his gentle, quizzical, and often unpredictable relationship with his audience. (*P.S. Jack Paar: An Entertainment*)

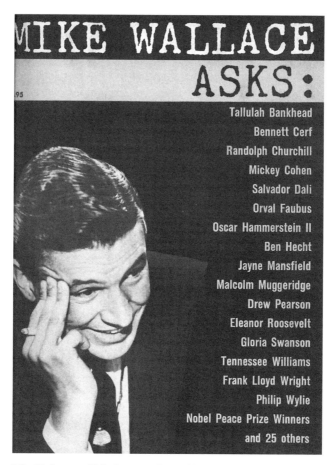

MIKE WALLACE ASKS:

Tallulah Bankhead
Bennett Cerf
Randolph Churchill
Mickey Cohen
Salvador Dali
Orval Faubus
Oscar Hammerstein II
Ben Hecht
Jayne Mansfield
Malcolm Muggeridge
Drew Pearson
Eleanor Roosevelt
Gloria Swanson
Tennessee Williams
Frank Lloyd Wright
Philip Wylie
Nobel Peace Prize Winners
and 25 others

Mike Wallace on *Night Beat*. On the starkly lit *Night Beat* set, Wallace's interviews were hard hitting but leavened by frequent flashes of wit and charm. (Cover of *Mike Wallace Asks: Highlights from 46 Controversial Interviews*)

Merv Griffin. Griffin cracks up in response to a deadpan remark by veteran radio and television performer Jack Benny. The ensemble talk of Benny's radio and television family was a direct precursor of the ad-libs and self-referencing talk of Griffin and also Johnny Carson, who was a guest host for Benny and inherited Benny's producer, Fred de Cordova. (Library of American Broadcasting, University of Maryland)

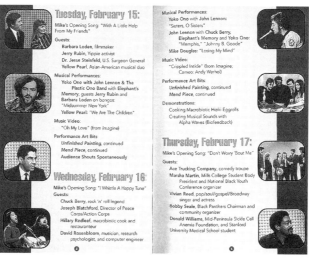

Mike Douglas (on left in first TV screen). During the week of February 14–18, 1972, Douglas invited singer-composer John Lennon and his wife, Yoko Ono, to cohost the show. Under Yoko Ono's leadership, the couple conducted a series of "conceptual" experiments and invited a range of unusual guests to explain the counterculture to a mass audience. (Spine and page from booklet of boxed set re-release, Rhino Video, 1998)

Dinah Shore. The predominant portrayal of Diana Shore was as the consummate "hostess" of 1970s television talk, as this full-page photographic portrait in *Ladies' Home Journal* indicates, but Shore was also portrayed as a woman with considerable clout in Hollywood in a *Time* magazine article, "Women of the Board." As in the case of Barbara Walters, who was leery of applying to herself the label of "feminist," portrayals of prominent women in TV talk in the 1970s did not always portray the split between work and home in simple terms. (*Ladies' Home Journal,* January 1972, pp. 100–101; *Time* magazine, "Women of the Board," October 16, 1972, p. 85)

Johnny Carson. Producer Fred de Cordova included this photo in his memoirs on his life with Carson and the *Tonight* show. It was a "gift" from Carson when de Cordova first joined the show, notifying the new producer of the host's well-known penchant for firing producers at turning points in his career. The names crossed out are those of Carson's four previous producers. (Fred de Cordova, "Welcome to the Tonight Show," in *Johnny Came Lately*, p. 25)

A pop pantheon, 1991. This cover of a 1991 *National Enquirer* special edition shows one of the ways in which popular magazines establish an iconography of stardom. This one shows magnitude of stardom by size and placement, and includes, counterclockwise from the left, Johnny Carson, Sally Jessy Raphaël, Arsenio Hall, Kathie Lee Gifford, Regis Philbin, David Letterman, Joan Rivers, Phil Donahue, Oprah Winfrey, and Geraldo Rivera. In the center are (left to right) "Dr. Ruth" Westheimer, Jay Leno, and Jenny Jones. (1991 *National Enquirer* Special Edition, "Secrets and Scandals of the Talk Show Stars")

VIDEODRONE THROUGH THE AGES
Bottom to top, right to left: Dave Garroway, Steve Allen, Jack Paar, Dick Cavett, Merv Griffin, Phil Donahue, Joan Rivers, Johnny Carson, David Letterman

A pop canon, 1986. This pyramid of TV sets represents talk-show hosts from five decades in an *Esquire* article by television critic Tom Shales. It attempts a historical canon of significant talk-show hosts rather than a simple pantheon of momentary popularity. ("Videodrone through the Ages," *Esquire,* November 1986)

THE TALK OF TV

Newsweek

SEPTEMBER 1, 1969   50c

Merv Griffin
Joey Bishop
Johnny Carson

The first late-night talk-show wars. This "prop" shot of Merv Griffin, Joey Bishop, and Johnny Carson (top to bottom) came out on September 1, 1969. Smaller insets of contenders David Frost and Dick Cavett along with pictures of "Permanent Second Fiddles" Regis Philbin, Ed McMahon, and Arthur Treacher appeared on the inside pages. This edition of *Newsweek* came out during the height of the first late-night talk-show wars. Magazine publicity of this kind hyped talk-show ratings and established wider recognition for the talk show as a genre. (*Newsweek,* September 1, 1969)

TONIGHT'S FIGHT CARD

RIVERS Vs. CARSON

And now you'll be able to tune in on Joan Rivers when Johnny Carson's on the air. She'll be on an independent television late night talk show next fall, head-to-head opposite the man who gave her the first big late-night TV break. **Full story on page 3**

Joan Rivers vs. Johnny Carson, 1986. This picture headline from the *New York Daily News* makes it seem as if there is a genuine ratings battle going on between Carson, the long-established "King" of late-night comedy, and contender Joan Rivers. In fact, given Carson's dominant position with his network affiliates and the fledgling status of Rivers' small number of Fox Network stations, Rivers never had a chance. (*New York Daily News*, May 7, 1986)

ISRAEL: RISE OF THE RABBIS
The Surge of the Religious Right

ewsweek

Trash TV

From the Lurid To the Loud, Anything Goes

Geraldo Rivera

Geraldo Rivera as an "action" reporter in 1972. He had been taught to wear his shirt collar open at the neck during a workshop at the Columbia School of Journalism by a veteran producer in the New York market, and was described in *Newsweek* magazine as "one of the hottest young reporters in the country." (*Newsweek*, July 17, 1972, p. 72)

Geraldo Rivera on the cover of *Newsweek*. Geraldo's nose was broken after a 1988 melee between an outraged African American civil rights activist and a representative of the White Aryan Resistance Youth. The picture became a symbol of the excesses of "trash talk." (*Newsweek*, November 15, 1988)

BILL MOYERS

A·WORLD·OF·IDEAS

Conversations with thoughtful men and women about American life today and the ideas shaping our future

Chinua Achebe
Nigerian novelist

Isaac Asimov
Writer

Mary Catherine Bateson
Anthropologist

Robert Bellah
Sociologist

Peter Berger
Sociologist

Sissela Bok
Ethicist

T. Berry Brazelton
Pediatrician

James MacGregor Burns
Historian

Noam Chomsky
Linguist

F. Forrester Church
Pastor

Henry Steele Commager
Historian

E. L. Doctorow
Novelist

Peter Drucker
Management professor

(continued on back)

Bill Moyers. Moyers looks thoughtfully out at viewer/readers from the cover of *A World of Ideas,* the book that accompanied his first PBS series of that title in 1989. The synergy created by best-selling books and videotapes enabled Moyers to receive major grants from private foundations and public television and put hundreds of hours of original TV talk on the air. (Cover of *A World of Ideas*)

Norman Mailer, Gore Vidal, Janet Flanner, and Dick Cavett at about the time they appeared together on the Dick Cavett Show of December 1, 1971. It was a combustible confrontation of three of the most accomplished conversationalists of their time —on one of the wittiest and most iconoclastic talk shows of its time. (*Time,* July 16, 1973, p. 60; *Atlantic Monthly,* March 1972, p. 85; *Newsweek,* September 8, 1971, p. 107; *Current Biography,* 1970, p. 75)

Larry King, with third wife, Sharon Lepore

Larry King, with fifth wife, Julie Alexander

"It's very hard for me to answer why people like me. I'm still amazed by it all."
— King quoted in The N.Y. Times

55

Larry King. A late-night radio personality turned national and later international cable host by a 1985 deal with CNN and Ted Turner, King was noted for his "softball" questions and story-telling ability, a relaxed habit of wearing suspenders on the air, and Hollywood-style serial monogamy. King is shown here in a 1994 article with two ex-wives and an "ex-flame." (*All Talk*, November–December 1994)

The New York Times Magazine

AUGUST 23, 1992 / SECTION 6

TENDER

Trap

THE
BARBARA
WALTERS
INTERVIEW

BY BILL
CARTER

Barbara Walters and Mike Wallace. They were the "Tender Trap" and "Grand Inquisitor," respectively, in cover stories written about them in the early 1990s. By this time they were the sole survivors on network television of the early founders of TV talk. (*New York Times Magazine,* August 23, 1992, and *TV Guide,* November 6–12, 1993)

TV GUIDE ®

Nov. 6–12
89¢

Sweeps Guide

- Lonesome Dove II
- Waltons' Reunion
- Julia Roberts Talks
- JFK Remembered

Inside
60
Minutes

25 Years of Tough Guys and Gritty Scoops

PLUS:
Mike Wallace by
Bob Woodward

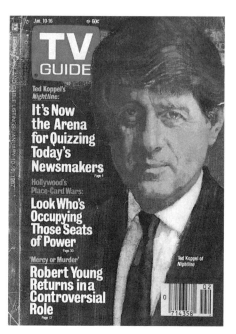

Ted Koppel. The consistency of these portraits is what sets them apart. Representing a period from January 1987 to February 1989, these carefully lit publicity portraits echo Koppel's public image as a statesman of television news broadcasting. (*TV Guide,* January 10–16, 1987; *The Washington Post Magazine,* February 26, 1989; *Newsweek,* June 15, 1987)

Phil Donahue. He was the recognized "king" of daytime talk in the 1980s and early 1990s. Press portraits included recurrent references to his religious Catholic upbringing and his microphone as a sacerdotal emblem as well as a directional signal for talk. (*TV Guide,* June 27–July 3, 1992, cover and picture from p. 6; *Washington Post TV Week,* November 15–22, 1992)

Oprah Winfrey. The sequence of photos represents moments in the drama of "Soap Oprah," as one headline writer put it. They appeared in 1993. Continually gaining in news-worthiness and stature through all of the twists and turns in her career, by January 2000 Winfrey had been named "woman of the new century" by *Newsweek* magazine, had her own production company (Harpo), and was the successful publisher of a mass circulation magazine. (*Redbook,* September 1993, p. 95; "*O*": *The Oprah Magazine,* September 2001)

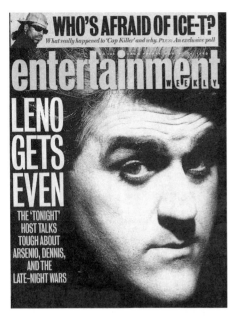

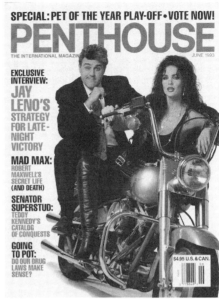

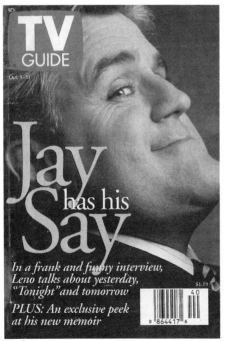

Jay Leno. The three front-page images here, from 1992, 1993, and 1996, cover three stages in the evolving press image of Jay Leno. At first, the press images of Leno were contradictory, contrived, and constrained. In the 1992 portrait he is seen as embattled, his face a sea of grain, trapped in the glare of a spotlight. A year later, Leno's flair for publicity was beginning to emerge more clearly. By 1996 he was the self-confident "co-king" of late-night comedy talk. (*Entertainment Weekly*, August 14, 1992; *Penthouse*, June 1993; *TV Guide*, October 5–11, 1996)

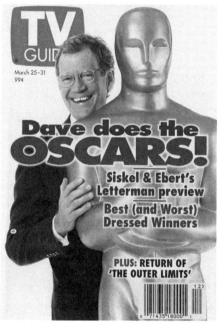

David Letterman in the 1990s. In contrast to the emerging consistency of Leno's image as a working comedian, press portraits of David Letterman during this period portray him as sad, beaming, startled—a man in conflict, who does not appear to be at home in his skin. (*Esquire,* September 1991; *All Talk* magazine, November–December 1994, p. 50; *TV Guide,* March 25–31, 1995, the year that Letterman hosted the Oscars)

Prop shots in the 90s. Press portraits in the 1990s often included props: here, for instance, Bill Maher (gleefully poised to launch a folded-up copy of the Constitution as a paper plane), Jerry Springer (made up as a victim of one of his own brawls), and Conan O'Brien when he first went on the air in 1993. His placard reads: "You don't know me. I was given the 12:30 a.m. talk slot on NBC and I'm going to need your help. . . ." (*U.S. News & World Report*, January 20, 1997; *Esquire*, January 1999; *Vanity Fair*, July 1993)

Garry Shandling. The self-reflexive comedian appears here as himself with an article about his on-air alter ego "Larry Sanders." (*Esquire,* July 1998)

Rosie O'Donnell. Rosie O'Donnell is proclaimed "Queen of Nice" in this *Newsweek* cover, a distinct contrast to the purveyors of Trash Talk like Jerry Springer who were still rolling up impressive ratings despite the opposition of many television critics. (*Newsweek,* July 15, 1996)

The Most Trusted Source for Campaign News.
(well, almost.)

The power and prejudice of political comedy.
By Marshall Sella

Jay Leno with political buttons, fall 2000. The two-to-one ratio of buttons was intended to support an article that argued that political jokes in TV talk were slanted by the politics of the comedy writers and hosts—and that Leno was a "liberal" comedy commentator. Leno said he believed exactly the opposite—that comedians go after "targets of opportunity." Here, however, he put the photo opportunity before his own opinion and obliged the *New York Times* with the image it wanted. (*New York Times Magazine*, September 24, 2000)

Arsenio Hall. For a while at the end of the 1980s, this "hip, hyperkinetic host" competed with Leno and Letterman for the top spot in late night. The first Black host to open up significant talk space for Black artists on TV, Hall was known for his trademarked gestures: two fingers pointed up and out (as pictured here on the cover of *Time* magazine) or a fist waving in the air in circles as he pumped up the energy of his "weeknightly party." (*Time,* November 13, 1989)

News, comedy, and politics converge: presidential candidate Bill Clinton plays the saxophone on the *Arsenio Hall Show* in June 1992; Al Gore debates Ross Perot on *Larry King Live* in 1992; a pop canon of political humorists living and dead—left to right, Will Rogers, Jay Leno, Bill Maher, Mark Twain, and David Letterman. (*All Talk* magazine, November–December 1994; illustration by Thomas Fluharty for *U.S. News & World Report,* January 20, 1997)

U.S.NEWS

JULY 25, 1994   & WORLD REPORT $2.50

INSIDE THE SEAMY WORLD OF TABLOID TV

A SPECIAL REPORT

O. J. Simpson. Simpson situated prominently among other characters of tabloid TV talk in 1994, only a month after his arrest. In 1995, with virtually all news and entertainment hosts covering the trial and eventual "not guilty" verdict, the O. J. Simpson case stoked a veritable talk-show industry, with O. J. Simpson as an African American male image now turned negative, balanced by a new "positive" African American male image: Johnnie Cochran. (*U.S. News & World Report,* July 25, 1994)

Regis Philbin and Kelly Ripa. Though a veteran TV talk personality, Regis Philbin's role as a successful TV talk game show host on *Who Wants to Marry A Millionaire?* catapulted him to new recognition, fame, and profitability in the early 2000s. Kathie Lee Gifford was replaced by Kelly Ripa, who proved to have the right "chemistry" with Philbin to sustain the dueling "couples" formula, a reprise of the romantic antagonism of screwball comedy and the "couple" shows of early TV talk. (*People Weekly,* February 19, 2001)

Jon Stewart was included on the cover of *Time* magazine as America's "Best TV Host" in 2001. Stewart's political news satires were recognized by a Peabody Award for his "Indecision 2000" series on *The Jon Stewart Daily Show.* The Peabody citation read: "No one was safe, and no topic was sacrosanct as they chased celebrities, political figures and ordinary people-on-the-street in their quest for unpredictable and hilarious 'news.'" (*Time,* July 9, 2001)

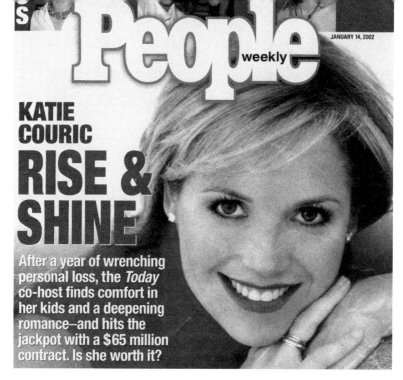

JANUARY 14, 2002

People weekly

KATIE COURIC

RISE & SHINE

After a year of wrenching personal loss, the *Today* co-host finds comfort in her kids and a deepening romance—and hits the jackpot with a $65 million contract. Is she worth it?

Katie Couric, seen here with NBC *Today* show coanchor Bryant Gumbel, achieved new status when she garnered a record-breaking $65 million four-year contract from NBC. Sympathy and interest in her personal life heightened over the decade with the death of her husband, her single-mother status, her new boyfriend (producer Tom Werner), and her new life as a talk-show celebrity. (*People Weekly,* January 14, 2002)

EIGHT
THE FIFTH CYCLE (1990–1995)
News as Entertainment

After fifty years on the air, the TV talk show was no longer a vague but somewhat undefined creation of live television. It had emerged as a full-fledged, critically recognized genre, and critics and viewers alike were now taking the talk show seriously.

In the hands of some host-producer teams TV talk hearkened back to earlier forms; in the hands of others it looked forward to experiments with new blends and directions as the decade came to an end. And in some cases shows simply took older forms and intensified or exaggerated them. Thus, talk shows during the 1990s could be characterized as "retro," "hybrid," or "baroque." Shows that institutionalized or consolidated older forms of talk would include the CNN television version of Larry King's long-standing late-night radio show, now called *Larry King Live*, and the *Tonight* show of Jay Leno, which preserved many of the elements of Carson's format in attempting to maintain his mainstream audience base. Another "retro" format was the morning comedy/variety show of Rosie O'Donnell and her producers, who consciously worked to re-create the atmosphere and staging of the successful syndicated daytime shows of the 1970s, particularly those of Mike Douglas, Merv Griffin, and Dinah Shore. At the same time, the news and public-affairs programs of John McLaughlin and Rush Limbaugh and the "reality-based" programming of Ricki Lake and Jerry Springer represented a "baroque" trend in which certain talk-show forms were pushed to their limits and past them. Hosts like Lake and Springer took

Donahue's audience-participation format into the realm of spectacle and carnival, turning it into emotional mud-wrestling in which dysfunctional couples and families aired their problems without the faintest desire to solve them. Audiences loved these shows. Finally, shows like Bill Maher's *Politically Incorrect,* and even more radically Garry Shandling's *The Larry Sanders Show,* experimented with new blends or hybrids of talk-show forms, sometimes mixing news and comedy in what might be called, as in the case of *The Larry Sanders Show,* television vérité.

While talk-show hosts and producers were blending, distilling, and pushing the limits of TV talk, the 1990s were witnessing convergence of technology and confluence of ownership in all forms of talk programming. New combinations of digital audio and video talk were springing up everywhere. While new talk products were multiplying and competing with each other in new technological forms, including the Internet, the ownership of these talk products and channels was becoming concentrated in fewer and fewer hands.

The economic consolidation of the broadcasting and telecommunications industries had begun in the 1980s when General Electric took over NBC, ABC–Cap Cities became the new corporate owner of ABC, and CBS was bought by Laurence Tisch from the Paley family interests.[1] By the end of the 1990s Rupert Murdoch's Fox Broadcasting had become a competitor to the three major networks and emerged as a fourth network. In the 1990s, Walt Disney purchased ABC–Cap Cities for $18.84 billion with its worldwide ESPN sports network, and Time Warner purchased Turner Broadcasting for $6.88 billion with its worldwide CNN (Cable News Network). Westinghouse merged with CBS in another $5.04 billion mega-deal.[2]

Despite the consolidation of financial interests represented by these large network sales, the traditional Big 3 — NBC, CBS, and ABC — and the new fourth network, Fox, now faced competition coming from cable and the burgeoning videocassette industry as well as other forms of new technology (computers, Internet channels, and videogames). Though network-advertising revenues doubled through the 1980s (from $5 billion in 1980 to almost $10 billion in 1992), cable profits grew even faster. Advertising revenues on cable television, only $45 million in 1980, exploded to almost $2 billion in 1992.[3] Public television expanded, too, with 349 stations on the air by 1992. Census data show the average yearly number of hours of network television watched by each person dropping from 1,000 hours in 1984 to 900 hours in 1992. During this same period average cable viewing grew from 185 hours a year in 1984 to 526 hours a year in 1992; home video use from nine to forty-six hours a year.[4] By 1990, 70 percent of all U.S. homes had videotape recorders and just under 60 percent had cable. Half of the cable homes subscribed to a "premium" service of some kind.[5] Dramatic and informational products flowed into this expanded and increasingly volatile market.

A lot of the new entertainment product was talk—sports talk, comedy talk, news talk, and specialized talk shows that covered health and exercise, home improvement, home shopping, finance, cooking, religious topics, and self-help programs of every kind. And people were talking to each other through computer monitors in other ways as well. By 1990, 27 percent of American homes possessed computers and an estimated 20 million homes subscribed to some form of Internet service.[6] By mid-decade 35 percent of American families and 50 percent of American teenagers had a personal computer at home, and thirty million people were on the Internet.[7] The speed of computer/video technology interface was picking up. As Nicholas Negroponte of MIT's Media Lab pointed out in his best-selling book, *Being Digital,* by mid-decade 90 percent of all new computers were being prepared for delivery pre-set with CD-ROM or modem capability.[8] Video "streaming" was increasingly discussed and put into practice by advanced communication organizations with broadband technological resources.

In the face of all this new competition the traditional broadcast networks' share of audience fell. From 1980 to 1990, the networks' share dropped from 90 to approximately 65 percent of the national prime-time viewing audience and nothing appeared to be reversing the trend.[9]

In the competitive environment of the 1990s network executives found themselves under increasing pressure to turn profits and pay off debts they had inherited in their takeovers.[10] Talk programming was one solution to their problems. It was relatively easy to produce, relatively low cost, and if the show managed to maintain itself on the air for a period of time, it could become a steady profit center. That had been Johnny Carson's selling point to NBC for years. Moreover, a successful national talk show became identified with the network that broadcast it, shoring up the network's institutional image with its affiliates.

In an era of concentrating ownership but intense media competition and fragmentation, this is exactly what the major broadcast networks needed. While their dominant position had been shaken, the networks still maintained an advantage over cable in reaching a mass audience, and they still commanded substantial advertising revenues, a third of the estimated $30 billion spent on advertising nationally and locally in 1992.[11] The networks were still the "massest" of the media, and they could reach the largest mass audience at any one time.

With the market so glutted with advertising pitches and informational and entertainment products, the "fresh talk" of national television served several purposes. Talk shows were a form of programming that depended on the present-tense engagement of their audience and were thus ideal for topical commentary and discussion. They were good forums for breaking news, and for parody and satire on the news. Talk shows like Bill Maher's *Politically Incorrect* that engaged in live or as-if-live debates contrasted vividly with the "canned" informational sources of news, commercials, or standardized entertainment products. When the O. J. Simpson verdict was announced in October 1995, national TV talk shows participated in a national talk event that was the most immediate source of coverage for most Americans. Viewers could watch "live" coverage on the O. J. Simpson verdict on every channel. Serving as a complement to next-day print media, the television talk show became the operational center of the "public sphere" during this time, elaborating upon, as well as filtering and channeling, the meaning of the event.

To summarize, the television talk of the last decade of the 1990s had three prominent thrusts. It institutionalized and consolidated older forms of TV talk. It experimented with previous forms of TV talk and pushed them to new extremes. It blended and created hybrids of previous forms of TV talk.

By the 1990s, the TV talk show was no longer a vague but somewhat undefined concomitant to live broadcasting. It was now a recognized cultural and ideological force within American society. With fifty years of history on the air, the talk show finally had emerged as a full-fledged, critically and commercially recognized genre of television.

LENO, LETTERMAN, AND THE LATE-NIGHT TALK-SHOW WARS (1992–1995)

Product wars bring attention to product lines and help stabilize them. This is especially true when the competition is between two product lines, like Pepsi and Coke, that dominate a market. Similarly, Jay Leno and David Letterman emerged as the two dominant late-night entertainment talk products of the 1990s, the competition between them centering at first around the question of who would succeed Johnny

Carson as "king" of late night. The first stages of the late-night talk-show wars did not, however, enthrone a particular host. What the late-night talk show actually accomplished was a more entrenched institutionalization of the late-night talk show itself.

Prelude

With Johnny Carson's announcement of his retirement in May 1991, a wide range of candidates entered the competition to succeed him. On August 16, 1992, a lead article in the *New York Times* "Arts and Leisure" section surveyed the field and announced: "Here's Everybody! After Carson, A Host of Late-Night Wannabes."[12] The article reviewed Carson's historical competitors, all of whom had faltered in their drive to best or "unseat" the king of late night. Joey Bishop (ABC, 1967–1969), Dick Cavett (ABC, 1969–1975), Joan Rivers (Fox, 1986–1987), Pat Sajak (CBS, 1989–1990), and Ron Reagan (syndicated, 1991) were mentioned. The article "handicapped" Carson's competition early 1990s. It gave each of them a label: Whoopi Goldberg (mass appeal), Dennis Miller (hip and quirky), Chevy Chase (flip prankster), David Letterman (sardonic style), Arsenio Hall (pop icon), Rush Limbaugh (radio conservative), Jane Whitney (intense reporter), and Jay Leno (affable comic).[13] David Letterman's name was mentioned as only one of many at this point. Indeed, by the end of the decade, Letterman seemed to be slipping, a talk product of the 1980s whose usefulness seemed to have outlived its time.

The *New York Times* article pointed out that Carson himself had only been averaging a 5 rating in his last years, well below his twenty-three-year average of 7.2 and his peak in the 1974–1975 season of 10. Jay Leno, Carson's replacement of only three months when the *New York Times* article was written, had maintained but not exceeded Carson's numbers. Was late-night television "oversubscribed?" the *Times* article asked.

A new audience for late-night talk in the early 1990s was an expanding base of young urban viewers with disposable incomes that was increasingly attractive to late-night advertisers. From 1970 to 1992 the late-night listening audience expanded from 18 to 27 million.[14] The networks were keenly aware of this audience, and national syndicators and the new Fox network were interested as well. By summer 1993, a year after the *New York Times* article, there had been a shakeout of the field of contenders for Carson's throne. Two had risen to the top: Jay Leno and David Letterman. Each had proved to advertisers and network officials that he could deliver a solid, profit-making, commercial talk vehicle. And the rivalry between these ex-comedy comrades and friends had inherent dramatic possibilities.

Leno and Letterman had known each other since their stand-up comedy days in Los Angeles, with Letterman introducing Leno to national TV audiences on his NBC *Late Night.* At first, Letterman seemed to have the upper hand. But despite early problems getting his new version of the *Tonight* show established, Leno was persistent and determined. By mid-decade Leno had caught up with Letterman in the ratings. He maintained Carson's basic format while adapting it to the demands of a post-Letterman generation of viewers. A look at the talk-show wars between David Letterman and Jay Leno shows us how publicity, business clout, and the clash of distinctive talk-show personalities advanced talk "products" in the 1990s while refining, rather than redefining, late-night talk as a subgenre.

Jay Leno

By the time he arrived on the set of *Tonight* in May 1992 as NBC's replacement for Johnny Carson, Jay Leno was known as "the hardest-working man" in show business. Typically he was on the road for as many as 250 engagements a year.

Born James Douglas Muir Leno on April 28, 1950, in New Rochelle, New York (three years after Letterman), Leno was the son of an Italian-American insurance agent from Andover, Massachusetts. At insurance company conventions, Angelo Leno gave the comic introductions of the vice president. Indeed, the senior Leno never missed an occasion to present his humorous take on life, and this ability impressed his son. While his father's side of the family were "boisterous, fun and food-loving Italians," Leno's Scottish relatives believed in restraint and keeping a lid on their emotions. His mother had immigrated to the United States from Scotland when she was ten. In 1959 the Leno family moved to Andover, where Leno acquired his working-class New England accent.

Leno, like Letterman, honed his comedy talent in his college years. A student at Emerson College in Boston, Leno chose a speech major because it allowed him to take oral final exams. He had a form of dyslexia that affected his ability to read, but he retained almost everything he heard in class. Rejected by the college's comedy workshop, he got together with classmate Gene Braunstein, later producer of the sitcom *Who's the Boss!*, to form a comedy team called "Gene and Jay" that played coffee houses and clubs in the Boston area. Later Leno soloed in a wide range of comedy clubs in the Boston and New York area. By the early 1970s he was a familiar presence on the New York comedy scene.

In 1974, the year before Letterman launched his own Los Angeles comedy career, Leno moved to Hollywood's entertainment capital. He faced a number of rebuffs. A William Morris agent told him he would never go anywhere, and an NBC casting director told him he should dye his hair and recast his jutting jaw. Leno persisted. A generous supporter of other comics, Leno also was fiercely competitive. "My slogan has always been: Sooner or later, the other person is going to have to eat, sleep, drink, go on vacation, have sex, do something. And that's when you catch him."[15] Along with his drive and durability, Leno was always accessible: to customers and people in the comedy clubs, to fellow comics, to the press. "I'm not one of those guys who run out the door once the show is over," he said in a 1996 interview. "I like people—I think that comes across. . . . If you're working a high-school gym in Des Moines, it puts things in perspective."[16] In addition, Leno was very analytical about his comedy routines. He would test them out in every conceivable comedy club and work late into the night to perfect a routine or series of jokes.

In an interview in the *Washingtonian* magazine in 1993, Leno explained his rules for political humor. The first, he said, was never to let people know how you feel politically. "And not to get personal," he added. "I once saw a comedian do a whole bit about [President] Reagan's neck, how it looked like a turkey's, and I told him afterward, 'That's not a political joke—a person can't help the fact that he's old. Go after what he says and does—that's political humor.'"[17] Another of Leno's rules: "Go after whoever's in power . . . you're not making fun of the man, but of the office. Whoever's vice president is going to catch it, and Quayle [Vice President to George Bush, 1988–1992] made it a bit easier with some of the things that happened. But it's never really personal."[18] When questioned about comedy's political influence and power, Leno said, "You don't change anybody's mind, you just reinforce what they already believe."[19]

Leno's remarks in the *Washingtonian* are a succinct statement of mainstream ideology in TV comedy. Some analytic case studies support Leno's observation. Constantinos Economopoulos, for example, came to a similar conclusion in his study of monologues from the *Tonight* show from July through November 1992. During this period of time,

George Bush, the sitting President, "was the subject of 154 jokes, more than twice that of Clinton. Further, the percent negativity for Clinton was 81 percent to Perot's 88 percent and Bush's 93 percent."[20] Thus, as a candidate seeking office, Bill Clinton had faired relatively well in comedy routines—and in public opinion polls as well.[21] The situation reversed itself six years later, when Clinton had been President for one and one-half terms and was the butt of a comedy onslaught at the time of the Monica Lewinsky scandal. Now, as sitting President, Clinton, the ensconced symbol of power, was the target.[22]

Leno's skills as a comedian were considerable and acknowledged by all. But his skills as a strategist within the business of broadcasting would be put to the test when he decided, with his personal manager, Helen Kushnick, to go for the job of host of the *Tonight* show.

Leno on *Tonight* (1992–1995)

Things did not look promising in Jay Leno's first days as host of the *Tonight* show. Some of Leno's problems stemmed from a show that was obviously quite raw and had not had time to find itself. Other problems came from Leno's producer, Helen Kushnick, whose aggressive take-no-prisoners style began to antagonize many.[23] Leno's "nice-guy" image did not seem to fit as the successor to the crafty, indomitable Carson. On the other hand, Letterman, a tireless and obsessive perfectionist, kept his nightly appearances sharp-honed. His press notices became increasingly positive in this early period as Leno's went downhill.

Washington Post critic Tom Shales, a long-time Letterman supporter, panned Leno's first *Tonight* appearance. He pointed to a series of awkwardnesses in the new show. Jeff Jarvis, reviewing Leno's show in his "Couch Critic" column of *TV Guide*, thought Leno pitiful—a man "begging to be loved."[24] *USA Today* ran a cover story on Leno entitled, "Taking It on the Chin: Leno Deflects a Barrage of Criticism." One *Newsweek* critic thought that the negative reviews had gone too far, and argued that the press should call off its "Jay-Bashing."

While Leno's press was not good, his relationship with the NBC brass was. Leno gained internal support by his hard work, loyalty to the company, and willingness to sell the show twenty-four hours a day. He had the support of network executives like Warren Littlefield, and he worked assiduously to develop affiliate support as well. Just as his father had sold insurance door to door, Leno crossed the country doing stand-up and talking to local NBC executives. "My attitude was to go out and rig the numbers," Leno said. "To go out and actually meet the customers who buy your product just seems like sound business."[25] As a result of his consistent salesmanship and willingness to work within the NBC system, Leno was often able to tweak the noses of his employers in his comedy act without causing lasting harm. He could do things that in retrospect sounded outrageous—like listening in secretly to negotiations by NBC executives discussing his future—and somehow make it right in the end.

All of Leno's hard work eventually paid off. The late-night talk-show wars of 1992–1995 featured so prominently in the news that *New York Times* critic Bill Carter wrote a book about the competition between Leno and Letterman that was made into an HBO docudrama. Within two years a remarkable transformation had occurred. The HBO docudrama, which detailed Letterman's early triumph, seemed badly dated. By November 1995, Jay Leno and his NBC *Tonight* show team had shifted the balance of power in late night.[26]

The ratings picture tells the story. At the beginning of 1995, Letterman had a commanding lead with 5.3 in the ratings (i.e., 5.3 percent of all TV households were tuned to CBS) and a 16 share (16 percent of all stations on at the time).[27] By the end of the year, Leno had reversed these numbers. Leno now had a 4.7/14 ratings/share ratio to Letterman's 3.9/12. Not only that, he had consistently scored better than Letterman in the crucial eighteen-to-forty-nine-year-old age group, a category in which Letterman had always done well.[28] Critical attention and awards were building for the *Tonight* show as well. In September 1995, Leno's version of *Tonight* captured the Emmy for Outstanding Variety, Music, or Comedy Series—the same award Letterman had won in 1994.[29]

Media critics cited CBS's faltering prime-time lineup as one of the causes of Leno's success. CBS had lost affiliates to the new Fox network, which further eroded its audience. Letterman pointed out that Leno's ratings had never "come up" to his; his own ratings had simply "gone down."[30] Indeed, the ten-month ratings trend from January to October of 1995 showed the combined late-night talk-show ratings of Leno and Letterman slipping from 9.9 percent of all TV households to 8.6 percent, while Ted Koppel's *Nightline* held surprisingly strong. In the Manichaean logic of this two-person "war" for the top spot in late-night comedy talk, Leno's fate was tied to Letterman's. As Letterman went down, Leno went up. And the press was beginning to weigh in on Leno's side. If Leno never showed his true feelings beneath his ironman comedy routines and a schedule that awed even his own staff ("I'm convinced Jay's an alien," his executive producer was quoted as saying. "He can outlast anybody. I don't think he has red blood . . ."[31]), Letterman was portrayed as a case of walking nerve ends. Even when Letterman was still ahead in the ratings in 1995, there was, said *Time* critic Richard Zoglin, "uneasiness in the kingdom of Letterman."[32] Letterman had expanded his monologue, and his show was in every way "bigger, louder, flashier." It was also significantly "less adventurous. . . . The grumbly, peevish Letterman of Studio 6A days could sometimes be a drag," said Zoglin, "but the upbeat Letterman who resurfaced on CBS seemed strangely 'defanged.'"[33]

Longtime Letterman enthusiast Tom Shales of the *Washington Post* also noted the strain on Letterman and his entourage. In June 1996, he reported a string of "woes" that had afflicted the Letterman show during the preceding year. Letterman's performance as host of the Academy Award ceremonies had been widely panned. The CBS executive who had wooed the star to CBS, Howard Stringer, had left the network. Letterman's longtime director, Hal Gurnee, had gone into retirement, and his head writer, Rob Burnett, was stepping down.[34] Soon, producer Robert Morton would be reassigned to another part of the Letterman organization. Signs of struggle and dissatisfaction appeared at the top of the organization, and the "triumphant" pictures of Letterman with cigar in hand were replaced by pictures of a host with a distraught, furrowed, and anxious look on his face. By the summer of 1996, the formerly reticent host gave a "Dave (Really) Talks" interview to *Parade* magazine. The cover read: "The usually guarded host of *The Late Show with David Letterman* reveals his feelings about his father, his loves, fishing, Indiana and whether he'll quit late-night TV."[35] It was all very embarrassing for many longtime Letterman fans.

Nothing Letterman did seemed to offset Leno's ratings and publicity success. If anything, the publicity coming out of the Letterman camp had the opposite effect. Leno had been, if nothing else, consistent. He had become the "terminator" of stand-up comedy, an unstoppable force. As Letterman's image zigged and zagged, Leno's solidified.

Critics tried to account for Leno's new success and plumb the mysteries of his show-business personality. Profiles of Leno dwelt on certain themes. There was Jay Leno the master satirist of consumer society. Then there was Leno the genial corporate trickster—a loyal company man who could get away with playing tricks even on his own boss. And there was Jay Leno the robo-comic: a man who on the surface was a warm, humane, compassionate comedian, but whose comedy persona masked an almost inhuman imperviousness to the pain, insults, and daily degradations of show business. Finally, there was Leno the comedy technician who worked on jokes the way he worked on engines in his fleet of motorcycles and cars.

Some attributed Leno's success to his famous work ethic. Subsisting on four hours sleep a night, Jay Leno was characteristically at his *Tonight* show office in Burbank by nine o'clock each morning and rarely got home before nine or ten in the evening. By midnight Leno's friend, *Tonight* show writer Jimmy Brogan, would come over to Leno's hillside mansion and work until two or three in the morning honing the next day's monologue. While Carson's contracts steadily expanded his days off, giving him the chance to recuperate from the grueling daily schedule, Leno argued with network officials to give him *less* time off.[36] He told interviewer Bill Zehme in 1995 that he was "miserable." "To me, a week's vacation just means you're now a week behind."[37]

On the surface a nice, warm guy who just wanted to get along well with everyone, Jay Leno was clearly more complicated than that. Just beneath the genial surface was a man so driven that he could erase "problems" as if they never existed. Referring to his long, intimate, and ultimately painful relationship with personal manager Helen Kushnick, he told interviewer Bill Zehme, "I look at that whole relationship as like a bad two weeks out of my life. Never happened."[38]

By 1996 Jay Leno had joined Letterman and Carson as a national comedy icon. He had proved his staying power and ratings clout. The late-night talk-show wars had come full cycle. Jay Leno was head to head with Letterman, and his stock was rising. Of course, the situation, which had changed before, could change again. American popular culture seemed enthralled with battles between name products and personalities: Coke vs. Pepsi, Avis vs. Hertz, Letterman vs. Leno. The producer of the Letterman show had commented during the mid-1980s writers' strike that the TV brass just didn't "get it." Talk shows are not simply packaged. They are built from the center, he said, around their hosts.[39] Jay Leno and his producers had worked hard to revise the show from its center, making the set, the monologue, and the sensibility of the show a successful product of the American television marketplace. They had succeeded.

NEWS TALK AS ENTERTAINMENT AND POLITICS:
McLaughlin and King (1992–1995)

In the early 1990s a number of television talk-show hosts rose to national prominence by combining news, public affairs, and entertainment in new or recycled talk-show formats. These hosts continued the pattern, begun in the 1980s, of narrowing the distance between news and entertainment, sometimes blurring the distinction entirely. Two of the most prominent of the news/entertainment talk-show hosts during this period were John McLaughlin and Larry King, and 1992 proved to be a significant year for each. This was the year that talk shows became one of the principal forums for all three candidates in the national Presidential elections: Republican incumbent George Bush, Democratic challenger Bill Clinton, and third-party Presidential candidate Ross Perot. Presidential candidates appeared regularly in entertainment talk as well as on news shows. Bush, Perot, Clinton, and Democratic Vice Presidential candidate Al Gore appeared on the David Letterman, Arsenio Hall, and Jay Leno shows. Bill Clinton, a product of the anti–Vietnam War movement, represented a different generation of American voters than George Bush, a veteran of World War II. Other generational battles emerged, and were featured in the talk-show "wars" of the period. Some contenders succeeded in dislodging their more veteran competition and others did not. Just as Oprah Winfrey had come to challenge and then often establish rating dominance over her predecessor in daytime talk, Phil Donahue, during this period of the early 1990s newcomer Ricki Lake, a role model for "Generation X," challenged Winfrey with flamboyant "trash talk" that garnered high ratings and increasing buzz within the talk-show industry. Eventually, Winfrey's decision to take the "high road"—and the diversification of her name and talent in other directions—enabled her to retain her star status. Lake remained on the air but a relatively minor figure later in the decade.

TV talk shows became national plebiscites in the identity politics of the era. This was the period in which Rush Limbaugh with his fanatical "ditto-head" following from radio rose to new prominence on radio and television and that television host Larry King achieved titan status when third-party candidate Ross Perot announced his candidacy on *The Larry King Show,* live, and to instant headlines.

Two new talk-show formats blurred the lines between the "real" world of news and the "entertainment" world of fiction and comedy.

Bill Maher's *Politically Incorrect* on the Comedy Channel fused news talk and comedy. Garry Shandling's *The Larry Sanders Show* etched satires of TV talk by using real guests playing themselves in situations that were often improvised. *The Larry Sanders Show* relied heavily on Shandling's experience as one of the main guest hosts of Johnny Carson's *Tonight* show at the end of the 1980s.

The shows cited above blended news and entertainment as they became new sites of political and cultural identification. Hosts built talk constituencies either in syndication or on cable networks that reached national audiences. They were often "outsiders," sometimes consciously positioning themselves, like Limbaugh, as "rebels" who stood outside traditional styles and formats of TV talk. They gave old formats new and sometimes controversial twists.

In news and public affairs, John McLaughlin took the traditional panel show and news commentary/interview show into new territory. McLaughlin specialized in baroque versions of news talk that blended news and entertainment, issues and gossip, raising the decibel level and also ratings. McLaughlin's work (and Rush Limbaugh's as well) paralleled what Ricki Lake and Jerry Springer were doing in daytime "therapeutic" talk. Both news and therapeutic "relationship" shows represented carnivalesque transformations of daytime talk that delighted daytime audiences and brought in new ratings. By extending radio formats into television, hosts like King and Limbaugh were complemented by others who participated in "retro" trends. Just as Jay Leno's *Tonight* show represented a conscious return to the proscenium-arch tradition of Johnny Carson and Rosie O'Donnell reinvented the daytime variety entertainment hour, shows like *Larry King Live* represented continuity as well as change. The news talk shows of the early 1990s were extensions of, or exaggerations of, previous talk traditions. They represented a swing of the pendulum back as well as an extension forward into TV talk's fifth cycle on the air.

John McLaughlin, Provocateur

Television critic Howard Kurtz ends the opening chapter of his book on the rise of sensationalized forms of news talk in the 1990s as follows:

> The power of talk has changed the very fabric of the country. What was once a rather stodgy collection of middle-aged media

men engaged in polite debate has become a raucous and hugely profitable business whose collective racket seems to grow more deafening each week.[40]

One of those most responsible for this transformation is John McLaughlin. Born to second-generation Irish-American parents in the summer of 1927—his father was a furniture store owner—McLaughlin attended a Christian Brothers high school and entered a small Jesuit novitiate in New England at the age of eighteen to train for the priesthood. Political interests ran in the family. One uncle was president of the Providence city council, and another was the Rhode Island state health director. His father, too, had a long-term interest in politics. McLaughlin got his B.A. and master's degrees in philosophy and education at Boston College and did advanced studies at Stanford University before starting to teach in Jesuit high schools in Lenox, Massachusetts, and Fairfield, Connecticut. He finished his Ph.D. in Communications at Columbia University while on leave from Fairfield.[41]

McLaughlin's journalistic career began as an editor of *America*, the Manhattan-based Jesuit weekly opinion journal. In the 1960s he became widely known as a lecturer on social and ethical topics, particularly on sexual and family mores from the standpoint of the Catholic Church. "Father McLaughlin knows more about the *Playboy* ethic than most dedicated playboys," the chaplain of one university where McLaughlin spoke told a reporter.[42]

In 1970 McLaughlin left the staff of *America*, plunging directly into politics by running against Rhode Island's Democratic senator John Pastore, and losing, and then joined the staff of the Nixon administration in Washington as a speechwriter. McLaughlin described himself as a "centrist," midway between speechwriters Pat Buchanan (on the right) and Ray Price. At the time of Watergate, McLaughlin briefly became a very visible figure on Nixon's defense team, staging his own press conference in support of Nixon and appearing on *Donahue*, Tom Snyder's *Tomorrow*, and the *Dick Cavett Show*. He also appeared in a series of televised debates with columnist Bob Novak, who recalls that McLaughlin was even then talking about launching a talk show with "a more conservative twist."[43] In 1975 McLaughlin renounced his celibacy and married Ann Dore, who worked as a high-level administrator in the Nixon and Reagan administrations and joined her husband in running a public affairs and media relations consulting firm in Washington.[44]

McLaughlin was tired of the traditional roundtable news discussion shows on television, like *Face the Nation* and *Meet the Press.* He thought they were boring and stilted. With financial backing from a wealthy friend in the Nixon White House and the politically conservative Edison Electric Institute, McLaughlin launched *The McLaughlin Group* in 1982. For his original "Gang of Five," as McLaughlin liked to call his panel, he chose two newspaper columnists, Jack Germond and Bob Novak, and two reporters, Judith Miller of *The New York Times* and Chuck Stone of *The Philadelphia Daily News,* both of whom were soon replaced by two more outspoken panelists—Pat Buchanan, McLaughlin's old colleague in the Nixon White House, and Mort Kondracke of *The New Republic.*[45]

Beginning his new talk-show program just a year after Ronald Reagan had taken office, McLaughlin reflected the conservative mood of the country, generally supporting conservative Republican positions and ridiculing the Democratic opposition. Despite token liberal opposition within the panel, McLaughlin would "provoke his panelists," goading them into hurling epithets at each other and making "brash statements they would never make in print."[46] The result lived up to McLaughlin's dream of talk at an opinion-maker's bar, and it caught on. By its sixth year the show was carried by 200 PBS stations and five NBC affiliates. McLaughlin also conducted a weekly Washington TV interview show (*One on One*) and continued to write for print, notably as editor and columnist for the conservative *National Review.*

Each of McLaughlin's cast of panelists developed his or her own character on the air. As Kurtz describes the show, McLaughlin himself was the overbearing, opinionated father; Fred Barnes the preppy favorite son; Eleanor Clift a liberal-leaning sister; Mort Kondracke the straitlaced brother-in-law; and Pat Buchanan the pugnacious uncle. Occasional guests—Clarence Page, Michael Barone, and Mort Zuckerman, for example—formed an extended family of cousins. The "family" structure of *The McLaughlin Group* and the verbal fireworks that occurred each week unquestionably made the show entertaining.

Another talk-show host who fused news and entertainment to rise to prominence during this period was Larry King.

Larry King, Talkmeister

Larry King's on-air persona was as casual and laid back as McLaughlin's was heated. King had built his reputation on dialogue, listening, and questions that probed the objects of his own curiosity in both news and entertainment, and by the early 1990s was a familiar presence on late-night radio. In 1985 he made a deal with CNN's Ted Turner to bring his late-night radio interview show to television. That program, *Larry King Live,* turned the veteran radio broadcaster into a national and international television success.

Fusing a relaxed style, a flair for storytelling, and an intense curiosity in the social world, Larry King made his name by re-marking talk's traditional boundaries on the air. Like Johnny Carson, he specialized in traditional one-on-one interviews, asking questions and listening closely to what his interviewee said. For King, like Carson, television was still a "window on the world," a pipeline to political and social reality—not a fun-house mirror of images. Like Carson he wanted not to construct a world of play out of public images, but to get behind the public image, to discover the personal opinions of the celebrity guests who appeared on his show. In that sense he represented a throwback to an earlier broadcast era. King gained his basic training in the low-cost environment of late-night talk radio on a midnight to 5:30 A.M. shift in which commercial pressures did not make every word so costly.[47] This broadcast environment allowed him to give more airtime to his callers and interview guests than was common.

When King brought his radio show to television on CNN, a twenty-four-hour news network devoted to longer forms of news talk, he gave his interview guests the luxury of thirty minutes on the air to express their views. He did not confront or press them but gently moved them along as a curious friendly presence on the air. He was not a debater or challenger, and never claimed to be. On the contrary, his famous "softball" questions gave his callers and studio guests time to chart their own responses and to get out a fuller version of what they wanted to say. For this reason his show became a favored spot in the 1990s for politicians, for members of the legal establishment (the prosecution and defense teams in the O. J. Simpson case, for example), and for entertainers of all kinds. What Larry King had rediscovered was, as Howard Kurtz put it, "the art of the schmooze."[48]

Born Lawrence Harvey Zeiger, in Brooklyn in 1934, Larry King worked behind a microphone for most of his adult life.[49] He started out on radio in 1957 at WAHR, a 250-watt station in Miami. His love of talk developed in his youth. His father, a Jewish immigrant from Eastern Europe, owned a bar and grill in Brooklyn, and young Larry enjoyed listening to the neighborhood people. His love of broadcasting included devoted listening to Red Barber announcing Brooklyn Dodger games.

Though the young Larry Zeiger had little formal education past a diploma from Brooklyn's Lafayette High School, he discovered that he had a talent for storytelling, talking, and radio. Within three years after high school graduation he was putting this talent to use on his own mid-morning talk show at WIOD from Pumpernick's Restaurant in Miami. He chatted with Don Rickles, Ella Fitzgerald, Danny Thomas, and Lenny Bruce, served as the emcee for Jackie Gleason's birthday party, and became a well-known Miami figure. King's late-night national radio talk show, out of Mutual's twelfth-floor studio in Crystal City, Virginia, was not the first in the country. Herb Jebco's show out of KSL in Salt Lake City in the 1970s certainly preceded him,[50] and on the Mutual Network longtime WOR-AM radio host Long John Nebel, working with his wife, Candy Jones, was on the national graveyard shift before King took the job.[51] But Larry King was the person who turned the late-night radio call-in show into an institution. When King began, Mutual radio officials were so uncertain about the show that they would not pay for an 800 number. Anyone who wanted to dial the show had to pay for the call. Slowly, over time, the show caught on. The timing was right. AM radio was in trouble when King went on the air. Music was dominating the FM channels, which were picking up more and more listeners. AM radio was looking for a new easy-to-produce programming format that did not need FM sound quality. King's talk show fit the bill.

King's late-night radio format was simple. He would line up a guest to speak with him for the first three hours of his five-and-a-half-hour show, and then open the phones and an assorted group of "insomniacs and graveyard-shift workers"[52] would light up the lines. Never doing any research or preparation before calls or interviews, King attributed his success to his own native curiosity and instincts. "You do not want to sit next to me on airplane," he told an interviewer, "because I'm going to find out an awful lot about you on an airplane." King once told an interviewer that he never consciously thinks of the audience when he is on the air. "I ask what I'm curious about, and hopefully enough of the listeners are curious about it too."[53]

Larry King began on the Mutual network on January 30, 1978, with twenty-eight stations. By the time he switched from late-night to daytime in 1992, the number had grown to 430 stations.[54] In between, he had signed a lucrative deal with Ted Turner's CNN in 1985—for $200,000, doubling his yearly income at the time—to bring his show to television in the nightly broadcast of *Larry King Live.*

Larry King Live on television was, of course, live, and it had the look and feel of a radio show. King began in a suit and tie, but switched back to shirtsleeves and suspenders, his tie loosened, his microphone visible. Close-ups on King and his guests promoted a feeling of intimacy as well.[55] At first, some politicians, business people, and celebrities did not want to appear on *Larry King Live.* They were not used to a situation in which they had to field questions from viewers by phone. Without a script they felt that the situation was potentially uncontrollable, too rife with the possibilities of on-air embarrassment. Eventually, however, the appeal of thirty minutes of uninterrupted prime-time exposure and King's soft, luring approach, began to melt the resistance. By 1988 the show was well known, but it was still not considered a site for serious news and public affairs. During the 1988 Presidential campaign, King couldn't get George Bush to appear on the program and Michael Dukakis refused at first but later changed his mind. It might have seemed the ideal forum for Vice President Bush after his highly publicized face-off with CBS's Dan Rather over the Iran-contra affair, but he felt a call-in show of this kind was too undignified for someone of his stature.[56]

The Presidential campaign of 1992 changed all that. One appearance—that of then unannounced independent Presidential candidate Ross Perot on the evening of February 20, 1992—provided the pivotal moment in Larry King's career and a turning point in the history of TV talk. On this show, in what appeared to be an unscripted response to a caller, Perot said he would toss his hat into the political ring if "drafted" by the people. As it turned out, the moment was not as unpremeditated as it looked. King had been told weeks before the program by Perot's friend and political advisor John Jay Hooker that Perot would be open to seeking the nomination. It had been set up. King would not have planted the question, he said, if Hooker hadn't told him Perot would say "yes."[57] No matter, in the eyes of the public and press it was "fresh talk," a revelation on the air. The announcement dramatized the power of talk on television when that talk was broadcast nationally.

By the time the election was over in November 1992, six Presidential candidates had fielded 122 viewers' questions on *Larry King Live,* with answers viewed by an average of 2.6 million households, according to King's ratings during this period.[58] News made on the Larry King show—like the Perot candidacy announcement—had a reverberation effect. *Larry King Live* made the front page of the *New York Times* fifty-seven times during the election year.[59]

In all, the candidates made nearly 100 talk-show appearances during the election year of 1992. Toward the end of the campaign, candidate appearances increased talk-show ratings an average of 40 percent, and a major network's advertising revenues from its political coverage made much more money for the network than it cost to cover the campaign.[60] For CNN the election was a windfall, giving the network its highest ratings since the Gulf War and extending its reach to other countries in the world interested in the results of the U.S. elections.

Larry King and Bill Clinton, 1992

One of the most adept politicians on the talk-show circuit in 1992 and in the televised Presidential debates that year was Bill Clinton. Clinton appeared in every talk format he could. For example, he made a highly publicized saxophone-playing visit (wearing green sunglasses) on the *Arsenio Hall Show*, and an appearance on MTV in which he was asked for his early rock music influences (Elvis), his favorite musician (Kenny G), his astrological sign (Leo), and whether he would inhale if he could replay his first marijuana experience ("Sure, if I could"). He was even questioned as to whether he wore briefs or boxer shorts (briefs). Clinton seemed ideally suited for an era in which hosts and audiences, from Larry King and his followers on down the talk-show "food chain," hungered for personal stories from public figures.

In a front-page article in *The New York Times* on July 27, 1992, Maureen Dowd pointed to the similarities between the speeches of the Democratic candidates for President and Vice President at the Democratic Convention and the themes of daytime talk shows that dealt with "dysfunctional relationships, marital troubles, addicted family members, self-help and recovery."[61] Bill Clinton told of the pain and agony of growing up with a father who was alcoholic and abusive. Al Gore told the story of his son's accident and subsequent recovery. These people seemed to belong on talk shows.

When Clinton faced Bush in the second Presidential debate, formatted to allow interaction and questions from the floor, Clinton showed himself masterful in speaking directly to audience members' concerns. When one person asked how the recession had affected each of the candidates, Clinton spoke about the pain of seeing people in Arkansas suffering from unemployment and the lack of self-confidence and self-esteem that came with that economic deprivation. In her book *Consumer Culture and TV Programming,* Robin Andersen argues that it was at precisely this moment that Republican candidate George Bush lost ground before a national TV audience.[62] Bush distanced himself from his audience rather than empathizing with it.

Indeed, the second Clinton-Bush Presidential debate, like John Kennedy's appearance in the 1960 Presidential debate against Richard Nixon, was a defining moment. The moment would be discussed, interpreted, and mythologized after the fact, but many felt Clinton had "won" this debate against Bush by his skill in the TV talk arena.

Clinton again proved skillful using television in his appearance on *60 Minutes.* Sitting next to his wife, he took a potentially damaging allegation of sexual liaisons and affairs while Governor of Arkansas and turned it to his advantage. Clinton repeated the performance less successfully on the grand jury tape of the Monica Lewinsky affair in 1998. The grand jury tape was made at first simply so jury members who were not present could see Clinton's testimony, but it was made public by the House Judiciary Committee in the fall of 1998. It was not a talk show, but it was a nationally viewed example of TV talk—one of the first examples of national TV talk in which a speaker appeared against his will, since the tape's release was court ordered. Again, however, Clinton's testimony helped him, by most accounts, win public support in his public relations battle to maintain his presidency through his impeachment proceedings.

In the 1992 campaign Clinton used another form of television talk: the video satellite tour, which was the equivalent of the old-fashioned whistle-stop train tour except that it was done from a television studio. Clinton recorded and sent a short version of the same message to selected television markets across the country through a live satellite feed. The following quotes were taken from a series of Clinton's messages on his "fidelity" problem. They were captured by independent filmmaker Brian Springer, in the repetitive "takes" in which they were recorded:

> Hello, Mike. If everybody in America who's had problems
> in their marriage and either wound up divorced or got back
> together votes for me, I'm a shoo-in.

Can you hear me? I figure if everybody in Maryland who's ever had trouble in their marriage and they're still together, or has ever been divorced votes for me, I'm a shoo-in.

Uh, hello, and you know, if every American couple who has either been divorced or had problems and stayed married votes for me, I'm a shoo-in for reelection. I think the American people are smarter [than that].[63]

During the campaign of 1992, filmmaker Springer recorded some 600 hours of live feeds off his dish (including moments between takes in which politicians did not know they were still on the air) and edited it all down to a one-hour documentary called "Spin" which provides fascinating glimpses into how "live" TV news talk was shaped on the air. The between-take footage, for instance, showed Clinton's enthusiasm for the marvels of the whistle-stop satellite tour and his new technologically enhanced ability to speak directly to voters without the filtering processes of broadcast journalists. Here are some of Clinton's off-screen comments:

> Clinton: This is great. I love these.
> Voice: We can do another hour if you want. We start doing Georgia tomorrow.

> Clinton: Can we do any more?
> Voice: We are setting up as many as we can.
> Clinton: Can we do some Maryland? Can we do those two Maryland?

The Springer documentary is also revealing when it shows the side conversations politicians have with Larry King on commercial breaks and King's off-screen attempts to become a power broker. King begins to tell Clinton a story on one camera break, and then tries to set up a Presidential appointment for his CNN boss, Ted Turner:

> King: I'm in Israel. I'm at the Wailing Wall. True story. . . . I'm with my brother. I'm Jewish, it's my culture. I'm standing there and I see an old rabbi, praying, a religious, Jewish man. He looks up at me and he says, "What's with Perot?" I swear to God, "What's with Perot?" in Israel.

Clinton: I love it.

King: It's crazy — Ted Turner changed the world. He's a big fan of yours.

Clinton: Is he?

King: He would — ah — serve you, you know what I mean?

Clinton: You're kidding.

King: Oh you'd be surprised. He's ready. What's he got left in life to gain? I'd call him after you're elected. Think about it. No dope.

Clinton: That's for sure.

King: Great guy to work for too.

Often handlers would come in to give advice, help the candidate "adjust" his answers or stay away from certain topics. Sometimes the host and candidate would work together to set up a bit on the air.

When Democratic Presidential candidate Al Gore was on *Larry King Live,* King and Gore engaged in pleasant banter and planned what Gore would say.

King (on commercial break): One of the problems with staying on the [campaign] bus too long is the two of you guys are so good on media.

Gore: You know what you ought to do? You ought to come out on the bus trip with us one day. We could do a joint interview from the bus.

King (leaning over): When we're out of time you can invite us on the bus. (Checks the camera. Sees that they are now back on the air)

King: Uh, we have plumb run out of time. Thanks for coming, Al.

Gore (voice strong with spontaneous enthusiasm now the camera light is on): I'd like to invite you to come on the bus with us, Larry.

One of the unspoken rules of television talk cited at the beginning of the book was that television talk is always to some degree structured. No clearer illustration of this could be possible than in these off-the-cuff exchanges when the participants thought the camera was off.

Though his popularity waxed and waned, Larry King maintained the national celebrity and prominence he had gained during the election year of 1992. He had become, in TV journalism critic Howard Kurtz's terms, "a worldwide TV star." Some felt King had never really changed. "If you took his ego away," said one person who knew him off the air, "you'd have the same 250-watt radio station hustler who just spent his last buck on a horse that went backwards. He is exactly the same man he was ten years ago."[64] But for a period of time in the mid-1990s, Larry Zeiger King had made his live television talk show the forum of choice for America's top political candidates, and, with the power of the broadcast satellite, that forum was now worldwide, available internationally through satellite in 151 countries.[65]

THE O. J. SIMPSON VERDICT AS A NATIONAL TALK EVENT (1995)

Occasionally a media event is so compelling that it captures the attention of the entire society. The highly publicized trial of African American celebrity O. J. Simpson was one such media event.

O. J. Simpson was a football hero, a handsome African American who was also famous for his Hertz car rental advertisements. His wife, Nicole Simpson, and her friend, Ron Goldman, were murdered. Simpson's wife had previously reported him for battering. Police claimed that a glove dropped at the scene of the murder matched one found in Simpson's house. Evidence against him appeared to be overwhelming, and the murder fit a pattern of batterers moving from hitting to killing. The issue of spousal abuse was important at that time, as women's groups were just beginning to open centers for battered women and working to get legislation passed that would protect women from abusers. Simpson hired a team of expensive lawyers. They challenged the prosecution evidence by uncovering evidence of racial bias on the part of the major police witness, claiming that the evidence had been planted, and arguing that Simpson loved his wife. The scene was set for drama in two major arenas—racial bias in police work and spousal abuse.

The trial lasted for months, and the news media's interest peaked in the trial's final days as news organizations from all over the world jockeyed for position to cover the verdict.

By the mid-1990s the TV industry had witnessed such an expansion of talk shows that no longer did it appear that any single network, sponsor, host, or show could have an impact on the culture as a whole. Only if a topic was picked up by the entire circuit of talk shows could it become truly national.[66] This was what happened as the O. J. Simpson trial neared its end.

The verdict came much sooner than anyone expected. Most commentators had predicted a long jury sequestration, and Judge Lance Ito's announcement on Monday, October 2, 1995, that the verdict would come the next day kicked off a frantic twenty-four-hour media watch. TV was not simply "reporting" the news at this point. It was helping to create it. The morning news information shows built anticipation and laid out scenarios for what might happen given a guilty or not-guilty verdict.

On the morning of October 3, 1995, NBC News announcer Tom Brokaw told his audience that the O. J. Simpson verdict had become "an enormous international magnet."[67] When the verdict finally arrived, the networks switched to the pooled coverage in the courtroom. A silent rustling in the courtroom filled television screens across the nation. The abrupt silence was startling and unsettling for viewers accustomed by now to nonstop talk. The judge asked the head of the jury to read the verdict, and the viewers heard, for the first time, the voice of a juror. The voice declared the celebrity in the dock "not guilty."

As the verdict was announced, members of the victims' families broke into tears and sobs, or simply held one another. The surveillance-like camera panned the table of the silent prosecution team and then a jubilant defense. O. J. Simpson himself broke into a broad smile and hugged his defense attorneys. Then the camera reversed itself, traveling back across the courtroom with the same impartiality with which it had originally uncovered the shock and grief. It was a moment of pure television, suspended in time, and showed the power of the televised visual image. At this moment a TV talk event was constituted as much by the images on the screen as the words that led up to it.

The silence did not last long, however. There soon resumed, on almost every talk show in every subgenre, a torrent of words as news and entertainment shows reacted to the verdict. African Americans were reported to be celebrating the not-guilty verdict; White Americans appeared to be stunned both by what appeared to many a miscarriage of justice and by the reaction of the Black community.

Consensus: Town-Meeting Shows

Immediately following the verdict two talk shows—*The Oprah Winfrey Show* on October 3, 1995, and Ted Koppel's *Nightline* "Town Meeting:

Where Do We Go From Here?"—abandoned their normal formats and became national "town meetings" of TV talk. Oprah Winfrey spoke as a host but also as an African American trying to come to terms with the trial and its verdict. Ted Koppel represented himself as a fair-minded explicator of the political and legal issues that surrounded the police investigation of the case. Both hosts had as little as forty minutes, not counting commercials, for their forums.

The Oprah Winfrey Show on the day of the verdict had no official guest panel. The few experts who had been invited sat mixed in the studio audience itself, not up front with Winfrey, a clear indication that this was to be an unusual community expression that did not elevate the professional or expert.

Winfrey guided, framed, and re-framed the themes and issues of the show. She responded to members of the audience in empathetic ways that derived from her own personal experiences. Oprah Winfrey's show was designed to reveal and debate the racial issues exposed by the trial, and to promote harmony and reconciliation for White as well as Black audience members.[68] Although she herself had been the victim of sexual abuse and had become a spokesperson for domestic abuse victims, she did not address the issue of domestic violence that had galvanized so many who watched the O. J. Simpson case on TV. She stuck to the issue of differing perspectives on the verdict according to race.

On ABC's *Nightline* the day after the verdict, host Ted Koppel also worked to create a sense of consensus around the issue of race. He began the show by using an edited news package to frame the question of the evening. The tape showed defense attorney Johnnie Cochran dramatically confronting the jury. "Who polices the police?" Cochran had declaimed. "You police the police. You police them by your verdict. You send the message." Was this the central result of the O. J. Simpson verdict, Koppel asked his audience, that the verdict sent a "message" to the police?

Koppel then introduced members of his invited guest panel—Los Angeles Police Department (LAPD) commissioner Daryl Gates, African American Congresswoman Maxine Waters, and several others. Many blasted the LAPD for its racial policies, but only Tammy Bruce, the guest panelist from the National Organization of Women (NOW), refused to limit the agenda to the issue of race but insisted on discussing domestic violence. Despite Koppel's repeated attempts to deter her, Bruce shifted the focus back to a discussion of domestic violence and gender imbalance within the LAPD. Koppel attempted to cut her off several times. She insisted that gender bias was as important as racial bias and persisted in saying that the defense team and the *Nightline* show itself had made race the sole issue.

It was in the rents of this generally smooth-running show—in the tension between well-managed discussion and rough-and-tumble guest reactions—that Ted Koppel's skill as moderator, arbiter of discussion, and framer of public debate came sharply into relief. At the same time, the rents in the show's smooth operation occasioned by Tammy Bruce's outburst were one of the things that enhanced its "live" energy.

Comedy Consensus

Late-night comedy shows like Jay Leno's *Tonight* and David Letterman's *Late Show* also focused on race in the wake of the verdict. The jury's decision of "not guilty" had shattered the presumption that a guilty verdict was the only logical conclusion to the trial. To the comedy commentators of late-night TV, the "not guilty" verdict was ludicrous.

A number of critics have pointed out that the jokes of late-night comedians like Jay Leno and David Letterman may have been more important in the shaping of public opinion in the 1990s than the words of network commentators. In the wake of the O. J. Simpson verdict, late-night comedians like Leno and Letterman were at the very center of television's national "court" of public opinion.

Filters were operating in national comedy as well as the news. Jokes in the late-night monologues worked to reassert conventional views in several ways. The jokes implied that O. J. Simpson was guilty from start to finish (the "scales of justice" were just temporarily out of kilter, joked Letterman); that race was the crucial issue of the day, not domestic violence; that the key players (the victims, the newly freed accused killer, and the star legal defense and prosecution teams) were true celebrities in a national, media-created melodrama that was entertaining and newsworthy.

Late-night jokes on the verdict fell into three categories: jokes that focused on the public obsession with everything connected to the case, jokes that centered on legal strategies within the case and flaws in the criminal justice system, and jokes that focused on race.[69] The issue of race held the day in the male-dominated subgenres of news and late-night comedy, and this comedy paid little or no attention to issues of domestic violence and gender bias in law enforcement in the days preceding and immediately following the verdict.

There were exceptions, however. For example, female late-night talk-show host Stephanie Miller, a newcomer who broadcast out of Los Angeles, presented a "woman's point of view." Miller's late-night comedy routines on the day of the verdict centered on lead prosecution attorney Marcia Clark. Most notable was a dramatic skit that parodied the moment the verdict was announced. This time the camera first focuses not on O. J. Simpson and his attorneys but on the smoldering prosecution attorney. Her eyes begin to burn not in shock or victimage but in explosive rage. With a banshee cry Stephanie Miller / Marcia Clark launches herself into a kick-boxer routine that takes out Simpson himself and his entire legal team.

Discussion of domestic violence was taboo in almost every talk venue other than the daytime audience-participation shows, where it was still mentioned. Miscarriage of justice and "race" jokes were the order of the day.

Media Heroes

On the night after the verdict Larry King interviewed lead O. J. Simpson defense attorney Johnnie Cochran. King was eager to explore the well-publicized tension that existed between the defense team's original coordinator, Robert Shapiro, and Cochran, who had taken over the leadership of the team from him. Shapiro had made clear his displeasure with the "race card" defense of Cochran.

Buried in the middle of *Larry King Live* that evening was a question that focused on domestic violence. King asked Cochran, "Are you a little surprised that the jury gave little credence to spousal abuse?" Cochran's reply took just thirty seconds. No, he said, the prosecution tried to make this "a burning fuse," but "the fuse kept going out." King accepted the response, and asked no follow-up questions about this.

Yet Cochran's own involvement in domestic violence had been documented and published. He had been formally charged by his first wife, Barbara Jean Berry, for assault—once in 1967 and again in 1977.[70] The avoidance of the question of Cochran's own record of spousal abuse on *Larry King Live,* and in the mainstream press in general, goes to the heart of the filtering process that occurs in the talk of the nation on TV at the time of a national media event. Anything that deviates too much from the main elements of the narrative, including the characterizations of its principal actors, tends to be minimized or ignored. Johnnie Cochran had become the hero of the day. Paraphrasing a newspaper editor in a classic John Ford western, when the facts contradict a legend that seizes the public imagination, the press "prints the legend." The omission of more penetrating questions on Johnnie Cochran's background was one instance of the ways in which talk-show hosts like Larry King, as consensus builders, print the legend.

Conclusion

Morning, daytime, and late-night talk-show hosts performed overlapping functions in the wake of the O. J. Simpson verdict. Each worked within his or her own distinctive talk tradition and format. Each remained "in character," anchoring the text of his or her show while guiding its principal themes and shaping sources of information for its viewing public. These texts created an intertext. In one sense each of the national talk-show hosts was performing the same role. Each strove to create a consensus within a national debate. What we see here is that TV talk is both text and intertext, and to understand the national TV talk show fully we must take into account the ideological unity that binds and often conceals the true diversity of political and cultural expression that surrounds an issue of national importance.[71]

NINE

THE FIFTH CYCLE (1996–2000)
Trash Talk, Nice Talk, and Blended Talk

RICKI LAKE AND THE NATIONAL "TRASH TALK" DEBATE

From a subgenre dominated by four major hosts in the mid-1980s (Donahue, Raphaël, Rivera, and Winfrey), the daytime audience-participation talk show had grown into a thriving industry of over twenty shows broadcast nationally by the mid-1990s. Daytime talk was a billion-dollar industry with an estimated fifty-seven million viewers a week. As an example of the kind of profits that could be made, *The Sally Jessy Raphaël Show* alone generated $40 million a year in sales and licensing fees. The expansion of the daytime talk show and the new competitive environment stimulated tabloid topics and sensationalism. Two widely circulated pictures dramatized this new sensationalism. The first was of host Phil Donahue wearing a skirt to spice up a show on changing gender roles. The second was of Geraldo Rivera with a massive bandage covering his nose, broken during a scuffle between White supremacists and their opponents and reported widely in press discussions of the new sensationalism, violence, and excesses of "trash talk." Both pictures represented the lengths to which talk-show hosts would go in order to garner ratings.

In March 1995 a guest on the nationally televised *Jenny Jones Show* was "ambushed" with the surprise announcement that his "secret admirer" was gay. The guest, Jon Schmitz, went back to his hometown in Michigan and murdered his gay admirer, Scott Amedure. Jenny Jones and her staff faced charges of legal culpability, and the case made national headlines.

The war of words over "trash talk" had by now reached policy levels. Former Education Secretary William Bennett, Democratic Senator Joseph Lieberman, and civil rights advocate C. Delores Tucker launched a national boycott of advertisers who supported tabloid-inspired talk shows. The shows "rot" and "degrade the human personality,"[1] Bennett charged, and during a "Talk Show Summit" in October 1995, Secretary of Health and Human Services Donna Shalala urged talk-show hosts and producers to exercise restraint and social responsibility in the topics they brought to the air. As a result of this public debate and criticism, advertisers and syndicators put pressure on talk shows to moderate themselves. And some did.

One that did not was *The Ricki Lake Show.* Entering the talk-show market in 1991, by the mid-1990s Lake was appearing in 212 markets around the country, and industry analysts were surprised to see that she had doubled her ratings from 1994 to 1995. She took second place in the daytime ratings behind Oprah Winfrey, and in some markets she was beating Winfrey.[2]

The segment titles of the Ricki Lake show telegraphed its "trash" appeal: "Get Real, Honey, Your Boyfriend Is a Dog"; "Pack Your Bags or You'll Wish You Were Dead"; "You're the Rudest Thing Alive . . . and I'm Sick of Your Attitude."[3] Whereas Phil Donahue, Oprah Winfrey, and Geraldo Rivera had come from journalism backgrounds, Ricki Lake had made her reputation as an actor, appearing in John Waters' movies and the television series *China Beach.* She and her producers had no qualms about producing a show that was designed primarily to entertain its young audience. As confrontation and "fight" scenes proved successful, the show was increasingly aimed toward its "money shot"—the moment in which tensions would build until a crying/scratching/fighting/shouting scene would break out as the studio audience chanted its approval.

Publicity in trade magazines and the popular press built Ricki Lake's reputation.[4] The show was on "a publicity roll," said *Variety.* Some critics were horrified. Articles in *Time, Newsweek,* and *The Washington Post* deplored the show's sensationalism and lowest-common-denominator approach to programming. In these articles, critics argued that Lake's soap-opera tactics and lower-class guests created patronizing and stereotyped portrayals. Journalists lamented the decline of the kinds of intelligent public-service programming that had characterized Arlene Francis, Barbara Walters, Phil Donahue, and Oprah Winfrey at their best.[5]

Some critics defended the show, however. *Time* critic Richard Zoglin argued that although Ricki Lake and her disciples had "achieved the impossible" by "lowering the standards of TV gabfests,"[6] they actually performed a public service by extending the limits of television talk. "Gone, for the most part, are the wacky transvestites, the bizarre tales of incest, the tearful AIDS victims," said Zoglin. Instead, Ricki Lake had opened the spectrum of television representation to "the vast expanse of anonymous Middle America, from trailer parks and ghettos, that TV has rarely shown so unvarnished."[7] From this point of view, Lake had delivered a "fresh twist on overworked" relationship shows.[8]

For *New York Times* TV critic Bill Carter, *The Ricki Lake Show* was simply about money. "Material that network executives say would never be acceptable in prime time, including graphic discussions of sex and highly abusive language, is routine on the daytime shows, which are supported by such prominent family-oriented advertisers as Procter and Gamble, General Mills, Sears, Roebuck and Company and American Home Products."[9] The ratings justified the programming for mainstream advertisers, Carter said. At its peak *The Ricki Lake Show* had the largest youth audience of any daytime talk show, with an estimated 22 percent of her audience representing a consuming public between the ages of two and seventeen, and approximately 600,000 viewers under the age of twelve.[10]

Narrative Structure

The Ricki Lake Show was based on a simple set of narrative conventions. A show of November 1995, for example, centered on the theme of "Women Who Dump Their Boyfriends for Another Lover." As three young women related stories to Ricki Lake about the boyfriends they were about to dump, the boyfriends sat, apparently mystified, in isolation chambers with earphones that cut the sounds of the studio. When they were let out to hear the news, the pain, discomfort, and confusion that registered on their faces was accentuated by the introduction on stage of their girlfriends' new love interests to the hoots and cries of the studio audience. Two of these new love interests were men; the third was a woman. Neither host nor audience could *believe* that these women would be willing to dump their boyfriends on national TV— especially when they were unsure if their new love interests would reciprocate. And sure enough in each case, as it turned out, the object of the woman's infatuation was *not* interested in returning the affection.

This all sounds a little absurd on the surface, a throwback to the most exaggerated nineteenth-century melodramas. Host, guests, and studio audience played their roles with glee. The audience reacted as they would at a professional wrestling event—on cue. They had many chances to indicate their disapproval of the "dumpers" and their sympathy for the nice young men who had been dumped. Ricki Lake relayed the "moral" at the end. "Remember," she said, "love only works if it goes both ways. Before you end one romance for someone else you think you're in love with, make sure that feeling is mutual . . . I think that the entire audience would agree that these guys are better off single. Am I right?" The studio audience roared its approval.

Ricki Lake and talk shows that were influenced by her staged "relationship" shows as spectacles. They were part of a growing trend toward "reality-based" shows. These shows were eagerly consumed by daytime audiences in much the same way that readers of the tabloid press consumed stories in the *National Enquirer* or *Sun*. Some media critics cited these shows as evidence of a growing public hunger for *Schadenfreude*, delight in the misery of others. These talk shows occupied the same slots in the daytime schedule as soap operas and were less costly to produce.

A generational shift was occurring. For a generation raised on Donahue, Winfrey, Rivera, and Raphaël, the issues discussed on "therapeutic" talk shows were ultimately solvable. The public-information, public-service model of daytime talk implied that if the public was given enough information about a particular personal or social problem, it could eventually be solved. By the mid-1990s shows like *Ricki Lake* no longer shared this optimism. For post-Letterman, "Generation X" viewers, some people were just too dumb to change, too mired in their own self-destruction. So viewers might just as well enjoy the *Schadenfreude* pleasures of watching "other people" make a mess of their lives. Of all the trash talk hosts of the 1990s, the triumph of talk-show host Jerry Springer, building on and extending what Ricki Lake had begun, was perhaps the most remarkable.

WHEN WORDS BREAK DOWN: Jerry Springer (1991–)

Jerry Springer was, like ABC's Ted Koppel, a child of Jewish immigrants who escaped Nazi Germany to England. Springer moved to New York with his family in 1947 at the age of five. His father had a business selling stuffed animals, and his mother worked as a bank clerk.[11]

By the time Springer graduated from Forest Hills High School and enrolled in Tulane University in New Orleans, he had become politically active in the civil rights and antiwar movements. After graduating from Northwestern Law School in 1969, he joined a Cincinnati law firm and entered local politics. In his early years in Cincinnati he worked on a referendum to lower the voting age in Ohio to nineteen.

Springer's political career was uneven. He ran for Congress at the age of twenty-five but lost to a five-term incumbent by a small margin. He ran again in 1971, this time for city council, gaining enough votes to be named vice-mayor. In December 1973 he married the former Micki Velten, an administrative aide for Procter and Gamble. Later that same year Springer's political career was caught up in a sex scandal. He had crossed the Ohio River to a Kentucky massage parlor, where he had employed the services of a prostitute. When vice cops discovered his secret, Springer resigned his post, stunning reporters in a 1974 press conference by revealing his true reason for leaving office.[12] Springer returned to electoral politics in 1977, however, and received more votes than any other councilman, becoming, at the age of thirty-three, the new mayor of Cincinnati.

As mayor, Springer worked to establish a new jail system and brought rock-and-roll to Cincinnati's Riverfront Stadium. He was an ardent advocate of the First Amendment, supporting the rights of a Nazi group to march in a local parade. His parents' advice, he said, was "Go ahead—this is America. Give the Nazis a lot of publicity, and people will see how vile they are."[13] Springer stepped down from his job as mayor in 1981 and launched an unsuccessful gubernatorial bid in 1982. That was also the year he went to work for Cincinnati's TV Channel 5 as a news commentator. Within five years the show was rated number one in the region.

As Springer's political and news career advanced, he experienced a personal crisis. His daughter, Katie, born in 1976, was legally blind at birth, deaf in one ear, and without nasal passages. Though she was later able to develop a life normal enough to make friends and enter public high school, this personal tragedy and the growing demands of Springer's political career strained the marriage. By the time he launched his talk-show career in 1991, he had been separated from his wife for over a year.

In October 1992, when Phil Donahue hosted his twenty-fifth anniversary special, Springer was introduced on the show as one of the "new generation" of talk-show hosts. "When I ran for political office,"

Springer said of his new talk career, "I wasn't scared—I always knew what I was talking about. But this is scary. I'm competing against some pretty major people."[14]

For a while Jerry Springer remained just one in a field of post-Donahue talk-show hosts. By May 1994, however, in a desperate move to maintain his ratings, he hit upon a new strategy with producer Richard Dominick, a former editor of the tabloid *National Enquirer.* "We were going into the May sweeps and the numbers were terrible," Dominick later explained. "We were told by them [the Multimedia Entertainment executives] that if it didn't get better by the end of the November book, the show would be canceled."[15] Dominick and Springer decided they would go after the college crowd. Host and producer would push for a show that was "interesting with the sound off," a show with enough "sizzle" that it would stop people from skipping through the channels. That meant physical action and spectacle. It called for a standard formula in American entertainment: sex and violence. In this case, the Springer team would stage sexual situations (strippers dipping themselves in chocolate, for example) and fights, lots of fights, as in the days when *The Ricki Lake Show* had earned its highest ratings.

When criticized, Dominick and Springer would maintain that they tried to stop the physical fighting as soon as it occurred, and that was true. Burly bouncers were hired to wrestle over-enthusiastic guests into submission. But it was the fights that drove the ratings. People seemed to relish the sight of people swinging at each other, breaking chairs (break-away prop chairs were used because they splintered more easily), and flying into bleeped insult matches. Still, Springer did not have complete carte blanche. The show was forced to temper its approach under Multimedia's watchful eye. In 1996, however, Universal Television Enterprises bought the show and told the producers the wraps were off again. "Just do your show, do your show," they told Dominick and Springer. "We'll worry about everything else."[16]

Suddenly, *The Jerry Springer Show* was the "hottest thing in television." Springer and his associates had learned the marketing lessons of the 1980s well. Their *Too Hot for TV* videotapes, featuring topless strippers and fight scenes edited from "break-out" moments on the show, became one of the most successful video direct-order marketing campaigns of the 1990s. By late fall of 1998, Springer's book (*Ring Master!* written with writer Laura Morton) had become a feature film. The book's Amazon.com Internet announcement proclaimed: "The man who has sold one million copies of his 'Too Hot for TV' video through direct response only, the man whose movie based on the show is due out for Christmas, for the very first time dares to remove the bleeps and bars that hide away the real action." The "real action" on *The Jerry Springer Show* was not the talk.

Like Ricki Lake and other trash talk hosts, Springer's on-air comments actually reinforced middle-class morality. While the studio audience would chant "Jerrreee, Jerrreee!" Springer himself would cling sheepishly to the periphery of the action, witnessing the fights from a posture of cool, somewhat bemused rationality. His commentary at the end would often include an appeal to the First Amendment:

> Please understand, because we show it does not constitute an endorsement of it, or any particular view or behavior, any more than a murder on the news, or a primetime movie about a rape is an endorsement of those horrors.[17]

While none of the lifestyles or manners depicted were "ones we would necessarily choose for ourselves," Springer told his audience, if there was no "outrageousness" how "boring" life would be. "Look," Springer ended his editorial at the end of the *Too Hot for TV* tape on a note of moral piety, "television does not and must not create values. It's merely a picture of all that's out there: the good, the bad, the ugly—a world upon which we then apply our own values learned and nurtured through family, church, and experience."

By 1999 Jerry Springer's combination of First Amendment flag waving and multimedia merchandising had put him at the top of the ratings. The show was sold to Barry Diller's Home Shopping Network[18] in 1998 in a move designed to position Springer against Oprah and Rosie O'Donnell in syndication. With his book out and a movie in theaters, with his bandaged face on the cover of *Esquire* magazine (a make-up artist's allusion to trash talk fights and Geraldo Rivera's broken nose), Jerry Springer had become a household name. The time was ripe for a reaction to trash talk, a show that would return audiences to the simpler and quieter pleasures of an earlier era of TV talk.

ROSIE O'DONNELL'S "NICE TALK" (1996–2002)

Rosie O'Donnell was introduced to talk-show viewers in June 1996, by one of the most successful promotional campaigns since King Syndication's campaign for Oprah Winfrey in 1986. The Warner/Telepictures public-relations/advertising campaign revealed an explicit awareness of the history of TV talk. O'Donnell was promoted as the reverential inheritor of the talk-show traditions of Mike Douglas, Merv Griffin, and Dinah Shore—all syndicated hosts who had entertained daytime audiences in the 1970s when O'Donnell was growing up. O'Donnell also acknowledged her debt to Johnny Carson. Her show was presented as an alternative to the excesses of the baroque trash talk style of Jerry Springer and others. She was quoted in the press as advocating a "kick-off-your-shoes-and-stay-awhile" mentality. "What I liked about Mike Douglas," the host was quoted as saying, "is that everyone who came on his show appeared to be his friend. No one looked nervous."[19]

The promotional package for *The Rosie O'Donnell Show* was shown to Sony, Disney, King World, Rhysher Entertainment, and eventually station managers and advertisers from across the country. As early as January 1996, six months before it was scheduled to air, stations were lining up to buy time on the show.[20]

One of the reasons Rosie O'Donnell as host and executive producer was considered a good bet by advertisers and promoters was that she had an established track record. She was well known for her character roles in Hollywood movies (*A League of Their Own* and *Sleepless in Seattle,* to name two of the most popular), and she also had a successful stand-up career. She had produced an HBO special and a Radio City Music Hall New Year Eve's Show. She was a frequent guest host and fill-in for Kathie Lee Gifford on *Live! with Regis and Kathie Lee,* standing up well to Regis Philbin's gibes and antic humor. She was the ideal candidate for a "retro" show because she genuinely idolized the popular culture and entertainment figures who appeared, and she had a photographic memory for show-business trivia.

From a young age Roseann O'Donnell had soaked in show business. Her mother took her to many film and theater productions. At the age of six Rosie had memorized all the lines from the movie version of the Broadway musical *Funny Girl* and would perform the Barbara Streisand songs in the kitchen.[21] Her mother's death on St. Patrick's Day 1973, when Rosie was ten, marked a turning point. "When a girl gets her period and her mom is not there to comfort her, it's incredibly painful," she told a 1997 interviewer.[22] The impact of the loss was compounded by her father's emotional removal. She looked to fill the void in the world of daytime TV—dramas and comedies like *Eight Is Enough, The Brady Bunch,* and *The Partridge Family,* and TV talk shows. She fantasized appearing as the guest of Johnny Carson, Merv Griffin, and

Dinah Shore. After completing high school in Commack, Long Island (she graduated as senior class president, homecoming queen, and prom queen), O'Donnell began a long apprenticeship in stand-up comedy, performing, and acting.

That career culminated in her talk-show deal with Warner/Telepictures in 1996, which put her in exactly the position she wanted. She received $4.5 million her first year in addition to a share of the profits through her Kid Ro Entertainment Production Company. She also had the use of the same 175-seat Rockefeller Center studio in New York in which Phil Donahue had talked, and the ability to have her son, Parker, in an adjacent nursery. When *The Rosie O'Donnell Show* went on the air it had been pre-sold with a 93 percent national market penetration.

The new show received good press. Critics like Tom Shales of the *Washington Post* praised its energy and exuberance. A July 1996 *Newsweek* feature spotted *The Rosie O'Donnell Show* as a trend. In a bold headline with a picture of O'Donnell crossing her fingers on both hands for good luck, *Newsweek* proclaimed the host "Queen of Nice" and someone who might single-handedly begin the task of "cleaning up trash TV."

The Rosie O'Donnell Show came at an opportune time. The industry was attempting to solve an image problem that had become increasingly troublesome. Even Geraldo Rivera was stepping back from the "trash" label, confessing flamboyantly in *Newsweek* that he had taken the "low road" and his show "was going to hell." It had gotten to the point, Rivera said, that "it was either change my daytime show or get out of the business." Echoing Republican majority leader Newt Gingrich, Rivera promised his audience to clean up his show in a "contract with America" in which "all guests would be treated with dignity, solutions would be emphasized over shock and heat."[23] Linking these developments to what was happening in late night, *Newsweek* said, "Nice is back, on TV and off. Leno is up, Letterman down." The ascension of Rosie O'Donnell in daytime talk was providing "relief from the freak-of-the-week sideshows" on *Jenny Jones, Ricki Lake, Sally Jessy Raphaël,* and *Jerry Springer.*[24]

NEW BLENDS

While hosts like Rosie O'Donnell and Jay Leno represented a throwback to an earlier era of TV talk, two new comedy hosts were establishing two successful new talk formats. Viewers had become increasingly sophisticated about how television worked and were responding increasingly to shows that blended forms or crossed the boundaries between news and entertainment, fiction and reality. Bill Maher's *Politically Incorrect* and Garry Shandling's *The Larry Sanders Show* were the two most successful new-blend formats in the TV talk of the mid- to late 1990s.

BILL MAHER AND *POLITICALLY INCORRECT* (1993–2002)

Though it sported ersatz Greek ruins in the background of the set, Bill Maher's *Politically Incorrect* was, in the words of one reviewer, anything but "Periclean." In the course of the 1990s it became a national comedy TV talk forum. Starting on Comedy Central in 1993, *Politically Incorrect* was within three years one of the channel's most popular shows. Merging serious news issues and comedy, each show featured four guest panelists, only one of whom was a professional comedian. Sometimes it was hard to tell who the professional comedian was, as the guests competed freely for one-liners as well as political and cultural insights. In its wide-ranging subject matter and eclectic mix of guests, *Politically Incorrect* recalled the early *Dick Cavett Show*. Critics began to take notice. In 1994 *Time* critic Richard Zoglin rated Maher and ex–*Saturday Night Live* comedian Dennis Miller as the two best comedy talk news commentators on television. "What other current comedian looks for humor in the GATT talks and China's most-favored-nation trading status?" Zoglin asked. The *Time* article credited both Miller and Maher with delivering not the "easy-to-take, non-partisan topicality of Leno and Letterman" but "informed, savvy, opinionated comedy about real issues."[25] By 1996 *Politically Incorrect* had won several Cable ACE awards for Best Talk Show Series and Best Talk Show Host. Finally, in January 1997, the show was picked by ABC to follow *Nightline,* and Maher's show received a fixed time slot on network television.

William Maher Jr. was born January 20, 1956, in Manhattan. His father was a radio announcer, and his mother worked as a nurse. He grew up in suburban River Vale, New Jersey, with a sister, Kathy, who became an English teacher. Maher describes himself as "an intense, serious, adult-like kid who always made lists and never watched cartoons." "I was snobby at five," he later said.[26] His mother was Jewish, but he was raised Irish-Catholic by his father in a house that encouraged reading, literature, and freewheeling discussion.

From the age of eleven Maher remembers watching Johnny Carson, and by the time he was a senior at Pascack Hills High School in New Jersey, he was the featured emcee of the school's talent show. He remembers the "adrenaline high" of that experience, but decided to finish college before seriously entertaining ideas about show business. Majoring in English literature at Cornell (one of his favorite books was *Heart of Darkness*), Maher graduated in 1978. His career as a stand-up comedian began soon after with appearances in comedy spots like Catch-a-Rising-Star in the early 1980s. A number of Maher's friends and fellow comics, including Jerry Seinfeld and Paul Reiser, went on to successful comedy careers.

In 1982 Maher's stand-up comedy talent was spotted by Steve Allen and a talent scout from *The Tonight Show*. He got his first guest appearance that year, and it led to dozens of future appearances. "I told the first AIDS joke," Maher said. Carson told him afterward that the punch line got him one of the "longest laughs" the veteran host had ever heard.

After appearing as a character actor in a musical by Steve Allen and in a number of Hollywood B-films,[27] Maher was invited to be a guest on several comedy specials on HBO, eventually getting his own special in 1992 and a short-lived (six-week) talk show. Maher's comedy work on HBO led to discussions with Comedy Central, and in 1993 *Politically Incorrect* was born.

The audience for *Politically Incorrect* on Comedy Central was at first relatively small. By 1994, however, the show was beginning to get more publicity and Maher appeared frequently on the *Tonight* show as a kind of "faux correspondent" covering events like the New Orleans Mardi Gras.[28] Maher himself described his show on Comedy Central as "the McLaughlin Group on acid." Instead of four newspaper critics battling over the meaning of the day's headlines, Maher and his staff of five talent bookers would enlist actors, rock singers, politicians, and citizen crusaders who would debate the news from a fresh angle. The results were often strained, but surprisingly substantial debates came out of this format as well. It was "outside the Beltway" talk, and it was refreshing after years of canned public-affairs discussion shows on television.

Also refreshing was Maher's stance toward the viewer. Maher was quite blunt about his lack of respect for the American electorate. "We deserve everything we get," he said on one show. "Farmers depend on subsidies, industries on bailouts, minorities on affirmative action and wrestlers on steroids." Once he told an interviewer: "It's always been the position of our show that the people aren't blamed enough."[29] On another occasion, in the midst of a series of comments on President Bill Clinton in the mid-1990s, Maher said, "Clinton was the right president because he's full of shit and we're full of shit. We claim we want one thing but we really don't. Or we claim we want two things that are diametrically opposed, like cutting taxes and saving entitlements."

Maher and his staff chose topics that were provocative: debates on the death penalty, hate speech, and the distribution of free needles to drug addicts to prevent AIDS. One program focused on the question: "If a woman can rent out her body for nine months as a surrogate mother, why can't she do the same for a half-hour as a prostitute?"

By the mid- to late 1990s, Maher had a widening national audience base on ABC, several books and videotapes on the market, and appeared to be following the tradition of such national public satirists as Mark Twain, Ambrose Bierce, Mort Sahl, and Will Rogers. His entertainment/news talk fusion was drawing an audience of 3.1 million viewers on ABC by the summer of 1997, 75 percent of the show's lead-in audience from *Nightline*.[30] In addition, Maher was beating *The Late Show with David Letterman* in seventeen major city markets.[31] "For the first time in anyone's memory," said ABC Vice President Alan Sternfeld, "we have a viable late-night franchise."[32] Five years later, however, *Politically Incorrect*'s run on ABC was over. A combination of factors, including a controversial remark after the World Trade Center bombing of September 11, 2001, led to its demise, but not until it had left a permanent mark on the landscape of commercial broadcasting and raised serious questions about the limits of first-amendment freedom of speech on commercial television.

GARRY SHANDLING AND *THE LARRY SANDERS SHOW* (1992–1998)

The Larry Sanders Show occupies a unique position in the history of TV talk. Although it follows a tradition of talk-show parodies that includes Bob and Ray, the satirical sketches of Jack Benny, *Fernwood 2-Night, Saturday Night Live,* and *SCTV, The Larry Sanders Show* was one of the most daring and intricate satires of TV talk. Garry Shandling and his associates employed a deliberate strategy to create an alternative talk universe, a para–talk show, with such a tightly interwoven texture of satirical exaggeration and show-business reality that it was frequently difficult to separate the two.

The host of the show, Larry Sanders, was closely modeled on Shandling himself. Larry Sanders was "70 percent" himself, Shandling once said. He mined facets of his own life and career to portray the monumental narcissism and insecurity of the host of *The Larry Sanders Show*. Sanders was, in fact, Shandling's show-business alter ego.

In developing his comedy act, Shandling had followed Woody Allen's work in film (an "enormous influence"[33]) and the autobiographical comedy of Steve Martin and Albert Brooks.[34] His own talk-show credentials were solid. He had been a frequent guest on Johnny Carson's *Tonight* show in the 1980s, starting with his first appearance in March 1981, and his guest hosting abilities had been well enough appreciated by Carson and his staff to earn him the "permanent guest host" position after Joan Rivers left the show in the summer of 1986.[35] With his experience on *The Tonight Show* and having finished his situation comedy, *It's Garry Shandling's Show*,[36] Shandling was ready to launch a new creative experiment in 1992.

The idea for *The Larry Sanders Show* began with an episode on his Showtime sitcom in which Shandling played a guest on a talk show. After his four-year run on Showtime was over, he received several offers to host talk shows. Tribune Entertainment asked him if he wanted to replace Dennis Miller. "I told my manager, Brad Grey, that if I had to choose—though I didn't have a commitment at that time to do *The Larry Sanders Show*—between a talk show and doing a show about a talk show, I'd rather do the show about the talk show," Shandling said. "I knew exactly what it would be."[37] What fascinated Shandling about doing a show about a talk show was the chance to expose the backstage machinations of TV talk, all the hypocrisy and maneuvering behind the scenes. "At home, you watch and can never guess whether the host likes the guest, doesn't like the guest, wants to date them, or wants to kill them." Now he would get a chance to show it all—the backstage venom, the petty egos, and the conflicts.

HBO president Michael Fuchs gave Shandling a go-ahead to develop a pilot with his cowriter Dennis Klein, the former head writer of *Mary Hartman, Mary Hartman* and writer/producer of *Buffalo Bill* and *Bakersfield P.D.* As the airdate neared, Shandling threw himself into all aspects of production, casting veteran actor Rip Torn as Sanders' amoral producer "Artie" and Jeffrey Tambor as his obsequious sidekick "Hank Kingsley." Shandling's real-life girlfriend, Linda Doucett, was Hank's assistant. When not on camera, Shandling remained on the set during all tapings, watching the monitor and working with Jim Kantrowe, a *Tonight Show* associate director of nineteen years, who supervised Garry/Larry's on-air scenes. As star, producer, and principal writer,

Shandling seemed to be on top of every script change, camera angle, and editing decision.

By the time the series aired in August, interest had grown. Shandling and his producing team invited comedy guests like Carol Burnett, Robin Williams, Dana Carvey, and Billy Crystal, who were skillful in blurring the lines between reality and fiction. Was the show a parody or a new kind of talk show, a new talk blend? Critics, fans, and publicists debated the issue. One of the first reviews of the show described it as creating a "parallel television universe" in which what was "real" and what was not was confusing even for those producing the show.

> There are dressing rooms in one building and sets built to look like dressing rooms in another. There are writers feeding lines to actors playing writers feeding lines to actors. There are makeup people making up actors playing makeup people, producers conversing with actors playing producers. And just across the parking lot from HBO's real *Larry Sanders Show* production office—a cluttered maze of ringing telephones, scattered notepads, and half-finished cups of coffee—is a painstaking replica of a production office—a cluttered maze of ringing telephones, scattered notepads, and half-finished cups of coffee.[38]

"We try not to think about it," one of the crewmembers was quoted as saying. "We're afraid that our head might explode."

For Garry Shandling, *The Larry Sanders Show* was a logical extension of a career based on autobiographical humor. Born in Chicago on November 29, 1949, the younger of two sons of a print shop owner and the proprietor of a pet store, Shandling moved with his family to Tucson when he was three. His brother, Barry, who suffered from cystic fibrosis, died eight years after the move, when Garry was ten. It was an incident that affected Shandling deeply.

Shandling went to the University of Arizona, where he studied electrical engineering before switching to marketing. Later he took courses in creative writing. A turning point came when he submitted examples of his comedy writing to George Carlin, who encouraged him to pursue a comedy career. In 1973 Shandling went to Hollywood and began writing comedy scripts.

In 1977 a traumatic car accident forced him to reconsider everything. He described this as a near-death experience, and it led him to believe that he should try to do what he really wanted to do, which was stand-up comedy. He felt that stand-up pushed him to self exploration. Shandling began exploring his new stand-up persona in clubs and in talk-show appearances, and then got his own situation comedy on Showtime.

In *It's Garry Shandling's Show*, Shandling played a star who repeatedly broke the frame of the story, the "fourth wall" convention of drama, by addressing the studio and viewing audience directly. *The Larry Sanders Show*, which started filming in 1992, was an extension of the comedy persona Shandling had been developing on his Showtime sitcom and in his stand-up routines. When asked what he considered the principal emotion of Larry Sanders, Shandling's alter ego talk-show host, Shandling didn't hesitate. He said that it was fear—fear that the show might be canceled and he might not be Larry Sanders, and if he was not talk-show host Larry Sanders, then who was he?

The Larry Sanders Show was both a commercial and a critical success, though it ended in exhaustion for the host and a legal battle with his former personal manager and partner, Brad Grey. By the time the show went off the air in May 1998, it had dominated the Cable ACE awards and earned more prime-time Emmy nominations than any other program in HBO or cable history.[39] It won the coveted Peabody Award, and the finale was named by *Time* magazine the number one show of 1998.

Reverberations from the show continued even after it went off the air. *Entertainment Weekly* named *The Larry Sanders Show* one of the ten best television series of 1998.[40] The fall after the show ended Larry Sanders' autobiography appeared, *Confessions of A Late-Night Talk Show Host*. The legal suit with former manager Brad Grey still unresolved at the time, the "real" world of Gary Shandling and the world constructed by Shandling/Sanders continued to intersect.

Jon Stewart, who had hosted his own late-night talk show and been cast as a "competitor" to Larry Sanders and then his succcessor in the show's final year on the air, now had his own show on Comedy Central. It was promoted in a full-page ad in *Entertainment Weekly* as "proudly making the line between news and entertainment even blurrier."[41] By the beginning of the next decade, the *Jon Stewart Daily Show* would itself win a coveted Peabody award. The marketing campaign for the new *Jon Stewart Daily Show* summed up one of the principal directions TV talk had taken in the last decade of the twentieth century. No longer did fiction and reality, news and entertainment simply alternate in TV talk. They were now interwoven.

CONCLUSION

News talk, entertainment talk, and the increasingly complex territory in between were alive and well at the end of TV's fifth decade. Some talk subgenres had consolidated. Some had reorganized. Some had disappeared. New forms and formats had arisen. Several talk stars—Mike Wallace and Barbara Walters, for example—had spanned the history of TV talk. Others were just beginning to appear on the horizon. As TV talk entered its sixth decade, the talk show continued to evolve, remaining one of popular culture and television's most fertile sites.

Talk itself was very old, but the broadcasting media of the twentieth century had turned talk into something else, something that was private and public at the same time. As the new millennium arrived, millions continued to experience talk worlds that were both virtual and real.

TEN
CONCLUSION

The discussion of the convergence of news and entertainment, fiction and reality on television in the 1990s concludes this fifty-year survey of the history of the TV talk show. This history has been designed to provide an overview of TV talk's unspoken rules, forms, and landmark figures, to describe the guiding principles of the TV talk show as they have evolved historically, and to provide a historical base for defining the TV talk show as a genre. In addition to close-ups, profiles, and case studies, the book explores the cultural role of the talk show in the United States as it both reflects and shapes public opinion.

Through a decade-by-decade description of five major cycles in the development of the TV talk show, we see how developments in TV talk were closely linked to developments within the television industry itself. Understanding the historical development of TV talk's unspoken rules, the social and economic forces that have shaped those rules, and the power the genre has to shape public opinion gives us a clearer understanding of what unites all TV talk shows. A periodic history of television talk helps us to see that the talk show is more than a simple personality-driven form of entertainment, that it is, in fact, a highly refined genre.

Certain talk-show hosts—the "auteurs" of television talk programming—appear as representatives of their audiences in ways that parallel elected political figures. In each decade, in both news and comedy, major talk-show hosts have come to represent the audience's "common sense" in public news and public humor. These hosts have become formative cultural figures.[1]

TV talk shows are now very much a part of the social matrix of our times. They parallel, reflect, or mirror social change. At times, they serve to balance or counterpoint changes in society. The 1950s, for example, described so frequently as an era of conformity and corporate homogeneity, brought American television viewers a series of strong-minded, flamboyant, and very independent and individualistic talk-show hosts: Murrow, Godfrey, Garroway, Francis, Wallace, and Paar. One by one, as the next decade approached, the founders of TV talk from the 1950s departed from the scene as network executives reasserted control over their shows. Only a few talk-show stars, tough negotiators operating within profitable network vehicles, survived. The hosts of the 1950s were removed by the networks for the same qualities of independence and feistiness that had made them stars in the era of strong sponsors. Indeed during much of the 1960s, when the civil rights movement, the youth movement, the anti–Vietnam War movement, and the early women's movement gained headlines, TV remained bland as the networks clamped down on controversy and dissent.

If the changes in the TV talk show of the late 1960s and early 1970s were not a matter of simple audience reaction to talk personalities, what did precipitate the changes? Three factors contributed: technological and economic shifts, new forces of competition within the television industry, and ideological splits within society. The big three networks were initiating hardly any new shows by the end of the 1960s, but national syndicators outside the networks quadrupled the output of TV talk at the end of the decade. The social and cultural ferment the networks nervously attempted to contain spilled over into syndication, and at times into late-night fringe time slots as well. Audiences were looking for escape, but they were also hungry for comedy and debate about the topics of the times: the "counterculture," the war in Vietnam, the civil rights movement, and the women's movement. This period coincided with sitcoms that often looked like talk shows (*All in the Family*, 1970–1979), and with the highly publicized late-night talk-show wars from 1967 to 1972 between Johnny Carson, Joey Bishop, Merv Griffin, David Frost, and Dick Cavett. These talk-show "wars" represented competing talk-show personalities, but they also represented conflicts in popular ideology. Carson and Cavett, for example, represented distinctly different points of view in the talk worlds they shaped and inhabited.

The 1970s were transitional for political, economic, and cultural institutions in the United States, and the television networks faced their own "legitimation crisis" in the political and legal turmoil of the Watergate era. Johnny Carson's reassertion of dominance in late-night television by the mid-1970s paralleled the U.S. government's reestablishment of its authority after Watergate, and though much of this may have been historical coincidence, television's exercise of power as a fifth estate was not. The nation watched television screens more and more as sets converted to color and the Vietnam War became a living-room war, contested in words and images as well as armaments. In the late 1960s and 1970s new technologies of production (cheaper television studios and lower production costs), new methods of distribution (satellite transmission and cable), and key regulatory decisions made nationally syndicated talk increasingly attractive to investors and opened up room for innovative hosts and formats like those of Phil Donahue in syndication and Bill Moyers on public television. Television became increasingly, during this time, the "talk of the nation."

In the 1980s and early 1990s, corporate takeovers and the deregulation of the Reagan and Bush administrations, combined with a willingness of advertisers to support hosts who appealed to racial minorities and new demographics, encouraged a range of new nationally syndicated shows with sensational topics, relationship themes, and ethnic hosts. Sally Jessy Raphaël, Geraldo Rivera, and Oprah Winfrey became national figures. National political campaigns contributed to the new prominence of talk shows. The 1992 Presidential contest between Democrat Bill Clinton, Republican incumbent George Bush, and independent H. Ross Perot paralleled the battle between late-night entertainment hosts for the time slot vacated by Carson. The second late-night talk-show war of 1992 and 1993 reflected the issues spotlighted by the 1992 national elections. A generational shift occurred in late-night and daytime TV talk (from Carson to Letterman and Leno, from Donahue to Ricki Lake) at approximately the same time it was occurring at the ballot box during the 1992 political campaign. In 1992 Democratic candidate Bill Clinton defeated George Bush and Ross Perot, with all the candidates attempting to parley talk-show appearances into votes. Some called Clinton the first talk-show President as viewers saw news and entertainment converge more and more on national television screens.

From the founders of the 1950s, through the institutionalization of major talk subgenres on network shows in the 1960s, through the experiments of syndicated talk entrepreneurs of the 1970s and 1980s, and finally through the work of innovators, blenders, and synthesizers of the 1990s, the TV talk show has been constantly evolving. It some-times reflects and sometimes counterpoints the surrounding social en-vironment. Though it normally takes place within the confines of a television studio, TV talk is always directed to a mass audience outside the studio. TV talk reflects a dual consciousness in this sense. It is both private and public, personal and mass. The talk show is a porous genre in a porous medium,[2] absorbing everything that comes its way: the eco-nomic climate, commercial trends and fashions, political and social movements. The talk show establishes new social rituals. As Michael Arlen has pointed out, talk shows maintain an almost obsessive form of television sociability at a time when traditional forms of hospitality are on the wane.[3] Videotape has made it possible to capture these sociable word rituals, and enjoy, analyze, and study them as social documents.

The survival of talk worlds past and present poses a special challenge for those who preserve, study, and interpret human communication. How can historical studies place the TV talk show in the context of earlier traditions of public talk? How can text studies by critics and scholars trained in film and other disciplines enable viewers to under-stand subtle but crucial distinctions that camera and direction make in the rhetoric of the TV talk show? In what ways can skillful editors putting together video compilations, commentaries, and critiques com-pare and contrast TV talk worlds from the same and different periods of television history? Such compilations and critiques would undoubtedly give us a more direct appreciation of what made certain hosts, guests, and talk worlds compelling for their viewers. How can political econ-omy and technology studies further our knowledge of this unique form of public talk at the end of the twentieth century? There is much work to do in studying and coming to terms with the contemporary tele-vision talk show, and this work is situated within a growing media lit-eracy movement that attempts to counter the power of the media by educating citizens to understand its forms.

To paraphrase W. E. B. Du Bois, the question of media literacy may turn out to be one of the fundamental questions of the twenty-first century. To the extent that this book encourages more specific under-standing and active engagement with a form of television that affects so many of us, it joins a much larger media literacy movement: a move-ment to understand the power of the media that politically, economi-cally, and culturally shape our future.

APPENDIX

A TAXONOMY OF TELEVISION TALK

By Robert J. Erler and Bernard M. Timberg

As this book evolved we realized that we had a double purpose: to explore the history of American "talk shows" but also something broader, to develop a taxonomy of television "fresh talk." Sociologist Erving Goffman applied the term "fresh talk" to talk that seems spontaneous but may in fact be quite planned or staged.[1] The term turned out to be very appropriate for the kinds of talk we were examining.

We felt that a taxonomy of television talk could be helpful to both scholars and ordinary viewers trying to understand television as more than the "one great, blooming, buzzing confusion" it often seems to be.[2] Classifying, as rhetorician James Kinneavy once said, is the beginning of theory.[3] And a taxonomy of television talk that can classify it into a unified system, we felt, would help people studying the genre. It would aid those trying to understand the medium to perceive the range of talk on television as part of a larger system conditioned by production practices and industry standards and shaped by economic and political as well as cultural constraints.

We make no judgments as to the "worth" of any of the kinds of television talk listed here. This talk is produced within a medium that is oligarchic—so much of it being controlled by major economic "players" and business interests. But it is also a democratic medium in one fundamental sense. Each of us is free to critique and evaluate television for what it does and does not bring into our lives. Viewers are free to satirize or lambaste television, even to turn it off. In other words, we see our mission as not only organizing what appears at present to be a hodgepodge of television talk into an organized whole, but also extending democratic discussion of the medium, something that becomes increasingly important as television wields growing economic and cultural power.

We found as we continued our work that the job we set ourselves was harder than we had thought it would be—that even what seemed at first a rather simple distinction, the line between spontaneous and scripted speech, was not so simple to draw in practice. We knew that comedians who appeared on talk shows wanted us to believe that their jokes had been created in the moment, spun out on the air. We knew, however, that in most cases, the comedian had worked hard and long in preparing those jokes—and had practiced them assiduously. Comedian Jay Leno was known as the "hardest-working man in show business" for the care he put into writing and practicing his casual-sounding routines. His "topical" jokes were always well rehearsed. And in this book we show how well rehearsed and carefully constructed were the premises of Letterman's "spontaneous" bits on his NBC show in the early and mid-1980s.

To draw the lines that separate the various forms of television fresh talk it seemed necessary to develop a taxonomy of television talk. We wanted to view television talk outside the traditional boxes of "talk show," "panel" or "cooking show" that separate one form of talk from another. We were taking a more unified approach to talk on television, so it would be necessary to develop a more unified way of organizing and classifying the traditional forms.

In the pages that follow we develop a series of terms that categorize all shows whose central interest is their talk, and we present a preliminary taxonomy of not just what are commonly referred to as "talk shows," but all television talk. We are well aware that because of the complexities involved in drawing lines between types and families of talk on television, along with the constantly changing character of the talk that occurs on the air, the categories we propose will be inexact at best. However, we hope to be as comprehensive in our taxonomy as is possible at the time the book appears.

First, we distinguish by their general purposes three broad subgenres of TV talk: news talk, entertainment talk, and socially situated talk. We believe that almost all television talk can be placed under one or another of these three headings. Though the narrative history of this book focuses on news and entertainment talk, socially situated talk, represented more broadly in the Guide, has its own fascination as an intersection of speech, social ritual, and television technology.

Although there are clearly many hybrids and blends, these broad subgenres have, at their roots, three separate aims: to provide information, to entertain, or to represent through various television formulas an array of social communication experiences—for example, legal proceedings, reunions, demonstrations of expertise and skills (such as cooking or home building), and competitive games of all kinds.

We can identify a TV talk show along a number of different lines. First, we classify shows by the rhetorical strategies or modes they employ. A monologue, talk from a single speaker who speaks directly to a studio audience or a viewing audience at home, is different from the talk that occurs among members of a panel or the kind of one-on-one dialogue that occurs in host-guest interviews. Here again, a blend or mixture of rhetorical modes characterizes most talk shows. A monologue begins a late-night entertainment show, but the monologue itself may be interrupted by banter between the host and the host's sidekick or band. Then the show shifts into the interview format that anchors most of the show, although the interviews are broken up by comedy skits, variety performances, sales pitches, and, of course, lead-ins to commercials and station breaks. One of the most important skills of a television talk-show host is the ability to shift modes, to execute one or more rhetorical modes in rapid succession. Johnny Carson's well-known comic grimaces, Joan Rivers' chatty asides, Jay Leno's winks, and David Letterman's playful encounters with the camera were trademark gestures of these hosts. Each established his or her own personal relationship to the viewing audience.

When rhetorical modes are organized into a particular structure or pattern for a show, they become a format: a hosted variety show, a panel discussion, an interview show, a satirical show, an instructional monologue. The rhetorical modes employed and the format of a show are influenced by the time of day the show airs. The industry's traditional day parts are early morning, daytime, evening prime time, and late-night fringe time. Formats are also influenced by the demographics of those who watch the show (women, men, couples, children, members of various ethnic groups). Most importantly, each host leaves his or her personal stamp on the rhetorical modes employed in a show. It is the host who establishes the tone and pacing of the show. For example, within the monologue format, a suave European on *The Continental* spoke alluringly through the screen to a largely female audience in the 1950s. This host established an entirely different ambience from the polemical monologue format of Rush Limbaugh or, to take another extreme, the mellifluous gentle tones of Mister Rogers as he spoke to his younger audience. Two hosts working within the same format (Phil Donahue and Oprah Winfrey, for example) may establish quite different tones.

We now have a series of parameters by which we can define a television talk show: the general aim or purpose of the show, the rhetorical modes it uses, the format which puts the modes together in a particular show, the time of day (still important, though now affected by video recording and "time shifting"), audience demographics, and the tone established by each host or team of hosts.

We found that in many shows the interview was the most important rhetorical mode, establishing a backbone structure for many of the news and entertainment shows we examined. Interview technique varied widely though. Sometimes interviews were technologically mediated. When Edward R. Murrow spoke on *Person to Person* to interviewees who existed merely on a screen in front of him, the interviews took on a somewhat genial, "removed" quality. Ted Koppel established a cerebral distance using a modernized version of this technological mediation. Barbara Walters specialized in relaxed modes of personal revelation by physically entering the domestic space of her interviewees. And Mike Wallace established an unusual form of third-degree intimacy within the stark glare of the studio "key" light on his early *Night Beat.* Some of his interviews verged on acts of aggression, the hunter pursuing his prey. The art of the interview was, in the cases mentioned above, central to the art of the show.

Some hosts shifted their on-air persona radically when they changed formats. In his earlier entertainment persona, Mike Wallace engaged in witty verbal repartee with his wife, Buff Cobb, as part of their early-morning talk show on CBS, *Two Sleepy People.* (Later, shows like *Live! with Regis and Kathie Lee* or its twenty-first-century version, *Live! with Regis and Kelly*, would extend and institutionalize this tradition of early-morning couples' banter.) However, in his news-related shows, *Night Beat* and *60 Minutes,* Mike Wallace developed a much harder, more intense, confrontational persona. Other hosts (Koppel, Carson, and Letterman, for example) were noted for the constancy of their host persona and tone over time, remaining with the same program categories that first brought them to national attention and instituting few changes in rhetorical mode and format.

Formats go in and out of style, just as hosts do. In the first decades of American broadcast television the panel show was the dominant form of TV talk. A group of celebrities would get together as a panel, using some sort of game or contest as a rationale for their witty conversation. *What's My Line?* and *I've Got a Secret* were two of the longest-running and most watched shows in early television, each of them airing well before the OED would make its first reference to "talk-shows" in 1965. Other varieties of game show became the pretext for talk, as in Groucho Marx's *You Bet Your Life* and *Hollywood Squares.*

Having established certain key terms and reviewed a wide range of talk programs over five decades of network television history, we now present an introductory map of the three main subgenres of TV talk, discussing some of each category's best known hosts and formats.

NEWS TALK

Television news talk in its earliest examples used already existing models. The press conference had already been modified on radio into a panel-interview format. *Meet the Press* is the oldest and longest-lived example of this type, which has proved to be one of the most unchanging of all news talk formats, although since Tim Russert's arrival the format has become looser. Similarly, prior models of debate and town meeting were used by television early on. In the 1980s Phil Donahue and Vladimir Pozner's *Citizens' Summit* extended the notion of town meeting to live intercontinental exchanges between Russian and American citizens as relations between the USSR and the United States warmed. In the 1980s Ted Koppel followed Edward R. Murrow's *Small World* example by institutionalizing trans-oceanic dialogue through live, satellite-feed interviews and international town meetings in countries such as Israel, the Philippines, and the Union of South Africa.

News talk includes forms that follow closely both the traditional talk events "borrowed" for television transmission and also the newer television-simulated or modified versions. The press conferences of the Eisenhower, Kennedy, and Nixon presidencies were often broadcast live, though frequently followed by television's own news talk creation: the "instant analysis" commentary from network reporters. Thus there are always strong consonances and parallels between "real" events and their televised cousins.

At the same time, similarities that seem obvious may be misleading. Although the live or as-if-live broadcasts of Senate investigative hearings, U.N. assemblies, Congress, and the British Parliament (as covered by C-SPAN and other networks) may appear to be purely re-corded public events, critics have noted that such broadcasts change the nature of the event, and some commentators have suggested that television and the Internet combined may actually become a new mode of community decision-making.

Other creations of radio and television are the discussion and newsmagazine of the air formats. Programs such as *Washington Week in Review, Nightline,* and *Today* echo older forms of talk, including Chautauquas and academic seminars, but these shows shape their communities of talk ("talk worlds") in new ways. For example, play-by-play descriptions and commentary at sports events are certainly fresh talk, although it is the sporting event itself that people tune in to watch. Here, sports commentary could be considered frosting on the cake. But how appealing is a cake without frosting? Talk may become important enough in a marketing sense to make or break a show. In the 1970s, people tuned in to hear Howard Cosell spar with Don Meredith on *Monday Night Football.* Sports reporting usually falls into the subgenre of news talk, even if an entertainment talk personality like Dennis Miller briefly tries his hand at the form (as he did in his *Monday Night Football* experiment in the early 2000s). But some sports, such as *DuMont Wrestling,* fall under the entertainment talk category, since the entertainment value of the talk supersedes the report on the game or contest.

ENTERTAINMENT TALK

The subgenre of entertainment talk is one of the most diverse and popular on television. It has its roots in earlier entertainment forms such as vaudeville, in magazine articles designed to provoke laughter or entertainment, and in a wide range of entertainment radio from the 1920s through the 1950s. Producers of TV talk entertainment "families" (which often include announcers, sidekicks, musical ensembles, and sometimes the production staff of the talk show itself) developed their own special combinations of traditional formats, parts of the audience day, audience demographics, and tones of approach (gentle, combative, informative, ludicrous, or bizarre).

Combinations of talk-show forms evolve through the years. From Steve Allen through Ernie Kovacs, Jack Paar, Johnny Carson, and Jay Leno, the late-night host-variety show *Tonight* (excluding its interregnum forms) has remained fairly stable. Yet it has evolved with each host, reshaping and reinventing itself each time. The daytime talk-variety show has numerous varieties within the format. Contrast *The Arthur Godfrey Show,* Don McNeill's *Breakfast Club, Art Linkletter's House Party, The Garry Moore Show,* and *The Morning Show* (CBS), for example.

The daytime audience-participation talk-interview show has also had numerous variations. The show has moved from a news/public-service orientation (the *Home* show) to unashamedly voyeuristic entertainment (*Jerry Springer*). Both *Oprah* and *Donahue* aimed initially at a daytime audience of women in a format that alternated or combined news and entertainment. *Jerry Springer* and *Jenny Jones* have come to appeal to a quite different "tabloid" audience and established quite different tones. Likewise, similarities may be found between Dick Cavett's interviews and those of Morton Downey Jr., but the audiences and tone are quite obviously different.

Parody and satire entertainment talk shows have included *Bob and Ray*, skits on *Jack Benny, Max Headroom, Dame Edna's Hollywood, America 2Night, The Larry Sanders Show, SCTV,* and popular segments on *Saturday Night Live.* The connections are most obvious when the satire is directly connected to a particular talk-show format or subgenre, as it frequently is.

Film or book review shows such as *Siskel & Ebert* and *Book World* also fall into the entertainment talk subgenre, because they are oriented toward books and films as entertainment primarily. *Captain Kangaroo* and *Romper Room* had educational purposes but used entertainment appeals to reach children. Recently, gender differences have been reestablished (and parodied) on such shows as *The View* and *The Man's Show.* And cable television has led to a proliferation of talk shows, which are hard to categorize. Sorting out these formats, subcategories, and reinventions of the talk show requires historical perspective. What we have attempted to do now for recent forms of TV talk might be much easier to accomplish ten years from now.

SOCIALLY SITUATED TALK

Of all the subgenres of talk the most diverse and in many ways the most interesting is socially situated talk. Here the event simulated for the television camera is the principal focus of the talk format. In some sense, all talk shows are socially situated. As Michael Arlen has pointed out, the entertainment talk show is based on a hospitality ritual in which a host invites a guest into his or her studio home for a visit.[4] (The hospitality rituals are even more consciously enacted when the studio mimes a home, as it did on the *Dinah Shore* talk show in the 1970s and for children in *Mister Rogers' Neighborhood*.) But the subgenre of socially situated talk shows also revolves around a particular "reality-based" social event. Thus, weddings produce *Bride and Groom*, beauty pageants bring us conversations with contestants, and judicial proceedings create *The People's Court* and *Judge Judy*.

The scholarly world of socially situated talk might include shows like *Author Meets the Critics, Bill Moyers' World of Ideas, Summer Semester*, and *What in the World*. The instructional lecture has become, within the world of socially situated talk, *Julia Child, This Old House*, and *Zoo Parade*. Religious socially situated talk has included various forms of preaching and prayer from Bishop Fulton Sheen to Oral Roberts, from Gene Scott to Billy Graham. *The PTL Club* is a hybrid of socially situated talk and entertainment talk.

All talk shows create "talk worlds," and those worlds, within socially situated talk, are various. How do we characterize *Juvenile Jury* or *Life Begins at Eighty*? Are advice shows such as *Consult Dr. Brothers* and *The Dr. Ruth Show* instructional, therapeutic, or forms of entertainment? Will the relationship shows like *The Dating Game* and *Blind Date* become grist for the mill of future cultural anthropologists? Finally, what do we do with the "reality" shows that thrive on intimate revelations of personal behavior (aggressive, sexual, mercenary) and sometimes embarrassment associated with that behavior, revealed before the camera. These shows range from *Candid Camera* through *Cops, Survivor*, and *Big Brother*. Very much in fashion in the late 1990s and early 2000s, these shows are clearly forms of entertainment within artificially constructed social situations that "test" their participants. For lack of a better term these might be called Schadenfreude shows: shows that allow the audiences to view and feel sorry for (or amazed at) the indignities people are willing to endure for their fifteen minutes of fame.

Though socially situated talk shows appear simple, usually based on a single premise or game, they are actually quite complex as categories of social experience and communication. What are the motivations to produce and participate in *This Is Show Business, Can You Top This?, The Price Is Right, Keep Talking, Hollywood Squares, Liars Club, To Tell the Truth, Queen for a Day, Family Feud*, and *Strike It Rich?* Are they "game" shows or "talk" shows, "relationship" shows, or something else? What kind of balance exists between the verbal competition that takes place and other forms of social competition that constitute the "game" of these shows? We have not attempted to go more deeply into the social meanings of "game" talk here, but we do argue that each show can be examined as socially situated fresh talk, forged in the crucible of competition.

Creating a taxonomy of fresh talk on television is an ongoing process. Formats shift and change. New fashions sweep the world of commercial broadcasting. What we have tried to present here is a framework on which to build. While it is commercially controlled, television is also created by its viewers. Its viewership is a mass, but also a collection of individuals, and it is conditioned by multiple perspectives. Television experience (what we make of what the commercial powers-that-be offer us) is as democratic and active as literate television viewers care to make it. It is ordinary viewers, as well as critics and producers, who make television history.

A GUIDE TO TELEVISION TALK

By Robert J. Erler

This appendix is designed to provide a basic understanding of important figures and programs in the history of talk television in the United States. As the book examines the transformations of television talk we rely on the definition of "fresh talk"—talk that appears to be spontaneous—as the principal key in delineating shows. At various periods in the history of television talk (understood in this very broad definition), the panel, instructional, and game shows have all played significant roles. At certain times, the press conference and government hearings have also stood out as significant examples of television "fresh talk." Recently, the return of the reality show, which goes back as far as *Candid Camera* and *Bride and Groom*, has begun to reshape spontaneous speech on television.

Each program entry consists of the dates the show was on the air and a brief description of its history. Each entry for an individual lists dates that cover the years the person was active in television talk and a chronological list of the programs on which the person regularly appeared. The list does not include radio or local TV shows. Names and titles in boldface have their own entries elsewhere in the list.

The list includes *only* programs that have a significant fresh talk element. For instance, the entry for Morey Amsterdam provides the dates 1948–1959 when he appeared on some shows, such as *Broadway Open House,* where fresh talk dominated the show, and others, such as *Battle of the Ages,* where fresh talk was a significant part. Amsterdam also appeared regularly on the *scripted* sitcom *The Dick Van Dyke Show* from 1961 to 1966, but, although mentioned in the paragraph, that show and its dates do not appear at the beginning of the entry because it did not have a significant fresh talk element.

The dates given are to some degree approximate in that reruns are not included and gaps of even a year or two in the careers of some individuals may not appear. These were often periods in which the personality searched for or prepared a show. No closing date indicates activity at the time this book went to press.

Some entries for major figures include only the name, dates, and shows but no paragraph describing that person. An entry for such a figure, for example David Letterman, includes a reference to the chapter in the text where that person is discussed. Most figures appeared nationally, but a few significant local figures, such as Joe Franklin, are also mentioned. One important factor in the selection of personalities is the number of years they were on TV. But some figures are included in this list because of an important aspect of their shows or careers. For example, Ronald Reagan is included because he became President, Max Headroom because he was a computer-generated character, and Wally George because of notoriety he received in the press.

Because of the historical character of our work and necessary limitations of space, some significant shows and personalities have not made it into this edition of the book. But readers who do not find a show they consider important can contact us and we will try to incorporate it into the next version of our work.

Allen, Steve, 1950–1986
> *The Steve Allen Show*
> *Songs for Sale*
> **Tonight!**
> *Talent Patrol*
> **I've Got a Secret**
> *Steve Allen's Laughback*
> *Meeting of Minds*
> See Chapter 3 for background on Steve Allen.

Allison, Fran, 1948–1957, 1967–1984
> **Kukla, Fran and Ollie**
> **The Breakfast Club**
> *The CBS Children's Film Festival*
> Fran Allison had been a radio singer and actress in Chicago for more than ten years when in 1947 she joined with Burr Tillstrom's pup-

pet group, Kuklapolitan Players, in a local Chicago television series. In 1948 the series began regional broadcasting as *Kukla, Fran and Ollie,* and it went on to become one of the most important TV programs of the early fifties. Beginning in 1950, Allison also appeared in her famous earlier radio role, which was Aunt Fanny on Don McNeill's *Breakfast Club,* whenever McNeill tried to bring his radio talk show to television. Allison attempted to expand to other roles: panelist on word-game shows, interviewing host in 1954 on *Let's Dance,* and, later, singing parts in TV specials. However for ten years she was essentially off the networks until CBS revived the Kuklapolitan Players on television in 1967 to introduce children's movies.

All-Star News, 1952–1953

ABC was much behind CBS and NBC in ratings during the early 1950s. It had no series in the top twenty until *Disneyland* in 1954–1955. In October 1952, ABC tried a daring experiment. Five nights a week it broadcast, during prime time, *All-Star News,* which was a half-hour long on two nights and an hour long on three. The program had no anchor and included not only headlines but also interviews and commentary from ABC reporters such as **Pauline Frederick** and Bryson Rash. Only the Sunday hour remained at the end of January 1953, and that disappeared in August.

American Bandstand, 1957–1989

American Bandstand first appeared as *Bandstand,* a local Phila-delphia afternoon show, with Bob Horn as host. When **Dick Clark** became host in 1956 the show was renamed. In 1957 it went on the ABC network five afternoons a week and also, briefly, as a Monday evening show. It continued daily until 1963 and later went to Saturday afternoon, where it stayed until 1987. Then it was in syndication for a year and finally ended on USA cable in 1989 with new host David Hirsch. Although the talk portion was less than substantial, it became a model for much similar programming aimed at teenage viewers, from *Soul Train* through MTV. Listening to age mates give their opinions about music influenced generations in their perspectives.

American Forum of the Air, 1949–1957

Theodore Granik, a Washington lawyer, started *American Forum of the Air* on the Mutual radio network in 1937 and brought it to the NBC television network in 1949. As producer and moderator, Granik attempted to provide a place where ideas important to the national community could be discussed seriously and without undue emotion. Clearly the model of speaking followed here came out of the long political tradition of the public forum. In 1953 ill health kept Granik from continuing as moderator, but not as producer. Stephen McCormick, a reporter, became moderator.

America's Town Meeting, 1948–1949, 1952

George V. Denny Jr., a sometime actor, sometime lecturer, began this series on radio as *America's Town Meeting of the Air* in 1935. It was broadcast from New York's Town Hall auditorium and proved immensely successful on radio during the politically charged 1930s. The format followed that of debates that had taken place in Town Hall for decades and was similar to some Chautauqua events. A panel of well-known figures with widely diverse but strongly held opinions were allowed briefly to present their views on a particular question; then the meeting was open to the floor. Frequently the discussion became loud and heated. **John Daly** sometimes replaced Denny as moderator. The show remained on radio until 1956.

America 2Night, 1978

America 2Night was a syndicated daily program that lasted little more than four months on the air. It was, however, the last of the Mary Hartman–Fernwood, Ohio, set of programs created by Norman Lear. It took a set of characters originally presented as satirical soap opera figures from Fernwood, Ohio, and who in 1977 appeared as the cast of a talk show in that town on the program *Fernwood 2-Night*, and moved them to Alta Coma, California, where they presented a nightly talk show whose guests were a mixture of the fictional world they inhabited and genuine celebrities from the real world, including Charlton Heston, **Steve Allen**, Robin Williams, Elke Sommer, and Martin Mull. Martin Mull, besides being a guest, also played the show's host, Barth Gimble, whose sidekick, Jerry Hubbard, was played by **Fred Willard**. The show was produced by **Alan Thicke**. Other shows even earlier in the seventies had satirized the talk-show genre, for example, *Saturday Night Live* and the syndicated *The Lohman and Barkley* [sic]. *America 2Night*, however, combined better than any other show of that decade the reality of being a talk show with looking at the forms of television talk from outside the frame.

Amsterdam, Morey, 1948–1959
> *Stop Me If You've Heard This One*
> *The Morey Amsterdam Show*
> **Broadway Open House**
> **Can You Top This?**
> *Battle of the Ages*
> **Keep Talking**

Morey Amsterdam was a radio and stage comedian (although not always stand-up, since he often delivered his jokes while playing the cello) with an important role in television talk. After having his own evening variety show starting in 1948, with Art Carney and Jacqueline Susann, in 1950 he became one of the initial hosts of *Broadway Open House*, considered by most critics to be the first network late-night daily talk-variety show. Because of his huge store of jokes, he was also a frequent panelist on shows such as *Can You Top This?* He is remembered by a later generation of viewers as Buddy Sorrell, one of the TV writers in the cast of *The Dick Van Dyke Show*.

Army-McCarthy Hearings, 1954

From April 22 to June 17, 1954, Senator Joseph R. McCarthy gave over the chair of the Senate permanent subcommittee on investigations in order to be able to appear as a witness in the subcommittee hearing looking into charges of subversive activity in the U.S. Army. The hearing, televised daily, became a sensation. The results, however, were far from what McCarthy had intended. He was censured for his behavior by the Senate, and public opinion solidified against him. The rhetorical devices used by the key figures were much discussed and imitated.

Art Linkletter's House Party, 1952–1969

The key element of this program was spontaneity. **Linkletter** and John Guedel, the producer of their weekly radio show *People Are Funny*, are said to have devised the format in one night, responding to a desperate executive. Linkletter would have no script, only an outline of when guests would be interviewed and a description of the various games that might be played with the studio audience. One feature that was on almost every show was an unpredictable conversation with five or six grammar school children. These conversations spun off into books and other TV series. The radio show started in 1945 and ended in 1967. A syndicated *House Party with Steve Doocy* appeared on television in 1990.

Author Meets the Critics, 1947–1954

Author Meets the Critics was first produced locally on New York radio by Martin Stone in the mid-1940s. It went on the Mutual radio network in 1946 and from 1947 to 1954 was broadcast on television at various hours by NBC, then ABC, and finally DuMont. During the initial fifteen minutes of the half-hour program, two well-known critics, one favoring the work and one opposing, debated the worth of a recent book (or occasionally a film or an article). The author could interrupt the critics by ringing a bell if he or she thought a false statement was being made. In the second half, the author could respond in detail to what the critics had said. The model of the show was that of the newspaper or magazine book review. The radio moderator was Barry Gray. On television that job was given at various times to John K. M. McCaffery, **Faye Emerson**, James Michener, and Virgilia Peterson.

Bakker, Jim & Tammy Faye, 1966–1987, 1996

The 700 Club

The P.T.L. Club

Jim J. and Tammy Faye

After starting out working for **Pat Robertson**, doing a Christian puppet show for children, and being the first hosts of *The 700 Club*, Jim and Tammy Faye Bakker created their own religious network in 1972 (along with a profit-making resort), becoming the **Johnny Carson** and Carol Burnett of televangelism (although the Bakkers' humor was less intentional). Their talk show *The P.T.L. Club* (short for "Praise the Lord") was produced in a clear imitation of **The Tonight Show**. After legal problems ended their network and their marriage and also sent Jim to prison, Tammy Faye attempted a brief commercial comeback with Jim J. Bullock on the Partner Stations Network. Both Bakkers continue to speak of future television revivals.

Barrie, Wendy, 1948–1952

The Wendy Barrie Show

Stars in Khaki and Blue

After being an early 1940s starlet in Hollywood, Wendy Barrie became in the first years of New York network television (on three different networks, sometimes on two at the same time) a charming and humorous interviewer, specializing in guests with artistic talent and/or social status. On *The Wendy Barrie Show* the interviews took place on a set meant to be Wendy's apartment. Her sign-off line was "Be a good bunny."

Barris, Chuck, 1976–1980

The Gong Show

The Chuck Barris Rah Rah Show

Having been the producer of the successful ABC shows *The Dating Game* and *The Newlywed Game,* Barris started his own production company and created more shows where contestants made bigger and bigger fools of themselves. In 1976 he started a show more foolish than any before, *The Gong Show,* and cast himself as the host. Having never been a professional announcer before, he demonstrated that he was ready to make a great fool of himself as well, as he introduced people who would give atrocious performances until a gong was sounded and a panel of professional show people mocked them. Barris continued this concept in prime time with *The Chuck Barris Rah Rah Show.*

Barry, Jack, 1947–1958, 1969–1984

Juvenile Jury

Life Begins at Eighty

The Joe DiMaggio Show

Twenty-One

The Generation Gap

The Joker's Wild

As a radio announcer in 1946, Barry created the show *Juvenile Jury,* on which he asked a panel of children three to twelve years old questions about how life should be lived that often elicited surprising and comic responses. He brought the program to television in 1947. Barry went on to produce, along with his partner Dan Enright, and sometimes personally to host numerous game and panel shows. He was highly successful until the quiz scandal that developed around his show *Twenty-One* in 1958. He returned to television in 1969 with *The Generation Gap* and in 1970 a syndicated version of *Juvenile Jury.* His career revived and continued until his death in 1984.

Bishop, Joey, 1958–1978

Keep Talking

The Tonight Show (substitute and guest host)

The Joey Bishop Show

Liars Club

Joey Bishop went from stand-up comic and TV panelist to frequent *Tonight Show* guest host. In 1967–1969 Bishop moved on to challenge **Johnny Carson**'s *Tonight Show* through his own ABC late-night talk show with sidekick **Regis Philbin**. Then Bishop returned to being a TV panelist and member of the Rat Pack.

Blind Date, 1949–1953

Blind Date and the later, very similar *The Dating Game* exemplify the re-framing for television of informal social encounters. On both shows eligible men answer questions from a woman who can hear the men but not see them. The woman then decides which man she will accompany for an evening on the town, provided by the show along with a chaperone. *The Dating Game* sometimes reversed the male-female situation and, like the similar *Love Connection* (1983–1999), would sometimes question the couples after their dates. *Blind Date* began on radio in 1943 with **Arlene Francis** as host and when it switched to TV in 1949, Francis became the first female television game-show host. The female player was usually a model or starlet and the males either servicemen or college students. The couples went to the Stork Club for their date. The TV version appeared on ABC through 1951, on NBC in 1952. When it moved to DuMont in 1953, the host was first Melvyn Douglas and then Jan Murray.

Bob and Ray, 1951–1955

    The Bob and Ray Show
    Club Embassy
    The Name's the Same

Although more famous for their over forty years of radio humor, Bob Elliott and Ray Goulding also shaped early television satire. Like the later SCTV programs, Bob and Ray offered parodies of all the other genres of television programming on their own service, which Bob and Ray claimed was the Finley Quality Network. They made fun of all the forms of television from commercials to soap operas, but their most incisive attention was given to the nature of the interview and the presentation of news. Their daily programs were well prepared but largely ad-lib. Their female coworkers were Audrey Meadows, before she worked with Jackie Gleason, and, for one summer, Cloris Leachman. In 1981 Bob and Ray joined Gilda Radner, Jane Curtin, and Laraine Newman for a one-night replacement special of *Saturday Night Live.*

The Breakfast Club, 1954–1955

On network radio from 1933 to 1968, Don McNeill's *Breakfast Club,* broadcast from Chicago, became the model for daily daytime broadcast talk-variety shows. There was a casual but energetic host with a family of performers and assorted characters plus celebrity visitors. There was a studio audience with whom the cast would often talk, and an effort to involve the non-studio audience through contests, letters read on the air, singalongs, and even shared prayer. Although there was no set script and much ad-libbing, there were many repeated and anticipated events. The hour was divided into four calls to breakfast, each with its own special format. The audience at home knew when to expect the raucous entrance of Aunt Fanny (played by **Fran Allison** of ***Kukla, Fran and Ollie***). **Arthur Godfrey**, although he owed much in inspiration to McNeill, kept up a feud. *The Club* first appeared weekly on television as a prime-time show, *Don McNeill's TV Club,* from 1950 to 1951. Apparently McNeill and television did not mesh, and the morning simulcast lasted only a year.

Bride and Groom, 1951–1958

Bride and Groom was a prime example of a television program centered on a formal social encounter. Each show interviewed a couple that had just been married in an offstage chapel. The couples had gotten to this point through an application and offstage interview process not usually talked about on camera. The on-camera interviews themselves were not rehearsed or scripted, but certainly questions were asked with knowledge that had been obtained in the off-camera process. John Nelson was host of the ABC radio version when it was on the air from 1945 to 1950 and continued to host the television version until 1954 on both CBS and NBC. The 1957–1958 season was cohosted by Robert Paige and either Byron Palmer or Frank Parker.

Brinkley, David, 1956–1998
  The Huntley-Brinkley Report
  David Brinkley's Journal
  News Magazine with David Brinkley
  This Week with David Brinkley

Upon his discharge from the Army in 1943, David Brinkley began working for NBC as a Washington correspondent, having been a reporter for United Press prior to World War II. In 1956 NBC's evening news became *The Huntley-Brinkley Report* featuring Brinkley co-anchoring from Washington and Chet Huntley from New York. In 1961, NBC began *David Brinkley's Journal*, which was broadcast weekly in prime time until 1963 and then occasionally until 1965. The *Journal* gave Brinkley the chance to comment more extensively in reports of his choosing and was an intermediate form of the developing serious television newsmagazine, situated in both time and format between **See It Now** and **60 Minutes**. Brinkley and his *Journal* won two Emmys and a Peabody. NBC expanded *The Huntley-Brinkley Report* to thirty minutes in 1963, giving Brinkley more opportunity for expanded commentary. After Huntley's retirement in 1970, Brinkley's role with *NBC Nightly News* shifted back and forth between co-anchor and commentator until he left the program in 1979. In 1980 and 1981, he hosted a new attempt by NBC to produce a prime-time newsmagazine, *NBC Magazine with David Brinkley*. This show covered either one or a few stories in the sixty minutes available, using a team of reporters with whom Brinkley could discuss the reports. Suddenly in 1981 ABC, in an effort to acquire major talent under Roone Arledge and David Burke, hired Brinkley away from NBC. In November 1981, *This Week with David Brinkley* took over the spot previously given to *Issues and Answers*, ABC's equivalent to *Meet the Press* and *Face the Nation*. After that, Brinkley interviewed newsmakers, discussed events with a group of journalists, and had time for his own commentary. After the 1996 elections Brinkley limited his appearances to brief weekly commentaries until finally retiring in 1998.

Broadway Open House, 1950–1951

Before *Broadway Open House* the networks had made very few attempts to provide regular late-night entertainment programming. Perry Como's **Chesterfield Supper Club** had been simulcast on Friday night for several months in early 1949. In late 1949 *A Couple of Joes* had been broadcast by ABC from 11:15 P.M. to midnight on Thursdays. The Joes were Joe Rosenfield and Joe Bushkin, and the show had music, jokes, giveaways, a singer, a basset hound named Morgan, and **Milton DeLugg** as musical director. **Faye Emerson** had her celebrity interview show on CBS Monday nights for two months in early 1950. Finally in May 1950, **Pat Weaver**, father of **Today**, **Tonight**, and Sigourney, had NBC broadcast *Broadway Open House* from 11 P.M. to midnight, Monday through Friday. Weaver had picked Don "Creesh" Hornsby to be host but "Creesh" died of polio two weeks before the show was scheduled to begin. So **Morey Amsterdam** took Monday and Wednesday nights and **Jerry Lester** the others. The show was a telecast stage show with skits, singing, and dancing—no desks and sofas. But unlike vaudeville, its greatest influence, it had continuity provided by the hosts from start to finish. The humor, although rehearsed, was open to improvisation. Lester had greater success at first, in part, because of the tall blond actress Jennie Lewis, who played his foil "Dagmar" and introduced a heavy sexual content (for the times) into the show. Amsterdam left in November 1950 and Lester in May 1951, in large part because of the conflict that had arisen between him and Dagmar. The music for both hosts was provided by Milton DeLugg. Jack E. Leonard took over and stayed on with Dagmar and DeLugg until the end in August. Weaver learned from the show's failure and came back with **Steve Allen** on *Tonight!* in 1953.

Brokaw, Tom, 1973–
> *Today*
> *NBC Nightly News*

Brokaw has hosted several news shows and specials, most importantly as anchor of the *NBC Nightly News* since 1982. He was also the principal figure on *Today* in 1976–1981, arriving two months after **Barbara Walters** was hired by ABC. Brokaw fit into the newsman-host pattern on *Today* but was definitely more sociable and good humored than his predecessor, John Chancellor. His tenure as *Today* host marked a period of transition from the *Today* show of the 1950s and 1960s, when it was the single dominant early-morning program, to that of the 1980s and 1990s, when the show often fell behind its competition.

Brothers, Joyce, 1957–1984
> *The $64,000 Question*
> *Sports Showcase*
> **Captain Kangaroo**
> *Dr. Joyce Brothers: Consult Dr. Brothers*
> *Tell Me Dr. Brothers*
> *Living Easy with Dr. Joyce Brothers*
> **The Gong Show**
> *The Love Report*

Dr. Joyce Brothers has one of the most peculiar and zigzagging histories in television talk. In 1957 she was a winning contestant on the infamous *The $64,000 Question* as well as its companion *The $64,000*

Challenge, answering questions about the sport of boxing. Because of her national fame, she got a job as a cohost of *Sports Showcase.* Since her doctor's degree was in psychology, she became a regular contributor of behavioral advice on various shows (including the children's show *Captain Kangaroo)* and also a frequent talk-show guest. In the 1960s she had her own syndicated psychological advice shows and in 1972 her own daily syndicated general talk show with a band and celebrity guests. From the mid-1970s through the 1980s, after joining the Screen Actors Guild, her television and film work was more self-satire. She was a frequent panelist on *The Gong Show* and guested on such shows as *One Life to Live, Sha Na Na,* and *Moonlighting,* usually providing advice to the regular players. Sometimes she was a guest on talk shows that were sequences on dramas or sitcoms.

Brown, John Mason, 1947–1949, 1955–1959
 Tonight on Broadway
 Critic at Large
 The Last Word
 A professional drama critic, Brown attempted television shows that were both intellectual and aimed at a general audience. On *Critic at Large* he led discussions on the arts with such figures as James Michener and Billy Rose.

Buchanan, Patrick, 1982–1985, 1987–1991, 1993–1995
 Crossfire
 When not serving as a speechwriter or running for public office, Buchanan has been the regular assertive conservative voice on *Crossfire* and a frequent guest on *The McLaughlin Group.*

Buckley, William F., 1966–1999
 Firing Line
 Because of his sharp wit, intriguing persona, and skill at debate, William F. Buckley was a frequent guest on television talk shows beginning in the 1950s. He presented a view melding the conservative and the libertarian. In 1966, starting on WOR-TV in New York and going into syndication, he founded his own talk show, *Firing Line.* At various times Buckley was interviewer, moderator, and panelist. Sometimes the show followed a formal debate structure between two people; sometimes it was a moderated panel discussion; sometimes it was an inter-

view. Although there was often humor, the matters under discussion were almost always approached seriously. The topics usually were related to recent politics. In 1971 *Firing Line* went to PBS and after that shifted back and forth between there and syndication, with its final show airing in December 1999.

Burke, Alan, 1966–1970
The Alan Burke Show
In the late 1960s the bearded Burke was one of the leading representatives of angry talk-show hosts, interviewing weird and outrageous guests. He operated out of New York in syndication.

Burrows, Abe, 1949–1958
This Is Show Business
Abe Burrows' Almanac
The Name's the Same
Burrows was a successful comic radio writer for Danny Kaye and *Duffy's Tavern*, but his high energy, "always on" personality led him into radio and television performing as well. Having authored *Guys and Dolls*, he was considered a Broadway personality. Although he had his own talk-variety show, his greatest TV success was as a panelist on *This Is Show Business*.

Camera Three, 1956–1980
Camera Three was a show without a format. What held it together was the effort made by its producers, Robert Herridge and later John Musilli, to present material that was, depending on your point of view, either high quality or high brow. More often than not, the material offered was not fresh talk but rather musical, poetic, dramatic, or cinematic performance art. However, on occasion, discussions of the highest quality in fresh talk forms dealing with artistic, cultural, and social issues varied the format. When the show originally appeared on WCBS-TV in New York in 1953, it was explained that the show's name derived from a television studio's camera three. Mounted in the rear of the studio, it was the most stable, and provided the widest picture. The show won an Emmy in 1966 and a Peabody in 1978. In 1979, CBS needed the show's time period on Sunday for their new *CBS News Sunday Morning. Camera Three* moved to prime time on PBS but was gone in a year.

Candid Camera, 1948–1953, 1960–1968, 1974–1980, 1987–1991, 1997–

Candid Camera consciously sets up contrived situations for spontaneous speech and action to take place. These are then recorded and edited. *Candid Camera* was originated by Allen Funt. Funt was an independent radio producer before World War II, worked with **Eleanor Roosevelt** on her broadcast commentaries, and was a gagman for *Truth or Consequences.* While in the Army during the war, he surreptitiously recorded the opinions of service personnel and broadcast them on Armed Forces Radio. In 1947 he transferred the idea of secretly recorded encounters to commercial radio with his program *Candid Microphone.* In 1948 he added an ABC television program called *Candid Mike.* He moved to NBC TV in 1949 and the program became *Candid Camera.* Since that time, the program has been on and off the air many times. It has been a part of other programs (*The Garry Moore Show*), has been used in advertising, has been syndicated, and has had its own network specials. Often more telegenic performers would accompany or substitute for Funt in presenting the candid snippets. Among these were **Jerry Lester, Arthur Godfrey**, Durward Kirby, **Bess Myerson**, Phyllis George, Dom DeLuise, and Allen's son, Peter. In 1963–1964, Funt produced *Tell It to the Camera,* hosted by Red Rowe. This program interviewed people on the street around the country, asking them to give their opinions about life. With the development of home video equipment, Funt's ideas have been carried on by such programs as *America's Funniest Home Videos.* Allen Funt became disabled in 1993 and died in 1999, but his son, Peter Funt, continued to produce and to cohost the show on which he had first appeared as a three-year-old shoeshine boy.

Can You Top This? 1950–1951, 1969–1970

Can You Top This? and the very similar *Stop Me If You've Heard This One* raised interesting questions about what fresh talk is and how it's constructed. Both shows dealt with the nature of the joke. Each had a panel whose members knew thousands of jokes. Audience members sent in their jokes; on the air their lines were read by a performer. On *Stop Me If You've Heard This One* the panel competed to finish the joke first. On *Can You Top This?* the panelists told jokes on the same subject as the joke sent in and a laugh meter measured the responses from the studio audience. In the first case, prizes were awarded to the joke submitter for each time the joke was completed incorrectly. In the second case, prizes were awarded for each time the submitter's joke got a better meter reading than a panel member's. The humor of the jokes seemed to depend on spontaneity of delivery; and yet the basic assumption of the shows was that the jokes were known previously to the panel. This same paradox exists in a less obvious way for all variety talk shows. Both programs had been popular on the radio during the 1940s.

Capp, Al, 1952–1954, 1968–1969
> *Anyone Can Win*
> *The Al Capp Show*

Capp created the Li'l Abner cartoon characters in the 1930s but he seemed to wish for more public visibility. In the early 1950s he was a quiz-show host, panel-show moderator, and frequent panel and talk-show guest. His politics switched from liberal to conservative in the 1960s and he hosted a syndicated but unsuccessful talk show in 1968–1969. General critical opinion felt it failed because Capp was loud, rude, and annoying. He might have been more successful in the early 1990s.

Captain Kangaroo, 1955–1984

Having unsuccessfully attacked the **Today** show in 1954 with **The Morning Show,** CBS decided on a flank attack on younger viewers by adding *Captain Kangaroo* to the engagement. The structure of *Captain Kangaroo* in many ways reflected the developing early-morning format: a host (the Captain), a supporting family of regulars, and various short segments presented in such a way that the viewers could come and go during the program without feeling they were missing continuity. Over the years certain guests, such as Bill Cosby and **Joyce Brothers**, made frequent visits. In 1981 CBS expanded *The CBS Morning News* in a renewed attack on *Today* through the adult audience. *Captain Kangaroo* was shortened and moved to earlier and earlier time periods. In 1982 the show was moved to weekends and in 1984 finally terminated. The Captain was always played by Bob Keeshan, who had been the first Clarabell, the clown, on *Howdy Doody*, in 1948–1953. After leaving *Howdy Doody*, Keeshan produced some local children's shows in New York before creating the Captain. In 1964–1965 Keeshan played a similar character on the Saturday morning show *Mister Mayor.*

Carson, Johnny, 1954–1992
> *Who Do You Trust?*
> *Earn Your Vacation*
> **The Morning Show**
> *The Johnny Carson Show*

Tonight
See Chapters 4 and 5 for background on Johnny Carson.

Cavett, Dick, 1966–1996
This Morning
The Dick Cavett Show
College Bowl
See Chapter 5 for background on Dick Cavett.

Chase, Ilka, 1948–1959
Celebrity Time
Glamour-Go-Round
Fashion Magic
Masquerade Party
Keep Talking

Chase, an actress, seemed to appear on almost every panel show in the first decade of network television. Her persona was that of the middle-aged, upper-class New York sophisticate. She also hosted two short-lived interview shows, *Glamour-Go-Round* and *Fashion Magic.*

The Chesterfield Supper Club, 1948–1950

From January to June 1949 *The Chesterfield Supper Club* was broadcast by NBC at 11:00–11:15 P.M. on Friday nights and thus became the first regularly scheduled network television late-night entertainment show. It was hosted by the singer Perry Como and began as a simulcast of his three-times-a-week radio program. Although music was the focus, over the years since the show was first heard in 1944, Como had developed a famous speaking manner—casual, friendly, and involving. He later became well known on television for the same approach to guests and audience. On *The Supper Club,* Como and the announcer, Martin Block, often engaged in comic repartee.

Child, Julia, 1962–1973, 1978–
The French Chef
Julia and Company
Dinner at Julia's
Cooking with Master Chefs
Baking with Julia
Julia and Jacques Cooking at Home

Julia cooked on television—cooked and talked. She talked to the crew, sometimes to guests; she talked to us, sometimes to herself. Julia had been on local TV in Boston for years before her network shows. Julia will always be cooking.

The Christopher Closeup (The Christopher Program), 1952–1987

Father James Keller founded a group called the Christophers, which had as its main purpose the promotion of moral behavior. Although run by Catholics, the group did not promote dogma but rather took the maxim "It is better to light one candle than to curse the darkness" as its guide. The Christophers gave yearly awards to people of any religious background for doing good works. In 1952 they also started a fifteen-minute syndicated television program, at first called *What Can One Person Do?* and then *The Christopher Program.* Although occasionally it presented short dramas, the program was usually an interview, often with a celebrity such as Rosalind Russell or Ed Herlihy. Whether drama or interview, the program did not hide its agenda, which was to change people's behavior. Over the years, the host and program length varied.

Chronoscope, 1951–1955

CBS presented *Chronoscope* at 11:00–11:15 P.M. Monday, Wednesday, and Friday. The program usually provided a discussion of an event or subject in the news that week. A panel of journalists and non-journalists were guided by a moderator. The moderators included William Bradford Huie, Edward P. Morgan, and Larry LeSueur. This program functioned much as **Nightline** did later, although it lacked the newer technical accessories.

Clark, Dick, 1957–

American Bandstand

Dick Clark's New Year's Rockin' Eve

The $25,000 Pyramid

TV's Bloopers & Practical Jokes

More than thirty network years of *American Bandstand* is certainly the most important feature of Dick Clark's involvement with talk television. On that show he was a host and also an interviewer of both the musical performers and the teenagers in the studio audience. Clark has also been a quiz and variety show host and a significant producer of varied shows.

Coates, Paul, 1955–1961
Confidential File
Tonight! America after Dark
Coates was one of the significant shapers of interview shows of the 1950s, working from Los Angeles, first locally and then in syndication. His shows were meant to be controversial, whether dealing with social, political, or entertainment topics. They often combined interviews with dramatic re-creations. Although often in the spirit of the tabloid, there was usually a serious tone. His network connection was in appearances on the *Tonight* interregnum between **Steve Allen** and **Jack Paar** in 1957.

Cobb, Buff, 1951–1955
All Around the Town
Two Sleepy People
Mike and Buff
Masquerade Party
In the early 1950s, Buff Cobb worked with her then husband **Mike Wallace** on some of the most original and fascinating of television interview shows. *All Around the Town* was often broadcast live from locations all around New York City. *Two Sleepy People,* so called because of its early broadcast time of 10 A.M., was one of the first network color telecasts. It could not be seen on most black and white sets; a special rotating disk was required for color. *Two Sleepy People* and *Mike and Buff* were in format very flexible and creative shows, ready to talk about any topic with intelligence and humor. Buff's family connections also placed her deep within the history of fresh talk. She was the granddaughter of the Kentucky humorist and teller of tales Irwin S. Cobb. Her husband, after Mike Wallace, was talk-show host and later CBS news division president Bill Leonard. Chris Wallace is her son.

Collingwood, Charles, 1948–1955, 1957–1971
People's Platform
The Morning Show (CBS)
Person to Person
Portrait
Charles Collingwood was one of **Edward R. Murrow**'s protégés in World War II, and in the 1950s and 1960s he became one of the principal CBS reporters. Besides being the moderator of many discussion shows, he succeeded Murrow as interviewer on *Person to Person.* He

had his own interview shows with both political and cultural figures. He hosted science shows and was the moderator of the yearly TV panel that brought together CBS bureau chiefs. From 1955 to 1957, he left CBS to work for U.S. Director for Mutual Security W. Averell Harriman.

Collyer, Clayton "Bud," 1948–1968
> *Winner Take All*
> *Beat the Clock*
> **Masquerade Party**
> **To Tell the Truth**

Bud Collyer had been a radio announcer and actor for more than ten years before entering television. His most memorable radio role was that of Clark Kent/Superman on *The Adventures of Superman,* although the fact that Collyer played the role was kept secret for six of the program's ten years. On television, he became one of the most significant game-show hosts of its first decades.

The Continental, 1952

In intent and format, *The Continental* was unlike any other network talk show. (There were some local imitators with female hosts.) For fifteen minutes at 11:15 P.M. on Tuesday and Thursday, the handsome, debonair, middle-aged Italian actor Renzo Cesana spoke directly to the camera as if it were a woman who had come to his apartment for a late-night visit. He would pour wine and offer it to his visitor. He would tell her how beautiful she looked and how well she did things. No voice answered, but he would go on as if there were a response. Here was an informal social situation, a seduction, offered with phrases that may have come from a well-developed repertoire, designed to produce, in the female viewer at least, the feelings of an actual spontaneous encounter. Cesana had done this sort of performance for several months locally on Los Angeles television before CBS put him on the network from New York. The show received considerable public attention and comment when it appeared, but it was gone in thirteen weeks. In a few months Cesana was back on the air with *First Date,* a show on which Cesana interviewed couples on their first dates. Although Cesana had no national show after 1953, Christopher Walken performed a *Continental* imitation several times in the 1990s on *Saturday Night Live.*

Cops, 1989–

Cops is variously linked to tabloid television and reality shows, but the most precise link is probably to cinéma vérité. On each *Cops* half-hour, camera crews accompany police on patrol in a selected city. The material shown is highly selected and edited, but the only narration is by the officers being accompanied. *Cops* is also unlike many similar shows describing crime and emergency incidents, such as *America's Most Wanted* or *Rescue 911*, in that no re-enactments or after-the-fact interviews are presented. Although much of the attraction of the show may involve physical pursuit and confrontation, most of the program is given over to actual dialogue among police, victims, suspects, and witnesses.

Cosell, Howard, 1957–1991
> *Sports Focus*
> *NFL Monday Night Football*
> *Saturday Night Live with Howard Cosell*
> *Battle of the Network Stars*
> *Sportsbeat*
> *Howard Cosell: Speaking of Everything*

Howard Cosell was educated as a lawyer and practiced for ten years before gradually shifting into sports broadcasting. Although he assisted in describing sports contests, his strength seemed to lie in interviewing and commenting on sports personalities. His success in those areas led him to even more general, but less successful, programming, including a live prime-time variety show (*Saturday Night Live with Howard Cosell*) and a general syndicated talk show (*Howard Cosell: Speaking of Everything*).

Costas, Bob, 1980–
> *NFL Live*
> *Later with Bob Costas*
> *Internight*

Bob Costas combined sports and general interviewing effectively from 1988 to 1994. In 1994 he gave the hosting of *Later* to Greg Kinnear and returned to sports, cohosting the 1996 Olympics.

Couric, Katie, 1990–
> *CBS Early Morning News*
> **Today**
> *Internight*

Katie Couric moved up from reading the news on *CBS Early Morning News*, returning to NBC, where she had worked before, to coanchor *Today* in 1991. It was a difficult time at *Today* for the female co-anchor because of conflicts that had developed in the transition from **Jane Pauley** to Deborah Norville and then at Norville's departure. Couric has become a figure whom the audience views with affection. She began *Internight*, an MSNBC show, in 1996.

Crane, Les, 1964–1965
>*The Les Crane Show*
>**Nightlife (ABC)**

Young, aggressive talk-show host Les Crane had proved popular in San Francisco, so ABC brought him to New York and gave him a studio where he could sit in the center on a stool with his shotgun microphone in hand to aim at audience members. ABC decided to use Crane to begin its intensive attack on **Johnny Carson**'s *Tonight* show, which in the two years of Carson as host had become a cash cow for NBC. *The Les Crane Show* lasted about four months and was succeeded by *Nightlife*, which had numerous hosts in less than another four months. Then Les Crane returned to lead *Nightlife*.

Cronkite, Walter, 1950–
>*Open Hearing*
>*Man of the Week*
>*You Are There*
>**The Morning Show (CBS)**
>*CBS Evening News*
>*Universe*
>*Dinosaur!*

Walter Cronkite came to CBS in 1950 after being a print and radio journalist covering both foreign and domestic news. He served CBS as Washington correspondent; an outgrowth of that was his moderating *Man of the Week*, though he left before the program had a needed name change in 1954 to become *Face the Nation*. Cronkite's best-remembered work from the 1950s is probably *You Are There*, a revival of the radio show that re-created historical events as if they were being covered by broadcast news people. Cronkite was anchor for everything from the fall of Troy to the crash of the Hindenberg, always ending with "What sort of a day was it? A day like all days, filled with those events that alter and illuminate our times . . . and you were there." Cronkite's strong performance in anchoring historical events may have led CBS to try him as the first host on its well-financed *The Morning Show* in opposition to **Today**. In 1962 he became the first anchor on *CBS Evening News*, the first network half-hour daily early-evening news program. He was anchor until 1981, covering many live events both on the show and in specials. His approach was not so much inquiring as involving. He cried on camera at the Kennedy assassination, delighted in observing space shots, interviewed heads of state, and became known as the most trusted man in America. After retiring from the *Evening News*, he continued to do specials and develop series of special interest to him for CBS, PBS, and A&E. Cronkite has hosted the Kennedy Center Honors Gala for more than twenty years.

Cullen, Bill, 1949–1988
> *Act It Out*
> *Matinee in New York*
> *The Bill Cullen Show*
> ***I've Got a Secret***
> *The Price Is Right*
> *$25,000 Pyramid*
> *The Joker's Wild*

Bill Cullen was one of the first to enter the pantheon of game-show hosts. Cullen had been a radio announcer and in 1946 became master of ceremonies on the radio version of *Winner Take All*. In his forty years on national television, he hosted more than a score of game shows. Like many game-show hosts, he also tried talk variety for a while but not very successfully. His most remembered appearances are probably as a panelist on *I've Got a Secret*.

Daly, John, 1948–1967
> ***What's My Line?***
> *It's News to Me*
> ***America's Town Meeting***
> *ABC News*
> *The Voice of Firestone*

John Charles Daly was the television figure who most successfully combined careers as a newsperson and as a panel-show member and host. Before leaving in 1949 and moving to ABC News, Daly had been a CBS radio correspondent for over a decade, anchoring the radio version of *You Are There*. In 1953 Daly became ABC's vice-president of news and public affairs and also anchor of the early-evening weeknight *John Daly and the News*, where he remained, with only brief absences, until he left ABC in December 1960. His other life as a TV panel-show personality began in 1948 as a panelist on *Celebrity Time* and reached its height as host of *What's My Line?* from 1950 to 1967. During that time he hosted and appeared on several other panel shows as well. His achievement in both fields was above average. He received an Emmy in 1954 as best news reporter or commentator, and *What's My Line?* was in the top twenty programs in ratings at various times in both the 1950s and 1960s. In an attempt to diversify, during 1949 and 1950, he also played Walter Burns in the television drama series *The Front Page*, and in 1958–1959 he was host/narrator of the musical program *The Voice of Firestone*. In all these roles, however, his same air of calm humor and urbanity came across. He headed the U.S. government's Voice of America in 1967–1968.

Dawson, Richard, 1969–1985
> ***Can You Top This?***
> *Laugh-In*
> ***Masquerade Party***
> ***I've Got a Secret***
> *Family Feud*

Richard Dawson was a comic actor, a panel-show member of the 1970s, and a game-show host. In the comedy format he is best remembered as Corporal Newkirk on *Hogan's Heroes* and as a 1971–1973 cast member of *Laugh-In*. As host of *Family Feud* he emphasized the humorous relationships of competing families. Dawson's role as Damon Killian, host of the deadly game show in the movie *The Running Man* (1987), repeats a number of mannerisms and attitudes from *Family Feud*.

DeLugg, Milton, 1949–1960, 1966–1967, 1974–1980
> *A Couple of Joes*
> *Abe Burrows' Almanac*
> ***Broadway Open House***
> ***The Tonight Show***
> ***The Gong Show***

Milton DeLugg is the model for all later talk-variety music directors. On television when the host talked to DeLugg, you knew Milton was a musician because he had his accordion around his neck. In 1966–1967 DeLugg was there with his accordion to joke with **Johnny Carson** on *The Tonight Show*. But DeLugg had been on late-night seventeen years before joking with *A Couple of Joes* and later with **Morey Am-**

sterdam, **Jerry Lester**, and Jack E. Leonard on *Broadway Open House,* and with Dagmar on her show *Dagmar's Canteen.* At other times of the day, he chatted with **Abe Burrows**, Doodles Weaver (Pat's brother), **Bill Cullen**, Fred Allen, and Paul Winchell. In the 1970s he was brought back by **Chuck Barris** as being perfect for musical director of *The Gong Show* and *The Chuck Barris Rah Rah Show.*

Donahue, Phil, 1969–1996
> *The Phil Donahue Show*
> ***Today***
> *The Last Word* (ABC)
> *A Citizens' Summit*
> *Pozner and Donahue*
> See Chapters 4 and 6 for background on Phil Donahue.

Douglas, Mike, 1953–1982
> *Club 60*
> *The Mike Douglas Show*
> Mike Douglas started out as a band singer from Chicago. He first appeared on television as a singer on Kay Kyser's show in 1949. Back in Chicago in the 1950s, Douglas sang nationally on *The Music Show* and *Club 60,* while hosting his own local shows, such as *Hi Ladies.* Near the end of the 1950s, he moved to Hollywood and worked as a piano-bar singer. In 1961 Douglas was hired by Westinghouse Broadcasting to host a daily talk-variety show in Cleveland. There Douglas developed his "guest cohost of the week format," in which he almost became the permanent sidekick for shifting hosts. The show became syndicated in 1963 and moved to Philadelphia in 1965 and to Los Angeles in 1978, keeping the same format but increasing the budget. In 1981 Westinghouse decided it needed a younger audience and younger host. It replaced Douglas with John Davidson. Douglas continued in other syndications and cable for a few years.

Downey, Morton, Jr., 1987–2001
> *The Morton Downey Jr. Show*
> *Showdown*
> *Downey*
> *The New Morton Downey Jr. Show*
> *Discovering Wall St.*
> Morton Downey Sr., an Irish tenor, had his own family entertainment talk-variety shows in 1949–1951. Downey Jr. developed a very dif-

ferent talk approach. Working on radio call-in shows around the country, Downey refined putdown, abuse, and anger. Politically he was called conservative, but ideas did not seem as important in his shows as emotion. His television show started on WWOR in 1987 and was syndicated the next year. The show would make the news often, especially if there was actual violence or threat of violence. The show ratings after a year were low and the program caused stations difficulty with various groups of viewers. Downey moved over to CNBC cable in 1989.

Downs, Hugh, 1949–
    Kukla, Fran and Ollie
    American Inventory
    Your Luncheon Date
    Home
    Concentration
    Tonight (sidekick and interim host)
    Today
    Not for Women Only
    Over Easy
    20/20
    My Take with Hugh Downs

Hugh Downs began his television career on NBC in Chicago. Downs was only the announcer on *Kukla, Fran and Ollie,* but that role often called for spontaneous response. In 1951–1952 he worked on two other Chicago shows where he began to develop the skills that he demonstrated later. *American Inventory* was a public-affairs show with panel discussions; on *Your Luncheon Date* Downs chatted in a casual manner with Nancy Wright. In 1954 NBC called him to New York to assist **Arlene Francis** in hosting *Home.* This was to be Downs' first lead on one of **Pat Weaver**'s big three magazine shows, *Today, Tonight,* and *Home.* From 1957 to 1962 Downs was **Jack Paar**'s sidekick on *Tonight.* When Paar left, Downs was one of the interregnum hosts of 1962. Downs had also begun to host the game show *Concentration* in 1958 and stayed with it until 1965. In 1962 Downs became host of *Today,* his third Pat Weaver show, and began his first of many years working alongside **Barbara Walters**, after she shifted from writer to on-screen presence in 1964. Downs stayed with *Today* until 1971. Downs worked during the 1970s on the syndicated daily talk show *Not for Women Only,* again with Walters. Then he was on the daily PBS show aimed at seniors, *Over Easy.* In 1978 Downs was suddenly called by *20/20* producer Bob Shanks to replace the disastrous hosts of the show's first week. Downs was with *20/20* from its second week until he retired from the show in 1999. He was joined by Barbara Walters as correspondent in 1981 and as cohost in 1984. The Guinness book of records has certified that Downs has had over 10,000 hours on commercial television.

Duke, Paul, 1975–1994, 1999
Washington Week in Review
After the death of Peter Lisagor, Paul Duke was moderator of *Washington Week in Review*, setting its serious journalistic tone and keeping the talk moving for twenty years. Duke worked for NBC before he came to PBS.

DuMont Wrestling, 1948–1955
All four early TV networks broadcast wrestling matches, but DuMont did it first and was the last to leave (before wrestling returned in the 1980s). Jack Brickhaus broadcast from Marigold Garden in Chicago on Saturdays and **Dennis James** broadcast from various arenas in New York on Mondays. James' commentary was the more flamboyant and attracted many viewers who had little interest in sport, for televised professional wrestling was in fact more mythic combat with humorous commentary than real sport.

Edwards, Ralph, 1950–1961, 1970–1972, 1987
Truth or Consequences
This Is Your Life
Ralph Edwards had worked in radio throughout the 1930s before devising and hosting the extremely popular radio show *Truth or Consequences* in 1940. The show was based on the parlor game of the same name, but its success on radio and later television depended on devising imaginative and usually embarrassing situations that were the consequences of not answering a question correctly. That real people were placed in genuinely awkward or ridiculous situations was the reason so many tuned in this program. Edwards hosted the TV version from 1950 to 1952, and others took over after that. Bob Barker hosted the daytime version from 1956 to 1974. There were brief revivals in 1977 and 1987. *Truth or Consequences* provided the base for Edwards to build a successful game-show production company. The idea of suddenly placing people in surprising situations was modified to create Edwards' next

show, *This Is Your Life*, which premiered on radio in 1948 and on television in 1952, both with Edwards as host. Here the situation of surprise was always the same. A famous person was suddenly put on stage, told "This is your life" in a melodramatic fashion, and presented one by one with people from his or her past who would tell intimate stories from the celebrity's life. The show stayed on network television until 1961, often being in the top twenty ratings, and was revived in syndication in 1970–1972 with Edwards as host and again in 1983 with Joseph Campanella hosting. Edwards hosted two specials in 1987, and in 1993 he handed over the show to Pat Sajak for some more specials. Edwards' production company has also been responsible for *Name That Tune* and **The People's Court**, among many other series.

Elliott, Gordon, 1986–
  A Current Affair
  Hard Copy
  To Tell the Truth
  The Gordon Elliott Show
  Door Knock Dinners
  Gordon Elliott came to the United States after hosting *Good Morning, Australia* in his homeland for six years. In the U.S. he worked on *A Current Affair* and was host of *To Tell the Truth* in 1990, before starting *The Gordon Elliott Show* in syndication.

Emerson, Faye, 1948–1960
  The Faye Emerson Show
  Author Meets the Critics
  I've Got a Secret
  Faye and Skitch
  Masquerade Party
  Faye Emerson was a Broadway actress whose tremendous success in the early years of network television was due to a combination of high intelligence, an interesting personality, and a sophisticated fashion sense that included low-cut gowns. From 1948 to 1956, she emceed a number of interview and talk-variety shows, some evening, some daytime, some with her then husband **Skitch Henderson**, some without, sometimes on two networks in the same week. She was able to host both serious discussion shows like *Author Meets the Critics* and entertainment shows like her own *Faye Emerson's Wonderful Town*, which was broadcast in prime time from a different city each week.

She filled in for **Edward R. Murrow** on *Person to Person*, as well as for **Dave Garroway** and **Arlene Francis**. As an actress, she appeared in various series and specials. However, from 1957 on, Emerson's appearances were mainly as a panel member on *I've Got a Secret* and *Masquerade Party*.

Entertainment Tonight, 1981–
Since 1981 *Entertainment Tonight* has been the nightly news for those interested in show-business personalities and events. There have been frequent shifts among the male and female cohosts; the longest-lasting were Mary Hart, Robb Weller, Leeza Gibbons, and John Tesh. Rona Barrett and Jeanne Wolf each served for a time as special gossip correspondent. **Robin Leach** did features that led to his *Lifestyles of the Rich and Famous*.

Evans, Bergen, 1951–1959
  Down You Go
  Of Many Things
  The $64,000 Question
  The Last Word
Bergen Evans is an example of what was possible in the first decade of television talk. Alongside his television career, Evans was a professor of English at Northwestern University and the author of scholarly books. On television he hosted three different panel game shows, one of which *Down You Go,* similar to the word game hangman, was broadcast from Chicago from 1951 to 1956, at one time or another on each of the four national networks. He was the on-air question authority on *The $64,000 Question* when it was the top-rated show and served the same role on two other shows. He also hosted his own serious interview program *Of Many Things* and the word-meaning discussion program *The Last Word.* On all these programs his demeanor combined the serious academic with the sprightly wit.

Evening Magazine. See **P.M.** *Magazine*

Fadiman, Clifton, 1949–1956, 1964
  This Is Show Business
  Information Please
Clifton Fadiman is a prime example of how in early television a figure seen as a member of the literati could also be a successful

television personality. Fadiman was an author and book editor of *The New Yorker* before he became a member of the radio show *Information Please* panel and later its TV Master of Ceremonies. Fadiman was also the host of several moderately successful panel shows aimed at general audiences, including *This Is Show Business,* which ran between 1949 and 1956.

Faulk, John Henry, 1951–1955, 1975–1982
    It's News to Me
    Leave It to the Girls
    The Morning Show (CBS)
    Hee Haw
    John Henry Faulk had been a radio host, a long-time TV panelist, and the permanent male defender on *Leave It to the Girls* when he was selected by CBS in 1955 to be host of their important *The Morning Show.* Faulk was also running for vice-president of the New York chapter of AFTRA, the performers' union, on a platform opposed to the rampant blacklisting by groups such as Aware, Inc. Faulk won the election, was dropped from *The Morning Show,* blacklisted by Aware, which suggested he was a Communist sympathizer (the HUAC hearings were still wrecking havoc in the entertainment industry), and found it impossible to get broadcasting employment. With his lawyer, Louis Nizer, Faulk filed a libel suit against Aware and its wealthy supporter Lawrence A. Johnson. In 1962, after six years of litigation, during which time he was unable to work because of the blacklisting, Faulk was awarded $3.5 million (later reduced to $550,000). After his victory, Faulk appeared as a guest on *Leave It to the Girls* but then had no permanent national television work until he had a regular feature telling tales on *Hee Haw* from 1975 to 1982.

Francis, Arlene, 1949–1975, 1983
    Blind Date
    What's My Line?
    The Comeback Story
    Home
    Tonight (interim host)
    The Prime of Your Life
    See Chapter 3 for background on Arlene Francis.

Franklin, Joe, 1953–1994

Down Memory Lane

The Joe Franklin Show

Joe Franklin is important to the history of television talk, but one really wonders why. Indeed he is in the Guinness book for the record number of continuous program years. He has been satirized on *Saturday Night Live* by Billy Crystal. Being on super station WWOR meant he was available nationally on cable. He may well have interviewed about 300,000 guests, including Bing Crosby, Marilyn Monroe, and Madonna. It would be interesting to analyze transcripts of his program to see how so much television talk could take place with so very little really being said.

Frederick, Pauline, 1948–1953, 1960–1961

Pauline Frederick's Guestbook

All-Star News

Purex Special for Women

Pauline Frederick was a rarity in early television, a woman journalist. She had been a foreign correspondent before doing her 1948–1949 *Pauline Frederick's Guestbook* on ABC, a live fifteen-minute interview with a political or cultural figure. After being a regular on ABC's *All-Star News*, she was NBC United Nations correspondent from 1953 to 1975. *Purex Special for Women* had her interviewing a doctor after a dramatization of some psychological or medical problem experienced by women.

Friendly, Fred W., 1984–1990

The Constitution: That Delicate Balance

The Other Side of the News

Fred Friendly is certainly remembered for more than his on-air work. Friendly produced **Edward R. Murrow**'s **See It Now** and **Small World** programs. When Murrow left CBS, Friendly started *CBS Reports*. Friendly was president of CBS News for two years and shared in ten Peabody awards. In 1966 Friendly became a Columbia professor of journalism and began working with the Ford Foundation to shape public television network news programming. On PBS in the 1980s, Friendly appeared as moderator of several series of discussions on public issues, following a format he had developed for seminars at Columbia.

Frost, David, 1964–1973, 1977–

> **That Was the Week That Was**
> The David Frost Show
> **The Nixon Interviews with David Frost**
> Headliners with David Frost
> The Next President
> Inside Edition
> Talking with David Frost
> Breakfast with David Frost (BBC)

David Frost is one of the few prominent trans-Atlantic television personalities. Frost's British 1963 weekly political satire *That Was the Week That Was* was imported and transformed by NBC into an American show the next year. Frost came along, first as contributor and then as host. Frost went back to London to do his chat show after *TW3* ended in 1965. Partly on the basis of his British work, Frost was hired by Group W in 1969 to do a daily show to replace **Merv Griffin**, who had been attracted away by CBS to challenge **Johnny Carson**. *The David Frost Show* was quite unlike either Griffin's or Carson's shows. The show scheduled only one guest per program, with Frost asking many probing questions, clipboard in hand, sitting opposite the guest in a facing chair. In 1971 Frost attempted another weekly program more like *TW3*, *The David Frost Revue*, in which satire and skits were aimed at a chosen topic, e.g., television talk shows. Frost also kept his weekend job in Britain. The daily show ended in 1972 after receiving two Emmys, the revue ended in 1973, and Frost was largely back on the other side of the Atlantic until negotiations began for *The Nixon Interviews with David Frost.* Since the success of these interviews, Frost has continued to have various shorter series or one-shot interviews broadcast in the United States. For three weeks in 1989, he was the initial anchor of *Inside Edition*, and then special interviewer for a month. He left with a reported $2 million contract settlement. He became Sir David Frost in 1993 and since then has been active mainly on British television.

Furness, Betty, 1945–1960, 1974–1990

> Fashion: Coming and Becoming
> Penthouse Party
> Meet Betty Furness
> **Today**

Betty Furness made over thirty B movies in the 1930s and then found a second career in the 1940s and 1950s as a television personality. Her most famous TV role was as the Westinghouse spokesperson, usually standing in front of a refrigerator or other appliance on the live *Studio One* set and explaining how we really would be much happier with one like it in our house. She represented Westinghouse from 1949 to 1960. But her video work was much more varied—not just commercials. In 1945 she appeared on an experimental DuMont program *Fashion: Coming and Becoming,* and among her TV acting jobs was her own series in 1951 as an espionage-fighting newswoman, *Byline— Betty Furness.* Furness hosted two talk shows. In 1950-1951 *Penthouse Party* supposedly took place in her penthouse apartment, where her guests would chat and perform, often doing something different from that for which they were famous, e.g., sultry actress Joan Blondell baked a casserole. In 1953 Furness had a more conventional interview show, *Meet Betty Furness.* After doing much local television in New York City during the early 1960s, Furness began a third career as a consumer advocate. She was appointed by President Johnson as his special assistant for consumer affairs in 1967. She continued in similar state and city positions in New York during the 1970s until she returned to television on the *Today* show in 1976 in an on-air tryout to replace **Barbara Walters** as cohost. **Jane Pauley** got the job, but Furness stayed with weekly reports on consumer affairs until 1992, thus combining two careers.

Garroway, Dave, 1949–1971
>   *Garroway at Large*
>   **Today**
>   *Wide, Wide World*
>   *Garroway*
>   See Chapter 3 for background on Dave Garroway.

George, Wally, 1983–1986
>   *Thicke of the Night*
>   *Hot Seat with Wally George*
>   Wally George's local Los Angeles talk show was designed to shout down and abuse people who disagreed with his very conservative views. Open discussion was not part of *Hot Seat with Wally George.* This approach, reminiscent of **Joe Pyne** or **Al Capp**, attracted **Alan Thicke**; he invited George as a frequent guest. That led to wide publicity with George's picture on many national magazine covers. So finally George was syndicated in 1985–1986. The program lasted less than a year, how-

ever, since people did not seem interested in watching abuse without discussion.

Gifford, Kathie Lee, 1977–
Name That Tune
Good Morning, America
Live! with Regis and Kathie Lee
Miss America Pageant
While still using her birth name, Kathie Lee Epstein, and attend-ing Oral Roberts University, Kathie Lee Gifford sang with the World Action Singers on *Oral Roberts and You* from 1972 to 1974. In Califor-nia she was a singer on Kathryn Kuhlman's CBS program *I Believe in Miracles* in 1975 and 1976. During these years, Kathie Lee also played Nurse Callahan on *Days of Our Lives.* Beginning in 1977 Kathie Lee Gifford appeared on several shows under her first married name, Kathie Lee Johnson. Under that name she was the La La singer on the syn-dicated *Name That Tune;* was a regular on *Hee Haw* and its spin-off, *The Hee Haw Honeys;* and after moving to New York a reporter and substitute for *Good Morning, America* cohost Joan Lunden. It was on that show that she met her second husband, Frank Gifford. In 1985 she became **Regis Philbin**'s cohost on his local New York program, *The Morning Show.* She married Gifford in 1986. In 1988 *The Morning Show* began syndication under the title *Live! with Regis and Kathie Lee.* Kathie Lee and Regis became the cohosts for the *Miss America Pageant* in 1991. The Regis–Kathie Lee talk team resembled in many ways the couple talk of such earlier figures as **Tex and Jinx** with their frequent reference to family, their tone more light than serious, their awareness of sexual differences, and their exchanging of slight digs within an over-all friendly atmosphere. In July 2000, Kathie Lee said good-bye to Regis and left the show.

Godfrey, Arthur, 1948–1972
Arthur Godfrey's Talent Scouts
Arthur Godfrey and His Ukulele
Arthur Godfrey Time
See Chapter 2 for background on Arthur Godfrey.

The Gong Show, 1976–1980, 1989–1990
Chuck Barris seemed to delight in making fun of the game-show genre. *The Gong Show* was a cross between *Major Bowes' Original*

Amateur Hour and **This Is Show Business**. Instead of looking for the best, Barris wished to present the worst. Instead of the panel giving helpful career advice, they specialized in abusive criticism. There were definitely notes of the postmodern in *The Gong Show*. After a year of Gary Owens as host of the network show, Barris himself took over as host, as he had already started doing on the syndicated version. He had never been a television performer before and knew he had no special talent for it. He selected a cast of odd fellows. The music was by the accordionist from the 1950s, **Milton DeLugg**. The panel included Dr. **Joyce Brothers**, Rex Reed, and Phyllis Diller. *The Gong Show* became a comment on the nature of television talk.

Good Morning, America, 1975–

Good Morning, America replaced *A.M. America*, which in ten months on the air had failed to make inroads on the **Today** show's audience. ABC decided to have as host a person with less news background and more of a "personality." The actor **David Hartman** proved a good choice. Hartman stayed with the show for twelve years, during which time the show moved up against *Today*. *Good Morning, America* placed more emphasis than its predecessor on features presented by personalities such as Rona Barrett, Jonathan Winters, and Erma Bombeck. Joan Lunden became cohost in 1980; Charles Gibson replaced Hartman in 1987; **Diane Sawyer** replaced Lunden in 1999. In the 1990s the show generally led in its time period. By following **Pat Weaver**'s original format for *Today* more closely than *Today* does, *Good Morning, America* did quite well.

Graham, Virginia, 1952–1972, 1978–1979

Food for Thought
Girl Talk
The Virginia Graham Show
America Alive!

Virginia Graham began on television as a panelist on many programs and host of the variety show *Summer in the Park* broadcast from Palisades Amusement Park. She developed her own serious but popular approach to television talk from a feminist standpoint over the series of three talk-variety shows she hosted, *Food for Thought* (1956–1961), *Girl Talk* (1963–1969), and *The Virginia Graham Show* (1970–1972). Graham stood along with **Arlene Francis** in those years as the rare woman talk-show host who combined the entertaining with the critical. She later appeared on *America Alive!* in 1978–1979 as a featured interviewer.

Granik, Theodore, 1949–1954
  American Forum of the Air
  Youth Wants to Know
  All America Wants to Know

Theodore Granik was one of the few important figures who shaped the beginnings of both radio and television talk in America. A Washington, D.C., lawyer, he became interested and active in radio in the 1920s. He eventually became a station owner. In 1937 he started the radio version of *American Forum of the Air.* Granik was committed to creating a place where the American public could hear political ideas discussed with as little emotional contamination as possible. In producing and moderating his programs he always withheld his own positions from view. In 1951 Granik began a simulcast *American Youth Forum.* It became *Youth Wants to Know* in 1952. Granik also moderated this program, but the format was different from his earlier one. Here a guest was asked questions by a select group of Washington high school students. Eventually this show was only on television. Granik became too ill to moderate his programs after 1954 but continued as producer until 1958.

Griffin, Merv, 1951–1986
  Robert Q's Matinee
  Keep Talking
  The Merv Griffin Show
  See Chapter 5 for background on Merv Griffin.

Gumbel, Bryant, 1975–
  NFL Pregame
  Games People Play
  Today
  Public Eye with Bryant Gumbel
  The Early Show

Bryant Gumbel's work for NBC began in covering sports—all sorts of sports: baseball, basketball, football, golf, Olympics, etc. In 1975 he became host of the NFL pregame program. In 1980–1981 he was host of the prime-time *Games People Play,* which covered such sports as taxicab demolition and belly flopping. In 1980 he began a thrice-weekly sports report on *Today* and in 1982 moved up to anchor. With diligence Gumbel overcame his lack of experience in non-sports areas and was able to do interviews of political figures that were quite good, winning an Emmy for his Senator Kennedy–Palm Beach incident work, as well as one for coverage of the Macy Thanksgiving Day parade. He also won other awards for foreign reporting. He left *Today* at the end of 1996 and moved to CBS. After his evening newsmagazine *Public Eye* failed in 1998, Gumbel returned to early-morning life, hosting *The Early Show* for CBS.

Hall, Arsenio, 1983–1997
> *Thicke of the Night*
> *The Late Show*
> *The Arsenio Hall Show*
> See Chapter 7 for background on Arsenio Hall.

Hall, Monty, 1952–1991
> **Strike It Rich**
> **Keep Talking**
> *Let's Make a Deal*

A native of Canada, Monty Hall produced and hosted the long-running Canadian game show *Who Am I?* before coming to the United States. After his move he was substitute host on the top-twenty *Strike It Rich* in the early 1950s and introduced Western films on *Cowboy Theatre*. Following that, he was the first host of *Keep Talking* in 1958. In 1963 Hall began producing and hosting the game show for which he is best known, *Let's Make a Deal*. Between 1963 and 1991, the show was on night or day, on NBC or ABC or in syndication, for all but nine of those years. The show has been produced in California, Las Vegas, Vancouver, and Orlando. Hall was host of all versions. Although Bob Hilton began as host of the 1990 Orlando version, Hall took over after a few weeks because of poor ratings. It was not the plan of the producers to have contestants wear strange costumes to the studio, but when a woman wearing a striking hat was chosen by Hall from the audience to play, people wanting to be selected latched on to the idea of unusual dress. Mathematics game theorists have named a problem "The Monty Hall Problem" because it can be applied to Hall's practice of gradually opening envelopes the contestant has not selected to see if the contestant will change his or her mind. Hall has been connected to many other less well known shows either as host or producer.

Hartman, David, 1975–1987

Good Morning, America

David Hartman was a stage/film/television actor during the 1960s. He was a star in *The New Doctors* (1969–1973) and the lead in *Lucas Tanner* (1974–1975). In 1975 Hartman found a new role as a morning talk-show host on *Good Morning, America* (see entry above). Since 1987 his appearances on television have usually been linked in one way or another to specials from his production company.

Hayes, Peter Lind, 1949–1952, 1958–1966

The Stork Club

Star of the Family

The Peter Lind Hayes Show (daytime)

The Tonight Show (interim cohost)

Alumni Fun

AND

Healy, Mary, 1949–1962

The Stork Club

Masquerade Party

The Peter Lind Hayes Show (daytime)

The Tonight Show (interim cohost)

Peter Lind Hayes and Mary Healy were a married couple and appeared in various media, usually but not always as a team. Unlike other couples such as **Tex and Jinx** or radio's Pegeen and Ed Fitzgerald, they were also actors, singers, and in Peter's case a comedian. The first network television they did together was *Inside U.S.A. with Chevrolet*, in 1949–1950. This was a revue variety show, based on the popular theatre musical *Inside U.S.A.* and utilizing Peter's background in vaudeville. Peter served as a minstrel touring America and discovering regional delights, including guests such as Lucille Ball and **Oscar Levant** and, of course, always, Mary Healy. Other of their shows attempted to combine sitcom and vaudeville (celebrities came to their house and performed at supper) or family interview and talent show. In 1950 they cohosted with Sherman Billingsley the thrice-weekly *The Stork Club*. Peter and Mary were particularly well suited for this interview show, since they belonged to the supper club milieu. After a number of short-lived daytime and evening, variety and sitcom shows, Peter and Mary were in 1962 interim cohosts on *The Tonight Show*. Hayes' last regular network program was *Alumni Fun,* a game show which he emceed from 1964 to 1965.

Henderson, Skitch, 1950–1966
> *Talent Search*
> *Faye and Skitch*
> **Tonight**

Skitch Henderson is remembered principally as the bandleader for numerous talk-variety shows. He worked with Eddie Albert, **Dave Garroway**, **Steve Allen**, **Ernie Kovacs**, and all the *Tonight* show 1962 interim hosts between Paar and Carson, and finally with **Johnny Carson** from 1962 to 1966. Sometimes he was used in skits, but there was often the sense he was being distracted from his main interest, the music. Henderson's early network non-musical video work was as host of the 1950–1951 *Talent Search,* as a panelist on *Where Was I?* in 1953, and as cohost in 1953–1954 with his then wife **Faye Emerson** of *Faye and Skitch.* Henderson has largely left television but continues as a frequent concert conductor.

Henson, Jim, 1957–1990
> **Tonight**
> *The Ed Sullivan Show*
> *The Jimmy Dean Show*
> **Today**
> *Saturday Night Live*
> *The Muppet Show*
> *The Jim Henson Hour*

Jim Henson is a bit difficult to fit into television talk categories. He developed an interest in marionettes and puppets (his term Muppets combining the two) while watching the shows of Bil and Cora Baird and Burr Tillstrom on TV. Certainly, *Sam and Friends,* the local Washington, D.C., children's show Henson and his future wife, Jane Nebel, started in 1955, would have qualified as fresh talk. Henson's early and frequent network appearances, beginning in 1957 with such variety hosts as **Steve Allen** and **Ed Sullivan**, were aimed at adults and often contained ad-lib material. Henson's first Muppet to make appearances on every show of a series was Rowlf, a dog. Rowlf was a regular on the prime-time *The Jimmy Dean Show* from 1963 to 1966. Rowlf and Dean would carry on what appeared to be spontaneous conversations. In 1967 Rowlf was the host of the comedy-variety show *Our*

Place. In 1969, *Sesame Street* began and the emphasis of Henson's work shifted again to children and set pieces. In 1975–1976 the Muppets were regulars on *Saturday Night Live,* where Henson was performing live with very adult material. The British production of *The Muppet Show* in 1976–1981 allowed Henson to experiment with many new adult forms. Around this time Henson's Muppet Kermit the Frog guest-hosted *The Tonight Show.* In the late 1980s Henson's work with children continued on *Sesame Street* and the newer *Fraggle Rock* of 1983–1988. In 1989 Henson himself appeared on *The Jim Henson Hour.* This show combined both child and adult elements and was Henson's last work completed before his sudden death in 1990. The sitcom *Dinosaurs,* whose development Henson had been deeply involved with, appeared in 1991. Henson's feature films can also be divided between family features like *The Muppet Movie* and darker, adult features like *Labyrinth.*

Hollywood Squares, 1966–1984, 1986–1989, 1998–

Hollywood Squares is tic-tac-toe played on a giant board inhabited by nine celebrities. The quizmaster asks a question of the celebrity whose square was chosen by a contestant. If the contestant says correctly whether the celebrity's answer was right or wrong, the contestant occupies the square as in tic-tac-toe. The next contestant then takes a turn. Seeing who wins the game holds some interest for viewers, but over the years more and more interest has developed around the humor and interaction of the celebrities, the center square celebrity playing a special role. Peter Marshall was host through 1982, and Paul Lynde was the most frequent celebrity for the center square. Other memorable squares from this period were **Charley Weaver**, Wally Cox, and George Gobel. In 1983–1984, *The Match Game / Hollywood Squares Hour* gave the first half-hour to "match" with **Gene Rayburn** as host. In the second half-hour, the contestants moved to the "squares" set, where Jon "Bowzer" Bauman was host and the panelists and Rayburn became squares. Bauman was also a special member of the "match" panel. In 1986–1989 John Davidson, a sometime square, became host, and Jim J. Bullock, **Joan Rivers**, and Shadoe Stevens were frequent squares. *Hollywood Squares* returned to syndication in 1998 with Tom Bergeron as host and Whoopi Goldberg as center square and executive producer.

Information Please, 1952–1953

Information Please shaped the panel program format into a prototype imitated for years. The panel show must always have an excuse for being. For *Information Please* it was an opportunity for the audience to send in questions that would stump the panel and in doing so win prizes. Then there is the real center of the panel show, an interesting group of people talking about certain stuff in a creative fashion. *Information Please* worked because the moderator, **Clifton Fadiman**, and regular panelists, John Kieran, Franklin P. Adams, and in the early years **Oscar Levant**, were joined each week by guest panelists, selected on radio by producer Paul Golenpaul. All together they became a group who produced conversation that a large audience wanted to hear. The show ran on radio from 1938 to 1948 but on television for little more than a year. The television show had the same host and panel but perhaps failed to find guests to match those on radio, such as Alfred Hitchcock, Mayor Fiorello La Guardia, Gracie Allen, Orson Welles, and Harpo Marx, who acted out his answers.

I've Got a Secret, 1952–1967, 1972–1973, 1976

I've Got a Secret was the most popular of all prime-time panel shows, being in the top twenty for five years of its first run. A contestant was asked questions by the panel to discover a secret about his or her life. It didn't matter too much whether the panel guessed the secret or not. (The contestant did get a somewhat larger reward if the panel failed.) People watched because the regulars were funny and smart and because the secret was often demonstrated on stage in an intriguing way. One contestant a week was a celebrity, for whom the secrets were sometimes contrived, e.g., when Monty Woolley, whose secret was that he slept with his beard under the covers, was asked why, he replied, "As a matter of fact I don't. That's merely the secret they decided upon for me." Allan Sherman, associate producer for Goodson-Todman, created the show and was often responsible for the presentation of the secrets. **Garry Moore** was emcee from 1952 to 1964, **Steve Allen** from 1964 to 1973, and **Bill Cullen** in 1976. Cullen had also been one of the early panel regulars. **Henry Morgan** was the only panelist on throughout the entire run of the show for all the years and probably the most rambunctious and sarcastic. Other regulars were **Faye Emerson**, Jayne Meadows, **Betsy Palmer**, **Bess Myerson**, **Richard Dawson**, **Gene Rayburn**, Nanette Fabray, and Pat Carroll.

The Jack Paar Tonight Show. See **Tonight**

Jackson, Greg, 1981–1988

Signature
The Last Word (ABC)
One on One
The Wilton North Report

Greg Jackson was an ABC correspondent and independent producer in the 1970s before beginning the interview show *Signature* for CBS Cable. On *Signature* Jackson used the technique of having the interviewee in close-up and himself off camera, concentrating attention on the person interviewed. In 1982 Jackson began hosting the hour-long *The Last Word* on ABC after **Nightline**. Jackson's interviews and news analysis were supplemented by taped interviews done by **Phil Donahue**. In 1983 *Nightline* was extended to an hour and Jackson's time was shortened to a half-hour. Donahue left and Jackson returned to his *Signature* interview technique on a program then called *One on One* that lasted only a few months. In 1987 Jackson returned to late-night television as one of the few serious-minded regulars on *The Wilton North Report*.

James, Dennis, 1946–1976

Cash and Carry
DuMont Wrestling
Okay Mother
The Dennis James Show
The Name's the Same
Club 60
People Will Talk
P.D.Q.
The Price Is Right

Dennis James was the first. In 1938, just out of college, James was the first emcee of a television variety series, *Television Roof,* and the first host and interviewer of a television sports series, *Dennis James Sports Parade.* These programs were broadcast on Dr. Allen B. DuMont's experimental New York station W2XWV. When television broadcasting resumed after World War II, James continued his association with DuMont and in 1946 hosted *Cash and Carry,* one of the first TV quiz shows. From 1948 to 1952, James became famous for his mocking but enthusiastic commentary on *DuMont Wrestling.* James did not disappear after the early days of television, but hosted his own prime-time and daily talk-variety shows and became known as a ready fill-in host when others became ill or left suddenly. By 1976 he had hosted more than a dozen different game or panel shows, the most noteworthy being *P.D.Q.* and the syndicated *The Price Is Right.* James was also the host of the Cerebral Palsy Telethons and of *Okay Mother,* an interview show of mothers of the well known, which took its name from a phrase James used often in his wrestling commentary.

Johns Hopkins Science Review, 1948–1960

Johns Hopkins Science Review was definitely a talk program in the academic tradition. Lynn Poole, a Johns Hopkins faculty member, was usually host. The topics, such as cancer or "Electrons at Work in a Vacuum," were presented by scholars and researchers, using diagrams and demonstrations as well as lectures. What is remarkable is that for seven of its years on the networks it was in prime time. Of course, it was usually scheduled against the most popular shows on opposing networks.

Juvenile Jury, 1947–1955, 1970–1971, 1983

Juvenile Jury was created by **Jack Barry** in 1946 for radio, where it lasted until 1953. The format was remarkably simple. Get five children between the ages of three and twelve as a jury and ask them to solve problems such as how much allowance a child should have or how old a girl should be to wear lipstick. Linkletter had already done something like it on his *House Party* show but not in such a concerted way. The audience loved the unexpected, often comic responses of the children. *Juvenile Jury* was Barry's first success as a producer, and he remained host even as his Barry & Enright Productions grew. After the quiz scandal involving Barry's show *Twenty-One,* he was unable to get his work on the air for over ten years. Shortly after Barry replaced Denis Wholey as host on the short-lived *The Generation Gap,* a new syndicated version of *Juvenile Jury* in 1970 became Barry's way of getting back on the air solidly as host and producer before going on to his later successes. The 1983 version was hosted by **Nipsey Russell** on Black Entertainment Television.

Keep Talking, 1958–1960

Keep Talking was a prime-time panel quiz show based on the ability of its players to simulate fresh talk. A phrase would be assigned to a panelist on one team, who would have to insert the phrase into ad-lib talk in such a way that the other team could not identify the phrase as not ad-lib. The regular members of the program were considered at the time to be the masters of fresh television talk. The successive quizmasters were **Monty Hall**, **Carl Reiner**, and **Merv Griffin**. The frequent panelists were **Joey Bishop**, **Ilka Chase**, Audrey Meadows, Elaine May, Paul Winchell, Danny Dayton, **Morey Amsterdam**, Peggy Cass, Pat Carroll, and Orson Bean.

Kefauver Crime Hearings, 1951

Senator Estes Kefauver was chair of a Senate committee that allowed live television coverage of its hearings into organized crime. The public became fascinated by the questioning of Mafia figures. In the case of Frank Costello, the interest was heightened by the restriction his lawyers obtained that his face would not be seen but only his hands. Although the hearings were carried in daytime, their ratings were high. Senator Kefauver received a special Emmy award for outstanding public service on television.

Kennedy Press Conferences, 1961–1963

John F. Kennedy was probably the most skillful of all the Presidents in using regularly televised press conferences. Dwight D. Eisenhower had been the first President to have a press conference televised, but he developed a reputation for answers of boring length, full of malapropisms. Kennedy's skill and wit with the press prompted him to hold televised press conferences with greater frequency than any President before or since.

King, Larry, 1983–
The Larry King Show
Larry King Live
See Chapter 8 for background on Larry King.

Koppel, Ted, 1979–
The Iran Crisis: America Held Hostage
Nightline
See Chapter 7 for background on Ted Koppel.

Kovacs, Ernie, 1951–1962
It's Time for Ernie
Ernie in Kovacsland
Kovacs on the Korner

The Ernie Kovacs Show
Tonight
The Ernie Kovacs Special

Ernie Kovacs is remembered mainly for his use of the visual possibilities of television to provide humor. In his last years on television
(1957–1962) he often used carefully constructed and rehearsed material,
but his prolific earlier work was notoriously unrehearsed and ad-lib; it
was more what today would be called performance art. Strong strains of
fresh talk appeared in many of his shows. Kovacs began his television
work in Philadelphia with a daytime cooking show, a fashion quiz program, and *3 to Get Ready* (broadcast on Channel 3), one of the first daily
television wake-up programs. A local show, *3 to Get Ready*, ended when
it was replaced by the network's **Today**. These local shows as well as
Kovacs' various daytime variety series and panel shows, local and network, often involved spontaneous talk with both audience and cast. In
October 1956, Kovacs became for five months the Monday and Tuesday night host of *Tonight*, when **Steve Allen**, the alternate host, needed
more time to prepare for his prime-time show.

Kukla, Fran and Ollie, 1948–1962, 1967–1984

Kukla, Fran and Ollie developed out of the puppetry of Burr Tillstrom, who, while working with the WPA in 1936, started his Kuklapolitan Players featuring the doll-like puppet Kukla. The Players were
first seen on television in 1939; in 1947 Tillstrom began the local Chicago show *Junior Jamboree*, which featured the Kuklapolitans. The Players were all hand puppets with voices supplied by Tillstrom. **Fran Allison** joined the Players and the show became *Kukla, Fran and Ollie* in
1948 and was carried on the NBC Midwestern network. In its first years
the show was telecast live five days a week in early-evening hours and
became popular both with children and with sophisticated adult viewers. The set was the puppet stage with Allison standing in front and
usually to the side, while talking with the other players, so to speak,
backstage. Occasionally, actual performances would be given of works
such as *The Mikado*. Outside of the productions, what was seen was ad-
lib conversations between Allison and Tillstrom in his various puppet
personae. **Hugh Downs** was the announcer in the first network years.
In 1954 the show moved from NBC to ABC, where it stayed until 1957.
A five-minute weekday version without Allison called *Burr Tillstrom's
Kukla and Ollie* was broadcast by NBC in 1961–1962. Allison returned
to the Kuklapolitans in 1967 to provide occasional and then weekly

introductions for *The CBS Children's Film Festival* and for a PBS version of *Kukla, Fran and Ollie* from 1969 to 1971. Another adult puppet talk show, unconnected to the Kuklapolitans but with similar humor and human puppet interaction, was *Madame's Place,* created by Wayland Flowers and syndicated briefly in 1982.

Kupcinet, Irv, 1957, 1962–1986
> *At Random*
> **Tonight! America after Dark**
> *Kup's Show*

Irv Kupcinet was a Chicago columnist who used his connections to celebrities to produce a local talk show starting in 1952. Kupcinet's local fame caused NBC to include him in the group of regulars that took over the *Tonight* time spot with *Tonight! America after Dark* in 1957 between **Steve Allen** and **Jack Paar**. Kupcinet's local show continued to develop, changing stations and title (from *At Random* to *Kup's Show*) and producing a quite distinctive format. Kup would sit back during his four-hour-long program and let his guests play out the themes they thought interesting. Kup's talent was bringing interesting talkers together. One 1972 show included F. Lee Bailey, Eugene McCarthy, William Saroyan, LeRoi Jones, and Xaviera Hollander, the Happy Hooker. When *Kup's Show* went into syndication in the 1960s, it was shortened to an hour. PBS picked it up in 1975.

Kuralt, Charles, 1959–1994
> *Eyewitness to History*
> *CBS Reports*
> *Who's Who*
> *CBS News Sunday Morning*
> *The CBS Morning News*
> *On the Road with Charles Kuralt*
> *The American Parade*
> *America Tonight*

Charles Kuralt began working for CBS in 1957, and in 1960 became the host for *Eyewitness to History.* This was the first of many CBS news shows on which he was a principal figure. It was in 1967, however, that Kuralt began the series of interviews that defined his television interviewing technique and brought him a gentle fame. *On the Road* was first an occasional feature on the *CBS Evening News* but later appeared on other CBS news shows, and during the summer of 1983,

On the Road with Charles Kuralt had its own prime-time half-hour. Kuralt's interviewing let the unique ordinary people of America speak of their passions in the locations they had shaped. Kuralt showed an interest in what they did and let them tell their stories. Kuralt's work earned him twelve Emmys and three Peabody awards, and it allowed him to host the relaxed *CBS News Sunday Morning* from 1979 till his retirement in 1994.

Lake, Ricki, 1993–
> *The Ricki Lake Show*
> See Chapter 9 for background on Ricki Lake.

The Larry Sanders Show, 1992–1998
> *The Larry Sanders Show* combined an intelligent sitcom about late-night talk shows with an actual talk show taped with well-known guests before a studio audience. Besides the usual sitcom interest in character interaction, the program displayed much interest in the day-to-day operation of a talk show. Larry Sanders was created and played by sometime talk-show host **Garry Shandling**.

The Last Word (CBS), 1957–1959
> At least two significant talk-television shows have had the name *The Last Word*. (For information about the 1980s late-night interview show with that name see the **Greg Jackson** entry above.) The 1950s panel show *The Last Word* was an attempt by CBS to dress up intelligent discussion of language and word usage as entertainment. The moderator, **Bergen Evans**, directed questions submitted by the home audience about grammar and linguistics to a rotating panel. The panel included personalities as varied as actress June Havoc and permanent member **John Mason Brown**. The discussion was witty and insightful.

Leach, Robin, 1981–
> **Entertainment Tonight**
> *Lifestyles of the Rich and Famous*
> *Fame, Fortune and Romance*
> *Runaway with the Rich and Famous*
> *Preview—the Best of the New*
> *Nitecap*
> *Robin Leach Talking Food*
> *Gourmet Getaways*

Robin Leach served as a reporter on *Entertainment Tonight* before he began producing and hosting the various interview-visit series with which he became associated. In 1984 Leach started the syndicated *Lifestyles of the Rich and Famous,* which in various later forms also appeared on ABC, daytime and late night. It has been noted that Leach's format of visits to the homes of celebrities had been used by others earlier, including **Edward R. Murrow** on ***Person to Person**. Leach's visits had a different character, however. They combined sycophantic praise and obsession with material wealth. *Fame, Fortune and Romance* followed the same pattern with a somewhat greater emphasis on love. *Runaway with the Rich and Famous,* instead of visiting celebrity homes, went on vacations with them. *Preview—the Best of the New* was produced by Leach for thirteen weeks in 1990 as a syndicated soft-news magazine show with Chuck Henry as host and Leach as one of several reporters. Because of his British accent and exaggerated manner of speaking, Leach may be one of the most frequently parodied television figures.

Leave It to the Girls, 1949–1951, 1953–1954, 1962–1963, 1981
This show was created for radio in 1945 by **Martha Roundtree**. It was seen on local New York television in 1947 and went to network television in 1949. A panel of four women discussed, with both seriousness and humor, topics of special interest to women. As the show developed, Maggie McNellis became its moderator and a male panelist was added to defend males; he was given a whistle to interrupt the women. The 1981 version was titled *Leave It to the Women* and moderated by Stephanie Edwards. In the early years, **Faye Emerson**, Eloise McElhone, Vanessa Brown, Harriet Van Horne, Robin Chandler, Eva Gabor, and Janet Blair were frequent panelists. **Henry Morgan** and **Morey Amsterdam** often played the male guest. In 1954 **John Henry Faulk** became the permanent male. He returned in 1962, as the first guest of the later series, to discuss his blacklisting during the years between.

Lee, Gypsy Rose, 1950, 1958, 1964–1966
Think Fast
The Gypsy Rose Lee Show
Gypsy!
A former striptease artist, Gypsy Rose Lee made the transition to being a panel and talk-show host on television. Lee succeeded Dr. Mason Gross as moderator of *Think Fast,* a show where panelists com-

peted to say the most without pausing on a subject they were suddenly given. Lee's own talk shows focused on witty and intelligent discussion with guests about everyday topics.

Lee, Pinky, 1939, 1949–1957

> *Pinky Lee and Co.*
> *Those Two*
> *The Pinky Lee Show* (daytime)
> *The Gumby Show*

Pinky Lee (Pincus Leff) began his career as a vaudeville comedian. Small and energetic, Lee would often attempt stage tasks beyond his capacities and fail in a humorous but appealing way. He brought his act to experimental NBC television in 1939. In 1950 Lee had a weekly prime-time show that cast him as a bumbling stagehand who also had opportunities to sing and perform in routines. From 1951 to 1953 Lee starred first with Vivian Blaine and then with Martha Stewart on *Those Two*, which was broadcast for fifteen minutes three evenings a week. The program was a loosely structured story of Lee's unrequited love for a nightclub singer, but was really an opportunity for both performers to joke with each other and sing, both solos and duets. From 1954 to 1956, Lee was host of his very popular daily children's show, where he restructured his vaudeville performances for a very young audience. One of the show's most memorable live moments was when Lee had an on-screen heart attack while performing a billy-goat dance. Lee's last network duties were as host of *The Gumby Show*.

Lehrer, Jim, 1973–

> **Watergate Hearings**
> Nixon Impeachment Hearings
> *The MacNeil-Lehrer Report*
> *The MacNeil-Lehrer NewsHour*
> *The NewsHour with Jim Lehrer*

Jim Lehrer was a newspaper journalist in Dallas before becoming executive director and on-air personality at KERA-TV, the Dallas public television station. In 1972 Lehrer moved to Washington, D.C., where he served in various roles in the world of budding network public television. In 1973 Lehrer teamed with **Robert MacNeil** to anchor the PBS coverage of the Watergate Hearings, and the next year Lehrer solo anchored PBS coverage of the Nixon impeachment hearings. In 1975 Lehrer was the Washington correspondent at the start of *The Robert*

MacNeil Report. The next year the program became *The MacNeil-Lehrer Report*. It was expanded to an hour in 1983, becoming *The MacNeil-Lehrer NewsHour*, and then in 1995, when MacNeil retired, *The NewsHour with Jim Lehrer*. Over the years the *NewsHour* developed several live formats for treating news topics in depth. Especially important were the panel of experts interviewed by the anchors and the review of current events by a pair of commentators with differing views, for example, David Gergen and Mark Shields. Lehrer worked with MacNeil in producing their shows but also worked alone as a novelist and playwright.

Leno, Jay, 1977, 1987–
    The Marilyn McCoo and Billy Davis Jr. Show
    Tonight (guest host and host)
    See Chapter 8 for background on Jay Leno.

Lester, Jerry, 1943, 1950–1955, 1962–1963
    Cafe Television
    Cavalcade of Stars
    Broadway Open House
    Candid Camera
    Pantomime Quiz
    The Jerry Lester Show
    Usually Jerry Lester is linked in television histories to his brief but spectacular fame as the alternating host of *Broadway Open House*, the short-lived late-night predecessor of **Tonight**. Lester may have been, seven years before that in 1943, the host of television's very first talk-variety special, *Cafe Television*, on DuMont's New York experimental station W2XWV. Lester was also the host of at least four prime-time variety shows, including *Cavalcade of Stars* (between Jack Carter and Jackie Gleason). In addition Lester was a regular player on *Pantomime Quiz*, a panelist on other shows, and an aid to Allen Funt on early *Candid Camera* programs. Lester had his own daytime show on ABC in 1953–1954 and a syndicated variety show in the 1960s. His style throughout remained rooted in vaudeville.

Letterman, David, 1977–
    Tonight (guest host)
    The David Letterman Show
    Late Night with David Letterman

TV's Bloopers & Practical Jokes
The Late Show with David Letterman
See Chapter 8 for background on David Letterman.

Levant, Oscar, 1950–1961
G.E. Guest House
Who Said That?
The Oscar Levant Show
Oscar Levant's principal career was in music as pianist and com-poser. Levant's individuality and wit made him both a radio personality and movie actor. In fact Levant was involved in a great deal of the star social life around Hollywood. Levant's connections and character got him onto several shows as host and panelist and, finally, as a much-watched frequent guest on **Jack Paar**'s shows in the 1950s. In the late 1950s Levant hosted his own syndicated talk show. His style as inter-viewer was often described as neurotic, but critics and viewers were still fascinated by him, and his work was highly praised by some.

Lewis, Jerry, 1950–
The Colgate Comedy Hour
Muscular Dystrophy Telethon
Tonight (interim and guest host)
The Jerry Lewis Show (1963)
The Jerry Lewis Show (1984)
Jerry Lewis came from a show-business family, performing in a Borscht Circuit hotel at the age of five. In 1946 at age twenty Lewis teamed with singer Dean Martin, playing mainly in nightclubs. Two years later they were guests on the first *Toast of the Town* and the first *Welcome Aboard*. They appeared frequently on other variety shows in performances characterized by lively spontaneity and interactions with hosts such as Milton Berle. In 1950 they became the most prominent of the rotating stars of *The Colgate Comedy Hour*, where they remained until their breakup in 1955. Martin and Lewis had already begun host-ing telethons together in the 1950s. In 1953 on ABC, they cohosted a Thanksgiving telethon for the Muscular Dystrophy Association. In 1956 the team even got back together to do another MDA telethon be-fore their permanent breakup in July of that year. Subsequently Lewis became chair of the MDA and did frequent video fundraisers. In 1966 he began his annual Labor Day Weekend series of MDA telethons. Lewis' MDA telethons have come to define the television talk-variety show

that lasts for a day or more. Lewis had several variety specials from 1957 to 1963, when he began his disastrous two-hour talk-variety show on ABC Saturday nights. A less grand comedy variety show on NBC in 1967–1969 proved more conventional and somewhat more successful. Lewis was a frequent guest host on *Tonight* and tried to establish a more permanent late-night presence both in 1962, when he hosted a week of *Tonight* during an interregnum, and in 1984 when, after *Thicke of the Night* collapsed, Metromedia allowed Lewis a week in that time slot. Both shows had Ed Herlihy as announcer, thus reflecting Lewis' talk-show host role in the film *The King of Comedy*.

Lewis, Robert Q., 1949–1964, 1969
    Arthur Godfrey's Talent Scouts (guest host)
    The Show Goes On
    The Robert Q. Lewis Show (late night)
    Robert Q's Matinee
    The Name's the Same
    The Robert Q. Lewis Show (daytime)
    Make Me Laugh
    Masquerade Party
    Play Your Hunch
    Maurice Woodruff Predicts

During the 1950s Robert Q. Lewis was one of the most frequently seen and even somewhat popular talk-show hosts. He often substituted for **Arthur Godfrey** on Godfrey's various shows. Lewis worked in radio before coming early to television. Rather than being just an announcer he was something of a comedian in the vein of **Henry Morgan**, but not so disturbing. Lewis often had more than one show going in the same week, e.g., *The Show Goes On*, a talent show, was on Thursday evening in 1950, while that year's *Robert Q. Lewis Show* was a comedy-interview program at 11 P.M. on Sunday, and *Robert Q's Matinee* was a weekday afternoon talk-variety show. Lewis' peak of success probably came in 1953–1954, when he had a well-received afternoon talk-variety program, *The Robert Q. Lewis Show*, and was hosting the popular evening panel quiz show *The Name's the Same*. From 1959 on, comedy decreased as an element of Lewis' work and the hosting and panel jobs became more ordinary, until in 1969 Lewis was merely the presenter for the psychic Maurice Woodruff on the syndicated *Maurice Woodruff Predicts*.

Limbaugh, Rush, 1990–1996

The Pat Sajak Show (guest host)
Rush Limbaugh, The Television Show

Rush Limbaugh III grew up in Missouri, son and grandson of prominent lawyers. His father was also a part owner of a 5,000-watt radio station in Cape Girardeau. In 1967, at the age of sixteen, Rush began working on air at the station. Through high school and college and on until 1979, he roamed the country doing many types of radio shows, but none with much success. After taking a job as publicist for the Kansas City Royals, he returned to radio in 1983 and finally developed the combination of politics and humor that made him one of the most successful radio talk figures of the 1990s. However, the format didn't seem to work so well on his syndicated television show from 1992 to 1996. He tried repeatedly to find a new TV niche for his linguistic creations (e.g., dittos and feminazis), but he never made it onto either Fox News or NFL *Monday Night Football* as a commentator.

Linkletter, Art, 1950–1970

Life with Linkletter
Art Linkletter's House Party
People Are Funny
Tonight (interim host)
The Art Linkletter Show
Hollywood Talent Scouts
The Lid's Off

Although Art Linkletter had many different television shows, they were almost all variations of one show, Linkletter talking to ordinary people who find themselves in a peculiar situation. He came to television from radio with his shows and with producer John Guedel in hand. Linkletter snatched *People Are Funny* away from Art Baker on radio in 1943 and in 1954 brought it to television, where it stayed until 1961. Linkletter took people from the audience and asked them to do unusual things, e.g., to give away money to passersby on the street. *House Party* started on radio in 1945, came to television as a prime-time show called *Life with Linkletter* in 1950, and switched to daytime in 1952 as *Art Linkletter's House Party*. It changed its name in 1968 to *The Linkletter Show* and lasted another year. The things the ordinary people did on *House Party* were less unusual than on *People Are Funny*, and often school kids would be brought by to chat, or celebrities might drop in. The youngsters also appeared on the syndicated *Art Linkletter and the Kids. The Art Linkletter Show* appeared on prime time in 1963, and the possible outcomes of people doing unusual things were guessed at by celebrities. Linkletter was assisted by **Carl Reiner** and Jayne Meadows. *The Lid's Off* was a syndicated interview show, again with ordinary people. Linkletter continued doing infomercials in later decades, along with an occasional religious program or educational special.

MacNeil, Robert, 1965–1995
> *The Scherer-MacNeil Report*
> *The Whole World Is Watching*
> **Washington Week in Review**
> **Watergate Hearings**
> *The MacNeil-Lehrer Report*
> *The MacNeil-Lehrer NewsHour*
> *The Story of English*

Robert MacNeil was born in Canada and worked for the CBC and Reuters before joining NBC as their London correspondent. By 1965 MacNeil was co-anchoring *The Scherer-MacNeil Report*, NBC's Saturday evening news program. In 1967 MacNeil worked for the BBC in England for a year, returning to the United States to do the PBS documentary *The Whole World Is Watching*. He then anchored *Washington Week in Review* and co-anchored, with **Jim Lehrer**, PBS coverage of the Watergate hearings. MacNeil worked again for the BBC in 1973–1974 but returned in 1975 to do *The Robert MacNeil Report* nightly for PBS. When that show became *The MacNeil-Lehrer Report* in 1976, MacNeil's newscasting career merged with that of Jim Lehrer in their formation of PBS's distinctive evening news. MacNeil did continue doing some outside work, such as narrating *The Story of English*, until his retirement in 1995.

Maher, Bill, 1990–
> *The Midnight Hour*
> **Politically Incorrect**

Bill Maher is an actor-comedian who has succeeded in bringing an original talk-show format out of cable and onto network. *Politically Incorrect*, which began on Comedy Central in 1993 and moved to ABC in 1997, combines humor and political comment with a roundtable structure and seemed to fit a groove in 1990s life. Maher's first network talk-show hosting was for a week on CBS's *The Midnight Hour*, a sort of very-late-night summer tryout program in 1990. In the summer of

1992 Maher also hosted the CBS comedy show *Say What?*, which added new dialogue to old newsreels.

March, Hal, 1951–1963, 1969–1970
>*Summer in the City*
>*The $64,000 Question*
>*What's It For?*
>**Tonight** (interim host)
>*Laughs for Sale*
>*It's Your Bet*

Hal March was one of the top character actors of early television sitcoms, featured on such programs as *The George Burns and Gracie Allen Show* and *My Friend Irma*. His first appearance in a variety series was the brief *Summer in the City*, which was cohosted by March and his comedy partner, Bob Sweeney. As Sweeney and March, they had had their own radio series and often appeared in other venues. In 1955 March had the apparent good fortune to be chosen as host of *The $64,000 Question*. After the show's scandalous end in 1958, March maintained a tenuous television talk career, being one of *Tonight's* interregnum hosts in 1962 and hosting several other comedy-based panel shows.

Marx, Groucho, 1950–1969
>*You Bet Your Life*
>*Tell It to Groucho*
>**Tonight** (interim host)

The stage and film history of Groucho Marx needs no review. However certain parts of Marx's radio career would be good to recall. In 1939 Groucho, his brother Chico, Ronald Colman, Carole Lombard, Cary Grant, and others formed *The Circle* around a specially built table. For an hour each Sunday night they discussed art, politics, life, and death, which may have made them the first spontaneous free-form talk radio show. In 1947 John Guedel, the producer of *House Party* and *People Are Funny*, persuaded Groucho to do a radio quiz show, *You Bet Your Life*, that relied not on rigid scripts but on ad-lib interchange. From 1950 to 1959 the show had slightly different radio and television half-hours edited down from hour-long studio tapings, removing both risqué and boring moments. The video version, often in the top ten, lasted until 1961. In 1962 Groucho did *Tell It to Groucho*, which was similar to *You Bet Your Life* in interviewing ordinary folks but with less emphasis on a quiz. Groucho was also one of the 1962 *Tonight* interregnum hosts and continued occasionally to emcee such shows as *Hollywood Palace* and *The Kraft Music Hall* until 1969.

Masquerade Party, 1952–1960, 1974–1975

Masquerade Party was one of the defining panel shows of television. It appeared on all three major networks and in syndication. A panel of attractive and witty people attempted to identify celebrities dressed in ornate costumes and masks who would answer questions through a voice-disguising microphone. Over the years the masters of ceremonies were **Bud Collyer**, Douglas Edwards, Peter Donald, Eddie Bracken, **Robert Q. Lewis**, **Bert Parks**, and **Richard Dawson**. Regular panelists included Phil Silvers, **Ilka Chase**, **Buff Cobb**, **Jerry Lester**, **Betsy Palmer**, Jonathan Winters, Jinx Falkenburg, **Faye Emerson**, Audrey Meadows, Sam Levenson, Ogden Nash, Dagmar, Bill Bixby, and **Nipsey Russell**.

McKay, Jim, 1951–

The Real McKay
Sports Spot
Youth Takes a Stand
Make the Connection
The Verdict Is Yours
ABC's Wide World of Sports

Jim McKay has emceed or appeared on *ABC's Wide World of Sports* since 1961. On the show and in his linked coverage of Olympic games, he has had to interview personalities, give enthusiastic descriptions of competition, fill time, and at the 1972 Olympics report on terrorist actions. It is fortunate that his earlier television career gave him a wide variety of preparatory experiences. After working as a print reporter, McKay in 1947 began producing, writing, and presenting the news and sports programming on WMAR-TV in Baltimore. Two years later he joined CBS and in 1951 had his own daytime talk-variety show, *The Real McKay*, and then a sports interview show, *Sports Spot*. In 1954 and 1955 McKay moderated the news interview and discussion show *Youth Takes a Stand*. In 1955 he emceed the prime-time quiz-panel show *Make the Connection*. From 1957 to 1960 McKay was the court reporter on *The Verdict Is Yours*. The show used real lawyers and judges to try mock cases with the audience as jury. The show used only a rough plot outline, with the actual dialogue being ad-lib. It was McKay's job to fill the viewers in on out-of-court and skipped events. Before going to ABC, McKay covered the Olympics for CBS in 1960.

McLaughlin, John, 1982–
   The McLaughlin Group
   See Chapter 8 for background on John McLaughlin.

McMahon, Ed, 1950–
   Big Top
   Who Do You Trust?
   Tonight
   Missing Links
   Kraft Music Hall
   Concentration
   Whodunnit?
   Muscular Dystrophy Telethon
   Television's Greatest Commercials
   Star Search
   TV's Bloopers & Practical Jokes
   Next Big Star

   Ed McMahon first appeared on network television as the hefty clown on CBS's *Big Top*, a children's circus telecast weekly from the Camden, N.J., convention center. In 1958 **Johnny Carson** needed a new announcer on his weekday game show out of New York City *Who* [later *Whom*] *Do You Trust?* McMahon was hired and commuted from Philadelphia. From then on McMahon stayed at Carson's side from his move to *Tonight* in 1962 to Carson's retirement in 1992. But McMahon was always finding additional work elsewhere. Besides commercials, McMahon hosted game shows starting with *Missing Links* in 1963 and ending in 1979 with the mystery solution contest *Whodunnit?* that included lawyers Melvin Belli and F. Lee Bailey as regular panelists. McMahon also hosted *Kraft Music Hall* in 1968, several *Television's Greatest Commercials* in 1982–1983, and, with **Dick Clark**, *TV's Bloopers & Practical Jokes* from 1984 to 1991. McMahon's greatest continuing success away from Carson was the weekly syndicated talent hunt, *Star Search*, which began in 1983.

Miller, Dennis, 1985–
   Saturday Night Live
   The Dennis Miller Show

Dennis Miller Live

Monday Night Football (Commentary)

After winning a comedian *Star Search* contest, in 1985 Dennis Miller joined *Saturday Night Live,* where he did the "Weekend Update" until 1990. In 1992 *The Dennis Miller Show* appeared as a syndicated late-night talk-variety show. Miller's humor with its somewhat obscure references to cultural figures was much admired by some but avoided by others. In 1994 Miller began the weekly *Dennis Miller Live* on HBO. The more specialized audience and intense preparation may be responsible for the success of the new show, which has won several Emmys. Miller also beat **Rush Limbaugh** in the competition to do the Monday night NFL commentary.

Miss America Pageant, 1954–

The annual *Miss America Pageant* has become a ritual for many Americans. About half the television homes in the country tune in each September. The show moved from network to network over the years, but from the first telecast to 1978, the host and interviewer was **Bert Parks**. Parks introduced the song "There She Is, Miss America" on the second program, in 1955. The key talk-television element was the interviews with the finalists, America watching carefully and judging every word and expression. Ron Ely hosted for two years and then Gary Collins until 1990. **Regis Philbin** and **Kathie Lee Gifford** became cohosts in 1991, but Philbin worked alone in 1996. After a couple of years of tryouts by other personalities, Donnie and Marie Osmond took over in 1999. In the 1990s the pageant became interactive, with phone-in votes counted. The first poll was to see if the swimsuit competition should be eliminated (it wasn't), and later poll results counted as if they were another judge's vote for one or another of the contestants.

Moore, Garry, 1950–1977

The Garry Moore Show

I've Got a Secret

To Tell the Truth

Garry Moore had been an important figure on network radio for more than ten years when he began his simulcast show five early evenings a week in 1950. In his twenties Moore learned the basics of radio comedy from old pro Ransom Sherman on *Club Matinee* out of Chicago from 1939 to 1942. On *Club Matinee* Moore met his long-time sidekick

Durward Kirby and also had his name changed from Thomas Garrison Morfit by a contest to Rename-the-Morfit, for which a listener won $50. During those years, Moore also emceed *Beat the Band,* a show where listener questions were addressed to the show's musicians, including Perry Como and the Ted Weems orchestra. In 1942, Moore had another naming contest for his new six-day-a-week morning show that was *The Show without a Name* until a listener won $500 for *Everything Goes.* In 1943 when Lou Costello was stricken with rheumatic fever, Moore was teamed with the semi-retired Jimmy Durante to replace Abbott and Costello. Durante and Moore proved a very popular radio duo, developing a program that combined Moore's writing with Durante's ad-libs. In 1947 Moore went on his own to host the quiz show *Take It or Leave It,* then the daily restaurant visit show *Breakfast in Hollywood,* and at last in 1949 *The Garry Moore Show,* which went to simulcast the next year.

On television during the 1950s Moore was one of CBS's biggest moneymakers and for a time the highest salaried. Moore's strength was a soft folksiness and, as can be seen from the earlier contests, contact with the home audience. The Moore show split into a popular daytime talk-variety show from 1950 to 1958 and a prime-time variety show in 1951, then from 1958 to 1964, and again in 1966–1967. The daytime show continued the history of contests, one awarding Durward Kirby to an Ohio family for a weekend, and became well known for the early TV appearances of important figures such as Don Adams, Carol Burnett, Wally Cox, George Gobel, Don Knotts, Leslie Uggams, Tuesday Weld, and Jonathan Winters. The daytime show also had more scholarly guests such as Ashley Montagu, Ivan Sanderson, and Frank Lloyd Wright. Moore wished to give up the daily grind in 1958 and switched to a once-a-week prime-time format that was quite popular and which lasted until Moore's semi-retirement in 1964. Another successful show emceed by Moore, which may have been the most popular TV panel show of all, was *I've Got a Secret.* It began in 1952 and was a production with Allan Sherman doing much of the creative work. The show required a panel that would interact in a spontaneous, interesting, and humorous way while questioning guests to discover their secrets. After some early trials the panel was **Bill Cullen** and **Henry Morgan** as the males and first Jayne Meadows and **Faye Emerson** and then **Betsy Palmer** and **Bess Myerson** as the females. Moore also left this show in 1964, and **Steve Allen** became emcee. Moore returned from semi-retirement in 1966 to do a new evening show, but it was up against *Bo-*

nanza and failed badly, being replaced by the Smothers Brothers. After that Moore emceed the syndicated *To Tell the Truth* from 1969 to 1977, when he went into full retirement.

Morgan, Henry, 1948–1967, 1972–1976
> *On the Corner*
> *The Henry Morgan Show*
> *Draw to Win*
> **I've Got a Secret**
> *Morgan and Company*
> **That Was the Week That Was**

For a comedian often considered too acerbic and uncontrollable, Henry Morgan had a rather long career with a bit of recognition. Perhaps Morgan's durability was due to *I've Got a Secret*, where he was a panelist in all its years—1952–1967, 1972–1973 and 1976—network and syndicated. On that show Morgan with his special wit was balanced against more congenial figures such as **Bill Cullen**, **Betsy Palmer**, and **Garry Moore**. Morgan's radio life began in 1931 as a page and then in 1933 as announcer at New York's WMCA. He wandered around the country during the 1930s, returning to New York and his own program of comedy and comment on WOR, *Here's Morgan*. Morgan's work, which was largely ad-lib, made fun of sponsors and station executives and was much admired by other broadcasters. After serving in World War II, Morgan had ABC and then NBC network shows from 1946 to 1950. Morgan also appeared as one of the male defenders on **Leave It to the Girls**. Morgan's first television show, *On the Corner*, was also the ABC television network's first show. Morgan thumbed through *Variety*, cracked jokes about the sponsor, and introduced a wide mix of performers. The show lasted five weeks. In 1951 Morgan had an NBC show (*Henry Morgan's Great Talent Hunt*) that at first, like **The Gong Show**, made fun of talent competitions but later changed to more straightforward variety, still with spontaneous comment. In 1952 Morgan hosted a panel quiz, *Draw to Win*; then came *I've Got a Secret*. For sixteen weeks in 1959, Morgan had his own syndicated show, *Morgan and Company*, on which he made fun of talk shows in a Letterman-like fashion. In 1963 and 1964 Morgan's skills were recognized by the producers of the American version of *That Was the Week That Was*, and he became one of their regular satirists. After *I've Got a Secret* left the air in 1976, Morgan returned to local New York radio.

The Morning Show (CBS), 1954–1957

In 1954, ABC and CBS entered into competition with **Today**. ABC used a simulcast of its long-term popular radio show Don McNeill's **The Breakfast Club**. It failed after a year. CBS also began, in direct competition with *Today*, the most remarkable morning variety show ever produced. *The Morning Show* had as its successive hosts for the three years it was on the air, **Walter Cronkite**, **Jack Paar**, **Johnny Carson** as guest host, **John Henry Faulk** until the time of his blacklisting, Dick Van Dyke, and Will Rogers Jr. Among those who appeared as regulars were one of the writers, **Barbara Walters**, and as singers, Edie Adams, Betty Clooney, and **Merv Griffin**. The show attempted every challenge to *Today* that fit within the variety/news talk range but it finally gave up. In 1955 CBS substituted **Captain Kangaroo** for the second hour of *The Morning Show*.

Moyers, Bill, 1971–
> *This Week*
> *Bill Moyers' Journal*
> *CBS Reports*
> *The CBS Evening News* (commentator)
> *Crossroads*
> *Bill Moyers' World of Ideas*
> See Chapter 6 for background on Bill Moyers.

Murrow, Edward R., 1951–1961
> **See It Now**
> **Person to Person**
> **Small World**
> *CBS Reports*
> See Chapter 2 for background on Edward R. Murrow.

Myerson, Bess, 1949–1967, 1972
> *Jacques Fray's Music Room*
> *The Big Payoff*
> *The Name's the Same*
> **I've Got a Secret**
> **Candid Camera**
> *What Every Woman Wants to Know*

Bess Myerson was the 1945 Miss America, nine years before the pageant was televised. Myerson appeared in 1949 on *Jacques Fray's*

Music Room, a program of concert and show music where critics gave their judgments on each performance. Myerson's later television work was more as personality than performer. She was greeter and model for several seasons on *The Big Payoff* quiz. She was a regular panelist on *The Name's the Same* in 1954–1955 and on *I've Got a Secret* from 1958 to 1967. Myerson assisted Allen Funt in hosting *Candid Camera* during 1966–1967. In 1972, Myerson finally got her own syndicated talk show, *What Every Woman Wants to Know,* a daily half-hour devoted to features helpful to women.

Night Beat, 1956–1957

Night Beat was a New York local show that offered a model of live television interviewing. For an hour each weeknight, **Mike Wallace** sat on a chair in a smoky studio holding a clipboard with notes and talking across an open space to a guest in another chair. On each show there were two such guests—politicians, entertainers, or cultural figures, such as Norman Mailer and Salvador Dali. Through astute camera work and tough questioning, the feeling sometimes came across that the guest was facing his or her final judgment.

Nightlife (ABC), 1965

During the fierce mid-sixties network battles and immediately after the rapid failure of the *Les Crane Show,* ABC made *Nightlife* its next challenge to **The Tonight Show**. Network executives tried a new host every week, including **Dave Garroway**, Pat Boone, and Shelley Berman. But after less than four months, they were back to Crane, this time with a less political, more show-business approach, and with **Nipsey Russell** as second banana. The show then shifted from New York to Hollywood, but still ended in another five months.

Nightline, 1980–

See Chapter 7.

The Nixon Interviews with David Frost, 1977

One year exactly after Richard Nixon received his pardon from Gerald Ford, Nixon signed a contract for $600,000 and 10 percent of profits with **David Frost** to broadcast four ninety-minute interviews. After taping twenty-eight hours of interviews at Nixon's San Clemente home, Frost set up a network of U.S. stations that covered 90 percent of the country. The four shows were broadcast in May 1977, and became some of the most highly watched news programs of all time. An hour-long fifth program was broadcast in October. The conversations fascinated, even if not much new was revealed. Many critics point to this as a rapid acceleration of checkbook journalism.

O'Brien, Conan, 1993–
  Late Night with Conan O'Brien
  Conan O'Brien had almost no previous on-air experience when he took over Letterman's *Late Night* spot on NBC. O'Brien had written for *The Wilton North Report* and *The Simpsons* and shared in an Emmy for *Saturday Night Live* writing. O'Brien's work reflects the insight of the experienced humor writer.

O'Donnell, Rosie, 1996–
  The Rosie O'Donnell Show
  Rosie O'Donnell had difficulty getting a talk show produced in the 1990s that was like the **Mike Douglas** and **Dinah Shore** shows she remembered from childhood. However, once her syndicated daytime show began in June 1996, she became an instant star with high ratings. The show updates the friendly daily talk show with Letterman-like bits, e.g., an audience consisting only of her look-alikes. After her rapid success, O'Donnell's earlier TV and movie work even began to get more attention. After competing on *Star Search*, she had appeared as a secondary character on the sitcom *Gimme a Break!* and, beginning with *A League of Their Own*, in several feature films, including the television-based *Car 54, Where Are You?* and *The Flintstones*. Flintstone vitamin tablets for children now include ones shaped like her character, Betty.

Olsen, Johnny, 1947–1985
  Doorway to Fame
  Johnny Olsen's Rumpus Room
  Fun for the Money
  Kids and Company
  The Strawhatters
  The Price Is Right
  Johnny Olsen is one of the most neglected and yet one of the best-remembered game-show figures. Some important television reference works even misspell his name as Olson. On radio Olsen emceed the popular daytime quiz *Ladies, Be Seated* as well as a 1945 experimental television version from the General Electric Schenectady station. From

1947 to 1949 he hosted the DuMont talent show *Doorway to Fame*.
From 1949 to 1952 he was very busy working for DuMont hosting a
daily game variety show, *Johnny Olsen's Rumpus Room*, and a Saturday
children's show with Ham Fisher in 1951–1952. He also worked on an
ABC 1949 game show, *Fun for the Money*. In 1953 he emceed the variety
show *The Strawhatters*. At this point Olsen became unforgettable but
almost invisible. Olsen was the announcing voice for **What's My Line?**,
I've Got a Secret, **To Tell the Truth**, *The Jackie Gleason Show*, and,
until his death in 1985, most memorably the voice that yelled "Come
on down!" on *The Price Is Right*.

The Open Mind, 1956–
  Professor Richard Heffner has kept this straightforward half-hour
interview show going for more than forty years, collecting his intriguing conversations with everyone from Martin Luther King Jr. to **William F. Buckley**.

Original Max Headroom, 1985–1987
  This is a little hard to explain. In 1984, British Channel 4 and
Chrysalis Records broadcast music videos introduced by a computer-
generated head that came to be called Max Headroom. A telefilm was
produced in Britain in 1984, giving the fictional story of how Max came
to be. The film has been called sometimes *The Max Headroom Story*
and sometimes *Rebus: The Max Headroom Story*. Cinemax showed
this telefilm in 1985. Max Headroom with the altered voice of Matt
Frewer began to do interviews for Channel 4 in 1985. In 1986 Cinemax
began cablecasting the British interview show as *Max Headroom*. In
1987 Cinemax cablecast its own U.S. interview show called *Original
Max Headroom*. This title change was made because, also in 1987, ABC
broadcast *Max Headroom*, a drama based on the telefilm. What makes
this relevant to television talk is the use of a computerized image doing
live interviews. When the shows came to the United States, Max even
appeared as a guest on talk shows like **David Letterman**'s.

Osgood, Charles, 1981–
  CBS Sunday Night News
  The CBS Morning News
  CBS News Sunday Morning
  Charles Osgood is the poet and songwriter of the newsroom. Be-
sides being a quite good news anchor for more than fifteen years, Os-

good composed Nancy Wilson's "Black Is Beautiful" and did "The Osgood File," a feature often including a poem, for radio and *CBS This Morning*. He seemed well suited to the casual atmosphere of *CBS News Sunday Morning*.

Paar, Jack, 1952–1965, 1973
    Up to Paar
    The Jack Paar Show
    The Morning Show (CBS)
    The Jack Paar Tonight Show
    The Jack Paar Program
    Jack Paar Tonite
    See Chapter 3 for background on Jack Paar.

Palmer, Betsy, 1956–1970, 1977–1979
    Masquerade Party
    I've Got a Secret
    Today
    Girl Talk
    Candid Camera
    Betsy Palmer as an actress had been one of the mainstays of early television dramas such as *Studio One*. But beginning in 1956, she became one of TV's most important panelists, first on *Masquerade Party* and from 1957 to 1967 on *I've Got a Secret*. In 1958–1959 Palmer was also one of the *Today* girls. In 1969–1970 Palmer succeeded **Virginia Graham** as host of the syndicated talk show *Girl Talk*. From 1977 to 1979, Palmer returned as cohost of *Candid Camera*.

Parks, Bert, 1947–1978
    Party Line
    Break the Bank
    Stop the Music
    The Bert Parks Show
    The Big Payoff
    Miss America Pageant
    Bandstand
    Hold That Note
    County Fair
    Masquerade Party
    Circus

Strike It Rich

Bert Parks was one of the pantheon of game-show hosts. Parks' radio work began when he was an announcer for the Eddie Cantor and Xavier Cugat shows and other programs. After Parks returned from World War II, he became emcee of some of the most popular radio quizzes, such as *Break the Bank* and *Stop the Music.* In 1947 Parks was TV quizmaster of *Party Line*, which gave $5 to anyone who could say what had just been shown on the program when called at a phone number picked from cards sent to the show. In 1948 Parks began bringing his popular radio quizzes to TV, where they lasted until 1957. His quiz show successes earned Parks his own daytime talk-variety show from 1950 to 1953. Other game shows came along, but from 1955 to 1978 Parks' greatest fame was as host of the *Miss America Pageant.* Parks hosted two more 1950s daytime variety shows, *Bandstand* and *County Fair,* and in 1971–1972 the syndicated weekly *Circus.* On these shows Parks' skills as a barker came to the fore. The shift away from talk may have come from the feeling viewers had that Parks never paid much attention to what people were saying to him.

Pauley, Jane, 1976–
Today
Real Life with Jane Pauley
Dateline NBC

Having been born in 1950, Jane Pauley represents the first generation of television figures who grew up with television all around them. She was a news anchor in Indianapolis and Chicago after graduation from college. *Today* was looking for a **Barbara Walters** replacement in 1976 and picked young, attractive Pauley from the candidates. Pauley fit in well as cohost with **Tom Brokaw** and then **Bryant Gumbel**. In 1989 Dick Ebersol brought in Deborah Norville as *Today* newsreader; it appeared that Pauley was about to be replaced with a younger "other woman." Pauley resigned from the show, and viewer sympathy went in her favor. In 1990–1991 Pauley got her own "softer" prime-time news and interview show, *Real Life with Jane Pauley.* In 1992 Pauley became one of the first cohosts of the prime-time *Dateline NBC.*

The People's Court, 1981–1993

The People's Court represented both the 1980s trend to "reality television" and a return to 1950s TV shows like *Four Square Court* and *Traffic Court.* The show's great popularity came from the fact that actual small-claims cases were being heard and decided on by a real judge. Judge Joseph A. Wapner brought years of experience on the California Superior Court and an apparent cranky interest in justice to each case. Here were real people angry at and really confronting each other. The show was framed by "reporter" Doug Llewelyn's interviews of the litigants. The producers also paid all settlements and a bit more to the participants.

Perkins, Marlin, 1950–1957, 1963–1985
> *Zoo Parade*
> *Mutual of Omaha's Wild Kingdom*

Marlin Perkins was television's animal man. In 1949 Perkins was Director of Chicago's Lincoln Park Zoo, and he asked local television to visit his animals; the next year people were watching *Zoo Parade* on NBC. Perkins explained animal life to the audience and on camera to Jim Hurlbut, the cohost. In 1963 Perkins returned to wild life on television, but for this show he was traveling around the world with Jim Fowler on *Mutual of Omaha's Wild Kingdom.* After going into syndication, the show received a waiver from the FCC's Prime Time Access Rule to allow it to use network reruns because they had sufficient "educational" value. Most people probably watched because they liked looking at animals and listening to pleasant Marlin Perkins.

Person to Person, 1953–1961

Edward R. Murrow is often associated with tough, principled news reporting. Murrow's *Person to Person* was different. Murrow used television to connect the viewers to people in their home environments. With his cigarette in hand, Murrow sat before his studio monitors looking at his interviewees in their homes, two visits for each half-hour show. The visited could hear Ed but not see him. The artifacts to be shown and the route through the house were all carefully worked out in advance. Murrow visited with Jackie Robinson, Harry Truman, Marilyn Monroe, and Maria Callas. Everyone wanted to see them, but what did they really get to see? How close can we get to another person with twelve minutes of television viewing a living room with Murrow asking questions? Sometimes it got very close. After Murrow left the show in 1959, **Charles Collingwood** took over the interviewing until 1961.

Philbin, Regis, 1963–1976, 1981–1982, 1988–
> *Philbin's People*

That Regis Philbin Show
The Joey Bishop Show
The Neighbors
The Regis Philbin Show
Live! with Regis and Kathie Lee
Miss America Pageant
Who Wants to Be a Millionaire?

Regis Philbin has been on and off national television over several decades, but, unlike that of most talk figures in that situation, his stature has grown. After local shows in Los Angeles, Philbin's first national appearances in the 1960s and 1970s started well, hosting his own talk shows *Philbin's People* and *That Regis Philbin Show*. The shows didn't last long, so Philbin became **Joey Bishop**'s sidekick on Bishop's late-night challenge to Carson in 1967–1969. After that there was some hosting of game shows and such through 1976 and then a return to local work. In 1981–1982, Philbin was on the national scene again with Mary Hart to do an NBC daytime talk show aimed at women, *The Regis Philbin Show*. Then Philbin was back to local television, but now in New York, working with **Kathie Lee Gifford** on *The Morning Show*. The combination proved effective, and in 1988 the show went into syndication as *Live! with Regis and Kathie Lee*. It is generally acknowledged that the show's attraction was maintained by the spontaneous interchanges between Kathie Lee and Regis about personal events. In 1991, Philbin became host of the *Miss America Pageant*, at first along with Gifford. In August 1999, Regis began hosting *Who Wants to Be a Millionaire?*, which soon became the high point of his video career. In July 2000 Kathie Lee left *Live! with Regis and Kathie Lee*, and in February 2001 Kelly Ripa replaced her, making the show *Live! with Regis and Kelly*.

P.M. East / P.M. West, 1961–1962

P.M. East / P.M. West was Westinghouse Broadcasting's attempt to challenge **Tonight** in the Paar years. The New York east segment was hosted by **Mike Wallace** and Joyce Davidson, followed by the San Francisco west segment hosted by Terrence O'Flaherty. Wallace seemed to regress from the acerbity of his interview shows to the couple-television of Mike and Buff. The show should be remembered as a platform for new talent: it provided the first national television appearances for performers such as Woody Allen and Peter, Paul, and Mary.

P.M. Magazine, 1977–1990

P.M. Magazine was a project of Group W, which took the developing magazine genre, combined it with local station production, and created a program individually shaped by each of the stations that broadcast it. In 1976 KPIX, the San Francisco Group W station, began Evening: The MTWTF Program. It was broadcast at 7:30 weeknights and contained three or four filmed segments of news or human interest connected by in-studio anchors. The next year all five Group W stations were producing Evening Magazine locally and sharing the segments among themselves. In 1979 Group W made agreements with stations around the country to supply them with feature segments for a large portion of each local station's P.M. Magazine, if the local stations would in turn supply their best locally produced segments, at least one a week, to go into the pool for national distribution. The rules set up by Group W were that all features contributed would be filmed on location by minicam and not in studio and that a certain format would be used locally—for example, two cohosts at each station. In addition to their choice of pool features, the local stations received use of the P.M. name, graphics, and expert advice. The project went well through 1980, many interviews and other features being used nationwide. The cooking of Chef Tell became one of the favorites. In the mid-1980s, competition developed when syndicated, completely packaged programs, designed for pre–prime time, became more common. Such programs as A Current Affair, **Entertainment Tonight,** and Wheel of Fortune attracted stations away from the pool, and P.M. Magazine went out of existence in 1990.

Politically Incorrect, 1993–2002

Politically Incorrect first appeared on Comedy Central with stand-up comedian **Bill Maher** as host. In 1997 it moved to ABC in the spot after **Nightline.** The intense interest in the show seems to come from having well-known people from show business, journalism, and politics talk freely about subjects not usually discussed on television. This suggests that in addition to setting the structure of talk, the accepted standards of television talk have also set limits upon the topics discussed.

Povich, Maury, 1986–
   A Current Affair
   The Maury Povich Show

Maury

Maury Povich was a Washington, D.C., news anchor before becoming host of *A Current Affair*. That show was one of the leaders in the tabloid television magazine genre. The program was produced for Rupert Murdoch's Fox stations; in selection of topic and treatment it resembled some of Murdoch's print tabloids, such as *The Star*. Use of videotape not originally intended for broadcast was highly sought after by the program and when obtained, as with the case of actor Rob Lowe making love to a sixteen-year-old girl, led to the desired publicity and uproar. Povich left *A Current Affair* in 1990 and started his daily syndicated talk program *The Maury Povich Show* the next year. On it Povich talked with the familiar assortment of troubled people but in a fairly gentle manner. In 1998, Povich switched his show from Paramount to Studios USA and shortened the title to *Maury*.

Pyne, Joe, 1965–1969

> *The Joe Pyne Show*
> *Showdown*

Joe Pyne anticipated many of the combative techniques of talk-show warriors of later decades. Pyne invited people to speak who held beliefs very different from accepted middle class norms. Then when they expressed their views, he would call them names and make fun of them. He became nationally famous when, on his local Los Angeles show, around the time of the Watts riots, Pyne and his militant Black guest both displayed pistols that they had hidden but close at hand. After this incident, Pyne got national syndication. Strangely in 1966 Pyne was also emcee on an NBC daytime game show called *Showdown*. Teams competed in answering questions. Contestants missing a question would fall to the floor on breakaway chairs.

Queen for a Day, 1956–1964, 1970

> *Queen for a Day* and **Strike It Rich** vie for the title of American TV's most maudlin game show. *Debt* is the major recent competitor for that title. *Queen for a Day* appeared on radio in 1945 before *Strike It Rich* in 1947, but came to television in 1956, five years later than its opponent's 1951. Originally broadcast on radio from New York with Dud Williamson as emcee, the show had the format (four or five women from the audience say why they should be crowned queen for a day, are judged by the audience, and given gifts) but not yet the tone (tears and suffering) that would be achieved when the show moved to Los Angeles

later in 1945 and Jack Bailey became emcee (until 1964). Bailey had been a vaudeville music man and World's Fair barker before going into radio, where he had hosted *Meet the Missus*. Bailey played on the emotions of the contestants and the audience. On radio, sometimes a contestant would win enough support from the audience to be crowned queen by expressing a whimsical desire or a good deed. By the time the show got to television, where it was at times the most popular daytime show, only a wish coming out of the saddest story and most difficult situation had any chance of being rewarded. The show returned briefly in 1970 with Dick Curtis as host.

Raphaël, Sally Jessy, 1984–
Sally Jessy Raphaël
    Sally Jessy Raphaël grew up traveling back and forth between Scarsdale, New York, and San Juan, Puerto Rico. Sally was her given name; Jessy is a nod to her father, Jesse Lowenthal; and Raphaël is her mother's family name. Like many talk television personalities, she had a long and varied radio career before settling into television. While a teenager she hosted "Junior High School News" from White Plains, New York. She acknowledges working for twenty years on local radio and television stations in twenty-four cities and being fired eighteen times before starting a successful network radio show in 1982. In 1984 her local St. Louis television show was syndicated nationally by Multimedia. Usually broadcast in the daytime, Sally followed the frequent Donahue format of a studio audience hearing the personal and often traumatic life stories of ordinary folk. Sally would listen with sympathy and attention as her guests told their often-tearful tales. In 1989 Sally received a Daytime Emmy as outstanding talk show host.

Rather, Dan, 1970–
    CBS Reports
    60 Minutes
    Who's Who
    CBS Evening News
    Campaign '84
    48 Hours
    Dan Rather worked in both print and broadcast journalism in Texas before joining CBS in 1962 as Dallas bureau chief. The Kennedy assassination thrust him into the center of the news, after which CBS assigned him to the Johnson White House and then to several foreign

posts. In 1970 Rather began anchoring some of the CBS weekend news reports, while also covering the Nixon White House, and soon hosted several Watergate-related special reports. Rather was *CBS Reports* anchor in 1974–1975, became a *60 Minutes* editor in 1975, and during 1977 a reporter-interviewer on its spin-off *Who's Who*. When **Walter Cronkite** retired in 1981, Rather left *60 Minutes* and became only the third person to be permanent anchor on CBS's evening news telecasts. In 1988 Rather took on the added duty of anchoring *48 Hours*. Rather has had numerous important interviews with major news figures, including Richard Nixon, George Bush, and Saddam Hussein.

Rayburn, Gene, 1953–1986
> *The Name's the Same*
> **Tonight**
> *Make the Connection*
> *The Steve Allen Show*
> *Dough Re Mi*
> *The Match Game*
> *The Amateur's Guide to Love*
> *Break the Bank*

Gene Rayburn is another of the television game-show pantheon. Rayburn developed his talent in radio, but post-television radio. Rayburn and his then partner Dee Finch did their New York morning drive-time radio comedy from 1946 to 1952. After their breakup Rayburn got into television as a panelist on *The Name's the Same*, as panel host of *Make the Connection*, and most importantly as **Steve Allen**'s sidekick/announcer in pioneering late-night and prime-time television formats. The Allen connection ended in 1959 and Rayburn plunged into game-show hosting. Rayburn is most closely associated with the various versions of *The Match Game* from 1962 to 1985.

Reagan, Ronald, 1953–1954
> *The Orchid Award*

Ronald Reagan's appearances as guest and panelist on **What's My Line?**, his numerous live TV acting appearances, his hosting from 1954 to 1962 of *General Electric Theatre* (in the early years live), hosting *Death Valley Days* in 1965–1966, appearances on **Joey Bishop**'s and Bob Hope's shows, and various debates would not quite qualify him as a television talk figure. But his hosting of *The Orchid Award* does. The fifteen-minute show was broadcast after **Walter Winchell**'s weekly news and gossip reports, on which Winchell often awarded orchids of praise. Reagan as Hollywood host alternated weeks in 1953–1954 with Donald Woods as New York host. Exchanging some words, Reagan would present the orchid to an entertainer, such as Rosemary Clooney or Eddie Fisher, who would then perform briefly.

Real People, 1979–1984

Real People began slow but became one of the most popular shows of the early 1980s. *Real People* falls within the television tradition of presenting in interviews non-celebrities who because of occupation, hobby, or special talent will interest viewers. However, the methods and tones of presentation within this genre vary widely. **We, the People** was almost patriotic, whereas **Charles Kuralt** was down-home and folksy. *Real People* tended to emphasize the humorous and outrageous. Although the personnel shifted over the years, each program had four or five hosts who would operate both in the studio, often going into the audience, and in filmed pieces done on location. Among the hosts were **Fred Willard**, Sarah Purcell, John Barbour, and Byron Allen. The show inspired many imitators, most notably *That's Incredible!*

Reiner, Carl, 1948–1984, 1991

> *The Fashion Story*
> *Fifty-Fourth Street Revue*
> *Eddie Condon's Floor Show*
> *Your Show of Shows*
> *Droodles*
> *Caesar's Hour*
> **Keep Talking**
> *Take a Good Look*
> *The Art Linkletter Show*
> *The Celebrity Game*
> *Sunday Best*

Carl Reiner is one of the most important of television comedy second bananas. He worked with Sid Caesar through the 1950s and was also the straight man to Mel Brooks' "The 2000 Year Old Man." Reiner was the creator/producer/writer of *The Dick Van Dyke Show* and also played the role of Alan Brady, the TV star for whom Van Dyke's character, Rob Petrie, wrote. And Carl is Rob Reiner's father. Although in the earlier shows there was a certain amount of spontaneous humor, what makes Reiner a television talk person is his forgotten work. Before *Your*

Show of Shows, Reiner was featured on three shows that combined talk and variety. On *The Fashion Story* he played a photographer who took pictures of the fashion models, who were at the center of the show. He moved up in 1949 to be a featured variety performer on *Fifty-Fourth Street Revue,* and in 1950 to host and interviewer on *Eddie Condon's Floor Show.* As a sideline in the Caesar years, Reiner was a regular panelist on *Droodles,* and after Caesar in 1958–1959 Reiner emceed *Keep Talking.* He was also a panelist on *Take a Good Look* in 1960–1961. In **Art Linkletter's** 1963 imitation of **Candid Camera,** Reiner played one of the shills. In the late 1960s he emceed *The Celebrity Game,* partly panel, partly quiz, but mainly a chance for comedians to joke back and forth. After several years' absence, he returned in 1991 to host *Sunday Best,* a very short-lived attempt to meld the television magazine format with comedy. In 1995 Reiner won an Emmy for Alan Brady's appearance on *Mad About You.*

Rivera, Geraldo, 1974–

> ***Good Morning, America***
> *20/20*
> *Geraldo Rivera: Good Night, America*
> Rivera-Llewelyn "events"
> *Geraldo*
> *Now It Can Be Told*
> See Chapter 7 for background on Geraldo Rivera.

Rivers, Joan, 1968–

> *That Show with Joan Rivers*
> ***Tonight*** (guest and permanent guest host)
> *Late Night Starring Joan Rivers*
> *The New Hollywood Squares*
> *The Joan Rivers Show*
> *Can We Shop!*

Joan Rivers is the only woman to have any success as a host of what has become the traditional late-night talk-variety format. Rivers was a member of the Second City troupe in the early 1960s. She began appearing on Carson's *Tonight* in 1965. In 1968–1969 Rivers had her own daily syndicated talk-variety show *That Show with Joan Rivers.* In 1983 she became the permanent guest host on *Tonight.* In 1986 she gave up that position to become host of Fox's *Late Night Starring Joan Rivers.* Because of poor ratings, Rivers left the show the next year and

Arsenio Hall eventually took over. From 1986 to 1988, Rivers was the center square on *The New Hollywood Squares*. From 1989 to 1993 she had her own syndicated talk show again, eventually offered live in the morning hours. After marketing on QVC, she experimented in 1994 with her own syndicated daytime shopping program, *Can We Shop?* Since 1995 she has interviewed celebrities outside the movie Academy Awards for E! Entertainment Television.

Roberts, Oral, 1954–
> *Oral Roberts*
> *Oral Roberts and You*
> *Miracles Now*

The television work of Oral Roberts, one of the pioneers of televangelism, is divided into two periods. From 1954 to 1967, Roberts usually appeared as a hands-on healer working in a large tent. Roberts dropped his programs for a year and in 1969 reappeared on *Oral Roberts and You*, which concentrated on preaching and religious music from an indoor studio or auditorium. In 1987 Roberts asserted that God would call him "back to heaven" if he failed to raise $8 million. Roberts didn't reach that goal and his audience declined sharply.

Robertson, Pat, 1975–1986, 1988–
> *The 700 Club*

Pat Robertson's Christian ministry in Virginia Beach ran WYAH, a UHF station, and in 1963 Robertson held a telethon to aid the beleaguered station, seeking 700 people to contribute $10 a month. The telethon was a success and in 1966 the station began broadcasting a talk show, *The 700 Club*, to honor the contributors. The host for the first six years was **Jim Bakker**, who left to begin his own TV ministry. Robertson took over as host, and in 1975 *The 700 Club* went national and in 1977 had its own network. So that he could run for U.S. President, Robertson handed the show over to his son, Tim, in 1986. Robertson returned in 1988 and continued to host the show with Ben Kinchlow as his sidekick and former Miss America Terry Meeuween assisting in a combined news and religious talk-show format. Kinchlow left the show in July 1997 to pursue his own ministerial mission.

Rogers, Fred, 1955–1956, 1967–1975, 1979–2001
> *The Children's Corner*
> *Mister Rogers' Neighborhood*

After getting a 1951 bachelor's degree in music, Fred McFeely Rogers worked in New York television production. In 1953 Rogers returned home to Pennsylvania to work for WQED-TV, the Pittsburgh educational station. In 1954 he began *The Children's Corner,* which went on NBC Saturday mornings in 1955–1956. Rogers produced, co-hosted, and served as puppeteer, introducing to children King Friday and Daniel Striped Tiger. The show lasted until 1961 on WQED. In 1963 Rogers was ordained a Presbyterian minister and began *Misterogers* [sic] on CBC. In 1966, Rogers brought *MisteRogers* [sic] to U.S. educational television, where it has stayed and grown ever since. For several years in the 1970s, no new shows were produced. Limited production began again in 1979 and ended in 2001. Rogers developed a television talk mode especially aimed at children that depends heavily on direct looks and slow speaking.

Roosevelt, Eleanor, 1950–1951
> *Today with Mrs. Roosevelt*
> *Mrs. Roosevelt Meets the Public*

Eleanor Roosevelt was one of the few important political figures who had their own political discussion programs. Others were Alben Barkley with *Meet the Veep* in 1953, the year after he was U.S. Vice President, and Adlai Stevenson with *Adlai Stevenson Reports* in 1961–1963 when he was U.S. representative to the United Nations. Roosevelt had appeared frequently on radio while her husband was President. Not only did she appear as a guest on programs like *America's Town Meeting of the Air,* but she also had her own series on both CBS and NBC, contributing any fees to charity. In 1948–1949 on ABC radio, Roosevelt had a program with her daughter, *Eleanor and Anna Roosevelt. Variety* called her "one of the standout commentators on the air." Roosevelt's television program for NBC featured informal talks with public figures. The guests on her first program were Albert Einstein and J. Robert Oppenheimer.

Rose, Charlie, 1978–
> *The Charlie Rose Show*
> *CBS News Nightwatch*
> *Personalities*

After receiving a law degree, Charlie Rose worked with **Bill Moyers** in producing some of Moyers' PBS shows in the 1970s. After other TV work, Rose began syndicating his own talk-interview show, first from Dallas and then from Washington, D.C. In 1984 he became an anchor of *CBS News Nightwatch.* In 1990 Rose departed CBS to host the daily syndicated interview show *Personalities,* but left after only a few weeks. He restarted his own show on The Learning Channel in 1992, moving to PBS the next year. Rose combines newsworthiness with personal involvement in interviewing figures from all areas of interest.

Roundtree, Martha, 1947–1957
> *Meet the Press*
> *Keep Posted*
> *Press Conference*

Martha Roundtree created both *Meet the Press* and **Leave It to the Girls**. Both programs began on radio in 1945 and moved to television in 1947. *Meet the Press* is the longest-running network program. Roundtree was the original moderator of both the radio and TV versions of *Meet the Press,* but she was bought out by her coproducer, **Lawrence Spivak**, in 1953, at which time Ned Brooks became moderator. Roundtree also hosted the similar *Keep Posted* (later called *The Big Issue*) from 1951 to 1954. After leaving it and *Meet the Press,* she moderated several other variations of those shows until 1957. Roundtree's creative work is no longer sufficiently well recognized.

Rukeyser, Louis, 1970–
> *Now*
> *Wall $treet Week*
> *Louis Rukeyser's Business Journal*
> *Louis Rukeyser's Wall Street*

Louis Rukeyser hosted *Wall $treet Week* on PBS from 1972 to 2002. He had been with ABC until 1973 as foreign correspondent, in 1968 as economic commentator and in 1970 cohosting its new series *Now.* In 1981 he also tried briefly a syndicated show. *Wall $treet Week* over the years stayed with the format of a brief, often humorous commentary on the week's business events, followed by interviews with experts in economics and investment. In 2002, Maryland public television and Rukeyser confronted each other, and the format moved with Rukeyser to his new CNBC program.

Russell, Nipsey, 1965–1975, 1980–1985
> **Nightlife** (ABC)
> *P.D.Q.*

Dean Martin's Comedyworld
Masquerade Party
Chain Reaction
Juvenile Jury
Your Number's Up

Nipsey Russell was one of the very few Blacks to be active in American television talk during the 1960s and 1970s and may be unique in that his presence was in the mainstream, unlike the specialized work of Tony Brown, Don Cornelius, and Ben Kinchlow, or various sports commentators. Russell had been a regular on the sitcom *Car 54, Where Are You?* and did stand-up routines on variety shows before becoming **Les Crane**'s sidekick on ABC's *Nightlife* in 1965. Russell served as a comedy correspondent, doing on-location spots, for *Dean Martin's Comedyworld* in 1974. Russell has been a regular or frequent panelist, known for his ad-libs, on *P.D.Q., Masquerade Party, Chain Reaction, Vaudeville, The Match Game,* and **Hollywood Squares**. Russell hosted a new version of *Juvenile Jury* on Black Entertainment Television in 1983 and emceed the NBC daytime game show *Your Number's Up* in 1985.

Russert, Tim, 1991–
Today
Meet the Press
The Tim Russert Show

Tim Russert's path to success is less typical than that of most talk-show figures. Although delivering pizzas while a student may be something he has in common with other hosts, receiving a doctor of law degree, being admitted to the bar, and then becoming, first, special counsel and chief of staff for a U.S. senator (Daniel Patrick Moynihan) and then counselor to a New York governor (Mario Cuomo) is not the usual way to television fame. The fact that Russert went on to become a network executive (NBC vice president, then Washington bureau chief) before appearing regularly on the tube is also a bit unusual. In 1990, Russert made his first appearance on *Meet the Press.* In 1991, he was a regular analyst on *Today* and the same year became host of *Meet the Press.* Under Russert, the tone of that show changed radically. In earlier years the press conference was the model: usually only one guest, a panel of questioners, and an atmosphere that allowed the guest to say much at the pace he or she wished. In 1992, the show expanded from half an hour to an hour and the number of guests was often three. Russert could speak directly to the interviewee, ask more frequent questions, and more easily interrupt answers. Russert's tone was not so much invasive as investigative. The changes he made greatly raised the program's ratings and earned him a contract in 2001 that would keep him as host of *Meet the Press* through 2012.

Sales, Soupy, 1955–1981
> *The Soupy Sales Show*
> **Tonight** (interim host)
> **What's My Line?**
> *Junior Almost Anything Goes*
> *Chain Reaction*
> **To Tell the Truth**
>
> After graduating from college in the 1940s, Soupy Sales (Milton Hines) worked as a writer and DJ at a small station in West Virginia, while traveling at night to do comedy in distant nightclubs. In 1950 Sales moved on to Cincinnati as a local television host, doing both a teen dance show and an adult comedy talk show. He continued his wanderings, moving to Detroit in 1953 where one of his popular children's shows was picked up briefly by ABC in 1955 and again in 1959–1961, moving to Los Angeles in 1960. Sales' shows involved comic dances and much slapstick, sometimes with puppets and especially with pies. This proved very attractive to various show-business figures. Bob Hope, Burt Lancaster, Frank Sinatra, and his friends all visited Sales' shows to participate in pie throwing. In 1962 Sales was one of the many *Tonight* interregnum hosts for a week. In 1964 he moved to New York, continuing his career with a combination of local, network, and syndicated shows. In New York, Sales repeated in 1965 a routine he had done before in other locales but which now attracted much more attention and got Sales suspended for a week: After New Year's Eve he asked his child viewers to send him "those green pieces of paper" that parents carried in wallets and purses. From 1968 to 1975 Sales was a regular panelist on the syndicated *What's My Line?* In later years, he also hosted the children's version of *Almost Anything Goes,* was a featured comic on *Sha Na Na,* and was a regular guest celebrity on *Chain Reaction* and the syndicated *To Tell the Truth.*

Sawyer, Diane, 1980–
> *The CBS Morning News*
> **60 Minutes**

PrimeTime Live
20/20
Good Morning, America

The daughter of a Kentucky Republican politician, Diane Sawyer was American Junior Miss in 1963. After Wellesley and a semester at law school, Sawyer became a TV "weather girl" in Louisville, Kentucky, sometimes reciting Emily Dickinson. In 1970, Lamar Alexander helped Sawyer get a job as chief assistant to Press Secretary Ron Ziegler in the Nixon White House, at times helping to present Watergate matters to the press. After President Nixon's resignation, Sawyer flew with him to San Clemente and aided him in producing his memoirs and preparing for the **David Frost** interviews. Sawyer began working for CBS News in 1978 and in 1981 became cohost of *The CBS Morning News*, at first with **Charles Kuralt** and later Bill Kurtis. In 1984 Sawyer moved up to become the first woman coeditor/correspondent on *60 Minutes*. After being linked romantically with Warren Beatty, Sawyer married director Mike Nichols. In 1989 Fox tried to woo Sawyer away from CBS with a $10 million deal, but she went instead with ABC's $6 million offer. Sawyer cohosted *PrimeTime Live* with Sam Donaldson, although the awkward format of the first weeks with both hosts before a live studio audience shifted to a largely taped interview format with Sawyer working out of New York and Donaldson in Washington. Among Sawyer's most successful interviews was one with Boris Yeltsin in his Kremlin office while the 1991 attempted coup was at its height. Her most-watched interview, but one of her most criticized, was in 1995 with Michael Jackson and Lisa Marie Presley. ABC has also used Sawyer to host 20/20, other newsmagazines and specials, and occasionally to fill in for Peter Jennings and **Ted Koppel**. She was also brought in, along with Charles Gibson, to rescue *Good Morning, America*.

Scott, Gene, 1975–
The University Network with Gene Scott

Dr. Eugene Scott is one of the most fascinating and eccentric of all televangelists and television talkers. Since 1975 Scott claims to have broadcast more than 50,000 hours, compared to **Hugh Downs'** commercial record of over 10,000 hours. Scott does about four to six live hours per day, seven days a week. The bearded Scott can usually be seen seated in front of the camera, a cigar in his mouth and a broad-brim hat on his head. Obviously well read, intelligent, and with a quick sense of humor, he may be writing on a blackboard and teaching about the lost tribes of Israel settling the British Isles. Or he may be interpreting biblical texts to show that there are no requirements set on human behavior except that we properly reward those who teach us the truth. Or he may just be staring at us for half an hour, waiting for us to pledge money to the number on the screen. Sometimes Scott will interrupt his monologue to show an old clip of gospel singing, or his stable of prize-winning show horses, or in the 1990s films of his beautiful model and actress friends performing in athletic activities around Los Angeles and throughout America. Scott's television talk is taped and then sent by satellite around the world twenty-four hours a day, while his words are also broadcast by short-wave radio to every nation. On one station in 1983, Scott was taken off the air, in mid-sentence, by the FCC while he was showing his audience a group of wind-up toy monkeys representing the FCC, with which he was in conflict.

See It Now, 1951–1958

Considered by many critics to be the most important and perhaps the best of all television documentary/interview programs, *See It Now* was developed by **Edward R. Murrow** (see Chapter 2) and **Fred W. Friendly** from their 1948 record album *I Can Hear It Now* and from the 1950 radio program *Hear It Now*. Murrow and Friendly were always experimenting with each new medium. Their album was a sound history of the years 1933–1945, but the radio program moved past history to catch the sounds of the moment—an atomic accelerator starting up, artillery shells in Korea. Their first telecast, directed by Don Hewitt, set Murrow in front of two TV monitors, one of which showed a live shot of the Brooklyn Bridge while the other showed the Golden Gate Bridge. It was the first commercial use of coast-to-coast live television. Each *See It Now* that followed focused on one subject. Sometimes the program was mostly filmed on location. Sometimes it was an interview, either live or filmed, always unrehearsed. At the end of each program, Murrow would face the camera from the studio and comment directly on what had just been seen. The most important *See It Now* programs were a series of three on Senator Joseph R. McCarthy. The first two showed film of McCarthy speaking and presiding over Senate hearings, along with Murrow's critical comments. On the third segment, McCarthy appeared personally to defend himself and to attack Murrow. These programs, together with the soon-to-follow **Army-McCarthy Hearings**, contributed greatly to McCarthy's fall from favor and censure by the U.S. Senate, although he remained a senator until his death. When *See It*

Now left the air, *CBS Reports,* sometimes with Murrow himself appearing, continued the tradition of focused, critical television journalism.

Sevareid, Eric, 1949–1984
>   *Capitol Cloak Room*
>   *The American Week*
>   *The Search*
>   *CBS Evening News* (commentator)
>   *Town Meeting of the World*
>   *Conversations with Eric Sevareid*
>   *Eric Sevareid's Chronicle*

In 1939 Eric Sevareid was recruited onto the CBS news team by **Edward R. Murrow**. Sevareid had worked as a print journalist in Minnesota and Europe before joining CBS to cover World War II in Europe and Asia. Sevareid's first regular television work was on the interviewing panel of *Capitol Cloak Room* (see **Televised Press Conferences** below). During the 1950s Sevareid hosted several CBS news shows and specials. After anchoring the *CBS Sunday Night News* in 1962–1963, Sevareid became permanent commentator on *The CBS Evening News,* staying until his retirement in 1977. Sevareid's commentaries were so different from the other segments of the news that there was a part of the FCC fairness doctrine, called the Sevareid Ruling, which exempted Sevareid-like commentary from the usual obligations associated with "personal attack." Also, whenever Sevareid's subjective commentaries ended the newscast, **Walter Cronkite** dropped his usual "And that's the way it is" ending. Sevareid is considered by many to have been the most elegant and poetic of television commentators. Sevareid is also remembered for moderating the 1964 *Town Meeting of the World* with Richard Nixon, Harold Wilson, and other world leaders; for his interviews in the 1970s with Peter Ustinov in the roles of Lord North and King George III; and for his 1975 *Conversations with Eric Sevareid,* informal chats with notable figures. After retirement from CBS, Sevareid continued doing syndicated and PBS series.

Shandling, Garry, 1983–
>   **Tonight** (guest host)
>   *It's Garry Shandling's Show*
>   **The Larry Sanders Show**

In the 1980s and 1990s, Garry Shandling was the comedian-writer who most deeply incorporated the paradoxes of television talk into his work. Shandling's two series bracket television talk. *The Larry Sanders Show* presents within a television sitcom what appears to be a genuine talk show with spontaneous speech, performed before a studio audience. *It's Garry Shandling's Show* was a sitcom about a TV comic who played himself and spoke directly to the studio and home audiences in what was meant to appear as real and spontaneous speech. At times the studio audience was asked to discuss the show's plot and action. In between these brackets, Shandling was a frequent guest host of *Tonight,* starting in 1983, and in 1986–1988 he was permanent guest host after **Joan Rivers** and before **Jay Leno**. Shandling also hosted the Grammy awards on TV from 1990 to 1994. The Shandling show ran on Showtime and Fox between 1986 and 1990 and seemed to influence strongly the creation of *Seinfeld,* which began in 1990. The Sanders show began on HBO in 1992, and by the time it ended in 1998, it had gained a reputation as one of the best television shows of the 90s. While shifting to film production and acting, Shandling continued TV work as a well-received awards show host.

Sheen, Fulton, 1952–1968
>   *Life Is Worth Living*
>   *Mission to the World*
>   *The Bishop Sheen Program*

Bishop Fulton Sheen was probably the most popular of all television preachers, certainly the only one to have regularly scheduled live shows in prime time on two major networks and to have won an Emmy for television personality of the year. All of Sheen's network and syndicated shows had the same format. Sheen stood talking for twenty minutes or so, occasionally drawing on a blackboard, winding up with a two- or three-minute memorized summary. Sheen would often introduce jokes that were more friendly than uproarious. Sheen wasn't continually asking for contributions or attempting to convert, but trying to get viewers to think about how to live their lives.

Shore, Dinah, 1951–1991
>   *The Dinah Shore Chevy Show*
>   *Dinah Shore Special*
>   *Dinah's Place*
>   *Dinah!*
>   *A Conversation with Dinah*

See Chapter 6 for background on Dinah Shore.

Simpson, O. J., 1977–1994

The Superstars

ABC Monday Night Football

NFL Live

O. J. Simpson was a collegiate and professional football player, winner of the Heisman trophy at USC. Even during his football years, Simpson began to develop broadcasting and acting careers. He served as a commentator on the trash-sports show *The Superstars* and competed on *Celebrity Challenge of the Sexes*. He had acting parts in *Roots* and the HBO series *1st & Ten*. He was also executive producer of several TV films, which he hoped to develop into series starring himself. In the 1983–1985 seasons, Simpson was one of the *Monday Night Football* announcers, appearing alongside **Howard Cosell**, Don Meredith, Frank Gifford, and Joe Namath. Later he was a commentator on NBC's *NFL Live*. Then in 1994 Simpson became a participant in a car chase shown simultaneously on more networks than any other live unscheduled event. In 1995 the decision in his murder trial and the immediate reaction to it was probably watched by more viewers, perhaps 150 million, than any other television event. The television talk that developed out of the trial may have set other records, but the measurements are difficult to make. Indicators, however, pointed to 600 hours of trial coverage by CNN; 700 by Court TV, which raised its ratings tremendously; 1,000 hours by E! Entertainment Television; and the assignment of thirty staffers to the case by *Hard Copy*.

Siskel and Ebert, 1978–1999

Sneak Previews

At the Movies

Siskel & Ebert

In 1975 Roger Ebert, writing for the *Chicago Sun-Times*, became the only critic ever to win a Pulitzer Prize for reviewing films. That was also the year that Ebert and Gene Siskel, who was criticizing films for the *Chicago Tribune*, began their television partnership, doing reviews on the local *Opening Soon at a Theatre Near You*. In 1978 they went on PBS as *Sneak Previews*. In 1982, when *Sneak Previews* was the highest-rated PBS show, Siskel and Ebert left to do their own syndicated show *At the Movies*. *Sneak Previews* continued with Jeffrey Lyons and, for three seasons, Neal Gabler, who was then replaced by Michael Medved. Since *Sneak Previews* retained the right to score movies with a "Yes" or "No," Siskel and Ebert switched to "Thumb Up" and "Thumb Down," which has certainly become more influential. In 1986 Siskel and Ebert moved again to their own show, *Siskel & Ebert*, taking their thumbs with them and leaving Rex Reed and Bill Harris to run *At the Movies* with a four-star system. Dixie Whatley succeeded Harris in 1988, and the show died in 1990. Siskel and Ebert did not reveal their opinions to each other before the taping, and their reactions to each other's views created a character or chemistry that separated them from their competitors and formed them into a single but complex icon. Siskel and Ebert went on as a team beyond their own review show. They made frequent appearances as a duo on shows such as **David Letterman**'s and *Saturday Night Live.* In 1990 Siskel and Ebert substituted for Pat Sajak on his talk show and had their own CBS prime-time special. After Gene Siskel's death in 1998, Ebert teamed up with another Chicago writer and critic, Richard Roeper, to transform the show into *Ebert & Roeper and the Movies.*

60 Minutes, 1968–

In 1967 Don Hewitt sent a memo to his higher-ups at CBS, writing, "Somewhere in all the minutes of make-believe—couldn't we make room for sixty minutes of reality?" And so 1968 introduced the *60 Minutes* that Hewitt had created with the aid of the many other **Edward R. Murrow** alumni still at CBS plus some new faces. Since then *60 Minutes* has become the paradigm for television newsmagazines. The formula is: have a crew of great reporter-interviewers like **Mike Wallace**, Harry Reasoner, Morley Safer, **Dan Rather**, Ed Bradley, **Diane Sawyer**, Steve Kroft, Meredith Vieira, and **Lesley Stahl**; have an off-camera staff that knows how to produce memorable images and find out hidden conspiracies; keep a consistent format but experiment a little with features like Andy Rooney's wry observations or short debates between conservative and liberal commentators; balance interviews of well-known figures, both political and cultural, with reportage on previously unknown scams and dangers. This format has made *60 Minutes* one of the longest-running prime-time programs on the networks; it has been the top show of the year in three different decades and won innumerable awards.

Small World, 1958–1960

Small World was one of the less well known creations of **Edward R. Murrow** and **Fred Friendly** but one of the high points of talk television. Around the world cameras recorded the simultaneous and spontaneous discussion of an important topic by some of those who knew the most about it. Murrow was the moderator in New York. For the first show the other participants were Aldous Huxley, Jawaharlal Nehru, and Thomas Dewey. Darryl Zanuck, Ingrid Bergman, and Bosley Crowther were another trio, and James Thurber, Siobhan McKenna, and Noel Coward a third.

Smith, Kate, 1951–1960
>   *The Kate Smith Hour*
>   *The Kate Smith Show*

Kate Smith is remembered best today for her singing of "God Bless America," which she introduced in 1938 on her evening radio show, having obtained exclusive rights to the song from Irving Berlin. However, she was also an important figure in radio and television talk. From 1938 to 1951, Smith, working with her mentor and announcer Ted Collins, produced *Kate Smith Speaks,* a noonday radio program of current news, casual chat, and comments on the passing world. *The Kate Smith Hour* (1950–1954) brought this spirit of down-home talk to afternoon television in one of its daily quarter-hour segments called "The Cracker Barrel," on which Smith and Collins talked with each other and a guest. The other three-quarters of the hour contained a variety of features, some musical, and others that later spun off as sitcom series, such as *Ethel and Albert.* Smith had evening variety shows in the 1950s and was a guest on specials and variety shows into the 1970s.

Snyder, Tom, 1973–1982, 1993–1999
>   *Tomorrow*
>   *Prime Time Sunday*
>   *Tom Snyder*
>   *The Late, Late Show with Tom Snyder*

In the 1960s Tom Snyder was one of those young men who wandered from television station to station across the country, anchoring the local news or hosting a popular interview show for a year or two, going from Milwaukee to Savannah, from Atlanta to Los Angeles to Philadelphia. Finally in 1973 NBC picked him for a new show, *Tomorrow,* an hour interview show broadcast on the coasts at 1 A.M. Snyder fit the show. He was a night owl, smoking away, casual and personal, joking with the stage crew, capable of understanding what was important, but wandering off in the middle of a thought. The show was popular in a late-night fashion. People could identify Snyder when

Dan Aykroyd parodied him. Snyder was given opportunities in prime time, hosting the newsmagazine *Prime Time Sunday* in 1979–1980 and trial specials of Snyder's own interview show. Then in fall 1980 *Tomorrow* took over Carson's vacated 12:30–1:00 A.M. half-hour and NBC brought in Rona Barrett as cohost. There were problems and clashes. In 1982 NBC replaced *Tomorrow* with *Late Night with David Letterman*. Snyder got work on ABC talk radio. In 1993, Snyder began a cable interview show on CNBC. Then in 1995 after Letterman's move to CBS, Snyder returned to major network late night in the post-Letterman hour on *The Late, Late Show with Tom Snyder*. Things were as they had been, except no smoke. In 1999, Snyder retired.

Spivak, Lawrence E., 1947–1975
> *Meet the Press*
> *Keep Posted*

Lawrence Spivak worked in publishing during the 1920s and 1930s. In 1939 he became publisher and later editor of *American Mercury*, a magazine of opinion. The young freelance writer **Martha Roundtree** came to Spivak with her idea for a radio program on which political figures would meet the press. Spivak helped Roundtree produce the show in 1945, and in 1947 they brought it to television in 1947, where it has been ever since, making it the longest-running network show. Spivak served as panelist-questioner on *Meet the Press* and worked with Roundtree in producing several other similar television shows. In 1953 Spivak bought out Roundtree's interest in *Meet the Press;* in 1965 he became its moderator. Spivak seemed familiar with the issues discussed but always appeared to have come from a definitely non-television world. For Spivak's departure from *Meet the Press* in 1975, Gerald Ford was the guest, becoming the first sitting President to appear on the show.

Stahl, Lesley, 1977–
> *The CBS Morning News*
> *Face the Nation*
> *America Tonight*
> **60 Minutes**

Lesley Stahl is one of television's leading interviewers, intelligent and probing but not unusually confrontational. From 1977 to 1979 Stahl cohosted *The CBS Morning News* along with Richard Threlkeld. From 1983 to 1991 Stahl moderated *Face the Nation* while also serving in various other roles as a Washington correspondent. In 1990–1991 along with **Charles Kuralt**, she co-anchored *America Tonight*, CBS's unsuccessful attempt at a late-night news program. In 1991 Stahl was named a co-editor on *60 Minutes*.

Stern, Bill, 1949–1954
> Trotting Races
> *Spotlight on Sports*
> *Remember This Date*
> *Star Night*
> *Bill Stern's Sports Quiz*
> *The Saturday Night Fights*
> *The Name's the Same*

Bill Stern was a sports talk broadcaster with one of the most popular shows in radio, *Colgate Sports Newsreel*. Nightly from 1939 to 1956, Stern would tell an unbelievable sports story with organ accompaniment, sometimes with the help of a guest like Orson Welles or Frank Sinatra. The stories were fascinating, but Stern was not much of a fact checker. In 1949 as NBC sports director, Stern began to appear on pre- and post-game shows as well as nightly sports reports. Like **Howard Cosell** in later years, Stern attempted every sort of program, day and evening quiz hosting, sports interviews, and variety, acting, and panel shows. Nothing clicked. Stern left NBC for ABC, but by 1954 he was gone from the national screen.

Stern, Howard, 1990–
> *The Howard Stern Show*
> *The Howard Stern "Interview"*
> *The Howard Stern Radio Show*

Howard Stern, wildly popular in certain markets as a radio shock jock, continues to attempt to find a suitable video format. Although he claims to be king of all media, he has not achieved great success on television, due in part to the difficulty of attracting sponsors. His syndicated *The Howard Stern Show* appeared in 1990–1991. On New Year's Eve 1993, Stern tried a highly explicit pay per view show. E! Entertainment Television cablecasts edited and delayed versions of his radio show. In 1998, some CBS TV stations began telecasting *The Howard Stern Radio Show*, which is in fact only a television show.

The Stork Club, 1950–1955

Sherman Billingsley opened a speakeasy during prohibition. It continued in the 1940s and 1950s as The Stork Club, one of the principal hangouts of New York glamour society. Seeking to promote himself and his club, Billingsley built an area in the club that served as the site of television broadcasts. From 1950 to 1952, several nights a week CBS televised Billingsley wandering from table to table, talking to his guests about what exciting things they were up to and where they had been lately. The first year Billingsley was assisted by **Peter Lind Hayes** and **Mary Healy** and then briefly by Johnny Johnston and Virginia Peine. In 1953 *The Stork Club* switched from a quarter-hour format to a half-hour once a week, and in 1954 it moved to ABC. Part of the show's attraction may have been seeing what the rich and famous looked like and what they wore; but listening to their meandering talk must have filled some need for many people.

Strike It Rich, 1951–1958, 1973, 1978

Strike It Rich was nominally a quiz show but, as with ***Queen for a Day,*** its real attractions were connected to hearing people talk of their hardships and difficulties in life. Walt Framer produced a radio version in 1947. Then in 1951 Warren Hull began hosting both daytime and evening video versions. Contestants were chosen from thousands of letters for the interesting nature of their woes. If the contestant failed to win enough in the quiz to ease their situation, Hull would ask viewers to call in on "The Heart Line." Many did phone in with gifts, including manufacturers of needed medical equipment or makers of furniture to replace what had been destroyed in horrible disasters. In 1953 the evening version was in the top twenty programs on TV. Many charities and government agencies criticized the program when it was shown that thousands of disadvantaged people had moved to New York to get on the program, but the daily show remained on the air into 1958. Unsuccessful attempts were made to syndicate *Strike It Rich* in 1973 and 1978.

Sullivan, Ed, 1948–1972

Toast of the Town (*The Ed Sullivan Show*)

Ed Sullivan was largely an introducer of the acts on his long-running variety show, but some talk did take place between Sullivan and his guests, both the performers and the famous in the audience, who would stand up, bow, and sometimes speak back.

Sunrise Semester, 1963–1980

   Sunrise Semester presented courses given for credit by New York University faculty. Broadcast on CBS at 6:30 A.M., the program began locally in New York in 1957. NBC's equivalent, *Continental Classroom*, which began at either 6:00 A.M. or 6:30 A.M., was broadcast from 1958 to 1964, and produced in cooperation with the American Association of Colleges for Teacher Education. The classes duplicated the forms of talk found in ordinary college instruction, though usually with no student response.

Susskind, David, 1958–1987
   Open End
   The David Susskind Show

   David Susskind was a television producer of quality programs as well as those of perhaps not such high quality. Susskind was responsible for an adaptation of *The Glass Menagerie,* but also for *Supermarket Sweeps.* In 1958 he started hosting his own talk show. It was called *Open End* because it started at 11 P.M. on Sunday night and went on until the participants finished talking, which might be three or four hours later. Susskind could do this because several of the few stations that broadcast *Open End* at first were the remaining members of a network that NTA (National Telefilm Associates) had tried to establish. Susskind later began selling an edited two-hour videotaped version. The show, which covered both highbrow and show-business topics, was enjoyed by a limited audience until in 1960 Premier Nikita Khrushchev of the USSR visited the United States and Susskind was the only broadcaster willing to meet the Premier's conditions for a lengthy interview. The Khrushchev performance proved so controversial that it prompted a fourfold increase in the number of stations carrying the series. Controversies about other performances also caused Susskind to switch his station of origin and required him to limit the program's length and to change its name to *The David Susskind Show.* The last program was produced in 1986 and shown in 1987, the year of Susskind's death.

Televised Press Conferences, 1947–
   Meet the Press was begun on NBC television in 1947 by **Martha Roundtree** and still continues, making it the oldest continuing network program. The show presented on a broadcast medium a type of daily event, reporters asking questions of people involved in events about which others wanted to know more. This format reappears often. *Capi-*

tol Cloak Room, which had been a radio program, was simulcast by CBS in 1949–1950. CBS then tried *Man of the Week* in 1951–1954. In 1954 Senator Joseph R. McCarthy was the first interviewee on *Face the Nation,* which continues on CBS. *Issues and Answers* was ABC's 1960–1981 version of televised press conferences. John Kennedy was probably the President who came closest to turning his press conferences into a regularly scheduled TV show.

Terkel, Studs, 1949–1952, 1971–1972
Studs' Place
Saturday Square
The Great American Dream Machine
Studs Terkel is a writer who places himself among the working class. He is also a Chicago radio interviewer and personality. In 1949 he created *Studs' Place,* a television program that set up a location—an eatery with a piano player where folks hang out—and that allowed Terkel and a small group of performers to improvise working-class philosophical conversations. In early 1950 "Studs' Place" was briefly part of a larger environment, *Saturday Square.* In April 1950, *Studs' Place* expanded to thirty minutes and continued on NBC and later ABC until 1952. In 1971–1972 Terkel re-created essentially the same environment as a feature on *The Great American Dream Machine.*

Tex and Jinx, 1947–1951, 1957–1958
Tex and Jinx
The Swift Home Service Club
Journalist John Reagan (Tex) McCrary and model and tennis player Eugenia Lincoln (Jinx) Falkenburg married in 1945. The next year they had one of the hit husband-and-wife radio shows of the period, *Hi, Jinx!* In 1947 Tex and Jinx began the first of their many television talk-interview shows. Tex and Jinx appeared as guests and panelists on many early television shows, not only as a couple but often individually. Tex was the more serious, politically interested figure, and Jinx was the glamorous but also intelligent society woman. The names of their shows often shifted, including words like "Close-up" and "Preview," but usually ending up as *Tex and Jinx.* One exception was 1947's *The Swift Home Service Club,* which is credited with being the first sponsored daytime network TV show.

That Was the Week That Was, 1963–1965

David Frost began *That Was the Week That Was* for British television in 1963 and brought it to NBC with a special that year and then with regular live telecasts from New York in 1964. *TW3*, as it was often called, gave an outstanding American cast and writers to a British show and became the model for much of U.S. television's later topical variety and satirical comedy shows, such as the Smothers Brothers shows and *Saturday Night Live*. Burr Tillstrom and **Henry Morgan**, who had done original work in early television, appeared regularly on *TW3*. Buck Henry was deeply involved, and Tom Lehrer provided some of his most memorable songs.

Thicke, Alan, 1983–
    Thicke of the Night
    Animal Crack-Ups
    Hope & Gloria
    Pictionary
    The All New Three's a Crowd

Alan Thicke's relationship to television talk has been quite involved. Thicke was a comedy writer in his native Canada and later one of Canada's most popular daytime talk-show hosts. He wrote comedy material for specials starring Richard Pryor and Bill Cosby. In 1977–1978 Thicke produced and wrote for the remarkable talk-show parodies *Fernwood 2-Night* and **America 2Night**. In 1983–1984 Metromedia provided Thicke with his own ninety-minute late-night talk-show disaster, *Thicke of the Night*. Thicke was well furnished with supporting talent. **Arsenio Hall** was Thicke's sidekick. Richard Belzer, Gilbert Gottfried, and the LA Connection provided comedy. The show, however, got poor ratings and bad reviews. It was constantly being revised. Thicke was said to be too laid-back. Fortunately for Thicke, he had a hit in 1985 as the star of the sitcom *Growing Pains*. From 1987 to 1990 Thicke also hosted *Animal Crack-Ups*, on which a celebrity panel asked questions about animal behavior and were then shown film taken from Japanese television where the answers were revealed by the animals themselves. In 1995 Thicke was featured in a new sitcom, *Hope & Gloria*, playing a self-obsessed local talk-show host. While frequently having acting roles in films and theater, Thicke maintained his TV talk presence, hosting the game shows *Pictionary* (1997–1998) and *The All New Three's a Crowd* (2000).

This Is Show Business, 1949–1956

This Is Show Business was an early and successful attempt to combine variety performance and interesting, spontaneous talk. The format was a panel of major show-business figures watching three different acts perform. After each act the performers asked the panel for advice. A great deal of the success of the program came from the selection of panel members noted for their wit and depth of knowledge. **Clifton Fadiman** was the moderator; the most frequent panelists were **Abe Burrows**, George S. Kaufman, Sam Levenson, Walter Slezak, and Jacqueline Susann.

Today, 1952–

Sometimes referred to as *The Today Show.* See Chapters 3–5 for background on the program.

Tonight / The Tonight Show, 1954–

Although always thought of as a single program created by **Pat Weaver**, over the years there have been variations in the format, time, and name of the program. On September 27, 1954, *The Steve Allen Show,* which had been a local program in New York City, became *Tonight!* and was broadcast nationally on NBC. At times, the exclamation point was dropped and the show was merely *Tonight.* When Allen left in January 1957, the show entered what is referred to as its first interregnum and became ***Tonight! America after Dark,*** which has its own entry below. In July 1957 **Jack Paar** took over the show and it was usually referred to as *The Jack Paar Show* or sometimes as *The Jack Paar Tonight Show* with frequent Friday repeats that were called *The Best of Paar.* When Paar left in March 1962, there was the second interregnum and the show, under numerous successive hosts, including **Art Linkletter, Joey Bishop, Merv Griffin, Peter Lind Hayes** and **Mary Healy, Soupy Sales, Jerry Lewis, Arlene Francis, Hugh Downs, Groucho Marx,** and **Hal March,** was called *The Tonight Show.* In October 1962 **Johnny Carson** arrived and until May 1992 the program was *The Tonight Show Starring Johnny Carson.* After Carson retired, **Jay Leno** came on and it was *The Tonight Show with Jay Leno.* See Chapters 6–8 for background on this program.

Tonight! America after Dark, 1957

Tonight! America after Dark is sometimes referred to as *The Tonight Show*'s first interregnum. It began January 28, 1957, after **Steve**

Allen's departure, and ended July 26, 1957, just before **Jack Paar**'s arrival. During the first interregnum the show became a tribute to American nightlife, with daily remote location shoots of festivals, nightclubs, and parties. At first Jack Lescoulie hosted from New York; columnists such as Hy Gardner, Bob Considine, **Paul Coates**, Earl Wilson, and **Irv Kupcinet** provided interviews, gossip, and commentary from New York, Chicago, and Los Angeles. Since Considine also summarized world news, the show was almost an amalgam of *Tonight* and *Today*. It did not do well in the ratings, and changes in structure and cast were frequent. In June, Al "Jazzbo" Collins, a popular radio DJ, replaced Lescoulie and broadcast from a studio called "The Purple Grotto."

The Tonight Show. See *Tonight*.

Tony Brown's Journal, 1968–

Tony Brown's Journal actually began on PBS as *Black Journal* with Bill Greaves as host-producer. Brown took over Greaves' duties in 1970, and the show changed over the years from more of a Black-affairs newsmagazine to an interview-commentary show. Many Black figures, such as Angela Davis, Bobby Seale, and Malcolm X, who had few opportunities to speak on mainstream television, were given time on the *Journal*. Brown took the program into syndication from 1976 to 1981, but returned in 1982 to PBS to stay.

To Tell the Truth, 1956–1977, 1980–1981, 1990–1991

To Tell the Truth was one of the most popular and longest-lasting panel shows. Its success rested more on the quality of the talk than the value of the prizes. Three contestants all claimed to be the same person. By asking questions, the panel would attempt to find out who was lying and who was telling the truth. The first host was **Bud Collyer**, followed by **Garry Moore**, Joe Garagiola, Robin Ward, **Gordon Elliott**, and **Alex Trebek**. Outstanding panelists were Polly Bergen, Dick Van Dyke, John Cameron Swayze, Tom Poston, Peggy Cass, Kitty Carlisle, Orson Bean, **Bill Cullen**, Phyllis Newman, **Joyce Brothers**, Hildy Parks, Hy Gardner, and Ralph Bellamy.

Trebek, Alex, 1973–
    The Wizard of Odds
    High Rollers
    Double Dare

The $128,000 Question
Battlestars
Jeopardy!
Value Television
Classic Concentration
To Tell the Truth

Alex Trebek is the most recent entrant into the pantheon of television game-show hosts. A Canadian, Trebek has hosted U.S. television game shows every year since *The Wizard of Odds* in 1973. In some recent years he has had two and three shows at the same time. He has also hosted *Value Television*, a home-shopping program. Trebek's greatest success has been the revival of *Jeopardy!* beginning in 1984. Trebek seems especially suited to the almost scholarly atmosphere of the competition and, unlike most game-show hosts, he seems as if he would be able to play this difficult game better than most of the contestants.

TV Nation, 1994–1995

Michael Moore, director of the 1989 documentary *Roger & Me*, created *TV Nation* and described it as a "nonfiction, comedic newsmagazine with a point of view." Moore and his correspondents, including Merrill Markoe, Janeane Garofalo, and Rusty Cundieff, set up interviewing situations with a different angle. For instance, Moore showed the Ford CEO demonstrating how to change oil in his cars.

TV Screen Magazine, 1948–1949

TV Screen Magazine may have been the first network magazine show. Hosted by John K. M. McCaffery, the show included interviews, musical performances, and a feature very popular in the early years of TV, fashion shows. Millicent Fenwick, later a New Jersey congressional representative, was also featured as an interviewer. Ray Forrest replaced McCaffery toward the end of the run.

TW3. See **That Was the Week That Was**

U.N. General Assembly, 1949–1954

CBS broadcast United Nations General Assembly sessions as an easy daily daytime filler that also provided public service. In 1949 the telecasts filled several hours in both morning and afternoon but by 1954 were down to a fifteen-minute report in the afternoon. Larry LeSueur was often the principal reporter.

Vanity Fair, 1949–1951

Vanity Fair was a very early CBS daytime series of woman's interest features. At first broadcast two afternoons a week, beginning in 1949 it was broadcast each weekday. Robin Chandler and Dorothy Doan were the hosts.

Vila, Bob, 1979–

This Old House

Bob Vila's Home Again

Bob Vila was the first host of PBS's popular home-improvement show beginning in 1979. Vila would often work on a year-long project, and in the 1980s he was assisted by carpenter Norm Abram. In 1989 when a dispute arose about endorsements that Vila had done on commercial television and which an underwriter of the PBS show did not like, Vila was forced to leave. Steve Thomas became the new host of *This Old House*, and Vila started a similar syndicated show, *Bob Vila's Home Again.*

Wallace, Mike, 1949–

Majority Rules

Two Sleepy People

I'll Buy That

Night Beat

The Name's the Same

The $100,000 Big Surprise

The Mike Wallace Interview

P.M. East

The CBS Morning News

60 Minutes

See Chapters 3 and 4 for background on Mike Wallace.

Walters, Barbara, 1963–

Today

Not for Women Only

ABC Evening News

The Barbara Walters Special

20/20

The View

See Chapter 4 for background on Barbara Walters.

Washington Week in Review, 1967–

From 1967 to 1970 *Washington Week* had a regular roundtable of three journalists—Peter Lisagor, Charlie Cordry, and Neil McNeil— with John Davenport as moderator. Almost every week since 1970, five leading Washington journalists have sat down at a television studio table in Washington, D.C., and shared with each other and their viewers what was the leading edge of the conventional wisdom about the important political stories of the week. One of the five served as moderator, usually Lincoln Furber, Max Kampelman, **Robert MacNeil**, or Peter Lisagor until 1976, and then **Paul Duke** until Ken Bode took over in 1994. In early 1999, a conflict arose about efforts to enliven the program and Bode was let go for resisting suggested changes. Support from the public for maintaining the program's basic format brought Paul Duke back as moderator for several months before Gwen Ifill was given the position in October 1999. While a complete list of journalists who have appeared on the show would be quite long, outstanding and long-lasting participants have been Elizabeth Drew, Hedrick Smith, Haynes Johnson, and Georgie Anne Geyer.

Watergate Hearings, 1973–1974

In 1973, ABC, CBS, and NBC took turns broadcasting the daily hearings of the Senate Select Committee on Presidential Campaign Activities with Senator Sam Ervin as chair. PBS assigned **Robert MacNeil** and **Jim Lehrer** to host evening replays of the complete hearings. PBS ratings and contributions increased greatly. The linguistic turns of the inquiries were repeated frequently enough to become clichés, such as "smoking gun" and "What did the President know, and when did he know it?" In 1974 the networks continued their coverage for the six days of the impeachment hearings conducted by the House Judiciary Committee.

We, the People, 1948–1952

We, the People was presented on radio in 1936 by producer Phillips H. Lord as part of *The Rudy Vallee Show*. It got its own time period later that year and began television simulcasts in 1948. Over the years the show had many host interviewers from Gabriel Heatter to Burgess Meredith on the radio and Dwight Weist and Dan Seymour on TV. What remained the same were interviews with the people telling their stories of human interest. Sometimes the people were celebrities, sometimes unknowns, even once an amnesiac who could not remember his own identity. The tales sometimes seemed naturally and spontaneously told, sometimes overly prepared and rehearsed. There were stories of humorous events or strange hobbies, of brave rescues or former slavery, but always told by the people directly involved.

Weaver, Charley (Cliff Arquette), 1952–1970
> *Dave and Charley*
> *Do It Yourself*
> *The Jack Paar Tonight Show*
> *The Charley Weaver Show (Hobby Lobby)*
> *The Roy Rogers and Dale Evans Show*
> **Hollywood Squares**
> *The Jonathan Winters Show*

Charley Weaver was the alternate personality of Cliff Arquette. Charley did the routines, appeared on the chair next to **Jack Paar**, and answered questions from one of the Hollywood squares. Arquette was somewhere, but seldom seen on television. Perhaps he was off with his talented granddaughters, Rosanna and Patricia. On radio since 1924, Arquette had the voice for playing old men. He was the Old Timer on *Fibber McGee and Molly* and usually did comic characters on such shows as *Lum and Abner, Point Sublime,* and *Glamor Manor.* In 1952 Charley appeared on TV with his partner Dave Willock, a younger radio actor, in *Dave and Charley,* a highly improvised daily quarter-hour comedy. In 1955 Charley and Willock did *Do It Yourself,* a show combining household maintenance and comedy. Willock would give instructions on projects around the house and Charley would try to help but fail. At the end everything worked out. From 1958 to 1962 Charley made frequent appearances on *The Jack Paar Tonight Show.* In 1959–1960, Charley had his own show, which started out as *Hobby Lobby,* where Charley talked with people about their hobbies. Some visitors were celebrities. **Gypsy Rose Lee** talked about sport fishing, and Zsa Zsa Gabor demonstrated fencing. After a couple of months the celebrities were visiting Charley in his make-believe home in Mount Idy and talking about the residents of the small fictitious town. Charley was featured in 1962 on Roy Rogers and Dale Evans' evening variety show, and in 1968–1969 on Jonathan Winters' comedy-variety show. Charley was also a regular on *Hollywood Squares* in the late 1960s.

Weaver, Pat (Sylvester L., Jr.), 1981–1982

Television: Inside & Out

Pat Weaver's only regular TV appearances were as a featured commentator on the magazine show about TV, *Television: Inside & Out*, discussing such questions as the usefulness of TV ratings. Weaver also appeared on the farewell episode of *Your Show of Shows* because he is regarded as that show's originator. In fact, Weaver is regarded as the creator of a great many basic television formats including some of the most important in television talk. After attending Dartmouth, Weaver worked for the CBS and Don Lee radio networks and then found a home in advertising. In 1949 at the age of forty-one, Weaver became vice-president in charge of NBC television programming and president of NBC from 1953 to 1955. During that time Weaver accepted Max Liebman's proposal for a television show based on the structure of shows that Liebman had produced at the Tamiment resort. Weaver took the idea, realized first, in 1949, as *The Admiral Broadway Revue* and then, in 1950, as the New York segment of *Saturday Night Revue*. This full night of variety was another of Weaver's ideas. The first Chicago segment was *The Jack Carter Show*, and the second was *Your Show of Shows*. Later, in 1950, Weaver put the late-night prototype talk-variety show **Broadway Open House** on NBC. In 1952, Weaver started **Today**, television's first and longest-lasting morning talk show. In 1953 after *Broadway Open House* failed, Weaver switched his late-night idea from slapstick to talking on a sofa and had **Steve Allen** start **Tonight** as a New York local late-night program that went network in 1954. *Home* also began in 1954. It was Pat Weaver's midday and last-in-place component to accompany *Today* and *Tonight*. Since *Home* was a magazine, **Arlene Francis** was made on-air editor-in-chief. She was aided by **Hugh Downs** and singer Johnny Johnston. Contributing editors included Natalie Cole for fashion, Poppy Cannon for food, and Ashley Montagu for family affairs, although changes and additions were frequent. In 1955 Weaver had **Dave Garroway** do the first *Wide, Wide World* with segments originating in Canada, the United States, and Mexico. In 1957 a show that Weaver had been working on since 1952, *The Wisdom Series*, finally made it to the screen. The series consisted of filmed interviews with mature figures around the world, e.g., Bertrand Russell, Carl Sandburg, Herbert Hoover, and Wanda Landowska. Weaver is also credited with creating the "special," and he was probably responsible to some extent for his brother's *The Doodles Weaver Show* in 1951. After Weaver left NBC in 1956, he worked on a variety of television projects that didn't come to fruition, from pay TV to a fourth network, and he also worked in advertising again. Weaver received the Academy of Television Arts and Sciences Governor's Award in 1983.

See also the first section of Chapter 3.

What in the World, 1951–1955

What in the World may have been the most scholarly of game shows. Each week a panel of experts examined several objects from around the world and back in time. They attempted to identify the pieces by usage, period of time, and place of origin. The program succeeded as television talk because the regular panelists, Carleton Coon and Schuyler Cammann, as well as the guest panelists, were witty, interesting people. Froelich Rainey moderated this Peabody Award winner from Philadelphia.

What's My Line? 1950–1975

What's My Line? is the paradigm of talk panel game shows. It was not the first, but it showed that if you put four or five interesting people together playing a game and let them talk freely, people would watch for decades. In this case, the game was asking yes-or-no questions to find out the job of a guest or, once a program, the identity of a celebrity. **Arlene Francis** was the panelist who stuck around the longest. Others included Dorothy Kilgallen, Bennett Cerf, **Steve Allen**, Fred Allen, and **Soupy Sales**. The first moderator was **John Daly**, who was followed on the syndicated shows by Wally Bruner and Larry Blyden.

Willard, Fred, 1977–1992
>   ***Fernwood 2-Night***
>   ***America 2Night***
>   ***Real People***
>   *Thicke of the Night*
>   *"What's Hot, What's Not"*
>   *Access America*

Fred Willard's career has ricocheted back and forth from sketch comedy to talk, with interesting combinations in between. The starting point was the 1973 *The Burns and Schreiber Comedy Hour* with its sketches and a stop off with the sitcom *Sirota's Court.* In 1977–1978 there were the remarkable amalgams *Fernwood 2-Night* and *America 2Night.* In 1979–1984 he went on to the human interest trendsetter *Real People.* The magnificent disaster *Thicke of the Night* followed in 1983–1984. "What's Hot, What's Not" was a half-hour infotainment news component of *Inday*, an attempt in 1985–1986 by Tribune Entertainment to supply a daily two-hour block of news to member stations. Willard cohosted along with Melanie Chartoff. From 1990 to 1992, Willard visited weird public access shows across America, and clips from the visits appeared weekly on Comedy Central's *Access America*. Willard continues to appear on various shows, including marrying Martin Mull in a gay wedding on *Roseanne*, a reunion special of *Real People*, and frequent guest appearances with **Jay Leno**.

Williams, Montel, 1991–
The Montel Williams Show
    After service as a naval intelligence officer, Montel Williams became a motivational speaker. In 1991 he began his daily syndicated talk show, which fit into the common pattern of the period—interviews and surprise confrontations with ordinary people living offbeat and often sex-charged lives.

Winchell, Walter, 1952–1960
The Walter Winchell Show
    Walter Winchell was never as popular on television as he was on radio. From 1952 to 1955 Winchell tried simulcasting his Sunday evening quarter-hour news program on ABC. His rather rough, unkempt appearance surprised and perhaps put off many viewers. In 1956 Winchell hosted a half-hour variety show on NBC that lasted thirteen weeks. Winchell returned to ABC in 1960 with a half-hour version of his news reports and comments, but it was gone in two months. The only television work of Winchell that proved lasting was his narration of *The Untouchables* from 1959 to 1963.

Winfrey, Oprah, 1986–
The Oprah Winfrey Show
See Chapter 7 for background on Oprah Winfrey.

NOTES

1. HISTORY OF TELEVISION TALK

1. Hal Gurnee made these remarks in a seminar cosponsored by the Museum of Television and Radio and the Directors Guild at the Museum of Television and Radio on May 26, 1992.

2. See pp. 145–146.

3. This follows the distinction linguistic theorist Ferdinand de Saussure made between *langue* and *parole,* a language system and the actual written/spoken acts that occur within a language. Thomas Schatz uses Saussure's terms *parole* and *langue* to describe the impact of certain Hollywood films on the "language structure" of Hollywood film genres. The same could be said of the impact of certain talk-show hosts. Their shows redirect the development of the "language" of the television talk show.

4. "The 400 Richest People in America," *Forbes* magazine, October 8, 2000, p. 298.

5. Jane M. Shattuc, *The Talking Cure: TV Talk Shows and Women* (New York: Routledge, 1997), pp. 52–54.

6. A good example of the limits of television talk can be seen in the career of talk-show host Morton Downey Jr. Confrontational and abrasive, an "in-your-face" kind of host, Downey had a loyal following for his 1980s show out of New Jersey that ran in national syndication. Though critics were frequently repelled by Downey as a personality, they also found him provocative and a welcome change from the blandness of most television. But Downey's antics annoyed "blue chip" advertisers, and they decided they did not want their products associated with him. His show was taken off the air.

7. Bernard Timberg, "Anatomy of a Television Talk Show: 'Late Night with David Letterman,' 1983–86," manuscript.

8. Robert Erler, "The History of *The Morning Show*," The *Morning Show* entry in *The Encyclopedia of Television*, ed. Horace Newcomb (Chicago and London: Fitzroy Dearborn, 1997).

9. Hal Erickson, *Syndicated Television: The First Forty Years, 1947–1987* (Jefferson, N.C.: McFarland, 1989).

10. Tim Brooks and Earle Marsh, *The Complete Directory to Prime Time Network TV Shows, 1946–Present* (New York: Ballantine Books, 1979), p. xii.

11. Alex McNeil, Preface to 2nd Edition, *Total Television: A Comprehensive Guide to Programming from 1948 to the Present* (New York: Penguin Books, 1984).

12. Michael Arlen, "Hosts and Guests," in *The Camera Age: Essays on Television* (New York: Farrar, Straus, Giroux, 1981).

13. Frank Mankiewicz, "From Lippmann to Letterman: The 10 Most Powerful Voices," *Gannett Center Journal* 3, no. 2 (Spring 1989): 81. Mankiewicz's historical survey of opinion makers shows a progression from the influence of newspaper columnists in the 1930s (Dorothy Thompson, Franklin P. Adams, and Heywood Hale Broun, for example) to that of radio commentators and cartoonists in the 1940s and 1950s (Gabriel Heatter, H. V. Kaltenborn, Paul Harvey, and Edward R. Murrow on radio; Ernie Pyle and Bill Mauldin in syndicated newspaper cartoons) to a mixture of cartoonists, newspaper columnists, and television personalities in the 1950s, 1960s, and 1970s (Walter Cronkite, William F. Buckley, Jack Anderson, Garry Trudeau). In the 1980s a decisive shift occurs, and television personalities head Mankiewicz's list: Dan Rather, Pat Buchanan, Ted Koppel, Johnny Carson, and David Letterman.

14. For a comprehensive discussion of the vigorous competition to publish the words of Samuel Johnson, see Pat Rogers, Introduction to James Boswell's *Life of Johnson*, ed. R. W. Chapman (New York: Oxford University Press, 1991).

15. A number of social critics addressed the issue of talk shows, representation, and democracy. For example, see P. Carpignano, R. Anderson, S. Aronowitz, and W. DiFazio, "Chatter in the Age of Electronic Reproduction: Talk Television and the 'Public Mind,'" *Social Text* 9 (1990): 33–55; Sonia Livingstone and Peter Lunt, *Talk on Television: Audience Participation and Public Debate* (London: Routledge, 1994); Robin Anderson, "The Television Talk Show: From Democratic Potential to Pseudotherapy," *Consumer Culture and TV Programming* (Boulder, Colo.: Westview, 1995), pp. 146–173; Peter Dahlgren, "Talk Shows: Elite and Vox-pop," in *Television and the Public Sphere: Citizenship, Democracy and the Media* (London: Sage, 1995), pp. 62–67.

16. The story of these corporate takeovers is told in Ken Auletta's *Three Blind Mice: How the TV Networks Lost Their Way* (New York: Random House, 1991).

17. Janie Baylis, "1995: The Year of the Merger," *Washington Post*, January 6, 1996, p. D-1.

18. Rory O'Connor, "How Independent Journalism Can Survive Globalization," *Nation*, November 29, 1999, p. 32, and Jessica Caldwell, "Viacom + CBS = 3rd Largest Global Media Corp," *Global Media News* 2, no. 1 (Winter 2000): 3.

19. The merger was announced January 10, 2000.

20. The case is made particularly strongly in Carpignano et al., "Chatter in the Age of Electronic Reproduction," pp. 33–55.

21. For example, the Zeitgeist Films documentary *Noam Chomsky and the Media* includes a glimpse of a fascinating debate on the Vietnam War between Chomsky and William F. Buckley on Buckley's PBS program *Firing Line* in 1969.

2. THE FIRST CYCLE (1948–1962): CBS

1. The *Oxford Etymological Dictionary* (1989) first lists the term *talk show* as appearing in the *Times Literary Supplement* in 1965 ("There are now literally thousands of talk-shows"). In England, however, programs featuring conversation were (and still are) more commonly referred to as "chat" shows. *The Third Barnhart Dictionary of New English* (1990) also lists 1965 as the first year the term appears in print ("'Talk shows have never been more popular than they are now,' *Harper's* 3:70, p. 116 [1965]").

2. The careers of early hosts often intersected in interesting ways. For example, in the first Arthur Godfrey simulcast in 1948, preserved at the Museum of Television and Radio, a viewer can hear Arthur Godfrey give Edward R. Murrow and Fred W. Friendly's record album *I Can Hear It Now* an important "free" plug on the air.

3. In spring 1949 at KFI-TV in Los Angeles, the hourly rate was $150 and a single one-minute commercial spot cost $25. However, the trend toward national programming in television was already in full swing, and network TV was attracting half of all advertising revenues. Advertising rates continued to rise at the end of the decade. J. Fred MacDonald, *One Nation under Television: The Rise and Decline of Network TV* (New York: Pantheon, 1990), p. 44.

4. Ibid., p. 52.

5. Ibid., p. 44.

6. Ibid., p. 61.

7. This was the title of J. Fred MacDonald's detailed history of the television industry, cited frequently in this book.

8. Alexander Kendrick, *Prime Time: The Life of Edward R. Murrow* (Boston: Little, Brown and Company, 1969), p. 79.

9. Ibid., p. 16.

10. Ibid., p. 81.

11. R. Franklin Smith, *Edward R. Murrow: The War Years* (Kalamazoo, Mich.: New Issues Press, 1978), pp. 91–94.

12. Charles Collingwood remembers that in television studios during commercial breaks "the make-up girl would come racing in and dab him down with a cloth or kleenex or whatever. . . . Ed, always, in a broadcast would perspire heavily." Gillard and Collingwood are quoted in Smith, *Edward R. Murrow*, pp. 86–87.

13. A. M. Sperber, *Murrow: His Life and Times* (New York: Freundlich Books, 1986), p. 354. *See It Now* joined CBS's Sunday "culture ghetto."

14. Murrow's relationship with Alcoa executives stood him in good stead during his confrontation with McCarthy, but sponsor loyalty waned over time. *See It Now* appeared less and less frequently going into the 1950s until the show was eventually canceled by the network.

15. From kinescope of *See It Now*, November 18, 1951.

16. Merrill Panitt, "*See It Now* Show Proves Worth of Cable," *Philadelphia Inquirer*, November 20, 1951. Cited in Sperber, *Murrow*, p. 355.

17. Ibid.

18. Much of this and other accounts of the Radulovich and McCarthy programs rely on Fred Friendly's descriptions of those programs in his book *Due to Circumstances beyond Our Control* (New York: Random House, 1967). The most detailed account is *To Strike at a King: The Turning Point in the McCarthy Witch Hunts*, by Michael Ranville (Troy, Mich.: Momentum Books, 1997). Archival materials on the making of the show are held by the Center for American History at the University of Texas at Austin.

19. From "McCarthyism and the Golden Age of Television: 1953–1960," in *Grolier's Electronic Encyclopedia* (Grolier, 1992).

20. This and other quotes from the program in this section are taken from the kinescope of *See It Now:* "The Case of Milo Radulovich," October 20, 1953.

21. "Edward R. Murrow: This Reporter," *American Masters* series on PBS, Executive Producer, Susan Lacy; Producer, Susan Steinberg.

22. It was Joseph Wershba's recollection that Murrow was in the shower at the time. "Edward R. Murrow: This Reporter."

23. Sperber, *Murrow*, p. 420. It is of interest here that the Air Force chose to communicate not by letter or statement over the phone, but by a *filmed* statement.

24. "Edward R. Murrow: This Reporter."

25. McNeil, *Total Television*, p. 508. It was hosted by Murrow until 1959, when Charles Collingwood took over.

26. Script of *Person to Person*, October 2, 1953, The Edward R. Murrow Papers 1927–1965, microfilmed from the original papers in the Edward R. Murrow Center for Public Diplomacy, Fletcher School of Law and Diplomacy, Tufts University, Microfilm Corporation of America, 1982; hereafter referred to as Murrow Papers.

27. Ibid.

28. Transcript of first *Person to Person* program with Campanella and Stokowski, Murrow Papers.

29. A list prepared by Murrow associate Palmer Williams in 1973 shows the titles, dates, and guests of all these shows. See Murrow Papers.

30. Kendrick, *Prime Time*, p. 364. Also see Jeff Merron, "Murrow on TV: *See It Now, Person to Person,* and the Making of a 'Masscult Personality,'" *Journalism Monographs,* Association for Education in Journalism and Mass Communication, 1988, pp. 11–12.

31. Quoted in Joseph E. Persico, *Edward R. Murrow: An American Original* (New York: McGraw-Hill, 1988), p. 350.

32. McNeil, *Total Television*, p. 595.

33. Bill Moyers, who consciously modeled himself on Murrow in many ways, had not reviewed the program when I interviewed him in the summer of 1994. He was making a note to himself to go to the Museum of Television and Radio and see it on tape. Telephone interview with Bill Moyers, June 22, 1994.

34. Merron, "Murrow on TV."

35. "Arthur Godfrey: Broadcasting's Forgotten Giant," a sixty-minute documentary in the Arts and Entertainment *Biography* Series, Executive Producer, Arthur Singer, 1996. Singer wrote a biography of Godfrey while working on the documentary.

36. Entry on Godfrey in *Les Brown's Encyclopedia of Television,* 3rd ed. (Detroit: Visible Ink, 1992).

37. Albin Krebs, "Arthur Godfrey, Television and Radio Star, Dies at 79," *New York Times,* March 17, 1983, p. D-20.

38. J. Y. Smith, "Arthur Godfrey, Popular Radio and TV Personality, Dies at 79," *Washington Post,* March 17, 1983.

39. Information from "Arthur Godfrey: Broadcasting's Forgotten Giant," Arts and Entertainment *Biography* Series, 1996. Arthur Singer, Executive Producer.

40. Ibid.

41. The car accident and its aftermath are reported in J. Y. Smith, "Arthur Godfrey, Radio and TV Personality, Dies at 79," *Washington*

Post, March 17, 1983, and in Tom Shales, "Godfrey, Goodbye," *Washington Post*, March 17, 1983. The quote was taken from a 1972 *Washington Post* interview.

42. The quote is from "Arthur Godfrey: Broadcasting's Forgotten Giant," 1996.

43. An article in *Television* magazine titled "AM-TV Shows Pay Off" underscored the economic benefits of this kind of arrangement. "Lipton's dual airing of *Arthur Godfrey's Talent Scouts*, reported to have an AM cost of $7,300, provides the sponsor New York TV coverage for around $3,000" more, the article said. The article provides a series of interesting details on how the broadcasting industry was attempting to take advantage of the new television medium. *Television: The Business Magazine of the Industry*, February, 1949, pp. 13ff.

44. The kinescope is in the collection of the Museum of Television and Radio.

45. These and all other quotes from the program are from "Arthur Godfrey Time: Rehearsal 11/23/48," CBS (60:00), with Tony Marvin, announcer, and Archie Bleyer and his orchestra, MTR # T76:0070. Picture and sound are often out of sync, and there is some video loss on this copy.

46. "Arthur Godfrey: Broadcasting's Forgotten Giant," 1996.

47. Ibid.

48. A detailed description of the events leading up to the LaRosa firing is given in *CBS: Reflections in a Bloodshot Eye* by Robert Metz (Chicago: Playboy Press, 1975), pp. 184–187. It is also described and played back (on audio) in "Arthur Godfrey: Broadcasting's Forgotten Giant." My account is drawn largely from these sources.

49. Getting an independent agent broke an unwritten rule in the Godfrey "family." According to LaRosa in a later interview, he was getting fan mail of up to 6,000–7,000 letters a week at the time he was fired (Metz, *CBS*, p. 185).

50. Godfrey did not act entirely spontaneously. He talked about it first with top people in CBS management. Godfrey said that Frank Stanton of CBS had actually suggested it to him. "You hired him on the air? Why don't you fire him on the air?" Godfrey said Stanton told him in a dinner meeting with Paley and Stanton. Metz, *CBS*, p. 186.

3. THE FIRST CYCLE: NBC AND DUMONT

1. "The Communicator," Part I, "Athens Starts Pouring In," *The New Yorker* "Profile," October 16, 1954, first page of "Profile."

2. Ibid., p. 64.

3. One of his clients at Young and Rubican was Fred Allen, who

was notoriously difficult to work with. Weaver "tamed" him, becoming a trusted creative partner.

4. Though Garroway did not register high grades in announcing school, he was recognized early in his career as showing unusual talent. In 1939, while working as a Special Events announcer at Westinghouse radio station KDKA in Pittsburgh, Garroway received the H. P. Davis Memorial Announcer's Award, bestowed annually on the person judged to be the best announcer among Pittsburgh's five radio stations. *NBC Transmitter*, December, 1939, p. 10. (This in-house NBC publication, found in the Library of American Broadcasting at the University of Maryland, includes a photograph of the young announcer.)

5. Robert Metz, *The Today Show* (Chicago: Playboy Press, 1977), p. 12.

6. Ibid., p. 13.

7. These anecdotes about *Garroway at Large* come from Metz, *The Today Show*, pp. 16–18. For a while Garroway's life was quite frenetic. In addition to *Garroway at Large* he had a half-hour show sponsored by the U.S. Army and a call-in show, *Dial Garroway*, sponsored by Dial Soap. Robert Metz says that Garroway got into the habit at this time of relying on a form of "speed," a concoction of vitamin B and molasses with a liquid pep-up mixed by a show-business doctor that worked faster than pills. Metz, *The Today Show*, p. 16.

8. Tom Shales, "Garroway's Great Gift," *Washington Post*, July 22, 1982.

9. The quote is taken from a clip of the first *Today* show on "*Today* at 35," January 14, 1987, at the Museum of Television and Radio.

10. Metz, *The Today Show*, p. 55.

11. Ibid., p. 75.

12. Ibid., quoting Matthew Culligan, p. 66.

13. Ibid., p. 67.

14. Ibid., p. 135.

15. Though Mili Lerner Bonsignori was an important member of Edward R. Murrow's *See It Now* team, her name does not appear in two standard biographies of Murrow's life and work (Alexander Kendrick's *Prime Time: The Life of Edward R. Murrow* [Boston: Little, Brown and Company, 1969] and Joseph E. Persico's *Edward R. Murrow: An American Original* [New York: McGraw-Hill, 1988]). She surfaces, as late as 1986, as a source for A. M. Sperber's *Murrow: His Life and Times*. Thereafter, she was recognized as one of the principal members of the *See It Now* creative team, and was later interviewed in the *American Masters* series documentary on Murrow, "Edward R. Murrow: This Reporter," for which Sperber served as a consultant. Bonsignori had two

levels of invisibility working against her: as a woman and as a film editor.

16. In an acidic review, Philip Hamburger, writing about these three women talk-show hosts in *The New Yorker*, April 18, 1950, distinguishes the "new-type woman" who had recently come on television from the dominant image of women in previous years. "American women are no longer the cool, calm, gingham-clad matrons of the big color advertisements—the all-electric-kitchened, all-wise mothers who can simultaneously baste a duck, pull a fishhook from Junior's hand, tell Sis the facts of life, and read the Book of the Month. No, siree! After studying the quarter-hour programs of Miss Faye Emerson, Miss Wendy Barrie, and Miss Ilka Chase, I should say that the new-type woman belongs to an entirely different breed. She is chic, tense, commercially minded, out all night, has that highfalutin manner of speech generally associated with imitators of British actors, and speaks, for the most part, nonsense."

17. Two other nominees that year were Sid Caesar and Groucho Marx.

18. The film was *Murders in the Rue Morgue*. "Friends Sign in at Tribute to Arlene Francis," *New York Times*, May 19, 1987.

19. The Columbia Workshop radio tapes on which she appears are dated 3/28/37, 8/1/36, and 4/18/37.

20. Six servicemen compete for a blind date with three "lovely girls" for an evening at the Stork Club. The lines Francis reads are clearly scripted, and the soldiers' responses may have been heavily "coached" as well. Francis is introduced on the program as "America's *Blind Date* gal," a "sparkling and delightful" star currently appearing in a Broadway hit. *Blind Date*, ABC-radio, 5/7/45, R77:0366.

21. Early episodes of *What's My Line?* found at the Museum of Television and Radio are from the following dates: 8/2/50, 3/18/51, and 6/28/51 (T76:0105, T76:0106, T76:0022).

22. She is the narrator of a history of NBC radio's first fifty years ("NBC: First Fabulous Fifty," 10/31/76, R77:0137), a participant and commentator on a *What's My Line?* retrospective ("Wide World of Entertainment Takes a Look at 25 Years of *What's My Line?*" May 28, 1975, Parts 1 and 2 [T78:0637 and T78:0638]), and one of the panelists, along with Hugh Downs, in an AFTRA-sponsored seminar on the history of television talk shows taped at the Museum of Broadcasting organized by Martha Roundtree in the 1980s.

23. This clip from the first *Home* show appears on the last, preserved in the Museum of Television and Radio in New York as Arlene Francis' *Home* Show (Last Show), 8/9/57, B:18400.

24. Taken from Kinescope of last *Home* show, August 9, 1957. Viewed at the Museum of Television and Radio.

25. Alex McNeil, *Total Television: A Comprehensive Guide to Programming from 1948 to the Present* (New York: Penguin Books, 1984), p. 44.

26. *Mike Wallace Interview: Arlene Francis*, February 24, 1959. All direct quotes are from this interview, viewed at the Museum of Television and Radio.

27. Arlene Francis and Florence Rome, *Arlene Francis: A Memoir* (New York: Simon and Schuster, 1978), pp. 160–161.

28. Ibid., p. 161. This is the way Francis described NBC's choice: "Back in the executive offices, some bright fellow came up with the thought that a hard-working script girl and occasional writer on *Today* ought to be given a crack at that cohosting job, so they tried her out and Barbara Walters was launched on one of the most spectacular careers that's ever happened in television."

29. Ibid., p. 160.

30. When it went on the air in September, Steve Allen's *Tonight!* was seen on 105 NBC affiliates as far west as Omaha. It was, for its first fifteen years, 105 minutes in length. Though few affiliates carried the first 15 minutes, the original sponsor of the show, Ruppert Breweries, insisted upon their inclusion. It was not until the late 1960s that, at Carson's insistence, the show was shortened to a more conventional 90 minutes. McNeil, *Total Television*, p. 667.

31. Head writer Steve O'Donnell studied old *Tonight!* shows of Allen, as well as Kovacs, and borrowed freely in his early work for the Letterman show.

32. Description and quotes taken from kinescope of first *Tonight!* show, viewed at the Museum of Television and Radio.

33. McNeil, *Total Television*, p. 667.

34. Ibid., p. 78.

35. Allen ran this show from July 27, 1953, until the beginning of the *Tonight!* show on New York's WNBC-TV. It ran from 11:20 P.M. to midnight. McNeil, *Total Television*, p. 666.

36. Jack Paar, *P.S. Jack Paar: An Entertainment* (Garden City, N.Y.: Doubleday, 1983), p. 46.

37. All of the direct quotes from Paar on the walk-off incident in the pages that follow are taken from *P.S. Jack Paar*, pp. 114–117.

38. Transcript of interview of Steve Allen with Hugh Downs on *Host to Host*, August 18, 1988, p.25.

39. Paar, *P.S. Jack Paar*, p. 116.

40. Ibid.

41. Ibid., p. 117.

42. *TV Guide*, November 6–12, 1993. The story on Wallace, "Mike Wallace: Grand Inquisitor of 60 Minutes," by Bob Woodward, runs on pp. 14–17.

43. Gary Paul Gates writes alternate sections with Wallace in their collaborative book on Wallace's career, *Close Encounters* (New York: William Morrow and Company, 1984). The description of Brookline comes on p. 12. Two other notable figures who came from Brookline were John F. Kennedy and Leonard Bernstein.

44. Ibid., pp. 12–13.

45. Ibid., p. 14.

46. WXYZ produced such popular dramatic series as *The Green Hornet* and *The Lone Ranger*.

47. Wallace and Gates, *Close Encounters*, p. 15.

48. *Mike and Buff* ran from August 20, 1951, to February 1953. McNeil, *Total Television*, p. 428.

49. Wallace and Gates, *Close Encounters*, p. 19.

50. Ibid., pp. 22–23.

51. Ibid., pp. 23–24.

52. Ibid.

53. "Hot Property," *Time* magazine, January 7, 1957.

54. "No Velvet Glove," *Newsweek*, December 17, 1956.

55. Ibid.

56. Wallace and Gates, *Close Encounters*, p. 53.

57. Ibid., p. 52.

58. Muriel Cantor, *Prime-time Television: Content and Control.* Beverly Hills, Calif.: Sage Publications, 1980.

59. *The Mike Wallace Interview*, which ran from 1959 to 1961 on the NTA syndication network. Hal Erickson, *Syndicated Television: The First Forty Years, 1947–1987* (Jefferson, N.C.: McFarland, 1989), p. 86.

60. J. Fred MacDonald, *One Nation under Television: The Rise and Decline of Network TV* (New York: Pantheon, 1990), p. 146.

61. Ibid.

4. THE SECOND CYCLE (1962–1974)

1. J. Fred MacDonald, *One Nation under Television: The Rise and Decline of Network TV* (New York: Pantheon, 1990), p. 149.

2. Erik Barnouw in *Tube of Plenty: The Evolution of American Television* (New York: Oxford University Press, 1977) and David Halberstam in *The Fifties* (New York: Villard Books, 1993) point out that as early as 1952 television played a key role in Eisenhower's bid for the presidency in a campaign guided by BBDO Advertising Agency and

Rosser Reeves of Ted Bates Agency. Democratic candidate Adlai Stevenson refused to participate in television advertising, and this was one of the key factors in his defeat.

3. Barnouw, *Tube of Plenty.* See pp. 270–277.

4. Ibid., p. 241. For a description of the "kitchen debate" and the "new diplomacy" of television in the late 1950s and early 1960s, see Barnouw, *Tube of Plenty,* pp. 238–241.

5. See *Merv: An Autobiography,* by Merv Griffin and Peter Barsocchini (New York: Simon and Schuster, 1980), p. 59.

6. Ibid.

7. David Halberstam, *The Powers That Be* (New York: Alfred A. Knopf, 1979), pp. 416–417, quoted in MacDonald, *One Nation under Television,* p. 152.

8. Back cover of *Here's Johnny: Thirty Years of America's Favorite Late Night Entertainment,* by Stephen Cox (New York: Harmony Books, 1992).

9. Though the term was applied to Jack Paar and others, Carson dominated late-night talk competition for so long that he came to be known as the undisputed champ. Looking back, for its 40th Anniversary issue in 1993 *TV Guide* named Carson the "all-time best nighttime talk-show host without hesitation." "Is there any doubt?" the magazine crowed. "He's the King—the chief of chitchat, the master of monologues." *TV Guide,* 40th Anniversary Issue, April 17–23, 1993, p. 46.

10. Kenneth Tynan, "Johnny Carson," "Profiles," *The New Yorker,* February 20, 1978, p. 83.

11. Paul Corkery, *Carson: The Unauthorized Biography* (Ketchum, Idaho: Randt and Co., 1987), p. 60.

12. Cox, *Here's Johnny,* p. 164.

13. Corkery, *Carson,* p. 66.

14. Kinescopes of this show, distributed commercially in the *TV Variety* series, reveal the Carson comedy/host persona essentially as it was to remain for the next forty years.

15. Interview with David Tebet, March 4, 1984, at the Dorchester Hotel in New York.

16. Terry Galanoy, *Tonight* (Garden City, N.Y.: Doubleday, 1972), p. 134.

17. Corkery, *Carson,* p. 100.

18. Ibid.

19. In a commencement address to his old high school in Norfolk, Nebraska, in 1976, Carson urged the graduating class to study the art of compromise, "which implied a willingness to be convinced by other people's arguments." Kenneth Tynan, "Johnny Carson," "Profiles," *The New Yorker,* February 20, 1978, p. 85.

20. Corkery, *Carson*, p. 102.

21. Ibid., p. 104.

22. It is interesting to note that the first show was ushered in by the same kind of well-orchestrated publicity buildup that accompanied Carson's last week on the air in May 1993. By the time it appeared on the air the first Carson *Tonight* show had garnered, in the words of biographer Terry Galanoy, "more press than the Second Coming of Christ." Galanoy, *Tonight*, p. 137.

23. Tynan, "Johnny Carson," *The New Yorker*, p. 60.

24. Ibid., p. 74.

25. Orson Welles, who was a relatively frequent guest on *The Tonight Show*, once described Carson as being "the only invisible talk-show host." Tynan, "Johnny Carson," *The New Yorker*, p. 51.

26. In the Alex Haley *Playboy* interview Carson attacked the CIA for hiring students to compile secret reports on campus subversives, condemned corporate espionage and financial hanky-panky, supported the newly insurgent Black movement for social and economic equality, and summed up the war in Vietnam as "stupid and pointless." The Haley interview is quoted in Tynan, "Johnny Carson," *The New Yorker*, p. 76.

27. Tynan, "Johnny Carson."

28. Ibid.

29. Mike Wallace and Gary Paul Gates, *Close Encounters* (New York: William Morrow and Company, 1984).

30. Ted Cott, the same executive who had been influential in the success of Mike Wallace's *Night Beat* in 1956 on Channel 5 in New York.

31. James Conaway, "How to Talk to Barbara Walters about Practically Anything," *New York Times* Magazine Section, September 10, 1972, pp. 40, 43.

32. She was one of eight writers on the *Today* show at that time. Robert Metz, *The Today Show* (Chicago: Playboy Press, 1977), p. 185.

33. Conaway, "How to Talk to Barbara Walters," p. 43.

34. Ibid.

35. Ibid.

36. From videotaped interview on "Interviews with Interviewers," with Skip Blumberg, 1985. This is a documentary available at the Museum of Television and Radio.

37. Robert Metz, *The Today Show*, p. 188.

38. "Interviews with Interviewers," with Skip Blumberg, 1985.

39. Deborah Tannen, *You Don't Understand: Women and Men in Conversation* (New York: Ballantine Books, 1990).

40. Even the combustible Jack Paar, the only founder of television

talk to survive in regular programming into the first three years of the 1960s, had learned to compromise and see it "their" way—eventually quitting because, as he made it clear, he got tired of living that way.

41. From chart of "Number of New Talk Shows Each Year 1939–87," compiled for the author by Adam Roffman using Vincent Terrace's 2-volume *Complete Encyclopedia of Television Programs, 1947-1976* (South Brunswick: A. S. Barnes, 1976) and Hal Erickson's *Syndicated Television: The First Forty Years, 1947-1987* (Jefferson, N.C.: McFarland and Company, 1989).

42. Joseph Turow's "Unconventional Programs in Commercial Television: An Organizational Perspective," in *Individuals in Mass Media Organizations: Creativity and Constraint,* ed. James Ettema and D. Charles Whitney (Beverly Hills: Sage Publications, 1982), pp. 107–129, gives an interesting account of the unusual circumstances at the television network that permitted the "innovation" of *All in the Family* in the context of late 1960s television.

43. The *Les Crane Show,* which ran only four months, from November 9, 1964, to March 5, 1965, was one such show. Bob Dylan made a rare appearance on the show, and Crane raised a stir with his "shotgun" microphone that allowed members of the studio audience to talk directly to Crane's guests.

44. Both quotes are taken from Jane Feuer, Paul Kerr, and Tise Vahimagi, eds., *MTM: Quality Television* (London: BFI Publishing, 1984), p. 3.

45. This show, *Town Meeting of the World,* is mentioned by Wayne Munson in *All Talk: The Talk Show in Media Culture* (Philadelphia: Temple University Press, 1993), pp. 59–60. It preceded Phil Donahue and Vladimir Pozner's *Citizens' Summit* by some twenty years.

46. Wayne Munson, the television critic who has done the most thorough historical investigation of talk radio's origins, describes them as, at best, "cloudy." But he goes on to document the surprising reach of talk radio in the 1960s. Factual information in the following paragraphs comes from Munson's book *All Talk,* pp. 37–49.

47. *Conversation Piece,* Donahue's radio show from 1963 to 1967 in Dayton.

48. Transcript of interview with Phil Donahue by Kathy Haley, used for "Still Talking after All These Years," an advertising supplement to *Broadcasting* magazine on the occasion of the twenty-fifth anniversary of the *Phil Donahue Show* in 1992, pp. 1–2.

49. Phil Donahue and Company, *Donahue, My Own Story* (New York: Fawcett Crest, 1981), p. 266. (The original hardcover edition was published in 1979 by Simon and Schuster.)

50. It was characteristic of Donahue that his autobiography was coauthored by members of his staff, and pictured on the inside front cover of the paperback edition were the seven people who formed the core of his producing "family" (McMillen and Mincer; producers Darlene Hayes, Sheri Singer, and Lorraine Landelius; press relations officer Penny Rotheiser; and director Ron Weiner).

51. Interview with Richard Mincer, 1984.

52. Transcript of Kathy Haley interview, p. 3–25.

53. Ibid., p. 3–12.

5. COMPETITIVE FERMENT IN THE LATE SECOND CYCLE

1. "Joey at the Summit," *Time,* February 22, 1960, p. 76.

2. Ibid.

3. Harriet Van Horne's pro-Carson article in *Look* stresses, among other things, that Mike Wallace spoke "pleasant, standard Americanese," but "Bishop," she says, "regrettably, has a harsh voice." "His speech pattern is somehow alien to the American ear," and though "this is, in no sense, a character flaw . . . it is simply that Johnny Carson is easy to listen to, and Joey Bishop is not." "Johnny Carson: The Battle for TV's Midnight Millions," *Look,* July 11, 1967, p. 86.

4. "Comedians: Country Boy," *Time,* January 28, 1966, p. 61.

5. "The Newest Host," *Newsweek,* August 4, 1969, p. 87.

6. Griffin was born in San Mateo, California, in 1925, the son of a tennis pro who catered to a rich clientele and lost the family home during the Depression. Griffin is characterized in a biographical profile by Marshall Blonsky as a man who was financially successful but artistically limited, the key to whose character was a desperate drive to be accepted by the rich and powerful. Marshall Blonsky, "Merv Griffin Dancing in the Dark," in *American Mythologies* (New York: Oxford University Press, 1992), pp. 261–287.

7. "Battle of the Talk Shows," *Newsweek,* September 1, 1969, p. 42. See also Hal Erickson, *Syndicated Television: The First Forty Years, 1947-1987* (Jefferson, N.C.: McFarland, 1989), p. 164. Most of the information for this and the following two paragraphs comes from the *Newsweek* article.

8. "Battle of the Talk Shows," p. 42.

9. Ibid., p. 42.

10. "Goodbye Hollywood, Hello New York, 1948–1957," in *Merv: An Autobiography,* by Merv Griffin and Peter Barsocchini (New York: Simon and Schuster, 1980). The New York period is covered on pp. 155–217.

11. *Merv: An Autobiography,* p. 146.

12. Ibid.

13. Alex McNeil, *Total Television: A Comprehensive Guide to Programming from 1948 to the Present* (New York: Penguin Books, 1984), p. 424.

14. Blonsky, *American Mythologies*, p. 270.

15. Dick Cavett and Christopher Porterfield, *Cavett* (New York: Harcourt, Brace, Jovanovich, 1974), p. 232.

16. The show was videotaped on November 17, 1971, and aired on ABC on December 1, 1971.

17. I am indebted to Professor Carolyn Byerly and a guest talk at Ithaca College in 1997 for my own "decoding" of these allusions. Mailer's obsession with Vidal and his encounter with him on the Cavett show did not end with the show. It occupies 20 pages of a remarkable 68-page essay on Mailer's history with television that appears in his collected essays from the 1970s (Norman Mailer, "Of a Small and Modest Malignancy, Wicked and Bristling with Dots," *Pieces and Pontifications* [Boston: Little Brown and Company, 1982], pp. 13–81; the 1971 Cavett show is described on pp. 55–75).

11. Paul Corkery, *Carson: The Unauthorized Biography* (Ketchum, Idaho: Randt and Co., 1987), p. 60.113.

19. Ibid., p. 114.

20. Ibid., p. 115.

21. Ibid.

22. *Time*, May 1967 (Corkery, *Carson*, p. 119).

23. Stark recalled years later: "I walked in thinking it was a routine matter pertaining to a forthcoming show. 'Art,' Johnny said, 'I want another producer, not associated with NBC, on the show.' 'When do you want me to leave?' 'Right now'" (Corkery, *Carson*, p. 118). Carson staffer Rudy Tellez took over Stark's job until 1970, when veteran director-producer Fred de Cordova took over. Cordova himself was cut off by Carson at the time of Carson's final shows on NBC in May 1992. Later David Tebet, Carson's longtime associate and friend from the early NBC days, was also cut off.

24. J. Fred MacDonald, *One Nation under Television: The Rise and Decline of Network TV* (New York: Pantheon, 1990), p. 196.

25. Says MacDonald: "Gone, too, were offerings with prominent Black characters liberally melded into familiar genres: the medical drama *The Interns*, the police series *The Silent Force*, the medical drama *Matt Lincoln*" (ibid., p. 96).

26. Again, exceptions should be noticed. Tom Snyder's *Tomorrow* went on the air in 1972 in the late-night slot after Carson. It represented the kind of feisty programming that had characterized Cavett's and Griffin's challenges to Carson in the late 1960s, now safely contained in a time slot when most viewers were in bed.

27. "Battle of the Talk Shows," *Newsweek*, September 1, 1969.
28. Ibid.

6. THE THIRD CYCLE (1974–1980)

1. "Barbara Walters Now 'Today' Co-Host," *New York Times*, April 23, 1974, p. 83.
2. Larry Michie, "It's a New Year, but Is It Happy?" *Variety*, January 9, 1974, p. 99.
3. *Broadcast Yearbook 1974*, summary of year.
4. Ibid.
5. "The Year of the Woman," *Newsweek*, November 4, 1974, p. 20.
6. "Girls Are On-camera from Coast to Coast," *Ebony*, June 1971, p. 169.
7. *Woman*, 1971, hosted by WOR radio talk-show host Sherrye Henry, and *What Every Woman Wants to Know*, 1972, hosted by Bess Myerson, were two other such shows designed for the same audiences.
8. For a discussion of the relative freedom of fringe time, see Jimmie L. Reeves and Horace Newcomb, "Fringe Television: A Challenge to Prime-Time Criticism," *Southern Speech Communication Journal* 52 (Summer 1987): 339–348.
9. "The Early Show," *Time*, October 29, 1973, p. 124.
10. *Broadcasting Yearbook 1974*, chart of television billings from 1948 to 1972, showing a steady rise each year.
11. "No one is in a better position to explain the bizarre events of the past year than Richard Nixon," said CBS news producer John Sharnik in describing the program. "CBS Program on Nixon to Use His Statements," *New York Times*, January 2, 1974, p. 75.
12. "Letting It All Out," *Time*, May 13, 1974.
13. Ibid. Barry Serafin played the President, Bob Schieffer played John Dean, and Nelson Benton was cast as H. R. Haldeman.
14. The networks released a study that attempted to prove that less than one of each local station's fourteen access half-hours was devoted to local-interest programming, over 65 percent to game shows. *New York Times*, September 20, 1974, p. 76.
15. Hal Erickson, *Syndicated Television: The First Forty Years, 1947–1987* (Jefferson, N.C.: McFarland, 1989), p. 162.
16. Tony Brown hosted *Black Journal* on PBS from 1970 to 1976, later syndicating it as *Tony Brown's Journal*.
17. Dick Cavett, "Those (Bleep) TV Censors," *Newsweek*, September 9, 1974, p. 15. Cavett gave a number of examples in his article, including the refusal of ABC to let him have African American activist Angela Davis on his show.

18. Erickson, *Syndicated Television*, pp. 158–171.

19. Lester David, "Mike Douglas: His Common-Sense Views on Sex, Love and Marriage," *Good Housekeeping*, March 1975, p. 24.

20. Mike Douglas, "The Master Host of Talk Shows Talks about his Appendectomy," *Today's Health*, July–August 1975, p. 45.

21. Mike Douglas' autobiography appeared in 2000, and his contributions to the talk show as a form received new recognition at this time. See Bernard Timberg, review of *I'll Be Right Back: Memories of TV's Greatest Talk Show* by Michael Douglas with Thomas Kelly and Michael Heaton (New York: Simon and Schuster, 2000), *Television Quarterly* 31, no. 1 (Spring 2000): 99–102.

22. David, "Mike Douglas," p. 26.

23. From the booklet accompanying *The Mike Douglas Show with John Lennon and Yoko Ono* video, p. 39.

24. Moyers' own words for the kind of discussion that leads to national policy and choice.

25. Ken Burns, "'Moyers: A Second Look'—More than Meets the Eye," *New York Times*, May 14, 1989, p. 33.

26. These series were produced between 1986 and 1990, but he had had working relationships with many of these producers before. They are listed by name in the acknowledgments section of *Bill Moyers: A World of Ideas II: Public Opinions from Private Citizens*, ed. Andie Tucher (New York: Doubleday, 1990).

27. "Dialogue on Film: Bill Moyers," *American Film* (June 1990), p. 44.

28. Ibid., p. 17. The information on the Tuchman program comes from this article.

29. Ibid., p. 20.

30. David Zurawik, "The Following Myth Is Made Possible by a Grant from Bill Moyers," *Esquire*, October 1989, p. 146. Moyers, in reply to these charges, said that he was indeed difficult, if difficult meant fighting "the thousand fiefdoms of [bureaucratic] resistance that rise up to say 'No, that's not a good idea.'" He had "learned that in Washington," working for LBJ.

31. "Taking CBS News to Task: Bill Moyers Blasts Its Show-Business Approach," *Newsweek*, September 15, 1986, p. 53.

32. "Edward R. Murrow: This Reporter," two-hour *American Masters* series on PBS.

33. Jon Katz, "Why Bill Moyers Shouldn't Run for President," *New York Times*, March 8, 1992, p. H-38.

34. Ibid.

35. *Bill Moyers: A World of Ideas II*, p. vii.

36. Ibid., pp. xiii–xiv.

37. This was one of the main themes of "Consuming Images," Part 1 of the three-part *Public Mind* series produced by Public Affairs Television in 1990.

38. Katz, "Why Bill Moyers Shouldn't Run for President," p. H-33. Ken Burns, "Moyers: A Second Look," p. 33.

39. *The Power of Myth* series included six one-hour shows.

40. Zurawik, "The Following Myth Is Made Possible by a Grant from Bill Moyers," p. 140, and Katz, "Why Bill Moyers Shouldn't Run for President," p. H-33.

41. Marc Gunther, *The House That Roone Built: The Inside Story of ABC News* (New York: Little, Brown and Company, 1994), p. 40.

42. Alex McNeil, *Total Television: A Comprehensive Guide to Programming from 1948 to the Present* (New York: Penguin Books, 1984), pp. 661–662.

43. Gunther, *The House That Roone Built*, p. 41.

44. Ibid., p. 38.

45. Ibid., p. 58.

46. Ibid., p. 42.

47. Ibid.

48. Ibid.

49. Ibid., p. 51+.

50. Ibid.

51. Ibid., p. 58.

52. Ibid., p. 154.

53. *Les Brown's Encyclopedia of Television,* 3rd ed. (Detroit: Visible Ink, 1992), p. 504.

54. Erickson, *Syndicated Television*, p. 269.

55. Bruce Cassiday, *Dinah! A Biography* (New York: F. Watts, 1979), p. 161.

56. Ibid.

57. Ibid., p. 166.

58. Ibid.

59. Kenneth Tynan, "Fifteen Years of the Salto Mortale," "Profiles," *The New Yorker,* February 20, 1978, p. 74.

60. Ibid., p. 86.

61. Ibid., p. 87.

62. Ibid.

63. Paul Corkery, *Carson: The Unauthorized Biography* (Ketchum, Idaho: Randt and Co., 1987), p. 154.

64. Ibid., p. 155.

65. Ibid., p. 156.

66. Ibid., p. 169.

67. J. Fred MacDonald's term to characterize the 1960s and 1970s

in network television. *One Nation under Television* (New York: Pantheon, 1990), p. 147.

68. Ibid., p. 218.

7. THE FOURTH CYCLE (1980–1990)

1. Hal Erickson, *Syndicated Television: The First Forty Years, 1947–1987* (Jefferson, N.C.: McFarland, 1989), p. 165.

2. Joe Flickinger, "Infotainment and the Question of Legitimacy: A Case Study of CBS News in the 1980's" (Ph.D. dissertation, University of Oregon, 1993), Figure 24, p. 295.

3. Carlin Romano, *New York Daily News*, March 19, 1981, p. M-2.

4. Ibid. Talk-show hosts appearing at the National Association of Television Program Executives (NATPE) convention in 1981 included Merv Griffin, Charlie Rose (an up-and-coming talk commodity on PBS), and "NATPE's man of the year," Phil Donahue, whose show was then available in 180 markets.

5. Rosemarie Lennon, *David Letterman: On Stage and Off* (New York: Pinnacle Books, Windsor Publishing Company, 1994), p. 15.

6. *Playboy* interview with David Letterman. "A Candid Conversation with the Gap-toothed Prince of Late-night Television," *Playboy*, October 1984, p. 68.

7. Lennon, *David Letterman*, p. 23.

8. Bill Carter, *The Late Shift: Letterman, Leno and the Network Battle for the Night* (New York: Hyperion, 1994), p. 19.

9. Caroline Latham, *The David Letterman Story: An Unauthorized Biography* (New York: Franklin Watts, 1987), pp. 14–15.

10. Later DeWitt was one of the stars of *Three's Company*, and Pearson headed an ad agency in Indianapolis.

11. Latham, *The David Letterman Story*, p. 31.

12. A clip from the period survives, showing Letterman as a bushy-haired wisecracking weatherman. Phil Donahue ran it as a "surprise" when Letterman visited his show.

13. Lennon, *David Letterman*, p. 32.

14. Ibid., p. 33.

15. During this period Letterman worked at home on scripts for the *Mary Tyler Moore* and *Bob Newhart* shows. Later he said he really didn't know what he was doing with these scripts. Carter, *The Late Shift*, p. 19.

16. Ibid., p. 20.

17. Latham, *The David Letterman Story*, p. 61.

18. Ibid.

19. Ibid., p. 81. Markoe, during and after her relationship with

Letterman, engaged in a wide range of comedy-writing projects, including writing scripts for the critically acclaimed situation comedy *Buffalo Bill*, with Dabney Coleman. After a number of attempts to keep it alive, their relationship ended in 1988.

20. Carter, *The Late Shift*, p. 24.

21. Latham, *The David Letterman Story*, p. 81.

22. Videotaped copies of Letterman's morning show are hard to find. I am indebted to Ron Simon of the Museum of Television and Radio for the opportunity to see this one.

23. Carter, *The Late Shift*, p. 25.

24. Lennon, *David Letterman*, p. 61.

25. Sixteen minutes and thirty seconds of each Letterman show were devoted to station breaks, network identification and promotions, and commercials.

26. Morton's notes, as well as the run-down sheets and scripts for this show (Show #814, Thursday, January 15, 1987) were supplied to me by staff.

27. In comedian Jay Leno's first appearances on *Letterman*, his acid references to brand name products frequently had to be leached from his satires of American consumer culture. This and other information on NBC's standards and practices department come from an interview with Drew Kastner of the NBC Compliances and Practices Department, December 4, 1986.

28. Interview with Drew Kastner. From feeling as if he was the butt of the joke and his initial reaction of anger and humiliation, Kastner eventually came to feel that this was a sort of "baptism by fire" and that he was expected to be "part of the joke." The show eventually won him over and, while not central to it, he explained in the interview that he came to feel like part of the Letterman "family" after a while.

29. Marc Gunther, *The House That Roone Built: The Inside Story of ABC News* (New York: Little, Brown and Company, 1994), p. 112.

30. Marc Gunther tells the story of how Arledge was appointed President of ABC News on May 2, 1977, in *The House That Roone Built*, p. 26.

31. *Who's Who in America 1992–93*, 47th ed., p. 1899.

32. Gunther, *The House That Roone Built*, p. 107.

33. Ibid.

34. *Who's Who in America*, 47th ed., 1993, p. 1899. It was as ABC diplomatic correspondent that Koppel got to know Secretary of State Henry Kissinger, forming a close relationship and logging close to 500,000 miles with the Secretary of State. Kissinger tried to hire Koppel as a spokesperson for the State Department at one point (Gunther, *The House That Roone Built*, p. 110), but Koppel declined.

35. Roone Arledge's new team at ABC News had put his ideas into practice soon after he arrived. When South Moluccan terrorists seized a school and train in the Netherlands, Arledge ordered the news division to cover the event with blow-by-blow coverage for twenty-one days. He "steamrolled" the story, as one producer put it, putting six crews and four producers on it continuously. He sent another army of ABC correspondents and film crews to cover the prison escape of James Earl Ray, the convicted assassin of Martin Luther King Jr., and soon after that he turned the capture of "Son of Sam" serial killer David Berkowitz in New York into another heavily promoted news event. Gunther, *The House That Roone Built.*

36. Ibid., pp. 97–98.

37. Ibid., p. 98.

38. The ABC News people were beginning to refer to it jokingly as "ABC Held Hostage."

39. Les Brown points out that the show's original length of twenty minutes prevented affiliates from taking the half-hour for more profitable thirty-minute syndicated shows, since syndicators generally did not distribute in twenty-minute segments. Only when the show had a secure audience base did it expand to a half-hour. *Les Brown's Encyclopedia of Television,* 3rd ed. (Detroit: Visible Ink, 1992), p. 394.

40. Gunther describes *Nightline* producer Bill Lord as "fearless" in the control room. "He was so comfortable with technology and so sure of himself that he would change the topic of *Nightline* at the last minute, shifting gears on the air. 'Lord was extremely adept at putting people on two tracks to do two *Nightlines* and then deciding very late what he wanted,' said correspondent Jeff Greenfield. He turned out to be an ideal complement to Koppel. Lord had gut instincts about the news, while Koppel was cerebral. Lord's technical know-how was vast; Koppel's was limited. Lord . . . liked Washington stories, politics, science, pop culture, and music, while Koppel's interests lay overseas. 'There was a fear that, if left only to Ted, we would do esoteric foreign policy stories every day,' said producer Lionel Chapman." Gunther, *The House That Roone Built,* p. 115.

41. William Henry III, "Ted Koppel: The Real News Success," *New York Daily News,* November 11, 1980, p. m2+.

42. Ibid.

43. Ibid.

44. Ibid.

45. N. Collins, "The Smartest Man on TV," *New York Times,* August 13, 1984.

46. *Les Brown's Encyclopedia of Television,* 3rd ed., p. 394.

47. My information was drawn from David R. Marples, *The So-*

cial Impact of the Chernobyl Disaster (New York: St. Martin's Press, 1988); Grigorii Medvedev, *The Truth about Chernobyl* (New York: Basic Books, 1989); and Richard F. Mould, *Chernobyl: The Real Story* (New York: Pergamon Press, 1988). Also: Dennis Holloway, "The Catastrophe and After," *New York Review of Books,* July 19, 1990, pp. 4–6.

48. *Nightline,* May 14, 1986. All subsequent quotes taken from video recording of that show.

49. *Star Wars* was released in 1977.

50. Quotes taken from video recording of the *Tonight* show with Johnny Carson, May 15, 1986.

51. The part of the Carson monologue not quoted here emphasizes, in joke form, the same kind of "duplicity" on the part of Soviet Premier Mikhail Gorbachev that was charged by Koppel in his report. For the kind of Manichaeanism that characterized television news talk in the 1980s, see Richard Campbell and Jimmie Reeves, "TV News Narration and Common Sense: Updating the Soviet Threat," *Journal of Film and Video,* special issue on "Close Studies of Television: Encoding Research," ed. Bernard Timberg and David Barker, 41, no. 2 (Summer 1989): 58–74.

52. This was a technologically updated version of the photograph caption routine that Carson had done for years.

53. Julia Klein, "The New Stand-up Comics: Can You Be a Funny Woman without Making Fun of Women?" *Ms.* magazine, October 1984, p. 120+. This issue of *Ms.* featured profiles of Rita Rudner, Abby Stein, Beverly Mickins, and Kate Clinton, as well as a longer article on Joan Rivers by Lee Israel.

54. Jerry Adler with Pamela Abramson and Susan Agrest, "Joan Rivers Gets Even with Laughs," *Newsweek,* October 10, 1983, p. 58.

55. Ibid.

56. Cliff Jahr, in *Ladies' Home Journal,* November 1983, p. 86.

57. James Wolcott, "I Know Why the Caged Bird Kvetches," *New York Magazine,* January 24, 1984, p. 51.

58. Ibid.

59. Ibid.

60. Aljean Harmetz, "Fox Plans a TV Program Service," *New York Times,* May 7, 1986.

61. "Can We Talk? (Crash, Click, Buzz)," *Newsweek,* May 19, 1986, p. 52.

62. Richard Zoglin, "The Joan vs. Johnny: Carson Gets a New Rival, and a 'Fourth Network' Is Born," *Time,* May 19, 1986, p. 98.

63. This theme continued to be played out well into 1988, when Fred de Cordova published an excerpt from his autobiography in *Red-*

book magazine detailing his own view of Rivers' "manipulative" behavior and behind-the-scenes decision to leave the show. Fred de Cordova, "Johnny and Joan: What Really Happened between Them? A Behind-the-scenes Look at the Johnny Carson–Joan Rivers Feud," *Redbook*, March 1988, p. 84.

64. Erickson, *Syndicated Television*, p. 365.

65. Norman King, *Everybody Loves Oprah! Her Remarkable Life Story* (New York: William Morrow and Company), p. 11. Another critic described her as "a roundhouse, a full-course meal, big, brassy, loud, aggressive, hyper, laughable, lovable, soulful, tender, low-down, earthy, and hungry." Howard Rosenberg, "Winfrey Zeroing in on Donahue," *Los Angeles Times*, September 12, 1986, quoted in King, *Everybody Loves Oprah!* p. 10.

66. King, *Everybody Loves Oprah!* p. 47.

67. Her account of this has been questioned by some family members, who denied her report, or saw it as an example of Winfrey's "exaggerations." See Nellie Bly, *Oprah! Up Close and Down Home* (New York: Zebra Books, Kensington Publishers, 1993). One version of Winfrey's account is given in King's biography, pp. 45–47, but it has appeared in a number of journalistic sources.

68. The program aired in 1985. See Leslie Miller, "Sexual Abuse Survivors Find Strength to Speak in Numbers," *People Weekly*, August 27, 1992, p. 6D, and King, *Everybody Loves Oprah!* p. 156.

69. *Scared Silent*, produced by filmmaker Arnold Shapiro, aired simultaneously on CBS, NBC, and PBS on September 4, 1992, and on ABC two days later.

70. King, *Everybody Loves Oprah!* p. 63.

71. Ibid., pp. 78–79.

72. Bly, *Oprah!* p. 43.

73. King, *Everybody Loves Oprah!* p. 85.

74. Ibid.

75. Ibid., p. 89.

76. Ibid., p. 91.

77. Ibid., p. 92.

78. Ibid., p. 96.

79. Ibid., pp. 115–116.

80. Ibid., p. 121.

81. Harry Waters with Patricia King, "Chicago's Grand New Oprah," *Newsweek*, December 31, 1984, p. 51.

82. The quote is from publicist Anne McGee. King, *Everybody Loves Oprah!* p. 159.

83. Ibid., p. 164.

84. *USA Today*, August 6, 1986, "Because of Others I Can Live the Dream," p. 7A. The box at the beginning of the interview notes that Winfrey was interviewed by *USA Today*'s Barbara Reynolds and that *The Oprah Winfrey Show* was scheduled to go into national syndication a month later.

85. King, *Everybody Loves Oprah!* p. 166.

86. King says the pattern began to emerge from the beginning. He gives the ratings for the Los Angeles market in the first three days of the competition: Monday, Donahue, 26 percent of the audience share; Winfrey, 23 percent. Then the balance went to Winfrey—30 to 18 percent on Tuesday; 29 to 22 percent on Wednesday. Ibid., p. 25.

87. John Dempsey, "Syndie TV Becoming Tower of Babel: Talkshows Elbowing Each Other for First Run Slots," *Variety*, November 26, 1986.

88. Jacobs, who had been working for Winfrey since she came to Chicago in 1984, became her full-time business manager in 1987. "As her career progressed, I was handling more and more of her business. It got to where I was spending 60 or 70 percent of my time working with her, so I shut down my practice, and came in-house in 1987." Jerry Jacobs quoted in Bly, *Oprah!* p. 55.

89. King, *Everybody Loves Oprah!* pp. 133–137.

90. Bill Zehme, "It Came from Chicago," *Spy*, December, 1986. Quoted in King, *Everybody Loves Oprah!* pp. 159–160.

91. *USA Today*, August 6, 1986, 7A.

92. King, *Everybody Loves Oprah!* p. 31.

93. Gloria-Jean Mascariotte, "C'mon, Girl: Oprah Winfrey and the Discourse of Feminine Talk," *Genders* 11 (Fall 1991): 100. She quotes Henry Louis Gates' discussion from *The Signifying Monkey: A Theory of Afro-American Literary Criticism* (New York: Oxford University Press, 1988), pp. 127–130.

94. Mascariotte, "C'mon, Girl."

95. I am indebted to Dr. Glenda Dickerson for drawing my attention to the big momma/Aunt Jemima dichotomy. Donald Bogle, Marlon Riggs, and others have addressed this dichotomy.

96. Geraldo Rivera with Daniel Paisner, *Exposing Myself* (New York: Bantam, 1992), p. 8.

97. Ibid., pp. 12–13.

98. Ibid., p. 13.

99. Ibid., p. 51.

100. Ibid., p. 88.

101. The Paramount *Arsenio Hall Show* was on the air from January 1989 to May 1994.

102. Veronica Chambers, "Leaving a Void in the Late-Night Laughter," *New York Times,* Arts and Leisure section, May 21, 1995, p. H-29.

103. "Move Over, David Letterman: The Night Belongs to Arsenio Hall," *Village Voice* cover, May 23, 1989; "Arsenio Hall, on a Late Night Mission: Targeting the MTV Generation and Gaining on Carson," *Washington Post,* cover of Style Section, July 10, 1989; "TV's Hip Host Grabs the Post-Carson Generation," *Time* cover, November 13, 1989; "TV Person of the Year: Arsenio Hall, Late-night Sensation," *TV Guide* cover, June 23–29, 1990; "Arsenio Hall Talks about His Friendship with Eddie and His Feuds with Madonna and Roseanne," *Ebony* cover, December 1990.

104. Chambers, "Leaving a Void in the Late-Night Laughter," p. H-29.

105. Laura B. Randolph, "Prince of Late-Night TV: Arsenio Hall Talks about His Feuds with Roseanne and Madonna," *Ebony,* December 1990, p. 54.

106. Mary Murphy, "I Have Helped TV Loosen Up," *TV Guide,* June 23, 1990, p. 7.

8. THE FIFTH CYCLE (1990–1995)

1. The story of these corporate takeovers is well told in Ken Auletta's *Three Blind Mice: How the TV Networks Lost Their Way* (New York: Random House, 1991).

2. Janie Baylis, "1995: The Year of the Merger," *Washington Post,* January 6, 1996, p. 1.

3. *The Statistical Abstract of the United States,* 114th ed. (Washington, D.C.: U.S. Bureau of the Census, 1994), p. 581.

4. Ibid., p. 568.

5. Joe Flickinger, "Infotainment and the Question of Legitimacy: A Case Study of CBS News in the 1980s" (Ph.D. dissertation, University of Oregon, 1993). Information taken from Figure 23, a chart of "The Electronic Media Competitive Environment." Data from *Broadcasting Marketing and Technology News,* 27 August 1990, p. 39.

6. Flickinger, "Infotainment and the Question of Legitimacy."

7. Nicholas Negroponte, *Being Digital* (New York: Alfred A Knopf, 1995), p. 5.

8. Ibid.

9. Flickinger, "Infotainment and the Question of Legitimacy," Figure 24, "Broadcast networks' prime-time audience share: 1980–1990. Nielsen Media Research (Northbrook, Ill: 1980–1990)."

10. At one point NBC President Robert Wright told a group of investment counselors that GE was not interested in losing tens of mil-

lions of dollars on NBC for sporting events even if those sporting events allowed the network to remain the leader in ratings (*New York Times*, January 20, 1992). At that time Wright felt NBC was likely to face continuing losses until its contracts with its most important sports rights holders, including major league baseball and National Football League, expired in 1993.

11. *The Statistical Abstract of the United States, 1994*, p. 580.

12. Jill Gerston, "Here's Everybody! After Carson, A Host of Late-Night Wannabes," *New York Times*, August 16, 1992.

13. Ibid., p. 21.

14. Prominent among late-night viewers was a "young, free-spending" group of 18-to-49-year-olds (a 5 percent increase in this group over 1970) who sent "visions of dollar signs dancing in the heads of advertisers, networks, and syndicators." Ibid.

15. Bernard Weinraub, "Jay Leno: Higher and Higher, Night after Night on *Tonight*," *Cosmopolitan*, May 1, 1996, p. 238.

16. Ibid., p. 180.

17. Victor Gold, "Why Jay Leno Thinks Washington Is Funny," *Washingtonian Magazine*, November 1993, p. 77.

18. Ibid., p. 117.

19. Ibid.

20. Constantinos Christos Vassilis Economopoulos, "Effects of Political Satire on Feelings about Government and Its Officials: A Study of Jay Leno Monologues" (Master's thesis, University of Georgia, 1993), p. 41.

21. "Clinton got a huge surge in public support coming out of the Democratic convention. At the peak, he was seventeen points ahead of Bush. During the time that he was leading most, he was being hit by Leno the least. . . . As the race continued, the gap slowly closed and so did Leno's ratio of Bush to Clinton bashing." Ibid., pp. 42–43.

22. Calvin Woodward, "Clinton: Hooted from Office? Presidential Melodrama Is Playing Out against a Riot of Ribald Humor," Associated Press article reprinted in the *Roanoke Times and World News*, September 27, 1998.

23. These problems were reported by *New York Times* television critic Bill Carter in his column and later in his book, *The Late Shift: Letterman, Leno, and the Network Battle for the Night* (New York: Hyperion, 1994). The book has a wealth of detail on behind-the-scenes negotiations during this period but is heavily weighted toward Letterman sources.

24. Jeff Jarvis, review of "Jay Leno's Tonight Show," *TV Guide*, June 27, 1992, p. 5.

25. Bill Zehme, "Leno Lives!" *Esquire,* October 1995, p. 104.

26. Steve Coe, "What the L? Leno Leads Letterman in Late Night," *Broadcasting and Cable,* November 11, 1995, p. 70.

27. Steve Coe, "Resurgent Leno Re-ups with NBC: Five-year Extension Follows Nine Weeks in a Row of Household Wins," *Broadcasting and Cable,* October 30, 1995, pp. 14f

28. Ibid. Letterman was getting a 2.3 rating for the 18–49 age group, Leno a 2.5. In the 25–54 age group, Leno was leading Letterman 2.8 to 2.4.

29. "Jay Leno: Nice Guys Sometimes Finish First—but Only If They Learn to Snarl," *People Weekly,* December 25, 1995, p. 68.

30. Tom Shales, "Letterman's Not So Prime Time: After 2 Years at CBS, the 'Late Show' Host Is Dogged by the Competition and Self-Doubt," *Washington Post,* June 27, 1995, p. E-6.

31. "Jay Leno: Nice Guys Sometimes Finish First," p. 68.

32. Richard Zoglin, "In the Kingdom of Letterman: After a Smash Olympic Performance, He Is Dominating Late Night. But He's Not the Same Old Dave," *Time,* March 14, 1995, p. 107.

33. Ibid.

34. Tom Shales, "Letterman's Not So Prime Time," *Washington Post,* June 27, 1996, p. E-1.

35. Dotson Rader, "I Love Nothing More Than Being in Love," *Parade* magazine, *Washington Post* edition, May 26, 1996.

36. NBC Entertainment president Warren Littlefield was quoted after Leno had signed his new five-year deal with NBC in 1996 as saying, "This is the first time we've had a star negotiate for *less* time." Bernard Weinraub, "Jay Leno: Higher and Higher, Night after Night on *Tonight,*" p. 180.

37. Bill Zehme, "Leno Lives!," *Esquire,* October 1995, p. 102.

38. Ibid. p. 103.

39. Letterman producer Robert Morton said this to me in an informal exchange.

40. Howard Kurtz, *Hot Air: All Talk, All the Time* (New York: Times Books, 1996) p. 19.

41. *Current Biography Yearbook,* 1987, p. 405.

42. Ibid.

43. Kurtz, *Hot Air,* p. 30.

44. Ann Dore McLaughlin went on to serve as assistant secretary for public affairs in the Reagan administration's Department of Treasury (1981–1984) and as an undersecretary in the Department of Interior (1984–1986). *Current Biography Yearbook,* p. 407.

45. Kurtz, *Hot Air,* p. 30.

46. *Current Biography Yearbook*, 1987.

47. These were the hours of his Mutual Radio Network show beginning in 1978.

48. Howard Kurtz's chapter on Larry King in *Hot Air* is called "The King of Schmooze."

49. Biographical information on Larry King in this section is derived from Howard Kurtz's chapter in *Hot Air*, unless otherwise noted.

50. Peter Laufer, *Inside Talk Radio: America's Voice or Just Hot Air?* (New York: Birch Lane Press, 1995), p. 99.

51. Ibid., p. 100.

52. Kurtz, *Hot Air*, p. 83.

53. Ibid., p. 105.

54. Ibid., p. 100.

55. Ibid., p. 87.

56. Ibid., p. 88.

57. Ibid., p. 90.

58. Ibid., pp. 92–93.

59. *Spin*, 1995, a documentary produced by Brian Springer and distributed by Video Data Bank, Chicago, Illinois.

60. Ibid.

61. Dowd's article is summarized in Robin Andersen's book, *Consumer Culture and TV Programming* (Boulder, Colo.: Westview Press, 1995), p. 225–228.

62. Ibid., p. 229.

63. *Spin*, 1995.

64. Kurtz, *Hot Air*, p. 94.

65. *Spin*, 1995.

66. An exception might be Ross Perot's announcement of his candidacy on *Larry King Live* in March 1992, itself a prearranged idea. It was not the announcement itself, however, but the announcement's multiple exposure through newspapers and talk shows that made it a national "event."

67. NBC, recorded October 3, 1995. The programs and quotes used in this section were taken from programs videotaped off the air October 2–4, 1995.

68. It is worth noting that this is exactly the ceremonial role of the news announcer or host predicted by Elihu Katz and Daniel Dayan, *The Media Event: The Live Broadcasting of History* (Cambridge, Mass.: Harvard University Press, 1992).

69. Once again television was simply amplifying American culture itself. For a detailed review of O. J. Simpson jokes during this time, and their place in American popular culture, see Chris Lamb, "The

Popularity of OJ Simpson Jokes: The More We Know, the More We Laugh," *Journal of Popular Culture* 28 (Summer 1994): 223–231.

70. The declaration filed May 1967, to obtain a restraining order, alleged that "on April 29, 1967, my husband violently pushed me against the wall, held me there and grabbed me by my chin. He has slapped me in the past, torn a dress off me [and] threatened on numerous occasions to beat me up . . ." Ten years later the declaration for a restraining order stated: "During the course of our marriage . . . [Cochran has] without any reasonable cause, provocation or justification physically struck, beat and inflicted severe injury upon the person of the Petitioner . . ." Information cited from feature article on Johnnie Cochran by Michael J. Goodman, *Los Angeles Times Magazine,* January 29, 1995, p. 11+.

71. It is not difficult to see that the news and entertainment industries engage in almost obsessive campaigns for national consensus and solidarity in times of war or perceived threat to the nation. The "Iran hostage crisis," the periods immediately before, during, and after the Gulf War, and the period after the September 11, 2001, attack on the World Trade Center are all cases in point.

9. THE FIFTH CYCLE (1996–2000)

1. Howard Kurtz, "Morality Guru Takes on Talk TV: Daytime Confessionals Are William Bennett's New Targets," *Washington Post,* C-1,6, October 26, 1995.

2. Richard Zoglin, "Talking Trash," *Time,* January 30, 1995.

3. Ibid.

4. Joe Flint, "Talk and Magazine Shows, A Rise out of Rick," in the "Road to NATPE" section of *Variety,* December 12–18, 1994. Under the pressure of the ratings war, the article points out, Winfrey kept to the "high road," but her show was undergoing a series of internal changes. Her long-time executive producer, Debra DiMaio, quit the show, as did her publicist, Colleen Raleigh, filing a lawsuit against her former boss.

5. *Washington Post* critic Tom Shales discussed the Jenny Jones murder trial as a symptom of "America's cultural pollution." "Nothing seems to excite [the audience] more than seeing guests go at one another—two women fighting over the same man, or two men fighting over the same woman, or two of anybody fighting over one or more of anything." "Hosts like Ricki Lake," said Shales, "feign disdain while suppressing delight that things have gotten so entertainingly out of control." *The Washington Post,* March 19, 1995, p. G-5.

6. Richard Zoglin, "Talking Trash," *Time,* January 30, 1995, p. 77.

7. Ibid.

8. Ibid.

9. Bill Carter, "Television: In the Rough-and-Tumble World of Daytime Talk, Advertisers Seek to Be Heard but Not Seen," a column that appeared in the *New York Times* in March 1995, the same month Schmitz, the guest on *The Jenny Jones Show,* killed his "secret admirer."

10. Ibid.

11. Mark Goodman, "Unsilent Springer," *People Weekly,* January 24, 1994, p. 73+.

12. Ibid.

13. Ibid.

14. Ibid.

15. Joe Schlosser, "Jerry Springer: Punching the Envelope," *Broadcasting and Cable,* December 15, 1997, p. 32(4).

16. Ibid.

17. Transcribed from "Too Hot for TV!" Heliotrope Productions, Studio USA Talk Video LLC, 1997.

18. This was a group of major-market UHF stations owned by Diller that was competing with VHF outlets around the country.

19. Gina Bellafante, *Rosie O'Donnell Show* review, *Time* 147, no. 26, June 24, 1996, p. 76.

20. *MediaWeek* 6, no. 3 (January 16, 1996), p. 25.

21. Gloria Goodman, *The Life and Humor of Rosie O'Donnell: A Biography* (New York: Bill Adler Books, 1998), pp. 3–4.

22. Melina Gerosa, "How the Heartbreak of Her Childhood Made Rosie O'Donnell the Nicest Person on TV," *Ladies' Home Journal,* February 1977, p. 106.

23. Geraldo Rivera, "I Was Going to Hell," *Newsweek,* July 15, 1996, p. 48.

24. Susan Miller and Jeanne Gordon, *Newsweek,* July 15, 1996, p. 45.

25. Richard Zoglin, "Politically Incorrect," *Time,* May 30, 1994, p. 67.

26. Gregory Cerio, "Maher the Merrier: *Politically Incorrect* Host Bill Maher Thrives by Bringing Together the Strangest Bedfellows," *People Weekly,* July 24, 1995, p. 145.

27. Maher had film roles in *Rat Boy,* 1986; *House II: The Second Story,* 1987; and *Cannibal Women in the Avocado Jungle of Death,* 1988.

28. Bill Carter, "Lots of Political Humor and No Morton Kondracke," *New York Times,* February 27, 1994, p. H-33.

29. Scott Shuger with Julian E. Barnes, "Comic Relief: Real Issues, Barbed Wit and Celebrities Galore, Bill Maher Is Turning Political Satire into a Formula for Success," *U.S. News and World Report* (cover story), January 27, 1997, p. 60.

30. T. L. Stanley, *MediaWeek*, July 7, 1997, p. 9.

31. Gina Bellafonte, "Politically Incorrect," *Time*, July 14, 1997, p. 76. Like Larry King, Rush Limbaugh, and other talk-show hosts of the 1980s and 1990s, Maher had adapted a multimedia approach to his career as a talk-show host. In addition to cameos and acting roles, Maher had published a comedy novel (in 1992), a book of monologues from his show (in 1996), and audio and videocassettes of his work.

32. T. L. Stanley, *MediaWeek*, July 7, 1997, p. 9.

33. R. Daniel Foster, "Hey Now! Interview with Comedian Garry Shandling," *Los Angeles Magazine* 39, no. 8 (August 1994): 26.

34. "Steve Martin, Albert Brooks and Woody Allen have never stuck to a formula. I don't know the level of my own talent, so I just have to keep working to find it. I hope I can amass a body of work that reflects a certain degree of range." Garry Shandling *Playboy* interview with David Rensin, *Playboy*, December 1994, p. 61+.

35. *Current Biography Yearbook 1989*, ed. Charles Moritz (New York: The H. W. Wilson Company), p. 520.

36. *It's Garry Shandling's Show* (1986–1990) was coproduced on Showtime with Alan Zweibel, the former head writer of *Saturday Night Live*.

37. *Playboy* interview, December 1994. Shandling also became one of the first choices of NBC to replace David Letterman toward the end of 1993. An inquiry was made and an offer discussed. Shandling considered the four-year, $20 million offer over a period of several weeks, but turned it down "at the last possible day" because the NBC show, which would have begun in September, conflicted with the final productions of his second season of *The Larry Sanders Show*. Bruce Fretts, "Garry On," *Entertainment Weekly*, June 4, 1993, p. 26.

38. Joe Rhodes, "Garry Does Larry: As Host of the Hot 'Larry Sanders' Talk Show, Garry Shandling Isn't Himself These Days," *Entertainment Weekly* August 28, 1992, p. 28+.

39. Ray Richmond, "Shandling Takes Air out of 'Sanders,'" *Variety*, January 26, 1998, p. 35.

40. *Time*, December 21, 1998, p. 80; *Entertainment Weekly 1998 Year End Special*, p. 124.

41. *Entertainment Weekly 1998 Year End Special*, Advertising Supplement.

10. CONCLUSION

1. Jeffrey Preiss Jones, "Talking Politics in Post-Network Television: The Case of 'Politically Incorrect'" (Ph.D. dissertation, University of Texas at Austin, 1999), pp. v, 22. Jones' findings refute communication scholar Michael Schudson's assertion that problem-solving talk

and sociable talk are wholly separate. Jones contends that such distinctions can no longer be maintained.

2. I borrow the term and concept of *porous* from the introduction to Michael Arlen's *The Camera Age: Essays on Television* (New York: Farrar, Straus, Giroux, 1981), pp. 4–5.

3. Arlen, "Hosts and Guests," in *The Camera Age*, pp. 307–319.

A TAXONOMY OF TELEVISION TALK

1. Erving Goffman, *Forms of Talk* (Philadelphia: University of Pennsylvania Press, 1981).

2. We are still "babes in the woods" when it comes to understanding television, and this phrase, referring originally to a baby's apprehension of reality, seems to fit here. The quote is from William James, *Principles of Psychology*, vol. 1, p. 488, cited by Walter Lippmann, *Public Opinion* (New York: The Free Press, [1922] 1965), p. 54.

3. From notes of Bernard Timberg, fall 1978, from remarks by Kinneavy in a graduate seminar.

4. Michael Arlen, "Hosts and Guests," in *The Camera Age: Essays on Television* (New York: Farrar, Straus, Giroux, 1981).

SOURCES

I consulted many sources in writing this book, including broadcasting histories, academic studies, popular journalistic accounts, show business autobiographies, and kinescopes and videotapes of the talk shows themselves.

A number of works were particularly insightful and helpful. My earliest inspiration for working with the popular genres of television was Horace Newcomb's *TV: The Most Popular Art* (New York: Doubleday, 1974). Also influential in my appreciation of literary and film genres was John G. Cawelti's *Adventure, Mystery and Romance* (Chicago: University of Chicago Press, 1976). Another basic book in my early lexicon was Thomas Schatz's *Hollywood Genres* (New York: Random House, 1981). Little did I know at the time, as a struggling graduate student who was very impressed with these attempts to master entire popular genres, that I myself would end up writing a genre book. But I know I was inspired, reading these early works by Newcomb and Schatz, and they became my mentors in my Ph.D. program at the University of Texas. At some point, after trying to define the genres of daytime television (I had chapters on TV news, commercials, and game shows in my dissertation, "Daytime Television: Rhetoric and Ritual," University of Texas at Austin, 1979) and writing an article on television soap operas that was included in the third edition of Newcomb's *Television: The Critical View* (New York: Oxford University Press, 1982), I wondered why no one had tried to tackle the TV talk show in any systematic way. Now, twenty years later, I know.

On my journey, I have discovered remarkably good insights and leads from television critics, working professionals, and television scholars alike. Michael Arlen's "Hosts and Guests," published in his collection of essays *The Camera Age* (New York: Farrar, Straus, Giroux, 1981), represents a particularly astute, intelligent, and sometimes piercing series of observations about the "host/guest" relationships on television talk shows, the social tensions they expose and cover up, and their effect on social discourse in the United States. I liked the way Arlen thought and wrote. I returned to this piece again and again as a model of television criticism as I attempted to get my own grip on the rituals of the TV talk show.

Certain biographies of major television talk personalities were also inspiring. Joseph E. Persico's *Edward R. Murrow: An American Original* (New York: McGraw-Hill, 1988) and A. M. Sperber's *Murrow: His Life and Times* (New York: Freundlich Books, 1986) were unusually detailed and rich: great biographies that complemented each other well. Another fine biography of Murrow was the American Masters PBS documentary, "Edward R. Murrow: This Reporter." I was lucky to have such rich documentation of the most influential news broadcaster and talk show host of his day.

Of the many sources I consulted on the career of Johnny Carson, the host who institutionalized the late-night entertainment talk show founded by Allen, Kovacs, and Paar, one biography stood out: Paul Corkery's *Carson: The Unauthorized Biography* (Ketchum, Idaho: Randt and Co., 1987). It was by far the most detailed and unvarnished account of Carson's personal and professional life, and, through the testimony of associates and ex-wives, helped me understand the choices Carson made at crucial junctures in his career. One the best pieces of television cultural history I have ever seen is Kenneth Tynan's "Salto Mortale," a long profile of Carson from the *New Yorker*, reprinted in Tynan's book *Show People* (New York: Simon and Schuster, 1979).

Howard Kurtz's *Hot Air: All Talk, All the Time* (New York: Times Books, 1996) was the essential source for my understanding of the increasingly baroque direction television news talk was taking in the 1990s. I relied on it heavily (perhaps too heavily), but no one else had done the same kind of detailed thinking and writing on this topic.

The works of television historians and scholars like Hal Himmelstein, Albert Auster, Patricia Priest, Brian Rose, and Ron Simon were valuable signposts along the way. I learned from their written works as well as from personal insights in phone calls and conversations.

Most important was my access to the television shows themselves, and here I have to credit the magnificent, and magnificently well organized and accessible, collection of the Museum of Television and Radio. Thanks to Curator Ron Simon's unflagging generosity as a host and friend to television scholars, I was able to spend long hours in the viewing carrels of the library, where I made some of my most important discoveries. At the Museum of Television and Radio I discovered an amazingly completely collection of the work of Edward R. Murrow, including rarely seen episodes of what is now considered by some to be Murrow's most important work, his *Small World* shows of 1958–1960. It was there that I learned what made Arthur Godfrey such a "household name," starting with his first wry simulcast on CBS radio and television. There I saw the last *Home* show of Arlene Francis, which gave me important insights into the refinement and intelligence of this major talk-show host and her remarkable hold on the audiences of her time. There I was able to see directly the work of Mike Wallace on *Night Beat,* which I had read about for years but never seen. It is still his best work, in my opinion. There I also found Jack Benny's parodies of Mike Wallace and Johnny Carson. Benny's ensemble established in many ways the repertory company and repartee that characterized later talk shows (like *Tonight*); his parodies remain some of the best TV talk ever produced. For a glimpse of some fascinating public discourse among women in the 1970s, Virginia Graham's *Girl Talk* (later re-dubbed *Women's Talk* under Barbara Walters) is available through the Museum's well-indexed retrieval system. It is safe to say that this book would not have been written without the Museum of Television and Radio.

Finally, some of my most important sources were not books or tapes but people. From the television industry itself a key source was Hal Gurnee, the director of *Late Night with David Letterman* at NBC in the 1980s, who gave me my first and most important entrée to the NBC Letterman show. Three long recorded interviews with Gurnee, whose career spans the history of television talk, were some of the most insightful I recorded. It was also through Gurnee that I was able to interview other members of the Letterman production staff over a three-year period, and came to understand how remarkably complex the act of recording a TV talk show really is. Letterman himself was an important unseen but benign presence. I met him only once, in the hallway, and although he was clearly reluctant to talk about himself, he said that if I wanted him to talk about Hal Gurnee or anyone else on the production staff who put the show on the air, he would be glad to. I imagine few other talk-show hosts would let an unknown and relatively unpublished television scholar hang out for three years without any visible product. Other members of the Letterman production team were unfailingly generous with their time and insights. It was from watching this show over a three-year period, in among my duties as a full-time teacher and father, that the organizing concepts for this book emerged.

Another major benefactor was David Tebet, by then a senior executive in Johnny Carson Productions. Tebet, who struck me at my first

meeting and interview as playing the padrone role to the hilt (his grav-
elly voice helped), had a number of important insights. "Next-day talk,"
he told me: it was by the level of next-day talk around the water cooler
that you knew you had a talk show that was going somewhere. Jack
Rollins, Letterman's personal manager, a consummate show-business
professional, also gave me an interview. But it was Tebet who gave me
what was at the time an unusual opportunity to visit the Carson set in
the mid-1980s (it was generally a closed set). There I interviewed producer Fred de Cordova, director Bobby Quinn, "sidekick" Ed McMahon,
and a number of other members of the Carson production team, and
saw how different the organizational structure was from that of the
Letterman show—and what a show that had been on the air for two
decades looked like next to a new, raw one, where every show was an
experiment.

On the *Donahue* show, public relations director Penny Rotheiser
enabled me to visit the show, observe tapings, and interview key members of the staff, including director Ron Weiner, producer Richard
Mincer, and others.

It was fun watching these shows, but it was more than that. I absorbed things watching the show from the set, the control room, and
behind the scenes that made me understand how difficult it is to structure spontaneity, in discrete units of commercial time, around the same
host, day after day, and keep it moving and fresh. Fresh talk could easily
get stale, and the best talk-show hosts had to constantly, in Kenneth
Tynan's terms, "reinvent themselves." I learned a lot from that.

None of the people I talked to did these interviews for gain. They
were often as interested as I was in the art of the TV talk show, frequently asking me what others had said about their show or others. The
people who put TV talk shows on the air are aware of the contributions
of each of the members of the talk-show team—contributions that are
invisible to the viewer at home.

The sources used for this book have been written and oral, archival and immediate. The ideas for the book emerged as much out of talk
as written material. And that is fitting for a form of expression as spontaneous and of the moment as the "fresh" talk of television, captured in
an electronic present for its immediate audience and then, through the
magic of film, kinescope, and videotape, made available in an eternal
present for generations of viewers to see and talk about again.

One last contributing source for this book should be mentioned—
the editors. I had a number of gifted editors read my manuscript, in
parts and in whole, as I was working on this book. Of those who responded to drafts with encouragement as well as tough-minded criticism, several stand out: Sally Sevcik, Horace Newcomb, Tom Schatz,

Chris Anderson, Ron Simon, Robert Erler, Frankie Westbrook, and Carolyn Wylie. They gave me ideas and inspiration, as well as cautions and incentive to rethink and rewrite sections as I went along, and they were equally good at pointing out what I had and what I lacked.

Bernard M. Timberg

In working on the entries for longtime TV figures, I sometimes used scores of sources for a single entry and hundreds for the whole guide, too many to provide in footnotes. Instead the three ways into this information which I used and which I believe will be most helpful to readers are given below: (1) a short list of those books that provide basic program descriptions, brief biographies, and essential facts; (2) a paragraph on the use of Lexis-Nexis; and (3) a short list of the most recent and helpful Internet sources.

(1) Only the most recent editions are listed:

Horace Newcomb, Cary O'Dell, and Noelle Watson, eds., *Encyclopedia of Television* (Chicago: Fitzroy Dearborn Publishers, 1997).

Alex McNeil, *Total Television: The Comprehensive Guide to Programming from 1948 to the Present*, 4th ed. (New York: Penguin Books, 1996).

Tim Brooks and Earle Marsh, *The Complete Directory to Prime Time Network and Cable TV Shows, 1946–Present*, 7th rev. ed. (New York: Ballantine Books, 1999).

Les Brown, *Les Brown's Encyclopedia of Television, 3rd ed.* (Detroit: Gale Research, 1992).

Vincent Terrace, *Encyclopedia of Television: Series, Pilots and Specials* (New York: Zoetrope, 1986).

Craig T. Norback and Peter G. Norback, eds., *TV Guide Almanac* (New York: Ballantine Books, 1980).

(2) The database Lexis-Nexis was very helpful, especially in providing information about recent program changes that took place in the years not covered by printed reference books. In some cases, however, newspaper and magazine interviews with people active in early television also resolved questions about programs from the 1940s to the 1980s. Other serial publication databases such as Ebsco and Proquest were also used but did not provide nearly as much material as the entertainment news source section of the Arts & Sports category in the General News division of Lexis-Nexis Academic Universe.

(3) Note that Internet sources change rapidly.

Teletronic at freespace.virgin.net/steve hulse (especially *The A to Z Guide* at freespace.virgin.net/steve hulse/atoz.htm)

Tim's TV Showcase at timstvshowcase.com

TV Chronicles, The Home of Television Information at www.tvchronicles.com

Classic U.S. Television Collective at www.tvcollective.com

About Talk Shows at talkshows.about.com

The Classic TV Database at www.classic-tv.com

The Museum of Broadcast Communications at www.Museum.TV

Robert J. Erler

INDEX

Italicized page references indicate appendix entries or extended discussions in text.

McMillen, Patricia, 70, 318n50
McNeil, Alex, 11
McNeil, Neil, 299
McNeill, Don, 201, 206, 212, 263
McNellis, Maggie, 250
Meadows, Audrey, 211, 258, 246
Meadows, Jayne, 243, 256, 261
Medved, Michael, 286
Meet Betty Furness, 234, 235
Meeting of Minds, 205
Meet the Missus, 273
Meet the Press, 20, 161, 199, 279–281, 289, 292
Meet the Veep, 278
Meeuween, Terry, 277
Meredith, Burgess, 299
Meredith, Don, 123, 200, 286
Merron, Jeffrey, 28
Merv Griffin Show, 75, 111
Metromedia, 77, 93, 254, 294
Metz, Robert, 38, 311n7
Michener, James, 209, 215
Mickins, Beverly, 131
Midnight Hour, 256
Mike and Buff, 52, 221
Mike Douglas Show, 94–95, 227
Mike Wallace Interview, 43, 54, 298
Miller, Dennis, 12, 151, 184, 187, 200, 259–260
Miller, Dorothy, 46
Miller, Judith, 161
Miller, Stephanie, 173
Mincer, Richard, 70, 318n50, 340
Miracles Now, 277
Miss America Pageant, 236, 260, 267, 268, 270
Missing Links, 259
Mission to the World, 285
Mister Mayor, 218
Mister Rogers, 278
Mister Rogers' Neighborhood, 202, 277
Monday Night Football, 123, 200, 223, 260
Monroe, Marilyn, 27, 142, 269, 233
Montagu, Ashley, 261, 301
Montel Williams Show, 303
Montgomery, George, 104

Mooney, Paul, 145
Moonlighting, 215
Moore, Garry, 113, 201, 217, 243, 260–262, 296
Moore, Michael, 297
Morey Amsterdam Show, 208
Morgan, Al, 64, 65
Morgan, Edward P., 220
Morgan, Henry, 243, 250, 254, 261, 262, 294
Morgan and Company, 262
Morning Show, 218, 221, 224, 232, 236, 263, 267, 270
Morra, Buddy, 115
Morton, Laura, 180
Morton, Robert "Morty," 118
Morton Downey Jr. Show, 227
Moyers, Bill, 2, 11, 23, 28, 57, 88, 90, 95–100, 108, 193, 202, 278, 309n33
Moyers, Judith, 97, 98
Moynihan, Daniel Patrick, 280
Mrs. Roosevelt Meets the Public, 278
MTV, 12, 165, 206
Muggs, J. Fred (chimpanzee), 38
Mull, Martin, 207, 303
Multimedia, 5, 94, 180, 273
Munson, Wayne, 146, 317n46
Muppet Show, 241, 242
Murdoch, Rupert, 133, 148, 272
Murphy, Eddie, 132, 144, 145
Murray, Jan, 211
Murrow, Edward R., xiii, 2, 9, 10, 17, 19–21, 39, 54–55, 96, 124, 284, 287, 306n13, 308n12, 311n15; biographies of, 338; "higher" vs. "lower," 28–29; Moyers' encounter with, 99. *See also Person to Person; See It Now; Small World*
Murrow, Ethel Lamb, 22
Muscular Dystrophy Telethon, 253, 259
Museum of Television and Radio (New York), 40, 85, 339
Music Show, 94, 227
Musilli, John, 216
Muskie, Edmund, 105